# INDIAN ART FROM AFGHANISTAN

# Indian Art from Afghanistan

THE LEGEND OF ŚAKUNTALĀ
AND THE INDIAN TREASURE OF
EUCRATIDES AT AI KHANUM

CLAUDE RAPIN

CENTRE DE SCIENCES HUMAINES

MANOHAR

2023

Extracts from Claude Rapin, *Fouilles d'Aï Khanoum VIII. La Trésorerie du palais hellénistique d'Aï Khanoum. L'Apogée et la chute du royaume grec de Bactriane* (*Mémoires de la Délégation archéologique française en Afghanistan, 33*). Paris, De Boccard, 1992

Text translated by Rashmi Patni



First published 1996
Reprinted 2021, 2022, 2023



ISBN 978-81-7304-162-4

*Published by*
Ajay Kumar Jain *for*
Manohar Publishers & Distributors
4753/23 Ansari Road, Daryaganj
New Delhi 110 002

*Printed at*
Replika Press Pvt. Ltd.

# CONTENTS

CHAPTER I

# Introduction[1]

Hellenistic expansion reached its furthest physical limits with Alexander's conquest of the Oriental satrapies of the Achaemenid Empire. Though this subjugation of the Central Asian provinces is frequently referred to by the historians of Alexander and of his immediate successors, yet material evidence of three centuries of Greek colonisation of this region is scanty. Recent excavations in Afghanistan and Soviet Central Asia have brought to light the ruins of the magnificent city of Ai Khanum, and the great sanctuary of Takht-i-Sangin. In Afghanistan, research undertaken by the French Archaeological Delegation from the beginning of the twenties has resulted in the discovery of the remains of the era of the Kushans, successors and heirs of the Greeks in Central Asia. In this regard, discoveries made at Begram, the ancient Alexandria of Caucasus, are exceptional and merit special mention because they have revealed a treasure of Graeco-Roman, Indian and Chinese works of art, piled up at the same site. The discovery of the large sanctuary of Surkh Kotal which shows the direct imprint of Greek influence on its architectural decoration is also significant in this context.

It was only about thirty years ago, in 1962, that Daniel Schlumberger had the good fortune of discovering a large Greek colonial city. Situated in the northern part of the country, at the confluence of the Amu-darya and the Kokcha, this city was excavated by Paul Bernard and his team till 1978. Its geographical location makes it a very important site for the study of the interaction between Iranian, Indian and Chinese influences. Remains found in the excavation of Ai Khanum

---

1 This work is the English translation of several extracts pertaining to India published in the volume by Cl. Rapin, *Fouilles d'Aï Khanoum VIII. La Trésorerie du palais hellénistique d'Aï Khanoum. L'Apogée et la chute du royaume grec de Bactriane (Mémoires de la Délégation archéologique française en Afghanistan, 33)*, Paris, 1992. Other publications concerning the treasury : P. Bernard, *CRAI* 1978, pp. 447-460 ; *CRAI* 1980, pp. 437-446, 448 ; P. Bernard, Cl. Rapin, *BEFEO*, 68, 1980, pp. 10-38, pl. 6-10, 29-31 ; Cl. Rapin, "Les inscriptions économiques de la trésorerie hellénistique d'Aï Khanoum (Afghanistan)", *BCH*, 107, 1983, pp. 315-372 ; Fr. Grenet, "L'onomastique iranienne à Aï Khanoum", *BCH*, 107, 1983, pp. 373-381 ; O. Picard, "Sur deux termes des inscriptions de la trésorerie d'Aï Khanoum", in *Hommages à Lucien Lerat*, Paris, 1984, pp. 679-690 ; P. Hadot, Cl. Rapin, "Les textes littéraires grecs de la trésorerie d'Aï Khanoum", *BCH*, 111, 1987, pp. 225-266 ; Cl. Rapin, "La trésorerie hellénistique d'Aï Khanoum", *RA* 1987, pp. 41-70 ; "Ellinističeskaja sokrovišnica Ajxanum", in *Gorodskaja kul'tura*, Tashkent, 1987, pp. 108-119 ; "The Greeks in Afghanistan : Ai Khanum", in *Greek colonists and native populations*, Canberra, Oxford, 1990, pp. 329-342. On the coins see P. Bernard, *Fouilles d'Aï Khanoum IV. Les monnaies hors trésors. Questions d'histoire gréco-bactrienne (MDAFA, 28)*, Paris, 1985. The following aspects of the original edition have not been taken up here: the study of the Begram palace in the Hellenistic period (*Fouilles AKh VIII*, pp. 383-385, pl. 49-51), the catalogue of Greek inscriptions from Central Asia (*Fouilles AKh VIII*, pp. 387-392).

bear witness to the fact that this zone, colonised by the Greeks and contiguous to what was later to be known as the Silk Route, though it developed independently of the traditional Mediterranean milieu, continuously maintained its cultural contact with it. These remains show a very pronounced influence of Greek civilisation, particularly of the Seleucid period, but they also bear the imprint of Iranian culture. In fact, the originality of the art, and particularly of Graeco-Bactrian architecture, revealed to the world for the first time by the excavation of Ai Khanum, may be attributed to the blending of these diverse elements.

Though the name under which this city was originally founded around 300 B.C. is not known, it saw its veritable apogee in the second quarter of the second century B.C., when Eucratides, the last king of Eastern Bactria, chose it as his capital and probably renamed it Eucratideia, after his own name. The choice of this town as a capital around 150 B.C. resulted in a major reconstruction programme of the big monuments like the royal palace, and the gymnasium. However, the considerable architectural activity which dominated the life of this city came to a sudden halt when, in 145 B.C, the Greeks surrendered control over the city to nomadic groups, without any effort at resistance.

One of the big buildings at Ai Khanum which was opened up substantially was the palace treasury. Its exploration took place in the course of two excavation campaigns in 1977 and 1978. This building, whose function was identified by its plan, and by the numerous objects found in it, had housed the coffers of the royal administration in the middle of the second century B.C. Items imported from the West are almost non-existent amongst these objects, which can be classified geographically into two distinct categories: one consisting of products from Central Asia, objects pertaining to Greek everyday life, foodstuffs preserved in big jars, precious stones, and Graeco-Bactrian coins of Attic standard; and the other being a rich collection of Indian merchandise, which was part of the treasure and probably war booty brought back by Eucratides from his expeditions to North-West India. Two of the major finds, which are described here in detail, form a part of this collection. These are an inlaid Indian disc in mother-of-pearl (legend of Śakuntalā), and a set of plaques in Indian agate inlaid with rock crystal which formed part of a rare Indian object – a throne or a luxurious bed – of which the only known parallel, which has enabled us to identify its function, is a similar find in the gardens of an imperial residence in Rome.

This study has been possible thanks to the confidence reposed in me by M. Paul Bernard, who permitted me, as a young foreign research scholar, to collaborate with him in the excavation of Ai Khanum, and who gave me all the help and encouragement necessary to publish the results of this research[2]. I would like to thank M. Claude Bérard, Professor of Classical Archaeology at the University of Lausanne, for his invaluable advice and for guiding this research project, leading to the award of a Doctorate by the University of Lausanne. I am also grateful to M. Maurizio Taddei, Professor of Archaeology and History of Indian Art at the Istituto Universitario Orientale of Naples and member of the Istituto Italiano per il Medio ed Estremo Oriente of Rome who also agreed to be

---

2 I would also like to thank the members of Paul Bernard's team, Osmund Bopearachchi, Frantz Grenet, Guy Lecuyot and Pierre Leriche as well as Bertille Lyonnet for their learned suggestions and for their friendly help.

a member of the jury for my thesis, and who reviewed the portion relating to India in detail, as well as to M. Raoul Curiel, ex-Curator of the Cabinet des Médailles in Paris, for his comments and corrections. Finally, I wish to acknowledge my gratitude to M. Charles Bonnet, member of the Conseil de la recherche du Fonds national suisse de la recherche scientifique, and M. Pierre Ducrey, Professor of Ancient History, University of Lausanne, for their moral support and for the material aid which I obtained through them, which enabled me to complete my studies, and also to complete this work.

## CHAPTER II

# GENERAL LAYOUT

The building to which the subsequent pages are devoted is part of the palace, the seat of political power in the city. Its identification as a treasury is confirmed on the one hand by its plan, which consists of a central court bordered on all four sides by a continuous row of rooms, apparently warehouses, and an annexe consisting of another series of warehouses opening into a corridor, and on the other, by the archaeological finds at this site which are evidence of its role as the depot of the city's royal treasure (fig. 3-4).

An extensive programme of reconstruction of the official buildings was undertaken at Ai Khanum during the last few years of Greek rule in the eastern part of Bactria. Parts of some of these buildings remained incomplete or were apparently seldom, if ever, used as may be observed in respect of the gymnasium[3] or the palace, inclusive of the treasury. The collapse of Greek power at Ai Khanum led to a rapid and permanent desertion of the city by the colonisers. The buildings of the Hellenistic period are, so to speak, the only architectural remains at the site and it is only in certain areas of the acropolis that probes have revealed a succession of constructions going upto the post Timurid period[4].

During some years following the abandonment of the city by the Greeks around 145 B.C., the inhabitants, probably natives, applied themselves with great zeal to looting building material : beams from the roofs, stones, wood, bricks and metal. The larger buildings were, of course, pillaged first. The palace, of which the walls belonging to the last phase of construction had been rebuilt on a plinth formed of four courses of baked bricks, was systematically razed, sometimes even upto the foundation level. Actually baked bricks, like limestone, were the preferred material of the plunderers, and the only walls above a certain height to have survived in the palace are constructed with unbaked bricks. All these walls are located in zones which, from the architectural point of view, belong to an earlier period and were not rebuilt in the last phase of architectural activity, e.g. the lateral units situated to the east and the west of the hypostyle hall *2* and the hall of reception *3* (fig. 3). The walls of the court and the treasury itself are among the surviving structures of the palace which, though reconstructed, escaped total destruction solely because of the use of unbaked bricks.

---

3 S. Veuve, *Fouilles AKh VI. Le gymnase. Architecture, céramique, sculpture (MDAFA, 30)*, Paris, 1987, p. 109 ; P. Bernard, "Gimnasij v Ajxanum", in *Gorodskaja kul'tura*, 1987, pp. 22-31.

4 P. Leriche, *Fouilles AKh V. Les remparts et les monuments associés (MDAFA, 29)*, Paris, 1986, pp. 101-102.

## THE PALACE

The treasury forms that part of the palace complex which extended to the west of the main street of the lower town over an area measuring 350 x 250 m (fig. 3)[5]. To the west of the palace there was a street running north-south, which provided a direct passage between the gymnasium area and the residential zone which lay to the south-west of the city and comprised of patrician houses[6]. This street was also bordered in the west by one or two still unexcavated buildings abutting on the western rampart. A large rectangular court in the south (*40*) separated the palace from the residential area of the patricians. The buildings explored in the eastern zone of the lower town are the sanctuary of the *temple à redans*[7] and the north-western part of a public building or a large residence[8]. Between these two buildings stretched a long and narrow depression whose function remains a mystery[9]. The access to the palace from the principal street running north-south, was by a broad road lying perpendicular to it which skirted the temple à redans and the funerary chapel (heroon) of Kineas, and which one approached through a large propylaeum on the side of the principal axis[10]. Undoubtedly this passage must have served other public buildings in the town centre as well, particularly the large quadrilateral space to the south of the gymnasium with a deep depression in its centre, and covering an area of 41.50 x 44 m. This "pool" was, no doubt, the chief drinking trough of the city.

The structures in the palace complex that the excavation has brought to light represent the state of architecture at the time when the town was abandoned by the Greeks. In this final stage, the

---

5 P. Bernard, *CRAI* 1968, pp. 264-271 ; *idem*, *CRAI* 1970, pp. 301-310 ; *idem*, *CRAI* 1971, pp. 385-406 ; *idem*, *CRAI* 1974, pp. 289-293 ; P. Bernard, M. Le Berre, in *Fouilles AKh I*, pp. 17-83, pl. 1-11, 20-84.

6 On the houses see P. Bernard, *CRAI* 1968, pp. 272-276 ; *CRAI* 1969, pp. 321-326 ; *CRAI* 1970, pp. 310-316 ; *CRAI* 1975, pp. 168-180 ; *CRAI* 1976, pp. 288-293 ; "Les traditions orientales dans l'architecture gréco-bactrienne", *JA* 1976, pp. 257-266, fig. 6-7 ; H.-P. Francfort, "Le plan des maisons gréco-bactriennes et le problème des structures de «type megaron» en Asie Centrale et en Iran", *Le plateau iranien et l'Asie Centrale*, 1977, pp. 267-280; G. Lecuyot, "Ajxanum. Žiliščnoe stroitel'stvo", in *Gorodskaja kul'tura*, 1987, pp. 59-67 ; *idem*, "Résidences hellénistiques en Bactriane, résidences parthes en Iran et en Mésopotamie. Diffusion ou communauté d'origine ?", *Mesopotamian history and environment Series I, Northern Akkad project reports*, 8, 1983, pp. 31-45, pl. 1-2: *idem*, forthcoming monograph in *Fouilles AKh.*

7 P. Bernard, *CRAI* 1969, pp. 327-354 ; *CRAI* 1970, pp. 303-307 ; *CRAI* 1971, pp. 414-431 ; *CRAI* 1974, pp. 294-298 ; "Les traditions orientales", *JA* 1976, pp. 266-273 ; H.-P. Francfort, *Fouilles AKh III, Le sanctuaire du temple à niches indentées, 2. Les trouvailles (MDAFA, 17)*, Paris, 1984 ; Cl. Rapin, "Les sanctuaires de l'Asie Centrale à l'époque hellénistique. Etat de la question", *Etudes de Lettres (Université de Lausanne)*, 1992, 4, pp. 101-124.

8 P. Bernard, *CRAI* 1980, pp. 449-452 ; S. Veuve and others, "Bâtiment public en bordure de la rue principale", *BEFEO*, 68, 1980, pp. 46-50, 93, pl. XXXIV.

9 J. Thoraval, J.-Cl. Liger, "Campagne de fouille 1978 à Aï Khanoum (Afghanistan) : V. Le palais : sondages sur la cour sud", *BEFEO*, 18, 1980, p. 44 ; commentary on the hypothesis of D. Schlumberger according to which this space was a stadium : P. Bernard, D. Schlumberger, "Aï Khanoum", *BCH*, 89, 1965, p. 597.

10 O. Guillaume, *Fouilles AKh II, Les grands propylées sur la rue principale (MDAFA, 23)*, Paris, 1983.

palace consisted of many units grouped around the southern, eastern, and western sides of a large court with a slightly asymmetrical peristyle (*1*), measuring approximately 137 x 108 m and consisting of a total of 118 columns[11]. The entry to this zone was provided by a large propylaeum opening into the northern portico of this court. In the south, opposite this propylaeum, a monumental porch with a triple row of columns provided access to the main part of the palace. The most striking element of this southern zone is a large square block, divided by two orthogonal corridors into four equal sectors forming two identical units, which comprised working and reception areas[12]. A set of two residential units, each with its own court, was situated to the west of this block[13]. The residential unit in the west was itself flanked in the north by a large court (*90*) bordered by porticoes with Doric columns[14]. To the east and the west of the large court *1* were located premises which were used for economic activities : to the east were perhaps warehouses, a preliminary excavation of which has revealed the initial section of the walls ; to the west, contiguous to the northern portico of the Doric court, lay the treasury which has been largely excavated and its annexe of which, as yet, only the southern portion has been identified.

11 P. Bernard, "Chapiteaux corinthiens hellénistiques d'Asie Centrale découverts à Aï Khanoum", *Syria*, 45, 1968, pp. 111-151. The form of this court was dictated by the establishment of the heroon of Kineas near the northern entrance of the palace. The asymmetry of its form thus does not derive from the age of the palace and the unsystematic manner in which it was constructed as we had stated in "The Greeks in Afghanistan", p. 333.

12 P. Bernard, *CRAI* 1969, pp. 314-321.

13 P. Bernard, *CRAI* 1971, pp. 406-414.

14 P. Garczynski, "Campagne de fouille 1978 à Aï Khanoum (Afghanistan) : IV. Le palais. La cour dorique", *BEFEO*, 68, 1980, pp. 39-43, 86-91, pl. XXXII-XXXIII.

## CHAPTER III

# PLAN OF THE TREASURY

In its final phase of construction, the treasury occupied the north-western corner of the palace. It comprised two buildings conterminous with the length of a corridor running north-south *114*, which was contiguous to the western portico of the large court *1* of the palace. The southern structure, which was the larger of the two, was the principal building (rooms *104-127*) and the second, in the north, constituted an annexe (rooms *128-129* : fig. 4) whose real function we have been unable to determine. The corridor situated on the eastern side (*114*) served as passage from one building to the other. The length of the complex from north to south measured 111.30 m and its maximum width from east to west, including the corridor *114* and the rear wall of the western portico of the large court *1*, was 55 m.

The construction was set around a court (*105*) in the form of an almost square lozenge with sides measuring 28.20 m each. Access to it was possible both from the south as well as the east. On each side was a row of warehouses. The southern side also included the vestibule *106* which, oriented towards the colonnade of the Doric court *90*, provided access to the treasury from the administrative and residential zones. This small vestibule was flanked in the east and in the west by long rectangular rooms (*104* and *107*) whose doors opened into the court. A narrow door permitted direct access from the hall *106* into the room *107* in the south-western corner. In the east lay a second entrance which permitted access to the treasury building from the large court *1* of the palace by a set of two doorways separated from each other by the corridor *114* running north-south. The first was placed in the enclosure wall of the court and the other in the rear wall of room *110*. A stone threshold found in the doorway in the western wall of the large court *1* suggests that it was possible to close the treasury area from this side. The rooms *104* and *107* as well as the other warehouses had a uniform width of 4.50 m. Both the eastern and the western wings contained five rooms each which were greater in length than in width (4.50 x 7.50 – 8 m, rooms *108* to *112* in the east and *115* à *119* in the west). Eight rooms opened into a long corridor running parallel to the northern wall of the court *105* and connected to it by a doorway built in the centre of the wall (*120* to *127* : 4.50 m x 14 m).

The provision of two entrances in a building which had to be very carefully protected from the outside is rather surprising and can perhaps be explained only in terms of the different categories of persons who came here. The southern entry was certainly a special entry used by the rulers and the high officials who resided in the palace. The eastern door of room *110*, which was linked by the corridor *114* to a network of other corridors, was undoubtedly utilised by the subordinate employees of the palace administration and, perhaps, also by the artisans. It is likely that it was through this second entrance that merchandise carried across the large court of the palace was delivered at the treasury.

# CHRONOLOGY

The exploration of the site of the treasury reveals three distinct architectural periods : periods I and II correspond to the Greek period and period III to its post-Greek occupation. Period I, the earliest, can only be surmised on the basis of traces of an occupation prior to the construction of the treasury and the extension of the palace in this area. Period II corresponds to the phase when the palace was in use and it dates from the last years of Greek occupation, thus being contemporaneous with period II of the gymnasium. Period III immediately succeeded period II and was marked by the abandonment of the building and its subsequent reoccupation and pillage by its non-Greek inhabitants, in a chronological sequence corresponding approximately to the later stages Ia and b of the gymnasium.

In view of its size, the renovation of the palace to which we have referred above was not accomplished in one year but probably in many stages with interruptions imposed by the harsh Bactrian winters. The abandonment of the city by its Greek population occurred before it was possible to complete certain sections. This state of incompletion has already been referred to in respect of the treasury. Most of the floors do not seem to have been laid, particularly in the southern portion (for example, court *105*, rooms *106*, *108*, *115*, *116*, *118*). In many parts, the walls did not receive the usual protective coating with cob and in certain inner corners of the walls, the corners of the bricks overhanging both the courses had not been cut off (room *115* in the south-east, court *105* in the north-west). Finally, the arrangements for storing goods in the treasury were only partially executed. The rooms of the treasury were, for the most part, never utilised by the Greeks. Only six of the twenty warehouses around the court functioned effectively. The major part of the royal treasure appears to have been confined in only two rooms. The first (room *104*), contained mainly raw material and the second (room *109*), contained finely worked objects as well as varied merchandise. The northern rooms *120* and *126* probably served as depots for liquids.

The treasury witnessed two distinct phases of destruction which have also been noted with regard to other buildings in the city. The first followed immediately after the city was abandoned by its Greek inhabitants around 145 B.C. It was marked by the fire in the principal depot (room *109*), the first rapid pillage of the building and, immediately afterwards, without any lapse of time, a relatively short phase of reoccupation by the local population whose principal activity consisted of the removal of building material. Whereas the later inhabitants razed whole sections of the palace (particularly the Doric court) to extract beams, baked bricks from the foundations of the walls and stone from the pillars, they left the treasury untouched, using many of its rooms as living and working quarters. Some of these post-Greek inhabitants worked at the retrieval of metals (gold and silver) as is revealed by the presence of numerous furnaces for welding and the discovery of gold and silver ingots in room *115*. A second pillage took place after the building had already been abandoned by these post-Greek inhabitants.

The most spectacular evidence of the first phase of pillage (period III b) is related mainly to the two warehouses *104* and *109*, though which of the two was broken into first could not be determined. The debris from these warehouses was found scattered all over the treasury. The warehouse *104* seems to have been the main depot for rough semi-precious stones but some categories like obsidian, garnet, turquoise and rock crystal seem to have been common to both the depots though the possibility that this intermingling was the result of the upheaval due to the pillage can not be excluded. One notes also that certain precious objects of warehouse *109* like the plaques with agate inlay and Indian coins are totally absent from room *104*. Similarly, of the two hundred fragments of alabaster plates discovered in the treasury and believed to have been stored in room *109*, only one fragment was found in room *104*. This pillage seems to have been preceded by an initial phase, only slightly earlier and of lesser importance (period III a), which resulted in the installation of small workshops for the recovery of metallurgic debris, particularly near the entrance of room *109*, in the vestibule *106* and in the rooms *111* and *117*.

CHAPTER IV

# THE ROYAL TREASURE[15]

## VESSELS FOR STORAGE

The principal function of the treasury was the storing of precious merchandise. The inscriptions on the vases used for this purpose not only constitute one of the richest sources of information on the working of Greek financial administration[16] but also make it possible to reconstruct some of the major events which marked the last years of the city.

The type of vessels most frequently utilised were ceramic vases. The warehouse in room *109* contained, for example, fragments of several large jars and some impressions of their bases were also found in alignment on the floor. We were not able to ascertain whether these vessels were used to store foodstuffs (liquid or grain) or precious objects, of which hundreds of fragments were found intermingled with the pieces of these jars. The most common vessels were undoubtedly pitchers with flat bases, with or without handles. Their modest dimensions must have facilitated transport.

## COIN DEPOSITS[17]

Inscriptions found on a certain number of these vessels allow us to know the administrative system and the inventory methods of the treasury. They comprise labels written by the officials in ink on those vessels which served as the cash boxes of the treasury indicating their contents, and guaranteeing them by their seal. The larger number of the group of texts refer to coin deposits. One of the most elaborate examples available to us is that of an uncovered pitcher, discovered in a dwelling near the temple à redans, where it must have been carried after the pillage of the treasury. This vessel has three inscriptions mentioning successive deposits (texts **4a**, **b**, **c**). The first (text **4 a**) refers to a deposit of 500 drachmas, transmitted by an official named Zeno to two other employees (Oxeboacus and Oxybazus), who were responsible for putting the sum in the pitcher and for sealing it. In all inscriptions of this type the first official named is always Greek and may be regarded as the director of the treasury whereas the other two bearing either Greek or Bactrian names were probably subordinate treasurers whose function was to manage and handle the royal treasure. The second and the third inscriptions on this vessel are written according to the same formula but the officials named in each case are different.

---

15 The catalogue, pp. 123-142, includes only a part of the Indian finds in the treasury cited and illustrated in this volume and does not include the Graeco-Bactrian finds.

16 A Greek administrative parchment was recently discovered in Afghanistan : see P. Bernard, C. Rapin, "Parchemin gréco-bactrien d'une collection privée", *CRAI* 1995 (forthcoming).

17 Cl. Rapin, *Fouilles AKh VIII*, pp. 95-115.

**Deposits of drachmas** (texts **4a, b, c**). Sanctuary of the temple à redans

These texts figure on an ovoid pitcher without handles, 41 cm in height (mouth cracked) and 28 cm in diameter. Five of the seven officials mentioned on these labels – Oxybazus, Philiscus, Aryandes, Strato and Hermaeus – are mentioned in other texts as well, thus confirming the hypothesis that the pitcher in the sanctuary was brought from the treasury. **a)** Complete text in five lines, 5.5 cm from the cracked mouth. Accolade in the margin. This text is the earliest in date of the three complete texts inscribed on the same vessel. **b)** Text of four or five lines, 6 cm below the cracked mouth and placed opposite the preceding text, accolade in the margin. Chronologically, it is the second text on the vessel. **c)** This text was the last to be affixed on the vessel, below the text **4a**, slightly towards the left.

**a.**

| | | | |
|---|---|---|---|
| 1) | Παρὰ Ζήνωνος | | "On behalf of Zeno |
| 2) | ἠρίθμηνται | | it was counted |
| 3) | διὰ 'Οξηβοάκου | | by Oxeboaces |
| 4) | καὶ 'Οξυβάζου δρχ φ' | | and Oxybazus 500 drachmas; |
| 5) | ἐσφράγισται 'Οξηβοάκης | | Oxeboaces had sealed." |

**b.**

| | | | |
|---|---|---|---|
| 1) | Παρὰ Τιμοδήμου | | "On behalf of Timodemus |
| 2) | ἠρίθμηται διὰ | | it was counted by |
| 3) | 'Οξηβοάκου καὶ | | Oxeboaces and |
| 4) | 'Ερμαῖου ταξανά | | Hermaeus *taxaena* (?) ; . . ." |
| 5) | – – – – – – – | | |

**c.**

| | | | |
|---|---|---|---|
| 1) | Παρὰ Φιλίσκου | | "On behalf of Philiscus |
| 2) | κασαπανα ταξαηνὰ | A | 10 000 *kasapana taxaena* ; |
| 3) | διὰ 'Αρυάνδρου καὶ | M | by Aryandes and |
| 4) | Στρα . . - - - | | Strato; . . ." |

While the first label mentions drachmas, the last two inscribed on this pitcher refer to currency designated by the formula κασαπανα ταξαηνά (text **4 c**) or ταξαηνά (text **4 b**). The first term κασαπανα is the Greek transcription of the Middle-Indian *kārshāpaṇa,* which designates Indian square punch-marked coins struck in India during the Mauryan period. The second term ταξαηνά is a toponymic adjective with the Greek suffix which is found in the names of the administrative subdivisions of the Seleucid world. The identification of the root ταξα- with the region of Taxila (Takṣa-śila) thus does not seem to us to be far-fetched, specially because 14 of the 24 coins collected in the treasury, as also 545 of the 677 specimens of a treasure discovered nearby in the administrative zone of the palace[18], have come from the workshops of this capital of North-Western India. The phrase mentioning these Indian coins is followed by a total sum indicated by of an M capped by an A, which corresponds in all the deposits to a sum of 10,000, showing thereby

18 On the discovery of the treasure in room *20* of the palace, i.e. the large hall contiguous to the south-western portico of court 1, to the west of the hypostyle hall *2* : *CRAI*, 1971, pp. 435-446 ; R. Audouin and P. Bernard, *RNum* 1973, pp. 238-289 : Indian coins; *idem*, *RNum* 1974, pp. 6-41 : Indo-Greek coins. On the coins found in the treasury see Cl. Rapin, *Fouilles AKh VIII*, pp. 106-107, 304-306 ; P. Bernard, *Fouilles AKh IV*, n[os] 76, 170, 185-190, 192, 194-209, 211 ; on Indian and Indo-Greek coins : pp. 72-78 : all the Indian punch-marked coins found at Ai Khanum come from the treasury and the treasure found in its vicinity, except n[os] 191 and 193 (sanctuary), 210 (house 2 outside the walls), 212 (theatre).

that the treasury received a large quantity of currency (Texts **4c**, **6**, **8d**, **9**, **10 11**, **12a**). Apart from the names of the currencies mentioned on the vases, the coins found in the treasury itself provide evidence of the diversity of the currencies in stock. These include Seleucid and Graeco-Bactrian, Indo-Greek and Indian coins. The diversity of standards demanded the services of a finance officer specialising in the verification of the coins in circulation. A label of the treasury attests that the deposit had been made in "legal money": δοκίμου ἀρ[γυρίου], and that the verification had been done by a *dokimastes* (δεδοκίμασται). It guaranteed that the contents of the vessel consisted of Graeco-Bactrian silver coins of Attic standard in contrast with Indian money of a different standard and often with only an external coating.

## STORAGE OF NATURAL PRODUCTS

A second group of inscriptions on the pitchers reveals that the responsibilities of the treasurers also included the storage of certain natural products[19]. Incense, a luxury good imported generally from the Near East or from Arabia figured in the inventories of the treasurers, as attested by the term λιβανῶτου mentioned on pitchers **21** and **22**[20]. The second example is furnished by the group of labels relating to the delivery and decanting of olive oil, found both on a pitcher and its lid. This product, which was an integral part of everyday Greek life, was all the more precious at Ai Khanum because it had to be imported from the Mediterranean region, Bactrian winters being too harsh to allow the culture of the olive tree. The two labels (texts **1 a** and **2 a**) were, no doubt, identical, but are incomplete. Their comparison helps in establishing the following text:

| | | |
|---|---|---|
| 1) | Ἔτους κδ'. [- - ] | "Year 24, the ... ; |
| 2) | ἐλαίου ἐλαίνου | (content) in olive oil; (the vase) |
| 3) | ἀποδεὴς α' τὸ μεταγγισθὲν | A partially empty ( of the reserve) of a |
| 4) | ἀπὸ κεραμίων δύο διὰ Ἱππίου | (*stamnos*) and a half (contains) the oil |

19 Epigraphic evidence of natural products at Ai Khanum includes, apart from incense and olive oil (see below), honey (O. Guillaume, A. Rougeulle, *Fouilles AKh VII*, p. 73, n° 1263, inscription on jar : μελι) and cinnamon (κίνναμον or κιννάμωμον : see the two alabasters found in the heroon of Kineas with the inscription κινν, engraved on the shoulder which probably designates its cinnamon contents : P. Bernard, in *Fouilles AKh I*, pp. 100-102 ; O. Guillaume and A. Rougeulle, *Fouilles AKh VII*, p. 12, alabasters 0139, κιν and 0141, κινν). A specimen of alabaster from Nippur also bears the inscription κιννα : H.-P. Francfort, *Fouilles AKh III*, p. 21, n. 15. Arrian VII, 20, 2 attributes the cinnamon to Gedrosia : see also J.I. Miller *The spice trade of the Roman Empire 29 B.C to A.D. 641*, Oxford, 1969, p. 176 and M.G. Raschke, "New studies in Roman commerce with the East", in *ANRW, II Principat, 9,2*, Berlin, 1978, pp. 652-654.

20 P. Bernard, *CRAI* 1978, p. 450 and n. 25 ; Cl. Rapin, *RA* 1987, p. 56. On Near Eastern sources of incense : J.I. Miller *The spice trade* ; N. Groom, *Frankincense and myrrh*, 1981 ; E.H. Schafer, *The golden peaches of Samarcand*, 1985, pp. 170-171 ; K. Nielsen, *Incense in ancient Israël*, Leiden, 1986. For a reference to incense on alabasters see C.B.F. Walker, "Some Mesopotamian inscribed vessels", *Iraq*, 42, 1980, pp. 84-86. The usage of incense at Taxila since the Greek period is attested by the discovery of incense burners and of *thymiateria* : J. Marshall, *Taxila*, Cambridge, 1951, pp. 595-596 ; for the spread of incense in India see J.I. Miller, *The spice trade*, pp. 102-104.

| | | |
|---|---|---|
| 5) | τοῦ ἡμιο[λ]ίου καὶ ἐσφραγισται | decanted from two jars by Hippias ; and have sealed: |
| 6) | [Μολοσ]σὸς τὸν α' καὶ Στ[ράτων τον β'(?)] | Molossus (?) the vase A and Strato (?) the vase B (?)". |

The label **1a** related to the storage of olive oil is one of the principal documents yielded by the excavation of the treasury for the study of the events marking the fall of the city of Ai Khanum, as it bears the only date furnished by the exploration of the city: ἔτους κδ' "year 24". This date probably refers to a regnal year or era which P. Bernard has identified as pertaining to Eucratides. If we accept Justin's view (XLI, 6) that this king and the Parthian king Mithridates I acceded to their respective thrones at the same time, then Eucratides must have come to power in Bactria around 171 B.C. The twenty fourth year of his reign would then be 148 B.C. In this year Strato and Molossus held office under the direction of Strato. Projecting on the basis of the number of names occurring in the inscriptions, that the term of the officer in-charge of the treasury was one year at the most, we can re-establish the order of succession among the different *gazophylakes* of the treasury: the period of Zeno, the earliest officer in-charge, as attested by the texts, may be fixed as 150 BC. He was followed by Timodemus in 149 B.C., by Strato in 148 B.C., by Philiscus in 147 B.C. and by Nikeratus in 146 B.C. We do not possess the name of any treasurer after this. If there were no gap in the sequence of names mentioned and if, according to the texts, the officers in-charge succeeded each other annually without interruption, then the destruction of the treasury must have occurred in 145 B.C.[21]. We know, in addition, on the basis of ten different labels, that the treasury had received deposits of Indian coins during at least three years (**4b**, **4c**, **6** and **8**). These annual receipts were undoubtedly the result of expeditions to India. This observation corresponds with the account of Justin who informs us that Eucratides was killed by his son when he was returning from his campaigns in India. The execution of this king is certainly connected with the arrival of the nomadic tribes, already assembled on the northern frontiers of the kingdom, who had used the frequent absences of Eucratides to seize Ai Khanum. The sudden disappearance of the king must have resulted in the ultimate decline of Greek power in Bactria.

---

21 See P. Bernard, *Les monnaies hors trésors*, pp. 97-105 ; O. Bopearachchi, *Monnaies gréco-bactriennes et indo-grecques. Catalogue raisonné*, Paris, 1991, pp. 66-88 ; *idem*, "Ménandre Sôter, un roi indo-grec. Observations chronologiques et géographiques", *Studia Iranica*, 19, 1990, pp. 39-85. Basing himself on a study of monograms and all other available historical sources-Indian and Chinese classical texts and archaeological findings, O. Bopearachchi presents a new approach to the historical problems relating to the Greek kingdoms of Bactria and India which contrasts with earlier studies, particularly that of W.W. Tarn and of A.K. Narain (see also the general bibliography in R.N. Frye, *The History of Ancient Iran*, München, 1984, pp. 177-178). The date 130 B.C. that A.K. Narain proposes for the destruction of the city and which corresponds with the period of Menander which begins in 155 B.C., is not sustainable (A.K. Narain, "The earliest Brāhmī inscription outside India", *JAOS*, 106, 1986, pp. 797-801 ; *idem*, "Notes on some inscriptions from Ai Khanum (Afghanistan)", *Zeitschrift für Papyrologie und Epigraphik*, 69, 1987, pp. 277-282, particularly pp. 280-282 ; *idem*, "On some Greek inscription from Afghanistan", *Annali dell'Istituto Universitario Orientale di Napoli*, 47, 1987, pp. 269-392). Actually the period between 155 and 128 B.C., which represents Chang Kien's passage in Bactria is not sufficiently long to accommodate the total of 26 years attested by the economic inscriptions, and the approximately ten years which separate the two nomadic attacks on Ai Khanum (see n. 112-114). Similarly the second date proposed by A.K. Narain, from the reign of Agathocles (190-180 B.C.) would leave too long an interval between the end of Greek occupation of Ai Khanum and the fall of Bactria.

## MATERIALS USED IN ADMINISTRATIVE WORK[22]

Calam and inkpot are objects of everyday use in a depot, necessary both for preparing documents as well as for labelling merchandise. Evidence of **writing materials** exists in most of the buildings of Ai Khanum. They consist of calams and inkpots[23], whose form, influenced by Mediterranean style, survived in the East even after the Hellenistic period, as attested by the finds at Begram[24] and Taxila[25]. The only evidence of the writing materials used by the officials in the treasury is provided by the discovery of a handle with a loop on top (**D3-1**, p. 123 and fig. 6). This type of handle, which is found only on certain inkpots at Ai Khanum and Taxila[26], makes it possible to identify with certainty the original object. Graeco-Bactrian craftsmanship, as reflected in the finds at Ai Khanum, is characterized by a standardization of types and techniques. However, the ink-pots found at this site present variations which suggest differences in origin and it is possible that some of them, particularly the ones in bronze, were imported[27]. Without trying to delve into the question of their origin it is our view that they were not Mediterranean products. Their sophisticated form, particularly the lead cylinder fixed under the lid, intended perhaps to

---

22 Cl. Rapin, *Fouilles AKh VIII*, pp. 131-137.

23 O. Guillaume and A. Rougeulle, *Fouilles AKh VII*, pp. 47-48 : ceramic inkpot from the large propylaeum (n° 0920), bronze inkpots from house 3 and the gymnasium (n$^{os}$ 0921-0922), stoppers of inkpots from house 1 and the large propylaeum (n$^{os}$ 0923-0924) and calam in bronze from house 1 (n° 0925) ; regarding n° 0921 see also P. Bernard, *CRAI*, 1978, pp. 461-463 and fig. 21. On the finds in the sanctuary see H.-P. Francfort, *Fouilles AKh III*, p. 68, tableau n° 37.4 with references nn. 9-11 (calam in iron) and p. 59, tableau n° 20.30 (bronze and ceramic inkpots). On writing and painting materials in Egypt see A. Lucas, *Ancient Egyptian materials and industries*[4], London, 1962, pp. 338-366.

24 J. Hackin, "Catalogue descriptif des objets découverts à Begram", in J. Hackin *et alii*, *Nouvelles recherches archéologiques à Begram (ancienne Kâpicî)(1939-1940) (MDAFA, 11)*, Paris, 1954 , p. 280, n° 80, fig. 353 (bronze inkpot) ; R. Ghirshman, *Bégram, Recherches archéologiques et historiques sur les Kouchans (MDAFA, 12)*, Le Caire, 1946, pl. XI, 1 (calam).

25 J.H. Marshall, *Taxila*, Cambridge, 1951, p. 597, pl. 176, n$^{os}$ 329-339 (inkpots) ; p. 598, pl. 173, n$^{os}$ 340 and 341 (brass calams). See also the references in O. Guillaume and A. Rougeulle, *Fouilles AKh VII*, pp. 48 and 88 (F6 : bronze ink-pot seen in the bazar of Kabul). On the production of ink in India see E.H. Warmington, *The commerce between the Roman Empire and India*[2], London, New York, 1974, pp. 204-205.

26 O. Guillaume and A. Rougeulle, *Fouilles AKh VII*, n° 0921. J. Marshall, *Taxila*, pl. 176, n° 330 : specimen from the early Śaka period. Apart from these examples, we do not know of other inkpots possessing a handle with a loop of this type : the only parallel that we can suggest of this type of handle is associated with a small vessel of bronze discovered in Cyprus and identified as a lamp by the excavators : O. Vessberg, A. Westholm, *The Swedish Cyprus expedition, IV, part 3, The Hellenistic and Roman periods in Cyprus*, Stockholm, 1956, fig. 33.28, pl. CLIII.4. It is sometimes difficult to distinguish lamps from ink-pots : see, for Egypt, the profile of a hanging ceramic lamp – "lampe veilleuse en forme de corbeille " – dated to the ancient Ptolemian period : Ch. Desroches, K. Michałovski, "Catalogue des objets", in *Fouilles franco-polonaises : Rapports, III, Tell Edfou 1939*, Paris, 1950, p. 232, n° 557, fig. 112, pl. XXXI, 9.

27 O. Guillaume, "Contribution à l'étude d'un artisanat bactrien préhellénistique", in *L'archéologie de la Bactriane ancienne*, Paris, 1985, pp. 257-272, particularly p. 258. The ceramic ink-pot with two holds for fixing a handle found in Ai Khanum : O. Guillaume and A. Rougeulle, *Fouilles AKh VII*, n° 0920, pl. XII.16, is also identical to a specimen from Taxila : J. Marshall, *Taxila*, p. 422, pl. 125.142, who attributes this model to the Sakas. It is possible that the ceramic hanging lamp mentioned above belongs to the same tradition.

prevent the ink from spilling or to stabilise the pot, is, as a matter of fact, found also in ink-pots from Taxila[28].

There are only a few finds in the entire site pertaining to **weights and measures**. They consist mainly of weighing pans, a complete balance with its beam, three pointers of the beams and half a dozen weights. The weighing pans are of bronze or iron, their diameter varying between 6 to 17 cm. The weights are in lead, bronze, iron and agate. Among the notable finds of the treasury is a pendant-weight in agate of 27 g. (**E17-1**, p. 123 and fig. 7). This has the form of an extremely stylised duck with its head turned backwards, a notch marking its neck and a groove indicating the wings. We have ample evidence in the oriental jewellery of ancient times (Near-East & India) of precious stone pendants with animal forms[29], but we do not know of a real parallel to this type of a duck. In addition, in contrast to the specimen from Ai Khanum, the ancient oriental statuettes of ducks are usually realistic. There is a long tradition in India at Mohenjo-Daro[30], and in the Near East and Iran[31], at Sumer, Ur, Assur, Babylonia, Susa[32] and Persepolis[33] of using them as weights of all dimensions including , for example, in the activity of goldsmiths : there is evidence of an artisan utilising an object of this type in his workshop in Larsa[34]. On the basis of the archaeological context of room *108*, in which most of the remains of room *109* were discovered, it appears that the duck of Ai Khanum came from the Indian treasure. It would then belong to an Indian tradition of the Mauryan or Śuṅga period and would thus be related to Indian metrology. It

---

28 J. Marshall, *Taxila*, pl. 176, n° 333, 334, 335 ; of note is the large diameter of these ink-pots in contrast with the opening which is narrow. Although they belong to a layer of the site which is post-Greek, these objects fit perfectly in the Hellenistic tradition : we can therefore not exclude the possibility that they were fabricated at an earlier date than their stratigraphic context allows us to suppose.

29 H.C. Beck, *The Beads from Taxila (Archaeological Surveys of India. Memoirs, 65)*, Delhi, 1941, pl. 1, 9 : lion and pl. 7, n$^{os}$ 3 sqq. : lions, elephants, ruminants. See also M.G. Dikshit, "Notes on some Indian amulets", *Bulletin of Prince of Wales Museum of Western India*, 1951-1952, No. 2 (1953), pp. 86-99. The carving of animal figurines in precious stones (lions and reclining bulls) was also known to the Elamite and the Achaemenid world as, for example, in Pasargadae : D. Stronach, *Pasargadae*, Oxford, 1978, p. 177, pl. 152, c-d : 3 lions in carnelian, amethyst, lapis-lazuli; in Persepolis : E.F. Schmidt, *Persepolis II : Contents of the Treasury and Other Discoveries*, Chicago, 1957, pl. 17 : agate seal in the form of a cow or bull; pl. 43.1 : cow in lapis-lazuli; in Susa : J. de Morgan, G. Jéquier and others, *Recherches archéologiques, deuxième série (MDP, 7)*, Paris, 1925, pl. XIII.13 : lion in agate and head of bull in lapis-lazuli. For a lion in amber found in tomb 5 of Tilia-tepe see V. Sarianidi, *Bactrian Gold*, Leningrad, 1985, p. 253, n° 7, ill. 76.

30 A.S. Hemmy, "System of weights at Mohenjo-daro", in *Mohenjo-daro*, ed. J.H. Marshall, London, 1931, pp. 589-598. On the weights used by goldsmiths in Mohenjo-Daro see E. Mackay, "Household objects, tools, and implements", in *Mohenjo-daro*, p. 461 and ch. XXIX : cubic weights of all dimensions in hard stone.

31 *La Terra tra i due fiumi. Venti anni di archeologia italiana in Medio Oriente. La Mesopotamia dei tesori*, Torino, 1985, p. 316, n$^{os}$ 130-142 : Ischali, Larsa.

32 The Louvre Museum possesses a duck in agate of the Elamite period (2nd millenium) from Susa : N.T. Belaiew, "Examen des documents pondéraux", in *MMAP, 25*, Paris, 1934, p. 135, fig. I.

33 E.F. Schmidt, *Persepolis II*, pp. 105-107, pl. 82.3 et 4.

34 *La terra tra i due fiumi*, p. 316, n$^{os}$ 130-141, pp. 384-385. See also J.L. Huot, "Le métier de l'orfèvre à Larsa", in *L'archéologie de l'Iraq du début de l'époque néolithique à 333 avant notre ère, Paris, 1978*, Paris, 1980, pp. 113-118. D. Arnaud, Y. Calvet, J.L. Huot, "Ilšu-Ibnišu, orfèvre de l'*E.Babbar* de Larsa. La jarre L.76.77 et son contenu", *Syria*, 56, 1979, pp. 1-64.

is therefore possible that it might never have been utilised as such in the administration of the palace[35].

## SMALL OBJECTS

Among the buildings of Ai Khanum, the treasury, along with the sanctuary of the temple à redans, is the richest in objects of all sorts[36]. Despite the dispersal of the contents due to the pillage of the building, we are in a position to identify the following categories : 1) Objects related to the building ; 2) Objects brought by later inhabitants ; 3) Objects from the royal treasure. The objects belonging to the first group are mainly of iron. They consist primarily of components of doors and miscellaneous items used in carpentry : nails, rivets, plates of locks and keys of the Laconian type. The items in the second group – ceramic vases, sundry objects of domestic utility such as mortars, implements used in the retrieval of metals, and arms – were, no doubt, brought into the treasury in the post-palatial period. The objects in the third group, which are the most numerous, consist of remains of the royal treasure and are generally characterized by the fine quality of the material used. They are rough precious stones stored for the purpose of processing and finishing at a later date, fragments of jewellery and fine utensils. There is a large range of materials here, both in what concerns precious stones – alabasters (gypsum and calcite), schists, rock crystals (colourless quartz or amethysts), agates, carnelians, lapis-lazuli, turquoises, beryls, garnets, sapphires, obsidians – and other materials such as diverse metals, glass, coral, mother of pearl, ivory, bone, wood, asbestos, etc.

## RAW MATERIALS[37]

The objects of the royal treasure consist of rough and unfinished materials stocked either with the intention of working on them in the royal workshops, or simply as goods to be exchanged in the market of raw materials. It is nevertheless to be noted that, but for some categories of objects such

---

35 At Taxila, the weights are spherical and in stone : J. Marshall, *Taxila*, pp. 508-512. If the object of the treasury is indeed of Indian origin, we do not know to what standard it refers. The average weight of Indian punch-marked coins struck in Taxila varies according to the treasures, but on the whole does not correspond to 27 g. which is the weight of this object, particularly if considered in the decimal system. The average weight of coins is, in fact, 3.4 g. in the treasures of Taxila and 3 g. in the treasure of Ai Khanum : see R. Audouin and P. Bernard, *RNum*, VI-15, 1973, p. 285, fig. 7. According to O.Bopearchchi, in the coins of the earlier Greek sovereigns in India there are some Indo-Greek bronze issues (struck in Taxila ?) of a standard which differs from the one used for silver coins ; for the coins of Demetrius I see M. Mitchiner, *The early Indo-Greeks and their antecedents I*, types 106 and 107 ; these bronzes are extremely worn out but O.B. attributes to them an original weight of approximately 27 g ; for the coins of Agathocles see *ibidem*, types 150 to 153 : average weight of 13.5 g. approximately, half of the weight of the agate duck at Ai Khanum. It we translate this into the Indian binary system, this weight would correspond to the unit of 8 *kārshāpaṇa* of Taxila : J. Marshall, *Taxila*, p. 511 : 424 grains or 27.56 grammes (see also the Harappan units, p. 512).

36 On the small objects of Ai Khanum see Ph. Gouin in *Fouilles d'Aï Khanoum I*, pp. 195-201; H.-P. Francfort, *Fouilles AKh III*; O. Guillaume, A. Rougeulle, *Fouilles AKh VII*; Cl. Rapin, *Fouilles AKh VIII*, p. 91 sqq.

37 Cl. Rapin, *Fouilles AKh VIII*, pp. 143-152.

as vases in stone or in glass, no luxury goods appear to have been fabricated at Ai Khanum. Most of the precious objects are undeniably from India, including ornaments made from local minerals like lapis-lazuli. The only artisanal objects, which were definitely produced in Bactria, if not at Ai Khanum, were glass objects and vessels in schist and alabaster. The excavation at the site has revealed a very special type of small shovel, practically unknown elsewhere, in the shape of a drain pipe made of these materials.

The minerals found as rough stones in the treasury such as lapis-lazuli, turquoise, garnet, beryl, rock crystal, amethyst, asbestos, as well as the metals (gold, silver, lead, iron) are mostly of Central Asian origin. The pieces of jewellery in mother of pearl, rock crystal, carnelian, sapphire and some of the pieces in agate and ivory were, on the contrary, imported from India[38]. A pendant carved in the form of the symbol of *nandipāda* proves that even coral which was traditionally imported from the Mediterranean came via India to Ai Khanum (**O33-1**, p. 126, fig. 21.1).

The majority of the finds in glass (**M7**) are in the form of splinters of ingots of crude glass[39]. The original depots of such glass were the two warehouses *104* and *109*, but as a result of the pillage the remains were scattered in most of the areas of the treasury as well as in the sanctuary of the temple à redans[40]. The quality of this glass is uneven, due to the presence of numerous bubbles. Most of the fragments have become extremely iridescent but the range of colours that can still be observed is very wide (red, yellow, green, black, blue, violet and white molten glass)[41]. This collection also includes the debris of crafted objects : vessels, jewellery and decorative plates. It is very difficult to establish a typology of these objects as they are extremely fragmented and greatly corroded. Many of the blue and violet coloured specimens lack iridescence. This characteristic is due to the predominance of potassic in the composition of the molten glass employed in these fragments. Ancient Mediterranean glass had a sodic base. It is therefore possible that the raw material of the glass of Ai Khanum was of Central Asian origin[42]. This contradicts the general view held on the basis of *The Periplus of the Erythraean Sea* (49) that at least during the Hellenistic period glass was only produced in the Mediterranean world, because glass in a crude form was

---

38 M.G. Raschke, "New studies in Roman commerce", pp. 604-1361 ; E.H. Warmington, *The commerce.* As classical sources on precious stones we will be using mainly Theophrastus, *De lapidibus*, ed. D.E. Eichholz, Oxford, 1965 ; Pline, *Histoire naturelle, Livre XXXVII*, text estab. transl. and comm. by E. de Saint-Denis, Paris, "Les Belles Lettres", 1972 ; the chief edn. of *The Periplus of the Erythraen Sea* transl. by W.H. Schoff, New York, 1912 ; see also *The Periplus Maris Erythraei*, ed., and transl. with comm. by L. Casson, Princeton, 1989. We will not be taking into account much of the new information contained in *The Periplus of the Erythraean Sea, by an unknown author*, trad. de G.W.B. Huntingford, London, 1980. Lastly, see Chr. Robin, "L'Arabie du Sud et la date du *Périple de la Mer Érythrée* (Nouvelles données)", *JA*, 279, 1991, pp. 1-30 ; G. Fussman, "Le *Périple* et l'histoire politique de l'Inde", *JA*, 279, 1991, pp. 31-38.

39 Cl. Rapin, *Fouilles AKh VIII*, pp. 147-148.

40 H.-P. Francfort, *Fouilles AKh III*, p. 78, tableau n° 40.75 sqq. and pl. XXXII (0.1278 : parallelopipedal ingot).

41 On the colouring of glass see A. Lucas, *Ancient Egyptian materials and industries*[4], London, 1962, pp. 179-194, particularly p. 184 sqq. ; R.J. Forbes, *Studies in ancient technology*, t. 5 (1966), pp. 112-236.

42 On Central Asian glass see particularly the references of M.G. Raschke, "New studies in Roman commerce", pp. 627-628 and nn. 398-401 et 416. See also S.R. Pidaev, "Steklo srednevekovogo Termeza", *ONU*, 7/1986, pp. 53-58 ; A.A. Abdurazakov, "Ximičeskie sostavy srevnix i srednevekovyx stekol Afganistana", *ONU*, 11/1986, pp. 36-39.

sent from Alexandria towards Barygaza (in West India)[43], probably for the fabrication of mirrors and vases. India certainly imported from the West, as proved by the glass of Begram which was brought to Central Asia during the period when the *Periplus* was written[44]. Although the Graeco-Roman origin of a part of the finds of finished or unfinished glass in Central Asia and India is certain, several examples similar to the glass of Ai Khanum are also known[45].

Asbestos (**M30**) is found in the raw state in the form of blocks of supple beige fibres[46]. Pliny (XIX, 19-20 and XXXVI, 139) emphasizes the inmense value of this non-inflammable material comparing it to the most beautiful beads. Due to this non-inflammable quality it was possible to weave it as serviettes or shrouds[47], among other fabrics, or the wicks of candelabras (Pausanias I, 26, 7). People in ancient times knew of the deposits of asbestos – chrysotile – at Carystos in Euboea (Strabo X, I, 6), at Cyprus, in Arcadia and in other places in Europe (Alps, Pyrenees, Corsica) but numerous other deposits also exist. Pliny also refers to deposits in India (XIX, 4) and

---

43 On the history of this important port in Nort-West India see B.G. Gokhale, "Bharukaccha / Barygaza", in *India and the ancient world : history, trade and culture before A.D. 650*, ed. G. Pollet, Leuven, 1987, pp. 67-79.

44 For glass at Begram see R. Ghirshman, *Bégram. Recherches archéologiques*, p. 48, pl. XXVII, B.G. 98/a and B.G. 99/a, from level I, and the references of M.G. Raschke, "New studies in Roman commerce", pp. 633-634, nn. 501-502. On the trade with the Far East see C.G. Seligman, H.C. Beck, "Far Eastern glass : Some Western origins", *The Museum of Far Eastern Antiquities. Stockholm. Bulletin*, 10, 1938, pp. 1-64.

45 On glass objects manufactured in India see R.G. Chandra, *Indo-Greek jewellery*, New Delhi, 1979, pp. 103-104 ; R.S.M. Ghosh, "The use of glass in ancient India", *JBORS*, 10, 1924, 194-201, pp. 194-201 ; B.S. Upadhyaya, *India in Kālidāsa*, 1947, pp. 207-208 ; B.B. Lal, "Examination of some ancient Indian glass specimens", *Ancient India*, 8, 1952, pp. 17-27 ; *idem*, "Studies in early and mediaeval Indian ceramics - Some glass and glass-like artefacts from Bellary, Kolhapur, Maski, Nasik and Maheshwar", *Bulletin of the Deccan College Research Institute*, 14, 1953, pp. 48-58 ; M.G. Dikshit, , "Studies in ancient Indian glass (I). Glass as mentioned in Kautilya's Arthasastra", *EW*, 1-2, 15, 1964-1965, pp. 62-68 ; U.P. Thapliyal, *Foreign elements in ancient Indian society*, New Delhi, 1979, p. 74 ; M.G. Raschke, "New studies in Roman commerce", p. 671, nn. 1550-1551. On the glass tiles of the stūpa of Dharmarājikā at Taxila, produced in India in the 3rd cent. B.C. see B.B. Lal, "Examination of some ancient Indian glass specimens", *loc. cit.*, p. 22. For the beads of Taxila, see H.C. Beck, *Beads from Taxila*, pp. 20-31, and for those of Arikamedu, B.B. Lal, "Examination of rods of glass-like material from Arikamedu", *Ancient India*, 14, 1958, pp. 139-143. See also M.G. Dikshit, "A brief study of the glass industry at Kapadwany", *Museum and Picture Gallery, Baroda*, 20, 1968, pp. 1-9.

46 The original depot of these fibres, confused for a long time with roots, might have been the warehouse *109*. Like numerous other objects found in this room, these specimens may also have been of Indian origin. On asbestos see E. Saglio in *DAGR*, s.v. "Asbestus" ; A. Nies in *RE*, s.v. "Amiantus" (1894) ; V. Ball, "A geologist's contribution to the history of ancient India (early notices of metals and gems in India)", *The Indian Antiquary*, 13, 1884, pp. 228-248 ; B. Laufer, "Asbestos and salamander : an essay in Chinese and Hellenistic folk-lore", *T'oung Pao*, 16, 1915, pp. 299-373 (reprinted in B. Laufer, *Sino-Tibetan studies*, 1987, t. 1, pp. 219-293) ; E.H. Warmington, *The commerce*, pp. 255, 270, 384 ; R.J. Forbes, *Studies in ancient technology*, t. 5 (1964), p. 63 ; J.P. Wild, *Textile Manufacture in the Northern Roman Provinces*, Cambridge, 1970, p. 21 ; E.H. Schafer, *The golden peaches of Samarcand*, 1985, pp. 199-200.

47 Shrouds in asbestos were found in tombs at Pozzuoli, Rome and Rhineland. On the subject of a towel in asbestos in the treasure of Khosru II (VIIth century) see A. Christensen, *L'Iran sous les Sassanides*, Copenhague, 1944, p. 466.

we know that Central Asia, particularly the Hindu Kush (Badakhshan or the region of Kabul[48]) and northern India are rich in these deposits. It appears that Syria and Egypt had exported finished goods towards China and perhaps also to India[49]. But, if we are to believe the *Mahāvaṃsa*, which reports that Aśoka sent objects of gold and serviettes of asbestos to the king of Ceylon in exchange of precious stones which the latter had sent, then Indians probably knew how to weave asbestos in the third century B.C[50].

The orpiment (ἀρρενικόν, **M31**) is a sulphide of arsenic found in the form of golden yellow blade-like branches, which is volatile and capable of being liquefied by a blow lamp[51]. It served as a colouring agent in paint[52], and could also be used in metallurgy[53] and in the composition of medicines and cosmetics[54]. It is found in Syria, Iran, Turkey, Kurdistan and Caucasia. According to the *Periplus* (49, 56), Romans re-exported it to Muziris and Nelcynda. Since it was unknown in India, the orpiment found at Ai Khanum could have either been of local origin or imported from the Near East. It is possible that, like coral, it might also have transited through India where it may have been stocked before being brought to Bactria by the Greeks[55].

The study of trade between the different centres of civilisation in the Near and Middle East since the proto-historic period is mainly based on the indestructible remains found during excavations – ceramic, metal and precious stones. The spread of lapis-lazuli, of which the only known deposit in antiquity was located in Badakhshan, makes it possible to reconstitute the network of important commercial routes which linked Central Asia to the Mesopotamian, Iranian[56] and Egyptian worlds

---

48 W.C. Brice, *An historical atlas of Islam*, map pp. 16-17. B. Laufer, "Asbestos and salamander", pp. 327-328, p. 366.

49 Chinese sources on fabrics in Syrian asbestos : W.H. Schoff, *Parthian stations of Isidore of Charax*, Philadelphia, 1914, p. 42 ; B. Laufer, "Asbestos and salamander".

50 V. Ball, "A geologist's contribution", p. 231, with reference to G. Turnour, *A history of Ceylon for twenty-four centuries from B.C. 543*, p. 70.

51 A. Nies, in *RE*, s.v. "Arsenicum" (1896) ; H. Blümner, *Die Römischen Privataltertümer*, München, 1911, p. 438 sqq. ; E.H. Warmington, *The commerce*, p. 270 ; R.J. Forbes, *Studies in ancient technology*, t. 9 (1972), p. 178 ; E.H. Schafer, "Orpiment and realgar in Chinese technology and tradition", *JAOS*, 75, 1955, pp. 73-89 ; *idem*, *The golden peaches of Samarcand*, pp. 213-214.

52 W. Fol in *DAGR*, s.v. "Color", p. 1326b ; A. Nies in *RE*, s.v. "Arsenicum" ; R.J. Forbes, t. 3 (1965), p. 227. Theophrastus, *De lapidibus*, 51 reports that it could replace ochre. It is present, for example, in Central Asia in the composition of yellow pigments in the frescoes of Pendžikent.

53 J. Ramin, *La technique minière et métallurgique des Anciens (Latomus, 153)*, Bruxelles, 1977, pp. 186-187.

54 As medicine for the treatment of abscess or as depilatory cream : Dioscorides V, 104 : *Pedanii Dioscuridis Anazarbei de materia medica libri quinque*[2], ed. M. Wellmann, Berolini, 1958, t. 3, p. 74 ; *Des Pedanos Dioskurides aus Anazarbos Arztneimittellehre in fünf Büchern*, transl. J. Berendes, Stuttgart, 1902, pp. 521-522. Orpiment based depilatory creams were used in Iran till recently.

55 The discovery of orpiment was made in the warehouse *109* of the treasury where the majority of the objects found were of Indian origin.

56 The excavations of the sites of Namazga-tepe in Margiana, Shahr-i Sokhta in Seistan, Mundigak in the south of Afghanistan, Tepe Yahya in Iranian Baluchistan have brought to light the remains of the workshops where, sometimes, semi-precious stones were initially worked upon before their eventual exportation : M. Tosi, "The

in the West and the Indian world in the South[57]. It was by these routes that mineral riches of the Indian world were exported towards the Near East. The palaces and the treasuries of the Achaemenid Empire received food stuffs and precious raw material produced in its most distant satrapies which have been listed in the "charter of Susa"[58]. A precise chronological framework is not often available for Central Asian and Indian sites for the periods which followed (Hellenistic and Kushana periods). In addition, the literature on semi-precious stones used in antique jewellery is even now difficult to interpret, either due to the non-availability of generalised mineralogical analyses, or due to the inability to locate ancient deposits. Despite these deficiencies, the excavation of Ai Khanum is capable of furnishing a chronological scheme for these materials which could provide the basis for reconstructing the position of Bactria in the system of cultural and commercial exchanges on the eve of the disintegration of Greek power. The finds in the treasury and in the sanctuary leave no doubt that an overwhelming majority of these materials came from deposits situated in Central Asia and India[59]. However, in contrast with the preceding periods, there is no proof that there was a well-established industry of semi-precious stones in pre-Kushana Bactria, and perhaps most of the jewellery in semi-precious stones of the Hellenistic period was made in West or North-West India.

---

Northeastern frontier of the ancient Near east", *Mesopotamia*, 8-9, 1973-74, pp. 43-45 ; J.-Fr. Jarrige, "A propos d'un foret à tige hélicoïdale en cuivre de Mundigak", in *De l'Indus aux Balkans, Recueil à la mémoire de Jean Deshayes*, Paris, 1985, pp. 281-292.

57 On the relations between Central Asia and the Indus valley in the bronze age in the light of the excavations of the sites of Shortugai in the plain of Ai Khanum and Sarazam in Tadžikistan see H.-P. Francfort, M.-H. Pottier, "Sondage préliminaire sur l'établissement protohistorique harappéen et post-harappéen de Shortugaï (Afghanistan du N.-E.)", *Arts Asiatiques*, 34, 1978, pp. 29-79 ; B. Lyonnet, "Découvertes de sites de l'âge du bronze dans le Nord-Est de l'Afghanistan : leurs rapports avec la civilisation de l'Indus", *Annali dell'Istituto Orientale di Napoli*, 37, 1977, pp. 19-35 ; Francfort, H.-P., *Fouilles de Shortugaï. Recherches sur l'Asie Centrale protohistorique (Mémoires de la Mission française en Asie Centrale, 2)*, Paris, 1989.

58 In the three known inscriptions of the "charter of Susa", the supply of gold was maintained by Lydia and Bactria, that of lapis-lazuli and carnelian by Sogdiana, that of turquoise by Chorasmia, that of ivory by Nubia, Sind and Arachosia : P. Bernard in *Etudes de géographie historique*, p. 9 n. 30 (p. 70) ; F. Vallat, "Deux inscriptions élamites de Darius Ier (DSf et DSz)", *Studia Iranica*, I, 1972, pp. 4-5 ; J. Wiesehöfer, "Beobachtungen zum Handel des Achämenidenreiches", *Münstersche Beiträge zur antiken Handelsgeschichte*, 1, 1982, pp. 5-15.

59 Regarding the deposits and the historical sources, both ancient and modern, of lapis-lazuli, turquoise, carnelian and garnets see P. Bernard, in *Etudes de géographie historique*. See also H. Blümner, *Technologie und Terminologie*, III, 1884, pp. 227-323 ; Among the precious stones of Indian origin, we can cite sapphires (Zanskar), emeralds (Udaipur, Ajmer), chalcedonies and agates (Rajkot, Broach, Rajmahal [North]).

## EXPENSIVE VESSELS[60]

The expensive vessels consist of glass containers, alabasters in calcite and gypsum, plates in calcite, schist and yellow soapstone, bowls in rock crystal and agate and fragments of small rhytons in worked ivory. Most of these objects are part of the treasure but the place of origin of each type – Iran, India or Bactria – is not certain.

Among the pieces related to India, the vessels in crystal are represented by the fragments of two bowls (**N15-1** and **2**, fig. 11 and p. 124), the lid of a bowl decorated with a star-shaped engraving (**N15-3**), the lid of a small pyxide (**N15-4**) and the bases of pyxides (**N15-5** to **8**)[61]. As for the vessels in agate, the only remains consist of a fragment of a cone-shaped cup (**N17-1**, fig. 12 and p. 124)[62]. These finds are all from the treasury where they were part of the treasure housed in room *109*. Inspite of their extremely fragmented condition and modest dimensions, they are the finest pieces among the vessels that belonged to the treasury.

Rock crystal and agate are among the hardest stones used in the fabrication of vessels. The vessels as well as the jewellery and inlay work, found at Ai Khanum display a tremendous mastery of the technique of cutting and polishing hard stones and a great ability to choose the purest stones among crystals and the most regular patterns in the veins of agates. The technique of making vessels from semi-precious stones is known since the early ancient period but we will confine ourselves here to its state during the Hellenistic period[63].

---

60 Cl. Rapin, *Fouilles AKh VIII*, pp. 153-165.

61 On the fragments of crystal found in the sanctuary at Ai Khanum see H.-P. Francfort, *Fouilles AKh III*, p. 77 and tableau n° 40. The fragments published by H.-P. F. probably came from the treasury : n° 68 is a block of quartz with one side sawed and tarnished as in many other findings in the warehouse *104* (**M15**) ; n° 69 is a fragment of a tubular, octagonal element from Indian furniture piece in the warehouse piece *109* ; see **S15**, fig. 27.2. The hypothesis that rock crystal objects were produced in Bactria is thus not supported by the finds at Ai Khanum.

62 An examination of the finds in the treasury leads us to correct some of the hypotheses formulated by H.-P. Francfort, *Fouilles AKh III*, pp. 74-75 and tableau n° 40. The specimen of rock crystal found in the sanctuary belong to two categories of objects which have now been clearly identified. The n[os] 25, 27, 28, 30, 31, 32b are fragments of the Indian furniture piece from warehouse *109* ; see **S17**, fig. 28 ; n° 32a is a fragment of a bracelet known on the basis of several finds made in the same warehouse ; see **S17-94** to **117**, fig. 28.3. The agate, like the onyx, the sardonyx and the carnelian belongs to the chalcedony group or microcrystalline quartz. The term agate has been generally used for all the finds of chalcedony presented here – banded agate or white agate – excepting carnelian.

63 On the technique of cutting see H.-P. Bühler, *Antike Gefässe aus Edelsteinen*, Mainz, 1973, pp. 32-33. On vases in precious stones from prehistory to the Hellenistic period *ibidem*, pp. 4-10. On precious stones, *ibidem*, pp. 2-3. See also E. Babelon in *DAGR*, s.v. "Murrhina vasa" ; E.H. Warmington, *The commerce*, pp. 237-242 ; A.I. Loewenthal, D.B. Harden, "Vasa Murrina", *JRS*, 39, 1949, pp. 31-37 ; A. Lipinsky, *Oro, argento, gemme e smalti*, Firenze, 1975, bibliography pp. 372-377 ; D.B. Thompson, "The Tazza Farnese Reconsidered. Das ptolemaische Ägypten", *Akten des Internationalen Symposions Berlin, 1976*, Berlin, 1976, pp. 113-121 (on the Persian origin of the shape of Ptolemian vases in precious stones) ; D. Venturo, "I vasi murrini. Il contributo delle fonti classiche", *Antiqua*, 11, 1978, pp. 45-48 (the murrhine vases are in fluorite and not in agate) ; C. Gasparri, "Vasi antichi in pietra dura a Firenze e Roma", *Prospettiva*, 19, 1979, pp. 4-13. On chalcedonies see the technical study of M. Martini, "Le gemme degli Horti Lamiani", in *Le tranquille dimore degli dei*, Roma, 1986, pp. 149-150.

The origin of the vessels in precious stones enumerated for the Graeco-Roman world has been the object of numerous controversies. The problems relate not only to the identification of the stones in classical sources (onyx, particularly "murrhine vases") but especially to the physical study of the vessels which belong to collections and museums.

Dating presents problems for the majority of these vessels in precious stones. The forms rarely correspond to the models of specimens in precious metal whose dating is well established, and could help in arriving at a rigorous typology. These objects have had an exceptional longevity, thanks to collectors in the ancient period and the Renaissance as well as to those who conserved these treasures. But having suffered all the vicissitudes of wars and of pillages, their geographical origin and, consequently, the identification of the workshops is very difficult to establish. By the time they arrived in Rome in sufficient numbers to attract attention, following the triumph of Pompey over Mithridates VI Eupator[64], and then, following the battle of Actium when the Ptolemaic treasures came to be known (Suetonius, *Augustus*, 71), these objects had experienced an extremely turbulent past.

During the third and the second century B.C. the direction of trade and the volume of importations varied according to the political, military and economic condition of the Greek kingdoms. Although several references of the Ancients indicate the presence of these vessels in the courts of the Seleucids and the Ptolemies, it is only the rare case that can be dated and it is possible that most of the vessels actually known to us belong, in fact, to the Roman period. The sites from which the rough stones were extracted and the routes by which they were transported towards the Mediterranean world are only known approximately. On the basis of a wide range of sources, it appears that the important regions which produced raw material and precious vessels, before the industry for the fabrication of vases in precious stones, cameos and gem stones developed in the royal workshops of Alexandria and Antioch[65], were the Parthian Empire (Carmania) and North-West India.

If, as we believe, the majority of the objects stored in room *109* were brought by Eucratides as booty, it is possible that the vases in hard stones at Ai Khanum are of Indian origin. From this point of view, their discovery in the city is important because they confirm the existence of a highly developed industry of precious stone vessels in India around the beginning of the second century B.C.

**Rock crystal** (**N15**)[66] **:** Whereas the vases in semi-precious stones from the Mediterranean world are often modelled on the classical forms of ceramic or metal vessels, the specimens from Ai Khanum seem closer to Indian models in stone or ceramic of the closing years of the Mauryan period or the Śuṅga period. Despite its resemblance to the lid of certain Graeco-Roman pyxides, the form of the lid in rock crystal **N15-4** (fig. 11) for example, is probably, influenced by Buddhist reliquary[67], from India, for which the use of the same material is frequently attested[68].

64 J. Van Ooteghem, *Pompée le Grand bâtisseur d'empire*, Namur, 1954, p. 281 sqq.

65 On the workshops see H.-P. Bühler, *Antike Gefässe*, pp. 30-31.

66 Cl. Rapin, *Fouilles AKh VIII*, pp. 161-165.

67 We do not know if the lid has a handle but it is certain that its general profile is the same as the cover of a pyxide (reliquary) from the stūpa of the palace of Taxila : J. Marshall, *Taxila*, pl. 36 ; see also a fragment of a

Similarly the profile of the bases of the cylindrical vessels **N15-5** to **8** (fig. 11) is identical to that of the reliquary in rock crystal found in a stūpa in the Sanchi region[69]. The Indian origin of this material was known to the Ancients as is confirmed by Pliny XXXVII, 23-29 and Strabo (XV, 1, 67).

**Agate** (**N17**)[70] **:** Like the vases in rock crystal, the fragment of brown agate with large white veins **N17-1** (sardonyx? fig. 12) is also of Indian origin. The material and the colours are those of the vases largely dispersed in the Mediterranean world from the end of the 1st century B.C. In classical sources, the terminology used for these vases in chalcedony is imprecise and one finds a number of terms - onyx, agate or "murrhine vases" – each used generally to denote stones of different types[71]. The "murrhine vases" represented vessels in polychrome stone. According to the *Periplus of the Erythraen Sea* (48) these vessels came from West India (Ujjain, the hills of Rajpipla) from where they were taken to Barygaza before being exported towards Egypt[72]. However this source deals with a relatively later period. The influx of "murrhine vases" in the Roman world had already been indicated by Pliny in connection with the triumph of Pompey[73], and as they were found in the booty of Mithridates Eupator, Pliny attributed them mainly to Carmania and Parthia. This apparent contradiction between the author of the *Periplus* and Pliny regarding the origin of "murrhine vases" could indicate that these vases were made of two different minerals[74]. In view of the minerals still found in Carmania today, the stone of the "murrhine

---

stone reliquary discovered at Sanchi : J.H. Marshall, A. Foucher, *The monuments of Sāñchī*, Calcutta, London, 1930, II, pl. 4.

68 See the specimens from the Sanchi region in A. Cunningham, *The Bhilsa topes ; or, Buddhist monuments of Central India*, repr. Varanasi, 1966, pl. XXIX. For the specimens of rock crystal from Piprāhwā, 3rd cent. B.C. : S.P. Gupta, *The roots of Indian art*, Delhi, 1980, pp. 307-308 and pl. 111.a. For those of Amaravati, 2nd cent. B.C. : *ibidem*, pl. 111.b. For the vessels of Taxila see J. Marshall, *Taxila*, p. 554, p. 498, n^os^ 95-96, pl. 141 *h* et *i* et 147 *a* : miniature vessels – rouge compacts ? – found at Bhiṛ Mound ; p. 144 and pl. 36 *a* : reliquary of large dimensions (diameter 25 cm. approximately). See also E.H. Warmington, *The commerce*, pp. 245-246 ; A. Oliver, "Rock crystal vessels in Antiquity", *Muse*, 7, 1973, pp. 29-35. On the deposits of rock crystal in India, see J. Marshall, *Taxila*, pp. 477-478.

69 Stūpa D of Bhojpur : reliquary with slightly arched and very thin sides discovered inside a vessel of black clay with a lid bearing the inscription "The saint" : see A. Cunningham, *The Bhilsa Topes*, pl. XXVI, fig. 7.

70 Cl. Rapin, *Fouilles AKh VIII*, pp. 161-165.

71 It was certainly not easy for a non-specialist to distinguish between the stones, specially because both in Iran and in India, the stones were subjected to treatment by heat in order to make the colours more vibrant ; see Propertius IV, 5, 26 : *murreaque in Parthis pocula cocta focis*. This technique is still used in India.

72 A. Lipinsky, *Oro, argento, gemme e smalti*, pp. 291-292 ; J. Marshall, *Taxila*, pp. 477-478.

73 XXXVII, 18-22 : 21 : "In size the pieces are never larger than a small display stand, while in bulk they rarely equal drinking vessels that we have discussed... They shine, but without intensity ; indeed, it would be truer to say that they glisten rather than shine. Their value lies in their varied colours : the veins, as they revolve repeatedly vary from purple becoming fiery or the milk-white becoming red as though the new colours were passing through the vein...". On murrhine vases at Rome see also Juvenal VII, 133 and Martial III, 82, 25.

74 If, in the two sources, the "murrhine vases" represented the same mineral (the Indian chalcedony for example), this would lead to the assumption that Parthia and Carmania were intermediate stations in the commerce between India and the Mediterranean. This hypothesis is not sustainable because, as Pliny well knew, the two regions, India and Carmania supplied different types of stones.

vases" mentioned by Pliny (XXXVII, 21-22) could well be fluorspar[75]. The one mentioned in the *Periplus* would then naturally refer to Indian chalcedony, of which a specimen found its way to Ai Khanum. In Pliny, the term onyx[76], might also apply to stones of various types as another type described by him appears to be marble or alabaster[77].

As far as we know, very few remains of vessels in rock crystal or in polychrome stone have been found in the treasury of Persepolis[78] for the Achaemenid period and in the treasury of Nisa[79] for the Parthian era. It is therefore possible that this category of vessels was not produced in the Iranian world before the end of the third century B.C. If there was a production of stone vessels in the Parthian world, its development was independent of India. The differences between the stones found in West or North-West India on the one hand and in Parthia on the other, seem to preclude the possibility of direct trade between these two regions during the Graeco-Bactrian period. The Indian finds at Ai Khanum, as already stated, came not in the form of commercial merchandise but as war booty, and precious stones sent towards Egypt and the Near-East do not appear to have passed through Central Asia. In our opinion, the route used for transporting this merchandise was more to the South, perhaps via the Indian Ocean, either towards the Red Sea or the Persian Gulf. As emphasized by us in the publication concerning the few Greek imports in the treasury[80], the

---

75 In Pliny XXXVII, 18-22, chalcedonies are described as being distinct from "murrhine vases", XXXVII, 90-91 : onyx ; XXXVII, 139-142 : agates – *achates*. It is clear that he could distinguish between Carmanian and Indian stones, more so because it was known that fluorspar came from Carmania where it is still found : H.P. Bühler, *Antike Gefässe*, n^os^ 16, 17, 58 ; E. de Saint-Denis, *Pline l'Ancien, Histoire Naturelle*, Paris, 1972, p. 137 ; D.E. Eichholz, *Pliny, Natural History*, vol. X, London, Cambridge, 1962. H.-P. Bühler, *Antike Gefässe* maintains a distinction between Indian chalcedony, pp. 4-5, and fluorspar / "murrhine vases" of Carmania, pp. 18-21 ; see also pp. 24-25. J. Ogden, *Jewellery of the ancient world*, London, 1982, p. 139, fig. 27 (vase in fluorspar). See also A. Lipinsky, *Oro, argento, gemme e smalti*, pp. 295-296. If we accept the figure, the 2000 vases of onyx and gold in the treasure of Mithridates VI Eupator mentioned by Appian XII, 115, rule out the possihlility that the term onyx refered to chalcedony. The reference here is probably either to fluorspar or alabaster of Iranian or Near Eastern origin. Attention may also be drawn to the description in Pliny XXXVII, 18-19, of an elderly consul, who by drinking repeatedly from a murrhine vase, which he had bought for 70,000 sesterces, wore out the rim. The vase in question cannot be of agate because it is one of the hardest stones, but rather of a much softer stone, like fluorspar, for example.

76 XXXVII, 90-91 : "Zenothemis mentions that the Indian onyx has several different colours, fiery red, black and that of horn, surrounded by white layer as in an eye, and in some cases traversed by a slanting layer". Quoting a little after Satyrus : "a genuine onyx has several bands of different colours combined with others that are milk-white, the colours as the bands shade into each other being quite indescribable as they are reduced to a harmonious and delightfully agreeable unity".

77 XXXVI, 59 : "at first only drinking-vessels were made of it, and then the feet of couches and the frames of chairs".

78 E.F. Schmidt, *Persepolis II*, p. 91, pl. 65.7 to 11.

79 See the reference of H.-P. Francfort to G.G. Lemlejn, "Fragmenty kamennyx izdelij iz raskopok v staroj Nise", *TrJuTAKE*, 8, 1958, pp. 381-389, particularly pp. 381-382, fig. 1 : cup in agate. We can only mention two finds in rock crystal : the first is the fragment of a vase : *ibidem*, p. 381 ; the second is a cylindrical piece which is perhaps a part of a moveable object (according to an oral description given to us by M.I. Filanovič).

80 Cl. Rapin, *Fouilles AKh VIII*, pp. 295-299.

discovery of vessels in precious stones at Ai Khanum does not prove, any more than the articles in ceramic, that a commercial route traversing Bactria linked India to the Mediterranean.

## ORNAMENTS[81]

Since the treasury was among those buildings which were most systematically pillaged, it is not surprising that, only very fragmentary and disparate remains are left of the most expensive merchandise which one could have expected to find here such as ornaments and art objects. However, with a total of approximately 240 fragments, the collection of pieces of ornaments in the treasury is equal to the total finds of the sanctuary (approximately 100 fragments) and those of the other excavations at Ai Khanum (approximately 140 fragments). We do not know if the objects stored in the treasury were originally preserved as mounted ornaments or as loose stones to be assembled later. Although the fragments were found greatly scattered not only in the building of the treasury itself but also in the palace and in the temple à redans, all of them most probably came from only two warehouses *104* and *109*.

Although in a highly fragmented state, the pieces of jewellery from the excavation at Ai Khanum constitute an extremely varied corpus comprising beads for necklaces[82], pendants and some inlays made in a wide range of materials : metals, glass, semi-precious or common stones, coral, sea-shells, mother of pearl, bone and ivory. The finds include some fragments of ornaments in metal (bronze, gold-plated bronze, iron), such as bracelets and rings. There is almost no silver. As proved by the discovery of a jeweller's mould[83], gold work including gold plating on bronze was done in local workshops. The many parallels between the finds of Ai Khanum and Taxila demonstrate that work on the finest precious stones is specific mostly to objects produced in North India. Also, in order to view the ornaments at Ai Khanum in the correct perspective it is necessary to take into account the historical context, as revealed by the excavation of the treasury, which

---

81 Cl. Rapin, *Fouilles AKh VIII*, pp. 167-182.

82 The corpus of beads at Ai Khanum is insufficient for the establishment of a typology but one can refer here to collections which have been well classified, particularly that of Taxila : H.C. Beck, *The beads from Taxila* ; of the Black Sea : E.M. Alekseeva, "Antičnye busy Severnogo Pričernomor'ja", *Arkheologija SSSR*, 1-12, 1982, pp. 5-103 ; or of Central Asia : B.A. Litvinskij, *Ukrašenija iz Mogil'nikov zapadnoj Fergany*, Moscow, 1973, beads pp. 93-153, pl. 11-15, bibliography pp. 173-208 and B.A. Litvinskij, A.B. Sedov, *Kul'ty i ritualy kušanskoj Baktrii*, Moscow, 1984, pl. V. On the technique of making beads from semi-precious stones see A. Lucas, *Ancient Egyptian materials and industries*[4], pp. 386-405 ; J. Boardman, *Greek gems and finger rings. Early bronze age to late classical*, London, 1976, pp. 379-382 ; P.W.M. Wright, "The bow-drill and the drilling of beads, Kabul, 1981", *Afghan Studies*, 3-4, 1982, pp. 95-101 ; J.M. Kenoyer, "The Indus bead industry : contributions to bead technology", *Ornament*, 10-1, 1986, pp. 18-23.

83 O. Guillaume and A. Rougeulle, *Fouilles AKh VII*, p. 79, references to Sialk and Susa, n° 1314 ; Fergana : B.A. Litvinskij, *Ukrašenija iz Mogil'nikov...*, pl. 19.2 ; Bujrapuš-tepe : E.V. Rtveladze, "Novye drevnebaktrijskie pamjatniki na Juge Uzbekistana", in *Baktrijskie drevnosti*, Leningrad, 1976, pp. 101-102, fig. 5.1. See also B. Musche, *Vorderasiatischer Schmuck zur Zeit der Arsakiden und der Sasaniden (Handbuch der Orientalistik, 7, Kunst und Archäologie. 1 : Der alte Vordere Orient, 2 : Die Denkmäler, B : Vorderasien)*, Leiden, New York, 1988, p. 250, pl. LXXXVI, 2.3. For the finds of Taxila see J. Marshall, *Taxila*, pp. 506-507, pl. 142, n^os^ 143-146.

suggests that a large part of the treasure came directly from India. Since the finds at our site are a mix of Indian, indigenous Graeco-Bactrian, Bactrian or nomadic productions, earlier ideas regarding the Graeco-Bactrian ornament industry will thus necessarily get modified.

Both Indian and Graeco-Bactrian ornaments[84], such as it is possible to observe at Ai Khanum, are characterized by a considerable use of polychromy. The use of polychromy it appears was not widespread in the West before the end of the second century B.C., Greek ornaments being mainly of gold, notwithstanding stories of the Diadochi[85] period, and studies such as those by Theophrastus which mentioned exotic materials which were little used in the West. It is true that when Alexander returned to Mesopotamia at the end of his expedition, the Greeks discovered all sorts of unfamiliar precious stones in the booty. This inflow of materials did not continue for long as, with the first Seleucids, following the agreement between Seleucus and Chandragupta, India was no longer linked to them by direct administrative and commercial ties[86]. The coming of the Parthians and the secession of Bactria in the middle of the third century B.C. certainly interrupted direct trade with Central Asia for a long time[87].

---

84 On jewellery see, for example, R.G. Chandra, *Indo-Greek jewellery*, New Delhi, 1979 ; A. Von Śaldern and others, *Greek gold : jewellery from the Age of Alexander*, Mayence, 1965, p. 10 sqq. ; G.M.A. Richter, *Engraved gems of the Greeks and the Etruscans*, London, 1968-1971 ; A. Greifenhagen, *Schmuckarbeiten in Edelmetall*, Berlin, 1970-1975 (2 vol.) ; G.F.H. Smith, *Gemstones*, London, 1972, bibliogr. pp. 544-556 ; A. Lipinsky, *Oro, argento, gemme e smalti*, 1975 ; R.A. Higgins, *Greek and Roman jewellery*, London, 1980 ; J. Ogden, *Jewellery of the ancient world*, London, 1982 ; on semi-precious stones : p. 91 sqq. ; B. Deppert-Lippitz, *Griechischer Goldschmuck*, Mainz, 1985, particularly pp. 205-296 ; G. Devoto, A. Molayem, *Archeogemmologia : Pietre antiche, glittica, magia e litoterapia*, Roma, 1990.

85 On the stones in the rich ornaments of an Indian woman see, for example, Diodorus XIX, 34, 4.

86 M. Cima, "Il 'prezioso arredo' degli Horti Lamiani", pp. 121-122. E.H. Minns, *Scythians and Greeks*, Cambridge, 1913, p. 403 sqq. One of the oldest finds of polychrome jewellery in the Hellenic world is from Artjukhov (Phanagoria) : numerous ornaments decorated with precious stones including garnets, agates, emeralds, carnelians : end of the 3rd-beginning of the 2nd cent. B.C. In general, there are few evidences of ornaments decorated with precious stones for the Hellenic period. E. Levy, "Trésor hellénistique trouvé à Délos", *BCH*, 89, 1965, pp. 537-539 : medaillon in inlaid gold dating from the 3rd cent., pp. 548-549 : ornament decorated with beads of various stones dating from the 2nd cent. See also B. Deppert-Lippitz, *Griechischer Goldschmuck*, pp. 205-296 ; J. Ogden, *Jewellery*, fig. 20, 106-107.

87 The collection of pearls from Ai Khanum reflects approximately, the corpus of Taxila published by J. Marshall, *Taxila*, pp. 729-750 ; at Bhiṛ Mound in the 4th cent. B.C., we find amethyst, beryl, garnet, malachite and onyx but in small quantities : p. 105 ; in the Mauryan period in the 3rd cent., the most common beads are of agate, carnelian as well as amethyst and, for the first time, coral : pp. 109-110 ; at Sirkap in the Greek period there are some rare beads in carnelian, agate, amethyst, lapis-lazuli, etc. : p. 130 ; in the beginning of the first Śaka period, beads specially in glass and proportionately a lesser number in carnelian, agate, onyx, lapis-lazuli, rock crystal, garnet, etc. : pp. 135-136 ; in the Śaka-Parthian period, lots of shells, carnelian, agate, rock crystal, lapis-lazuli, garnet but little of coral, beryl, turquoise, etc. : pp. 204-205. The publication on the beads of Rajghat-Varanasi deals with 2472 specimens, especially of agate, carnelian, glass and terracotta but also of amethyst, coral, rock crystal, garnet, lapis-lazuli : A.K. Narain, P. Singh, *Small finds (Excavations at Rājghāt [1957-58 ; 1960-65] part III)*, Varanasi, 1977, pp. 44-45, tableau p. 21. See also the inventory of Indian stones in Kauṭilīya, *Arthaśāstra*, II, 11 (ed. and transl. by R.P. Kangle, Bombay, 1972, 2nd ed.).

Inlaying ornaments with precious stones is basically an oriental tradition. This is confirmed by the finds in Mesopotamia[88], in Iran which imported beads or rough materials from India and Central Asia (Pasargadae[89], Susa[90], Persepolis[91]). In India where the cutting of coloured beads is attested since prehistoric times[92], turquoise is an exception. Being from the north, this stone, along with garnets and corals, came to be used much later in ornaments. The finds in the necropolises of southern Russia and in general, of the Parthian, Śaka and Kushana periods in the Near East and in India[93], provide evidence that it was probably through the nomadic peoples who seized Iran and Greek Central Asia, that the technique of polychromy really spread in the West[94].

Rock crystal (**O15**, fig 14 and p. 124)[95] is almost solely used for vessels and in plaques for inlay. Except for a few necklace beads, it does not figure in the jewellery (**O15-3**[96] and **O15-4**).

The ornaments in agate (**O17**, fig. 15 and pp. 124-125)[97] consist of about fifteen beads (**O17**), a series of bracelets (**S17-94** to **117**, fig. 28.3, pp. 130-131) and a pendant weight (**E17-1**, fig. 7, p. 18 and 123). Generally, the beads in agate have forms which are common to the Oriental world from the Mediterranean to the Far East but it is on Indian sites that they are the most numerous. Along with carnelian beads, they also naturally figure in most of the excavations of the Hellenistic and Kushana periods in Central Asia[98]. Though workshops for the fabrication of agate beads

---

88 One of the largest collections of beads was discovered at Ur : see C.L. Wolley and others, *Ur excavations, vol. II, The Royal Cemetery*, New York, 1934, pp. 366-375.

89 The jewellery of Pasargadae is represented mainly by a treasure found hidden in a jar buried in the time of Alexander containing 1162 fragments of ornaments from the 5th and 6th cent. : D. Stronach, *Pasargadae*, p. 168.

90 Lapis-lazuli, turquoise and carnelian : J. de Morgan, "Découverte d'une sépulture achéménide à Suse", in *MDP, 8*, Paris, 1905, pp. 53-56.

91 Lapis-lazuli, turquoise and carnelian : E.F. Schmidt, *Persepolis II*, pp. 76-80, pl. 43-44.

92 E. Mackay, "Personal ornaments", in *Mohenjo-daro*, ed. J. Marshall, London, 1931, pp. 509-548. Imports in Susa in the third millennium : P. de Miroschedji, "Fouilles du Chantier Ville Royale II à Suse (1975-1977). I. Les niveaux élamites", *Cahiers de la DAFI*, 12, 1981, particularly fig. 39, pp. 110-111.

93 On one of the most important recent finds, that of Tilia-tepe in Bactria, see V. Sarianidi, *Die Kunst des alten Afghanistan*, Leipzig, 1986, pp. 301-327 ; *idem, Bactrian gold*, 1985.

94 M. Rostovtzeff, *Iranians and Greeks in South Russia*, Oxford, 1922, pp. 181-191. A.K. Narain, P. Singh, *Small finds*, pp. 34-35.

95 Cl. Rapin, *Fouilles AKh VIII*, p. 172.

96 There is evidence of facet cutting in beads of chalcedony, carnelian, agate, garnet at Taxila : H.C. Beck, *The beads from Taxila*, pl. 2, n$^{os}$ 41 to 43 : Bhiṛ Mound, 4th and 3rd cent. B.C. ; Sirkap : 1st cent. A.D. ; pl. 6, n° 30 : garnet from Sirkap ; 1st cent. A.D. ; beads in crystal and jasper of the same form were found at Hastinapura : B.B. Lal, "Excavations at Hastināpura and other explorations in the Upper Gangā and Sutlej basins 1950-52", *Ancient India*, 10-11, 1954-1955, pl. LV and fig. 29.16-17, p. 94 : around 4th to 2nd cent. B.C. On the rarity of rock crystal in the jewellery of the classical world see A. Lipinsky, *Oro, argento, gemme e smalti*, pp. 293-295. Perhaps the same observation can be made with respect to Taxila.

97 Cl. Rapin, *Fouilles AKh VIII*, pp. 172-174.

98 The specimens in barrel form **O17-5** to **7** (fig. 15) are very common : for Failaka see A. Caubet, J.-Fr. Salles, "Le sanctuaire hellénistique (B6)", in *Faïlaka. Fouilles françaises 1983*, Lyon, 1984, pp. 118-119, n° 342 and p. 142, n. 74 : treasure of agate beads dating from period 2, first half of the 2 nd cent. B.C. For specimens in the form of tear-drops **O17-8** to **12** see the sanctuary of Ai Khanum : H.-P. Francfort, *Fouilles AKh III*, tableau n° 40.24, pl. XXXV, n° 94 (with error of n°) and the palace : O. Guillaume and A. Rougeulle,

existed in the Near East, the most beautiful beads came mainly from India, from Cambay for example, where the earliest workshops date from the Harappan period. These workshops not only fabricated beads from local minerals like agate and carnelian but imported other minerals like lapis-lazuli, turquoise and coral[99] as well. The most complex specimens of agate (**O17-16** and **17**, fig. 15) are cut in the form of flowers with six petals (lotus ?), with the base pierced so that they could be strung in a necklace. We do not know anything about the mounting of these beads but it is possible that they were arranged in pairs on both sides of a round bead. Nos. **S17-94** to **117** are fragments cut in the form of segments of tubes with a diameter of 7.5 to 10 cm on an average and straight or slightly curved out ends. As revealed by the complete profile of a sample found in the sanctuary[100], they were not used as vessels or as elements for inlay but as bracelets.

The cylindrical bead **O17-3** (fig. 15) is of a different type with a hole measuring 3 mm in diameter through which a metal wire rather than a thread was supposed to pass. Similar types of elements were put together to serve as perfume stands in Taxila. This object consists of 14 agate pieces strung from end to end of an iron wire measuring about 32 cm in length and a base with a diameter of 1 cm[101].

Despite the hardness of these stones, the technique of cutting agates permitted as much variety in the forms as was possible in rock crystal (vessels, ornaments, furniture inlay). The vessels in agate and in rock crystal might have been stored in the same depot of the treasury (warehouse *109*) and have a common Indian origin. This is certainly also the case with respect to the bracelets, the pendant-weight, the beads **O17-16** and **17** with their typically Indian motif, and the object **O17-3** which might be a stand for Indian perfume. On the contrary, it is not possible to link agate beads with warehouse *109* because of their dispersion in the treasury. Since, in all likelihood, they were not part of the Indian booty stocked in this warehouse, these ornaments might well have circulated outside the treasury in the Greek period. The arguments advanced in favour of the Indian origin of the majority of the finds in room *109* are thus not applicable in this case and, consequently, the hypothesis that these agate beads, or at least a part of them, were cut in Bactria itself cannot be totally ruled out[102].

---

*Fouilles AKh VII*, n° 1103 (carnelian) ; Pasargadae : D. Stronach, *Pasargadae*, p. 206, fig. 88.19-20 ; Taxila : H.C. Beck, *The beads from Taxila*, pl. 3.12) ; Xalčajan : G.A. Pugačenkova, *Xalčajan*, p. 54, and fig. 31. Large formats such as **O17-1** and **2** are more rare but belong to the same geographical area : **O17-1** in Pasargadae : D. Stronach, *Pasargadae*, pp. 230-231, fig. 100, n° 6, dated to the end of the Achaemenid period, and in Ahichchhatra : M.G. Dikshit, "Beads from Ahichchhatrā, U. Pradesh", *Ancient India*, 8, 1952, p. 36, fig. 1.22, 8th to 9th cent. ; **O17-2** in Failaka : A. Caubet, J.-Fr. Salles, "Le sanctuaire hellénistique (B6)", pp. 118-119, n° 342a, and in Persepolis : E.F. Schmidt, *Persepolis II*, p. 77, fig. 13 C and D.

99 R.G. Chandra, *Indo-Greek jewellery*, pp. 104-105 ; G. Possehl, "Cambay beadmaking : an ancient craft in modern India", *Expedition*, 23-4, 1981, pp. 39-47 (bibliography) ; V.A. Janaki, *The commerce of Cambay from the earliest period to the Nineteenth Century*, Baroda, 1980. For Chanhu-daro see E.J.H. Mackay, "Bead making in ancient Sind", *JAOS*, 57, 1937, pp. 1-15. At Ujjain (Madhya Pradesh) a site dating from the 3rd-1st cent. B.C. was discovered in which a pile of agate cubes was found : *Indian Archaeology, 1956-57, A Review*, p. 27, pl. XXXIII B. On the use of flint in the cutting of beads see also Cl. Rapin, *Fouilles AKh VIII*, p. 251, n. 975.

100 H.-P. Francfort, *Fouilles AKh III*, pp. 74-75, fig. n° 40.32a, pl.26 ; its suggested identification as a vase here is definitely erroneous.

101 J. Marshall, *Taxila*, pp. 507-508, pl. 147, n° 153 : Taxila-Sirkap, Parthian period.

102 H.-P. Francfort, *Fouilles AKh III*, p. 74.

Carnelian (**O19**, p. 124) is a chalcedony like agate[103], but it differentiates itself from the latter by the uniformity of colour which varies from orange to brownish red. When seen against the light, certain samples present dark veins. The deposits of carnelian extend from the Near East to India and exist also in Central Asia, but most of the finds in Ai Khanum are, like the agates, probably of Indian origin (north-west of the Deccan, near Cambay, for example). The technique of cutting and polishing is the same as for other hard stones. It was mainly used for the fabrication of small objects. The elements of jewellery consist of beads, inlays and ring-stones. The forms of the beads are as follows : parallelepiped (**O19-1**, fig. 16), cube with corners dressed to form a polyhedron with fourteen sides (**O19-2**, fig. 16)[104], biconical or oval beads (**O19-3** and **4**, fig. 16)[105] ; disc with a concave edge (**O19-5**, fig. 16) ; spherical (**O19-6** to **8**)[106]. The plaquettes **O19-12** and **13** (fig. 16) were inlays of ornaments or of small pieces of furniture[107]. The figurines **O19-9** and **10** (fig. 16) which are definitely of Indian origin, were carved in relief on thin plaquettes of carnelian : the first represents a standing bird, the second, perhaps, the branch of a tree. Although they were found at a great distance from each other, these fragments probably belonged to the same object which might have been the appendage of a bead cut from the same block of carnelian rather than an isolated inlay in a metal ornament. This hypothesis is based on an almost identical figurine, in which a bird is perched on a branch sculpted on a parallelepiped bead, from Taxila dating to the third century B.C.[108]. More than any other stone sculpture, this fragile object, whose fabrication must have demanded great finesse, is evidence of the technical level which had been attained by the artisans of the Mauryan period.

The ring stones **O19-14** to **53** (fig. 16) are from warehouse *109*. We are however not in a position to locate the original depot of the other finds due to their dispersal in the treasury.

---

103 Cl. Rapin, *Fouilles AKh VIII*, pp. 174-175. The term is used by Theophrastus to describe this stone, *De lapidibus*, 30, *sarda* in Pliny XXXVII, 105-106 : the description applies perfectly to the finds of Ai Khanum : "In India ... there are red stones, those known as *pioniae*, or *fatty stones*, because of their greasy lustre [...]. The Indian stones are translucent, whereas the Arabian are somewhat opaque", and W.H. Schoff, *Periplus*, 49 and pp. 193-194. See the general study of P. Bernard in *Etudes de géographie historique*, pp. 9-10 and p. 71, n. 37-38 ; H.-P. Francfort, *Fouilles AKh III*, pp. 74-75 ; A. Lipinsky, *Oro, argento, gemme e smalti*, pp. 292-293 ; D. Whitehouse, "Carnelian in the Persian Gulf", *Antiquity*, 49, 1975, pp. 129-130. E.H. Warmington, *The commerce*, pp. 237-238 ; D. Fleming, "Darius I's foundation charters from Susa and the Eastern Achaemenid Empire", *Afghan studies*, 3-4, 1982, pp. 81-87, particularly p.84.

104 For a similar but cruder bead in beryl see O. Guillaume and A. Rougeulle, *Fouilles AKh VII*, p. 57, n° 1086.

105 O. Guillaume and A. Rougeulle, *Fouilles AKh VII*, p. 57, type c, n$^{os}$ 1072-1078 ; H.-P. Francfort, *Fouilles AKh III*, tableau n° 40.50.

106 O. Guillaume and A. Rougeulle, *Fouilles AKh VII*, p. 56, type a, n$^{os}$ 1054-1062.

107 On the practice of combining inlays of carnelian with those of onyx and lapis-lazuli in Persepolis : E.F. Schmidt, *Persépolis II*, p. 71 ; P. Bernard in *Études de géographie historique*, pp. 9-10, regarding the supply of provisions in the Achaemenid palaces of Susa and Persepolis.

108 H.C. Beck, *The beads from Taxila*, pl. VII, 14 ; Stronge and others, *A golden treasury*, London, 1988, p. 18, n° 9 : alamandite garnet, probably from Taxila ; M.G. Dikshit, "Notes on some Indian amulets", *Bulletin of Prince of Wales Museum of Western India*, 1951-1952, No. 2 (1953), p. 97, pl. XV.17. The fragment of a bi-coloured agate bead cut in a feline form was found in the palace at Ai Khanum as an inlay : O. Guillaume and A. Rougeulle, *Fouilles AKh VII*, p. 58, n° 1102.

Lapis-lazuli comes from the mountains of Badakhshan, situated in the mountainous region to the south-west of the plain of Ai Khanum where the only mines known in the ancient period were located[109]. This stone occupies an important place among the finds at Ai Khanum because of the hundreds of fragments, weighing in all a total of about 130 kg, recovered in the treasury (**M20**)[110]. Their place of storage was definitely warehouse *104* where the majority of these fragments were found in a compact pile which had probably been stored earlier in a bag or a box. Contrary to what the large volume of raw material might lead us to suppose, manufactured objects found at Ai Khanum are particularly few in number : about 15 beads in the treasury (**O20**, p. 124), three in the sanctuary[111] and three in the houses n° 1 and 3[112]. The specimens of the treasury are as follows : the fragment of a flower shaped bead with opened out petals (lotus?) (**O20-1**, fig. 17), an unpierced bead with pentagonal sections (**O20-2**), fig. 17, a hexagonal bead (**O20-3**, fig. 17), three half-beads (**O20-4** to **6**, fig. 17) and nine small, spherical beads cut unevenly. The larger beads are cut from stones of an extremely good quality, excepting the hexagonal bead **O20-3**. The flower shaped bead **O20-1** is probably of Indian origin like the specimens of agate which have been described earlier (**O17-16** and **17**, fig. 15). The hemi-spherical beads were arranged in pairs on both sides of a disc of a different colour. They belong to a type common in Mesopotamia and also found in Taxila[113]. It is possible that the small beads with an uneven form were produced locally, as they seem to come from warehouse *104* and not room *109* where the objects stored were mainly of Indian origin. Since the mines were in the hands of the Greeks of Bactria, it might have been expected that a flourishing industry of lapis-lazuli would be located in this region, yet, paradoxically, the most beautiful beads found at Ai Khanum were manufactured in India.

During the period of Bactrian dependence on the Achaemenid Empire, Oriental productions of lapis-lazuli in the form of beads, figurines, inlays or vessels were mainly known in Sumer, Assur, Babylonia and particularly at Susa[114] and Persepolis[115]. Their spread continued, but on an apparently much smaller scale, as revealed by most of the excavations of the Hellenistic, Parthian

109 Cl. Rapin, *Fouilles AKh VIII*, pp. 175-176. On lapis-lazuli see P. Bernard in *Études de géographie historique*, pp. 9-10 and 49-51, notes pp. 95-97 (map 3 : map of the mines of Badakhshan) ; V. Ball, "A geologist's contribution", *The Indian Antiquary*, 13, 1884, pp. 234-235 ; A. Lucas, *Ancient Egyptian materials and industries*[4], pp. 398-400 ; A. Lipinsky, *Oro, argento, gemme e smalti*, pp. 297-301, 375-376 ; D. Fleming, "Darius I's foundation charters from Susa", *Afghan studies*, 3-4, 1982, pp. 81-87 ; A.B. Delmas, M. Casanova, "The lapis-lazuli sources in the Ancient East", in *South Asian Archaeology 1987*, Rome, 1990, pp. 493-505. The production of lapis-lazuli in the bronze age is attested by the finds of Shortugai (plain of Ai Khanum) and Sarazm (Tadžikistan).

110 Many fragments were also found in the sanctuary : H.-P. Francfort, *Fouilles AKh III*, p. 77, tableau n° 40.1 to 9.

111 H.-P. Francfort, *Fouilles AKh III*, p. 77, tableau n° 40.56 to 58.

112 O. Guillaume and A. Rougeulle, *Fouilles AKh VII*, n[os] 1060 (spherical, of a small size), 1087 (polyhedric), 1091 (in the shape of a diabolo), 1104 (pendant in the shape of a drop).

113 H.C. Beck, *The beads from Taxila*, pl. 6.21, specimen dating from the 1st cent.

114 D. Fleming, "Darius I's foundation charters from Susa", pp. 81-87. The precious stones to which the charter of Susa allude are used in the composition of plates for doors or articles of furniture. But, in contrast with Persepolis, where such finds were made, the excavation of the palace of Susa did not yield fragments of this type : E.F. Schmidt, *Persépolis II*, p. 71.

115 E.F. Schmidt, *Persepolis II*, pl. 43.31, 43.47, 44.8.

and Kushan periods[116]. Although it is mentioned as an article of importation in the Mediterranean world – the *Periplus*, 49, refers to its transit through Barbarikon – this stone does not seem to have been as intensely sought by the Romans as the chalcedonies for the fabrication of intaglios or vases, probably because of its grain[117].

The beryl is one of the few stones in this collection which can properly be called precious. It was found only in the treasury and the palace[118], where it is represented by half a dozen fragments of rough stone (**M22**), an unfinished parallelepiped bead and a pendant (**O22-2**). The colour of the specimens of Ai Khanum ranges from greenish to sky blue but this stone, which belongs to the same group as emeralds and aquamarines, can be extremely diversified in colour. It is found in Bactria, in the Ural, the Altai and Nuristan[119], but classical sources attribute it chiefly to India[120]. Like most Indian stones, the beryl came to the West with the conquest of Alexander but its real spread began only in the post-Imperial period. It is not possible for us to be more specific with respect to the place of origin of the fragments of the rough stone in Ai Khanum but both the general context and the quality and the polish of the pendant point to an Indian origin.

The garnet is one of the most represented semi-precious stones in the ornaments of the treasury in particular and in Ai Khanum in general. Like the turquoise, this stone was found in both the warehouses *104* and *109* in the form of small lumps of rough stone or fragmented in cubes (**M23**)[121]. The worked objects comprise ring-stones (**O23-1**, fig. 18, p. 126), plano-convex

---

116 On the treasure of Tilia-tepe see V. Sarianidi, *Bactrian gold*, tomb 2, pp. 110 and 232-233, n° 15. On Tepai-Šakh : B.A. Litvinskij, A.V. Sedov, *Tepai-Šakh*, Moscow, 1983, pl. XXXIII, 6 et 10, p. 152. On a block of rough stone discovered in Begram see J. Hackin, "Catalogue descriptif des objets découverts à Begram", in J. Hackin *et alii*, *Nouvelles recherches*, p. 312, n° 195.

117 Regarding lapis-lazuli, see the commentary of Pliny XXXVII, 120 : *caerulae et sappiri ... inutiles intervenientibus crystallinis centris* ("they are useless for engraving, because core like rock-crystal interfere with this"). That Romans did not have knowledge of the origin of this stone is gleaned, for example, from Pliny who attributes it to Media (*ibidem*). See also E.H. Warmington, *The commerce*, pp. 251-252.

118 O. Guillaume and A. Rougeulle, *Fouilles AKh VII*, p. 57, n° 1086 : cubic bead with corners cut, similar in form but bigger than the carnelian bead in the treasury **O19-2**.

119 J. Marshall, *Taxila*, p. 478 ; M. Wheeler, "Arikamedhu : An Indo-Roman trading-station on the East Coast of India", *Ancient India*, 2, 1946, pp. 121-124 ; P. Bariand, J.-F. Poullen, "The pegmatites of Laghman, Nuristan, Afghanistan", *The Mineralogical Record*, sept.-oct. 1978, pp. 301-308 ; E.H. Warmington, *The commerce*, pp. 113-114, 250-251.

120 Pliny XXXVII, 76-79 : "Many people consider the nature of beryls to be similar to, if not identical with, that of emeralds. Beryls are produced in India and are rarely found elsewhere. All of them are cut by skilled craftsmen to a smooth hexagonal shape, since their colour, which is deadened by the dullness of an unbroken surface, is enhanced by the reflection from the facets. If they are cut in any other way they lack brilliance. The most highly esteemed beryls are those that reproduce the pure green of the sea (*aquamarine*) [...]. The Indian are extraordinarily fond of elongated beryls and claim that they are the only precious stones that are preferably left without a gold setting" (a description of the forms worked upon follows). See also Diodorus II, 52, 3 : ... *smaragdi* (emeralds ?) and *beryllia* ; Strabo XV, 1, 69 : ... τὰ πλεῖστα σμαράγδοις καὶ βηρύλλοις καὶ ἄνθραξιν Ἰνδικοῖς.

121 A fragment of rough was found at the sanctuary : H.-P. Francfort, *Fouilles AKh III*, tableau n° 40.15.

inlays (**O23-2** to **11**, fig. 18) and beads (**O23-12** to **17**)[122]. The geographical spread of this mineral is as large as that of beryl : we find it in Badakhshan, Baluchistan, Swat and India. It is present in ancient jewellery from India to the Mediterranean, with a predominance among the populations of the Steppes[123], but as far as the Hellenistic period is concerned, it does not appear to have played a significant role before the end of the second century B.C. The rough garnets of Ai Khanum are perhaps locally produced. The beads and the inlays, on the contrary, might have been worked in India, as suggested by the similarity of form between certain specimens of Ai Khanum and Taxila[124].

The sapphire – a blue corundum – which is traditionally attributed to Ceylon is probably represented by only one find : a small inlay carved in the form of a leaf (**O24-1**, fig. 19, p. 126) similar to the specimen of carnelian **O19-11** (fig. 16, p. 125)[125].

Almost all the elements of coral (**O33**) found at Ai Khanum come from the treasury, particularly the warehouse *104*[126]. They include beads and fragments of coral reef with a diameter of 1 to 4 mm. sometimes with ramifications. The colour varies from pale red to reddish orange but the original colour might have become modified. The shapes of the beads are oval (**O33-2** to **4**, fig. 21), spherical (**O33-5** to **15**) or cylindrical (**O33-32**), and they are generally polished. The branches of the reef **O33-16** to **18** (fig. 21) are pierced at one end. The most elaborate specimen is the pendant-bead **O33-1** (fig. 21) carved in the form of *nandipāda* (symbol of the sacred bull)[127],

---

122 H.-P. Francfort, *Fouilles AKh III*, tableau n° 40.44 and 45. With the exception of one ringstone, no garnet piece was found in other sites. For **O23-12** see E.M. Alekseeva, "Antičnye busy Severnogo Pričernomor'ja", pl. 39.40.

123 For a study of garnets and rubies see P. Bernard in *Etudes de géographie historique*, p. 10 and p. 72, n. 39. See also A. Lucas, *Ancient Egyptian materials and industries*[4], pp. 389-390 and 394-395 ; J. Marshall, *Taxila*, p. 478 ; E.H. Warmington, *The commerce*, pp. 249, 252-253 ; A. Lipinsky, *Oro, argento, gemme e smalti*, pp. 305-313, bibliography pp. 373-374 ; H.-P. Francfort, *Fouilles AKh III*, pp. 74-77 ; M. Martini, "Le gemme degli Horti Lamiani", in *Le tranquille dimore degli dei*, pp. 147--148 : mineralogical study of the finds in Rome. On the discovery of garnets in a reliquary see *Indian Archaeology, 1953-54. A review*, pl. XVIIB. On the mention by Pliny of vessels in garnet : H.-P. Bühler, *Antike Gefässe*, p. 2. The necropolis of Tilia-tepe is particularly rich in gold ornaments inlaid with garnets : V. Sarianidi, *Bactrian Gold.*

124 H.-P. Francfort, *Fouilles AKh III*, p. 75 with reference to a specimen from Lindos from the archaic period, tableau n° 40.44 : pendant bead from the sanctuary identical to a specimen of carnelian from Taxila : H.C. Beck, *The beads from Taxila*, pl. 4.11 dating from the 3rd cent. B.C. H.-P. Francfort, *ibidem*, tableau n° 40.45 : barrel shaped bead with narrowed ends similar to one of the coral beads in the treasury (**O33-2**) and to the agate beads from Taxila : H.C. Beck, *The beads from Taxila*, pl. 3.18, dating from the 3rd cent. B.C., and carnelian beads : *idem*, pl. 6.20, dating from the 1st cent. The hexagonal form **O23-17** in garnet and **O16-2** and **3** in amethyst is also found in the garnet beads from Taxila : *idem*, pl. 6.31, Sirkap ; 1st cent. B.C. Another form also present in the treasury (garnet **O23-15**) is the disc with concave edge (carnelian **O19-5**). The inlay **O23-11** resembles an inlay in carnelian found in house n° 1 : O. Guillaume and A. Rougeulle, *Fouilles AKh VII*, n° 1093. Thus these finds from Ai Khanum, including coral, were probably manufactured in India.

125 On sapphire in general see E.H. Warmington, *The commerce*, pp. 248, etc. ; mineralogical study of the finds in Rome : M. Martini, "Le gemme degli Horti Lamiani", pp. 145-146.

126 Cl. Rapin, *Fouilles AKh VIII*, pp. 180-181.

127 There is evidence in Taxila-Bhiṛ Mound from the beginning of the 4th cent. B.C. of the *nandipāda* motif : J. Marshall, *Taxila*, p. 105 ; see also p. 747, n. 4 the commentary on the *nandipāda* and the *triratna* (also

which seems to confirm the Indian origin of the entire range of specimens as well as the use of coral in the fabrication of amulets. The red coral, such as it is observed from Italy to China, is of Mediterranean origin (Pliny XXXII, 21-24)[128]. Believed to possess magical properties, the coral, both in the form of reef and bead sand inlays is, like the garnet, one of the most sought after materials for ornaments at Pasargadae[129] and Persepolis[130] in Iran, for nomadic jewellery in Central Asia[131], at Khorezm[132], at Kojkrylgan-Kala[133], Tepai-Šakh[134], Kampyr-tepe, Dal'verzin-

M. Bénisti, "A propos du triratna", *BEFEO*, 64, 1977, pp. 43-81, particularly p. 51 sqq.) ; O. von Hinüber, "Das Nandyāvarta-Symbol", in *XVIII. Deutscher Orientalistentag (ZDMG*, Suppl. II), ed. W. Voigt, Wiesbaden, 1974, pp. 356-365 ; V. Moeller, "Das *Nandyāvarta*-Symbol ?", *ZDMG*, 129, 1979, pp. 149-154 ; A.L. Srivastava, *Nandyāvarta. An auspicious symbol in Indian art*, Allahabad, 1991 (references proposed by P. Callieri). On the beads of Taxila see H.C. Beck, *The beads from Taxila*, pl. 8.7 : shell from Bhiṛ Mound, 3rd cent. B.C. ; pl. 1.25 (?) : blue serpentine from Sirkap, 1st cent. A.D. ; pl. 3.19 : agate from Bhiṛ Mound, 3rd cent. B.C. representing the *nandipāda* ; pl. 4.21 : carnelian from Bhiṛ Mound, 3rd cent. B.C. ; 22 : carnelian from Sirkap, 1st cent. A.D. The last two specimens are regarded as *triratna* (the three sacred jewels of the Buddhists : the Buddha, the Dharma and the Saṃgha) ; see perhaps also pl. 10.14 : bone from Sirkap, 1st cent. A.D. ; also a specimen of lapis-lazuli from Sirsukh, pl. 6.33 : garnet from a reliquary of the Dharmarājikā stūpa, 1st cent. A.D. On a specimen of green jasper from Rajghat, Varanasi, of the 4-6th cent., see A.K. Narain, P. Singh, *Small finds*, pl. VIII, 17.

128 H. Blümner, *Technologie und Terminologie*, Leipzig, 1879, II, pp. 378-381 ; A. Lucas, *Ancient Egyptian materials and industries*[4], pp. 392-393 ; E. de Saint-Denis, *Pline l'Ancien, Histoire naturelle, Livre XXXII*, Paris, "Les Belles Lettres", 1966, pp. 87-89 (§ 21-24 of Pliny) ; E.H. Warmington, *The commerce*, pp. 263-264, 386 n. 4-5 ; J. Marshall, *Taxila*, p. 740 ; A. Lipinsky, *Oro, argento, gemme e smalti*, pp. 321-322, bibliography p. 378 ; E. Tartamella, *Corallo, storia e arte dal XV al XIX secolo*, Palermo, 1985. On Indian coral (white not red "organ pipe" coral) see Theophrastus, *De lapidibus*, 38. On literary sources with references to Mediterranean coral : S. Lévi, "Alexandre et Alexandrie dans les documents indiens", in *Mélanges Maspero, II, Orient grec, romain et byzantin*, Le Caire, 1934-1938, pp. 161-164. Kauṭilīya, *Arthaśāstra* II, 11, 42. On Chinese coral see E.H. Schafer, *The golden peaches of Samarcand*, pp. 246-247. For the Black Sea see E.M. Alekseeva, "Antičnye busy Severnogo Pričernomor'ja", pp. 27-28, pl. 43.30-32, 42. For the rough or pierced branches found at Delos see Ph. Bruneau, Cl. Vatin *et alii*, *L'îlot de la Maison des Comédiens*, Paris, 1970, pl. 38, C303. See also L. Robert, *Noms indigènes dans l'Asie Mineure gréco-romaine*, Paris, 1963, pp. 280-281.

129 Fragment of a rose coloured coral reef, length of branch 2.2 cm : D. Stronach, *Pasargadae*, pl. 157 d.

130 Bead : E.F. Schmidt, *Persepolis II*, pl. 43.51.

131 Branches of pierced coral : *Pamjatniki skifo-sarmatskoj kul'tury (MIA, 115)*, Moscow, 1962, pp. 248, 269, fig. 7.1 ; on turquoise and coral in the tombs of Southern Russia see M. Rostovtzeff, *Iranians and Greeks*, p. 135.

132 S.P. Tolstov, *Trudy Khorezmskoj Ekspedicii*, I, Moscow, 1952, p. 113.

133 S.P. Tolstov, B.I. Vajnberg, *Kojkryl'gan kala*, Moscow, 1967, p. 332.

134 B.A. Litvinskij, A.V. Sedov, *Tepai-Šakh*, pl. XXXIV, 10, p. 157.

tepe, Qol-i-Nader[135], and at Begram[136], Taxila[137], Rājghāt[138], Maski (South Deccan)[139] in the south of the Hindu Kush. As attested by the finds in the treasury, the coral which was marketed in the Orient in the second century B.C. did not come by the direct route through Iran but probably via one of the ports in India where, like amber, it was imported from the West[140].

Shells and mother of pearl (**O34**, figs 22-23, p. 125), the other materials of animal origin, are also represented in the jewellery. The finds comprise a bracelet carved from a large shell of *Xancus pyrum* (**O34-1**, fig. 23)[141], a mother of pearl bead in an uneven form (**O34-2**, fig. 23), a series of small natural shells pierced or cut in flattened spheres, as well as a fossil (**O34-13**). There is no doubt that the bracelet and the bead are from India[142]. We do not know if the latter was from the Ganges region[143] where beads of a mediocre quality are in fact produced, or from West India. Beads (margaritae) constituted one of the principal commercial products of India in the Roman period. This production along with the production from the Persian Gulf was concentrated in Barygaza before being re-exported towards the Mediterranean in exchange of coral and amber. This commerce was limited to Egypt in the Hellenistic period, beads being unknown to the Greeks who rarely used them in their jewellery[144]. However, following the triumph of Pompey and the victory of Actium, they were imported in large quantities by the Romans who considered them as the most precious stone, second only to diamond (Pliny IX, 106 ; XXXVII, 62).

---

135 Like most of the other finds in the stūpas, this find dating to the 2nd cent. A.D. was wrapped along with relics consisting of fragments of bone, precious stones (turquoise, coral, ruby, agate and various types of beads) in small packets deposited in boxes of enchased gold and silver : J. Meunié, "Qol-i-Nâder, une petite fondation bouddhique au Kapiça", in J. Hackin *et alii*, *Diverses recherches*, pp. 115-127, particularly pp. 123-125 ; the precious stones placed along with the gold and silver in Buddhist reliquaries represented the "five" or "seven gems" : p. 125.

136 13 beads : J. Carl, "Le Bazar de Begram (chantier I, 1936), in J. Hackin *et alii*, *Diverses recherches*, p. 95, n° 96.

137 Rough beads in branches from the Dharmarājika stūpa, 1st cent. B.C. : H.C. Beck, *The beads from Taxila*, pl. 10.32

138 A.K. Narain, P. Singh, *Small finds*, pp. 31-32.

139 From the beginning of the first period (chalcolithic) : probably from the Indian Ocean.

140 See the references of the *Periplus*, 28, 39, 49, 56, concerning trade between Mediterranean and Indian products at Barbarikon, Barygaza, etc. : W.H. Schoff, *Periplus*, p. 168.

141 This specimen presents a close parallel to the finds at Taxila : J. Marshall, *Taxila*, pl. 201, n° 21, p. 672, etc. See also a bracelet carved and decorated with incised lines found at Begram : R. Ghirshman, *Bégram*, pl. XLVII, B.G. 557/a. On shells see also p. 54, nn. 200-202.

142 On beads and shells see E.H. Warmington, *The commerce*, pp. 167-174. See also A. Lipinsky, *Oro, argento, gemme e smalti*, pp. 313-319.

143 W.H. Schoff, *Periplus*, 63. The beads come from the rivers in the eastern part of Bengal.

144 Little known to Theophrastus, who has described them as transparent, *De lapidibus*, 36. Elian XV, 8, reports that during the period of Eucratides, which is precisely the period which interests us, the bead industry of Perimula (which, however, we are not able to situate) was located in a region ruled by a king named Soras : A. Dihle, "Die entdeckungsgeschichtlichen Voraussetzungen des Indienhandels der römischen Kaiserzeit", in *ANRW, II, Principat, 9,2*, Berlin, New York, 1978, p. 554.

Among the finds in bronze attention may be drawn to the presence of an anthropomorphous pendant-plate (**O3-3**, fig. 13 and p. 123)[145].

## ORNAMENTAL OBJECTS AND TOILET ARTICLES[146]

The finds of the treasury comprise some rare ornamental objects, toilet articles and surgical objects. Of particular note are :

**Surgery : P3-4** (*"Decapitator"* ?, fig. 24, p. 127) : This instrument consists of a pointed bronze blade folded back in the form of a pruning knife ; the middle portion is thickened by a joint. The inner edge has a small perforation near the end, which is broken. The function of this object is not clear. It is probably not a decorative element (strand of hair, feather or tuft of hair of a statue) because two objects of the same form and length, independent of any support, as in Ai Khanum, have been found in Taxila[147].

**Perfumes :** Perfumes are attested by the presence of alabasters, of thymiateria in the sanctuary a redans[148] and the element of agate which we had identified above (**O17-3**, fig. 15) as a perfume stand in the treasury. For the ingredients likely to be used in the preparation of cosmetics, medicines and perfumes, reference may be made to the inscriptions pertaining to olive oil, cinnamon and incense as well as to orpiment[149].

The curved plaque in ivory **R35-3** (fig. 25) probably formed, with three other similar plaques riveted at right angles, the lid of a square pyxide. A hole is pierced at the apex, in which a button of prehension, represented perhaps by the figurine **R35-2** (fig. 25), was supposed to be inserted. This figurine consists of the trunk of a small figure clasping an ovoid object in front of his chest. The identification of this figure is not easy because of the deterioration in the ivory. The head seems to be protected with a helmet like a human head[150]. The face is however grotesque and has a sort of beak or a hooked snout like that of a monkey. The figurines of monkeys, particularly of monkey musicians are very common in classical and oriental art[151] but the object held by the

145 For highly stylised anthropomorphous Indian amulets and their evolution towards the motif of *śrīvatsa* and *triratna* see P.K. Agrawala, *Early Indian bronzes*, Varanasi, 1977, p. 38, fig. 87 : specimen of Ahichchhatra ; S.P. Gupta, *The roots of Indian art*, pp. 325-326 ; chronology of Ahichchhatra : pp. 140-141.

146 Cl. Rapin, *Fouilles AKh VIII*, pp. 183-184.

147 Bhiṛ Mound : 3rd-2nd cent. B.C. : J. Marshall, *Taxila*, pp. 599-600, pl. 177, n^os^ 357-358 : while examining the object of Ai Khanum we did not remark that the inner edge was sharper than the outer but it is true that the object was extremely oxidised. In his catalogue, J. Marshall compares this object with a type of instrument also found in Taxila and utilised in obstetrics called *decapitator* : pl. 177 and 185, n^os^ 359-360. On this type of instrument see also J. Milne, *Surgical instruments in Greek and Roman times*, Oxford, 1907, pp. 152-154, pl. L, n° 2 ; G. Mukhopādhyāya, *The Surgical instruments of the Hindus*, Calcutta, 1913, pp. 225-226, pl. LIX. We do not know of any exact parallel of the model in small format found at Ai Khanum and Taxila.

148 H.-P. Francfort, *Fouilles AKh III*, pp. 81-84.

149 Cl. Rapin, *Fouilles AKh VIII*, p. 107, n. 246, pp. 151-152, 184 (for orpiment see above p. 22).

150 Cf. J. Hackin *et alii*, *Nouvelles recherches*, fig. 167 : small atlantes of Begram with luxuriant hair.

151 W.C. McDermott, *The ape in antiquity*, Baltimore, 1938. For India see M. Taddei, "Two notes on Gandharan iconography. 1. More on the meditating monkey from Tapa Sardâr", *EW*, 35, 1985, pp. 271-272 (ref. of P. Callieri). For Mesopotamia see C. Mendleson, "More monkey business", *Anatolian Studies*, 33, 1983, pp. 81-

figurine seems to be a vase rather than same musical instrument like a tambourine. The closest parallel might be found in Indian iconography, where monkeys are frequently the subject[152]. Of particular note is a monkey holding a vessel in his hands who figures in the illustration of the Miracle of Vaiśali on the northern toraṇa of the stūpa 1 of Sanchi[153].

## TOOLS

The tools and instruments discovered in Ai Khanum belong to types common to Central Asia and the classical world in general[154]. Of special note is the discovery of a point in agate **I 17-1** (fig. 8 and p. 123), which is probably a head for polishing small objects in gold and silver of the type found in the same stone (sardonyx, banded agate), the same slender form and approximately the same dimensions (6-10 cm. in length) in Rajghat (Varanasi)[155] and Taxila[156].

---

83 : monkey tamer in terracotta. For Central Asia see B.Ja. Staviskij, *La Bactriane sous les Kushans. Problèmes d'histoire et de culture*, Paris, 1986, p. 252 and H.-P. Francfort, *Fouilles AKh III*, pp. 39-40.

152 See the references of H.-P. Francfort (above) on the finds at Taxila, Charsadda, Shaikhan-Dheri ; for the Dharmarājikā stūpa of Taxila dating from the 1st cent. B.C. a bead in earthenware in the form of a monkey can be added : H.C. Beck, *The beads from Taxila*, pl. 7, n° 2. The closest parallels are the figurines of a squatting monkey holding a vessel found at Rajghat (date later than the 4th cent.) : A. K. Narain, P.K. Agrawala, *Terracotta human figurines (Excavations at Rājghāt [1957-58 ; 1960-65] part IV)*, Varanasi, 1978, pl. LXIX, 2-12 and LXX, 1-4.

153 *Sâñchi*, pl. 36c, 2, p. 219 ; the monkey is a langur : Skt *go-lāṅgula*. The description of this Miracle which took place near Vaiśali (Basarh, in the north-west of Patna) depicts how a monkey took his begging bowl to the Master after filling it with a drink similar to that extracted by the monks from the palm which they had a right to drink before it had fermented.

154 Cl. Rapin, *Fouilles AKh VIII*, pp. 249-263.

155 Specimen identified as a punch-mark : *Indian Archaeology 1964-65 – A Review*, ed. by A. Ghosh, New Delhi, 1969, pp. 44-45, pl. XXXVIII B, n° 71 : "Excavation at Rajghat, District Varanasi".

156 J. Marshall, *Taxila*, pl. 142 and 146, n° 118 ; pl. 146, n° 119 a and c, p. 501 with ref. to W.M.F. Petrie, *Objects of daily use*, pl. LVI, 33-35.

CHAPTER V

# THE INDIAN THRONE

(fig. 26-29)

It is probable that the 600 or so specimens of rock crystal and agate which were recovered mainly from room *109* of the treasury, and about 30 found in the sanctuary of the *temple à redans* where they were carried by the plunderers[157], belong to a throne or a *kline*, unique in its opulence and its dimensions. These fragments can be divided into two groups: tubular elements and discoidal or polygonal plaquettes.

## Tubular elements.

The tubular fragments of rock crystal, with all the sides polished because of the transparency of this material, have an octagonal or cylindrical section. It is possible to classify them into two distinct modules on the basis of the thickness of their walls and their inner diameter :

— **1)** a small module, of which the diameter varies from 1 to 1.3 cm (**S15-8, 16** and **17** : types C and E with octagonal section ; **S15-18** : type F cylindrical)[158]

— **2)** a big module, of which the inner diameter varies between 1.8 and 2.3 cm (**S15-9** to **11** : type D with octagonal section ; **S15-19** to **25** : types G and H cylindrical). A specimen of each type is arched (**S15-11** and **17**). The tubes had a perforation which allowed them to be nailed on the central portion of gilded wood and thus to assemble them (**S15-10** and **25**).

There are tubular elements in agate also which can be classified into two groups :

— **1)** a module with thick walls and polygonal section with the external corners rounded (**S17-58** to **61** : type L, whose diameter varies at the opening between 3.6 and 4.0 cm) or cylindrical (**S17-62** to **77** : type M, whose maximum diameter at the opening varies mainly between 2.3/3.4 and 4.2/5.0 cm)

— **2)** a module with fine walls but with a larger diameter (**S17-56** and **57** : type K : 10-12 cm).

This entire lot of tubular elements was probably strung on cylindrical supports and might have formed the uprights – legs or struts – of furniture. The rock crystal specimens were nailed to a support of gilded wood of which a fragment was found (**S36-1**). The inner wall of the

157 H.-P. Francfort, *Fouilles AKh III*, pp. 74-75, tableau n° 40.27 to 42, pl. XXXIII. Among the finds are two fragments which are absolutely identical to certain plaquettes of the treasury : the specimen of pl. XXXIII, to the lower right of fig. 34 (inv. n° of the sanctuary III 75/2.66), corresponds to the series **S17-39** to **53** ; the triangular specimen of pl. XXXIII, fig. 27 is perhaps the part of another fragment found in room *109*.

158 The types A to M refer to the catalogue below pp. 127-130.

cylindrical pieces in agate is unpolished with turning marks which must have facilitated its adherence to the support[159].

## Flat inlays.

The second group of elements consists of discs and plaquettes of 1 to 3 mm thickness belonging to one or several flat, circular panels of rock crystal and agate and polygonal panels solely of agate.

— **1)** The discs in rock crystal (**S15-1** to **7**), with diameter varying between 2 and 12 cm, were certainly fixed either on a support which was decorated with open-work or was gilded. Like the tubular elements they are polished on both the sides. The edges of certain pieces were chamfered to enable them to be fitted in a frame (**S15-1** to **4**). The face of the agate discs (**S17-13** to **18**) is slightly convex and carefully polished; the reverse side of the element **S17-13** is unpolished. We can still see the fine crack where the plaquette was detached from the main block during cutting.

— **2)** The polygonal plaquettes, in agate exclusively, are in diverse forms and sizes : trapezoidal (**S17-1** to **4**), triangular (**S17-5** to **9**)[160], oval (**S17-10**)[161], rectangular (**S17-19** to **38**), rectangular with convex edges (**S17-39** to **53**)[162]. The obverse is finely polished but the reverse was left unpolished, perhaps to reinforce their adherence to the support. Their edge is always smooth but not polished, and often bears the imprint of cutting with pincers. The edges of the plates **S17-39** to **53** were cut with pincers but not given a final polish. A resin must have, in all probability, masked the irregularities of the contours when they were assembled.

— **3)** The elements consisting of strips of agate (**S18-1** to **37**), mostly with one side and one edge polished, must have been used to decorated the edges of panel[163].

## Fixing techniques.

A putty or a resin was certainly used to fix the agate plaquettes on their supports. In the warehouse *109*, a series of rivets (**S3-1** to **23**) and small bronze nails (**S3-26** to **44**) as well as a series of grey schist nails in conical form (**S14**) were discovered. These elements which have been found only in the treasury might have served to reinforce the fixing of the inlays. In general, the bronze rivets are in the form of a horizontal H and were fabricated by folding a slender rod of bronze. The length of the central bar (4 to 6 mm) seems to correspond with the thickness of the inlay plaquettes.

---

159 The elements with a large diameter **S17-94** to **117** were carefully polished on both sides and should rather be considered as bracelets. For similar finds of cylindrical "tube sheaths" **S17-56** and **62** sqq. at Nisa see G.G. Lemlejn, "Fragmenty kamennyx izdelij iz raskopok v staroj Nise", *TrJuTAKE*, 8, 1958, pp. 383-385, fig. 2 ; on the cutting technique p. 384 and fig. 3.

160 Only one of these plaquettes has a hole for fixing it (**S17-11**). For a fragment found in the sanctuary see H.-P. Francfort, *Fouilles AKh III*, tableau n° 40.34, pl. XXXIII.

161 For a fragment found in the sanctuary : *ibidem*, tableau n° 40.33, pl. XXXIII.

162 A plaquette of the same collection was found in the sanctuary : *ibidem*, tableau n° 40.34, pl. XXXIII.

163 Six identical strips were found in the sanctuary : *ibidem*, tableau n° 40.35 et 40.40-42, pl. XXXIII.

### The support.

Fragments of carbonised wood which might well have belonged to the frame of the furniture piece on which the inlays were fixed were discovered in room *109*. Among the specimens analysed were a mortise of pine wood (**S36-2**) and a splinter of a pear tree (**S36-5**)[164]. The wood under the crystal elements was probably gilded (**S36-1**).

### Agates.

Among the agates, the following qualities can be distinguished :

— **a)** beige agates with brown veins (**S17-13** and **11**, for example) ;

— **b)** agates with brown and beige transparent veins alternating with white or creamy veins (**S17-1**, **2**, **16**, for example) ;

— **c)** banded brown agates with opaque white veins (**S17-39** to **53**) ;

— **d)** black agates with opaque white veins (**S17-24**, for example) ;

— **e)** certain black agates which are partly crystalline and transparent (for example **S17-21**) ;

— **f)** white opaque agates with the appearance of porcelain (**S18-1** to **37**).

The form of plaquettes is often related to the pattern of their veins (see, for example, **S17-1**, **2**, **13**, etc.). The colouring of brown and white agates is certainly natural. The black agates with white veins were artificially coloured. They are, for the most part, extremely fragmented. The technique of colouring by heating is surely responsible for their fragility. Certain plaquettes seem to have undergone a similar modification because of the fire in room *109* : the fragment **S17-44** is from the same lot of agate as the brown plates **S17-39** to **53**, but it bears the traces of the fire in the premises due to which the colour of the veins transformed itself into black and opaque white ; the fine creamy white veins of several other plaquettes have become a very pronounced opaque white.

### Cutting technique.

The piece **M17-2** is a fragment of circular inlay (fig. 9 and p. 123)[165]. The reverse is marked by a series of very narrow (less than a millimetre) parallel, evenly spaced furrows which were traced when a series of plaquettes were made out of a block of agate by sawing vertical slices. After sawing, these plates were detached from the block to which their base still adhered by breaking. A saw with multiple blades was probably the instrument utilised for this cutting process. The pieces **S17-39** to **53** which have veins identical to those in other groups of inlays were all

---

164 Analyses done by A. Plu of the Museum national d'histoire naturelle (Paris). Perhaps the fragment of wood from the pear tree does not belong to this object which is of Indian origin, as will be shown later, since this wood is not mentioned anywhere in the fabrication of thrones in India : J. Auboyer, *Le trône et son symbolisme dans l'Inde ancienne*, Paris, 1949, nor in studies relating to the culture of trees in ancient India : O. Viennot, *Le culte de l'arbre dans l'Inde ancienne*, Paris, 1954.

165 On the technique of cutting hard stones in general and, for example, the utilisation of a tubular drill which was probably used for cutting the tubular elements belonging to our object, see A. Lucas, *Ancient Egyptian materials*, p. 84 sqq.

drawn out from the same hemispherical block. Their length varies between 4.8 and 7.8 cm with an average height of 3 to 3.5 cm. The longest slices belong to the middle portion of the block where the diameter was maximum. The shortest slices belong to the sides. These pieces are slightly trapezoidal in profile, the thickness being 4 to 5 mm at the base and 3 mm at the top. This gradual thinning might have resulted from the longer exposure of the top to the friction of the blade of the saw, as compared with the base of the furrow. Near the base, on one side only, at the spot which corresponds to the last stage of cutting, a curved mark which was formed by the balancing movement of the saw can be seen. The white agates **S18-1** to **37** were also cut from the same block whose curvature can be observed at the ends of the batons **S18-1**, **2** and **11**. The marks of the saw and the pincers are still visible on the fragment **S18-3** and **6**.

Figure 10 makes it possible to reconstruct the principal stages in the making of the plates :

— **1** represents the preliminary cutting of the block into two half spheres.

— **2** illustrates the simultaneous cutting of several plaquettes. As is possible to deduce from the evenness of these plaquettes, the saw was undoubtedly equipped with blades rather than metallic wire which would have resulted in an undulating cut.

— **3a** and **3b** show two types of cutting finish : in the example 3a, the plate is sliced along the entire height of the demi-block which seems to have been done in the case of the plaquettes **S17-39** to **53** ; in the example 3b, the block is sawed upto a demi-centimetre from the base, as in the case of the disc **M17-2** described above. The slices thus formed were detached with a wedge. The base of the block, the one opposite the side which had been sawed for the cutting of plaquettes, could in its turn be utilised as inlay.

The mechanical technique of piercing beads utilised throughout the ancient world is not entirely absent and is attested by the turning marks in the tubular elements of rock crystal and agate and in the small holes made in certain elements for fixing them. But it is of interest to note that the cutting of plates was a manual operation using a saw with straight rather than circular blades, the only technique which probably made it possible to assemble multiple blades on a single tool.

### Identification and comparison.

It is not possible to reconstitute the piece of furniture to which these elements originally belonged exactly as they are too scattered and the attempt to combine the plaquettes themselves to reconstruct the decor would be equally futile. The latter, in any case, presented a particularly astonishing polychromy in which the gilded elements, enhanced by a decoration of rock crystal and agate, were found side by side with large flat surfaces having brown, black and white stripes. Not a single element of hinges having been found in the treasury, it appears that the support of these inlays was not a box or an almirah but rather a piece of furniture with legs and perhaps arms, as in a throne or a *kline*[166].

The association of agates and rock crystal in the same piece of furniture was confirmed by the discovery of a rich collection of stones with inlays in agate and tubes made of rock crystal in the *Horti Lamiani*, one of the large residences in Rome situated in the Esquilin quarter – the Piazza

---

166 Among other pieces of furniture, it is also possible to imagine tables or side boards (*abacus*).

Vittorio Emanuele II of today[167]. In the inventory prepared at the end of the excavation, the lot of precious objects consisted, in particular, of metallic elements (plates in gilded bronze, nails etc.), 441 gems, 296 plaquettes of agate (265 specimens of these still exist), 28 fragments of rock crystal (of which 24 have perhaps been analysed until now).

Roman agate plaquettes can be mainly classified into two groups according to the quality of the agate: the first type with brown, beige and white veins (type **b** of Ai Khanum)[168] and the second with black and white veins (type **d** of Ai Khanum). These also have only one polished side. Their forms are the same as already described for the treasury: triangles, rectangles, trapezoids, polygonal elements and discs. They distinguish themselves from the specimens of Ai Khanum in certain details : their edges were also cut with pincers but none of the plaquettes was smoothened as in the series of agates **S17-39** to **53**. The batons of white agate **S18-1** to **37**, which were used as a border in one of the panels of the piece of furniture in the treasury, are not there in the Roman treasure though there are some similar specimens in banded agate. To these differences it is necessary to add the find consisting of a fragment of inlay in banded agate, cut very carefully in the form of a vine or acanthus [169]. The rock crystal fragments are tubular elements formed by turning, and resemble those of Ai Khanum in their inner diameter. Their external wall, with its decoration of mouldings and vertical lines, is however different[170]. As for the system of fixing, bronze rivets twisted in the form of an H and schist nails of the type found at Ai Khanum were also not observed.

Achaemenid Iran has provided ample evidence that the technique of inlaying hard stone is of Oriental origin[171]. We can surmise its existence at Susa on the basis of the reference to precious materials in the foundation Charter of the Apadana and it is attested at Persepolis by diverse finds in the treasury where the facing was done with the help of inlays in ivory, lapis-lazuli, agate and carnelian[172]. There are very few specimens of rock crystal used as inlay in the excavations. Apart from the fragments which we have already mentioned, fragments of plaques with engravings or intaglios were also found in the treasure of the Esquilin[173]. A certain number of disc-shaped inlays found in Asia Minor and in Greece seem to have been used as earrings[174]. Other specimens, like

---

167 Discovered in 1875 and 1879, this find was presented during an exhibition at the *Musei capitolini :* M. Cima, "Il «prezioso arredo» degli Horti Lamiani", in *Le tranquille dimore degli dei, La residenza imperiale degli* horti *Lamiani, Roma, maggio-settembre 1986, Campidoglio, Palazzo dei Conservatori* (a cura di M. Cima ed E. La Rocca), Roma, 1986, pp. 105-144. A study of the gems in M. Martini, "Le gemme degli horti Lamiani", *ibidem*, pp. 145-150 ; E. La Rocca, "Il lusso come espressione di potere", pp. 30-31.

168 M. Cima, "Il «prezioso arredo»", p. 110, fig. 19.

169 On the discovery of a Corinthian capital worked in *opus sectile* in the same region of the *horti Lamiani* see M. Cima, "I pavimenti", *ibidem*, pp. 64-65 and p. 63, fig. 6.

170 M. Cima, "Il «prezioso arredo»", pp. 110 and 142-144.

171 For Asia Minor see, for example, the finds of the richly inlaid furniture of Gordion : R.S. Young, *The Gordion final reports, I, Three great early tumuli*, Philadelphia, 1981, pp. 259-281.

172 E.F. Schmidt, *Persepolis II*, p. 71, pl. 40.

173 M. Cima, "Il «prezioso arredo»", pp. 141-142 and ref. n. 3.

174 These crystal discs are often confused with modern magnifing glasses but they are definitely of ancient origin : F. Brein, "Ear studs for Greek ladies", *Anatolian Studies*, 32, 1982, pp. 89-92, pl. XXIII-XXIV, with references to the finds of the Artemis of Ephesus and analogous finds made at Thasos, Paros, Chios, Samos, etc.

one of the finds in the palace of Ai Khanum have often been confused with optical lenses[175]. This stone is represented in Nisa solely by an arched cylindrical element with several holes pierced along its length for the passage of a thread or a metallic wire. The use of agates in inlays is equally rare : about ten specimens, of which the majority is conserved in the Vatican Museum, were found in Italy and in particular, at Pompei. In Central Asia, the excavation of Koj-Krylgan-kala has furnished two specimens of discoidal plano-convex inlays. Two tubular elements at Nisa could well have belonged to a piece of furniture of the type at Ai Khanum (above n. 159).

As in the case of vessels in agate and rock crystal, it is in India that we should look for the precise origin of this type of inlay. Numerous plaques with agate inlays were recovered in a jar in a treasure concealed under the floor of house 4 of Sirkap, dating from the Parthian period[176]. Attributed to a goldsmith or a lapidary, the contents of the vessel consisted of pieces of silver and gold and hard stones, among which figured about ten plano-convex, banded agate discs, four discs of rock crystal and three fragments of small discs in white agate. The banded agate discs belong to the same type as those in Ai Khanum. But the most interesting observation relates to white agate which J. Marshall calls *porcelain-agate* because of its likeness to this material[177]. This stone has only been found at Taxila and the analysis of the finds have confirmed the siliceous composition of this material which might be of volcanic origin, and its identity with natural agates. The quality and technique of polishing being the same as for the batons **S18-1** to **37** of Ai Khanum, it is possible that these white agates of Taxila come from the same workshops.

Although it was not possible to identify the deposits of these stones, the finds of Taxila make it possible to attribute the throne of Ai Khanum to North-West India. This object constitutes the most significant piece in the treasury. Like the punch-marked coins of Taxila it must have been brought here as tribute or booty following one of the Indian campaigns of Eucratides.

The similarity between the finds of Ai Khanum and those of Rome and Nisa makes it possible to assign to them also the same Indian origin. The interpretation of the iconography of thrones in Graeco-Roman and Indian sculpture is difficult. Although their construction is almost identical, the appearance of the thrones at Rome and at Ai Khanum must have been perceptibly different due to the form of their legs. The fragments of the legs of the Roman specimen are no different from the type usually found in antique furniture as a whole in Greece[178], Iran[179] or

---

175 O. Guillaume and A. Rougeulle, *Fouilles AKh VII*, p. 79, n° 1329 (from the palace). Although the rounded form of these objects in crystal resembles optical lenses, it appears that the known parallels were never anything but elements of inlay : See L. Gorelick, A.J. Gwinnett, "Close work without magnifying lenses? A hypothetical explanation for the ability of ancient craftsmen to effect minute detail", *Expedition*, 23-2, 1981, pp. 27-34 ; "Discussion of suggestions from readers of Expedition", *Expedition*, 23-4, 1981, pp. 15-16. On magnifying glasses see also G. Lafaye, in *DAGR*, s.v. "Pila", p. 478. According to Pliny XXXVII, 64, "when *smaragdi* that are tabular in shape are laid flat, they reflect objects just as mirrors do. The Emperor Nero used to watch the fights between gladiators in a reflecting *smaragdus*" : we suppose that the surface of this emerald was concave and that Nero utilised it like a mirror in which the spectacle was reflected and not as a lens which he attached to his eyebrow.

176 J. Marshall, *Taxila*, pp. 188-189, 505-506, pl. 147 (dépôt E).

177 For the description and mineralogical analysis of this agate see J. Marshall, *Taxila*, pp. 478, 505-506.

178 G.M.A. Richter, *The furniture of the Greeks, Etruscans and Romans*, London, 1966[2].

179 P. Bernard, "Sièges et lits en ivoire", p. 337.

India[180]. In Indian iconography, the legs of thrones are generally moulded but the octagonal form of the legs of the specimen from Ai Khanum is nevertheless also attested in the bas-reliefs of Bharhut[181]. In the latter, the legs of the throne are octagonal with a bell-shaped capital, a direct influence of the columns in the architecture of Bharhut or Sanchi.

Like many objects of luxurious construction, this article of furniture has also no doubt had a long life. The date of the fabrication of the throne of Esquilin could thus well be close to that of the throne of Ai Khanum. It is, however, not possible to reproduce the itinerary followed by this object before its arrival in Italy. As noted in respect to the vessel in semi-precious stone, it was perhaps the Hellenistic kingdoms which were responsible for its importation in Rome, after the latter entered into contact with them. According to Appian (XII, 115), the treasure of Mithridates of Pontus in the city of Talauri contained "2000 drinking-cups made of onyx welded with gold, and many cups, wine-coolers, and drinking-horns, also ornamental couches and chairs, bridles for horses, and trappings for their breasts and shoulders, all ornamented in like manner with precious stones and gold. The quantity of this store was so great that the transfer of it occupied thirty days. Some of these things had been inherited from Darius, the son of Hystaspes ; other came from the kingdom of the Ptolemies, having been deposited by Cleopatra at the island of Cos and given by the inhabitants to Mithridates ; still others had been made or collected by Mithridates himself, as he was lover of the beautiful in furniture as well as in other things"[182]. Vessels and furniture inlaid with precious stones are of course mentioned also by Pliny in his narrative relating to the triumph of Pompey over Rome in 61 (*H.N.* XXXVII, 17 : *gemmata potoria et uaria supellectilis genera*). These riches generated a taste for fine goods among the Romans, who immediately began to fight over murrhine vases (Pliny XXXVII, 18 : *myrrhina (...), quae protinus ad hominum usum transiere*), as well as over stands (or 'trays') and tableware fabricated in this material (*abacis etiam escariisque uasis expetitis*). The victory of Actium in 31 B.C. once again brought a large quantity of merchandise to Rome drawn from the rich treasures of the Ptolemies which have been eulogised by Athenaeus (V, 194c-203b)[183] and Lucan (*Bell. civ.* X, 111-126) and which we know abounded in luxury goods from India.

Interestingly, during the period of Caligula or Commodus, the surroundings of the imperial residence at Esquilin where the throne of agate and rock crystal had been installed, consisted of a nymphee dedicated to Dionysos, the conqueror of India, but this is perhaps a pure coincidence. In

---

180 See, for example, the representation of the throne with the legs thrust out and richly decorated panels in a relief of stūpa I, western toraṇa, of Sanchi : *Sāñchī*, pl. 3. The seated personage is a king recognisable as such by his turban, by royal symbols such as the umbrella and the fly whisk and by the presence of his spouse seated facing him. See also I. Gobert, *La vie publique et privée dans l'Inde ancienne*, pl. 27 sqq. On turned and moulded legs of thrones in Gandhara sculpture see K.K. Murthy, *The Gandhāra sculptures*, pl. XVII, fig. 2-4; at Nagarjunakonda, the mouldings of the legs of thrones are ribbed : K.K. Murthy, *Nagārjunakoṇḍā*, p. 158 sqq., fig. XI.

181 A. Cunningham, *The Stûpa of Bharhut*, London, 1879, pl. XXIX, 4 ; I. Gobert, *La vie publique et privée dans l'Inde ancienne*, pl. 2, fig. 1.

182 *Appian's Roman history*, transl. by H. White, vol. II, pp. 463-465. M. Cima, "Il «prezioso arredo»", pp. 122-124. On Mithridates see Th. Reinach, *Mithradates Eupator König von Pontos*, transl. by A. Goetz, Leipzig, 1895, pp. 284-285 (ed. rev. and augm. by the author of *Mithridate Eupator roi de Pont*, Paris, 1890 ; also *Mitridate Eupatore re di Ponto*, Milano, 1960).

183 E.E. Rice, *The grand procession of Ptolemy Philadelphus*, 1983. On the procession : V, 197c-203b.

fact, the area called *horti* in the Esquilin zone consisted, from the beginning of the first century B.C., of group of luxurious residences and parks. These *horti*, including those of Mecena and L. Aelius Lamia, became Imperial property shortly after Augustus. Caligula transformed the latter into a luxurious residence and, following the Alexandrian tradition, built monuments dedicated to the divine cult of the Emperor here. As noted by E. La Rocca[184], under Commodus, this cult seems to have taken the form of a nymphee decorated with a group of sculptures representing the triumphal procession of Dionysos on his return from India – similar to the procession that Ptolemy II Philadelphus had organised on his so called return from Asia – with the intention of associating the image of Dionysos to his family's memory (Athenaeus V, 200d).

The conservation of thrones or pieces of furniture in precious materials seems to be a constant phenomenon in the archaeological findings in ancient warehouses and treasures. We will limit ourselves to the mention of Hellenistic ivory furniture in the Parthian treasury of Nisa[185], the Indian thrones in the palace of Pāṭaliputra[186] and of Begram[187], and the throne in syenite and asphalt of the Parthian residence in Babylon, whose original depot was identified by R. Koldewey in the sanctuary of Esagila[188]. Graeco-Roman[189] and Indian[190] sources are full of allusions to thrones and furniture pieces decorated with inlay work, but archaeological finds of these are relatively rare[191]. With respect to agates and rock crystal, no written evidence is available of their use in the objects which we have now been able to identify at Ai Khanum and Rome[192]. In the

184 E. La Rocca, "Il lusso come espressione di potere", p. 10 and 32.

185 P. Bernard, "Sièges et lits en ivoire", with references.

186 Stone elements in the form of griffins found in the palace of Pāṭaliputra (3rd cent. B.C.) : S. Piggott, "Throne fragments from Pāṭaliputra", *Ancient India*, 4, 1947-48, pp. 101-103. On the excavation of the palace see R.E.M. Wheeler, "Iran and India in Pre-Islamic times : a lecture", *ibidem*, pp. 96-100.

187 J. Hackin *et alii*, *Nouvelles recherches archéologiques à Begram* ; J. Hackin *et alii*, *Diverses recherches archéologiques en Afghanistan*. Let us not forget also that the ivory statuette of Pompei was probably part of an article of a furniture (small table or stool?) : E.C.L. During Caspers, "The Indian ivory figurine from Pompei – A reconsideration of its functional use", *South Asian Archaeology 1979*, ed. H. Härtel, Berlin, 1981, p. 341 sqq. Illustration : M.R. Borriello, "Gli avori e gli ossi lavorati", in *Le collezioni del Museo Nazionale di Napoli*, Roma, 1989, pp. 112-113 (statuette of Lakṣmī).

188 R. Koldewey, *Die Tempel von Babylon und Borsippa*, Leipzig, 1911, p. 46 sqq. ; *idem*, *Das wiedererstehende Babylon*, Leipzig, 1925$^4$, pp. 216-217. F. Wetzel, E. Schmidt, A. Mallwitz, *Das Babylon der Spätzeit (WVDOG, 52)*, Berlin, 1957, pp. 34-35.

189 Athenaeus V, 202b : thrones of ivory and gold in the procession of Ptolemy II Philadelphus ; Lucan, *Bell. civ.* X, 122 : beds scintillating with jewels in the description of Cleopatra's treasure ; Pliny XXXVII, 17 : "[Emperor Nero] had sceptres, actors' masks and travellings couches adorned with pearls". For thrones and beds in hard stones see also M. Cima, "Il «prezioso arredo»", pp. 110 (n. 15 of p. 128), 123-124.

190 For Indian sources see J. Auboyer, *Le trône et son symbolisme*, p. 10 sqq.

191 See G.M.A. Richter, *op. cit.* Among the attested archaeological specimen see the ivory throne in the tomb of Philip II at Vergina, the only one presently known for Greece : *Τὸ Ἔργον της Ἀρχαιολογικῆς Ἑταιρείας 1987* (Athens, 1988), fig. 48.

192 In our initial hypotheses, we were hesitant to associate agate and rock crystal in the same object. L. Lanciani, at the beginning of the century, and the authors of the catalogue on the *horti Lamiani* had expressed similar doubts with regard to the Roman find, by attributing agates to a mural facing and rock crystal to articles of furniture : E. La Rocca, "Il lusso come espressione di potere", p. 31. M. Cima, "Il «prezioso arredo»", pp. 122-124, was able, however, to develop a very rich study on thrones from the hypothesis that agate and rock crystal were

description of Strabo, XV,1, 69, relating to large Indian processions, where the royal treasure was paraded, tables, thrones, tall cups for drinking and vases for ablutions were mostly inlaid with precious stones, but the only ones mentioned are emeralds, beryls, garnets and rubies.

---

combined in the same object. On the cult of the throne and the theatrical function of the display of luxury by Hellenistic kings and emperors as a demonstration of power cf M. Cima, pp. 122-128. See Also E. La Rocca, pp. 3-35. With respect to the importation of Indian furniture in Italy see the case of the ivory statuette of Pompei above n. 187.

## APPENDIX TO CHAPTER VI ON THE INLAID SHELL PLAQUE

Fig. 29b

For a new example of Indian engraving technique similar to that of the vase of Gundla (pp. 67-71), mention must be made of the frieze decorating a cylindre of horn discovered in the Graeco-Bactrian sanctuary of the Oxus at Takht-i Sangin in Tadžikistan : I.R. Pitschikjan, *Oxos-Schatz und Oxos-Tempel. Achämenidische Kunst in Mittelasien (Antike in der Moderne)*, Berlin, 1992, pp. 38-41, Abb. 19-20. In contrast with the hypothesis presented in this publication, where it is considered as Assyrian, P. Bernard attributes to this object an Indian origin ("Le temple de Takht-i Sangin en Bactriane : Temple du feu ou pas ?", *Studia Iranica*, 23, 1994, pp. 112-113). The scene represented belongs to an Indian myth, probably related to the Hinduist pantheon (Cl. Rapin, "Hinduism in the Indo-Greek area: notes on some Indian finds from Bactria and on two temples in Taxila", in *Mesopotamia*, Turin, forthcoming).

CHAPTER VI

# THE LEGEND OF ŚAKUNTALĀ ON AN INLAID SHELL PLAQUE

Fig. 30-60

## A) *INTRODUCTION*

In this collection of Indian objects deposited by Eucratides I in the treasury of Ai Khanum, the "Indian plāque", along with the throne decorated with precious stones, is a masterpiece by virtue of the originality of its imagery as well as by the technical quality of its inlay decoration. A reconstruction of this plaque will be attempted in the following pages, on the basis of the fragmentary elements furnished by the excavation[193].

### 1) Place of discovery.

Almost all the elements[194] constituting this object come from an excavated zone in court *105* with a width of 2 m, in front of the warehouses *116* and *117* in the western wing of the treasury. The dimension of these elements as well as the colour of some of them (plaquettes of shells) makes it difficult to distinguish them, and it was possible to retrieve most of them only by a process of sieving and washing the rubble taken from a depth of about 15 cm. Only two fragments were discovered away from this group ; one on the floor of the court in a probe carried out at a distance of 4 meters from the wall opposite the rooms *116* and *117* (plaquette I-2), and the other, in the rubble resulting from the destruction of warehouse *111* in the eastern wing (plaquette I-10).

### 2) Characteristics of the object and technical comparisons.

By gradually piecing together the fragments until the possibility of all other combinations was ruled out, it was possible to restitute a circular plaque with a diameter of about 20.5 cm, formed by an assemblage of plaquettes cut from shells and juxtaposed against each other on a support which has disappeared. Alveoles were made in these plaquettes which were filled with minute inlays of coloured molten glass and circled with strips of gold forming a decoration of vibrant colours, which have retained their original freshness. Only a few of these inlays still adhere to the plaquettes. The function of this very luxurious object, of which no other parallel is available, is not certain. However, its dimensions make it clear that it could not have been an ornament. We see it rather as an object of feminine toiletry, the back of a mirror or the lid of a small box, for which the iconographic subject that we will be analysing below seems particularly appropriate.

---

193 Earliest publications : P. Bernard, *CRAI*, 1980, pp. 443-447 ; *idem*, *BEFEO*, 68, 1980, pp. 29-36 ; Cl. Rapin, *RA*, 1987, pp. 62-63 ; *idem*, in *Greek colonists and native populations*, 1990, p. 337, fig. 4 ; *idem*, *Fouilles AKh VIII*, pp. 185-232, 358-366, pl. 86-95, 121-124 and 126. See also the appendix p. 50 and fig. 29b.

194 For the catalogue of fragments see pp. 132-142.

Of the approximately 65 plaquettes which comprised the original plate only 33, in complete or fragmented state, were found (fig. 30). Their form is generally rectangular except in certain parts of the edges where some of them are cut in a triangular or trapezoid form (plaquettes I-30, I-31, etc.) ; their dimensions vary between 1.5 to 3 cm and they are extremely fine (2 to 3 mm in thickness). In most of the cases, their sides are strictly rectilinear so that the joints could be assembled exactly and would not be too visible ; only in rare cases do contiguous elements have chinks between them, as for example, between plaquettes I-31 and 32, 32 and 33, or 8 and 11 ; these chinks must have been filled by the stuff which was used to fix the plaquettes on their support (gum, putty ?).

A fragment with a semi-cylindrical section, 2 cm wide and 8.5 mm thick, with a slight curvature in its length, belonged to an annular border with bulges which appears to have served as a frame for the disc[195]. The inner edge is slightly flattened as if to allow a better adjustment with a contiguous surface (fig. 30.1). It is possible to project two different reconstitutions of this border ; it might have been placed either on the same side as the inlaid plate whose diameter would then have increased to 24.5 cm (A), or on the opposite side, where it would have delimited a reflective area of 16.5 cm (B)[196].

---

195 Although in the present case the curvature of the fragment excludes the possibility of its having served as the decoration of a handle, it should be noted that at Ter (a district of Osmanabad) there is a handle made of shell which is dated to the 2nd cent. A.D. : *Dawn of civilization in Maharashtra - Prince of Wales Museum of Western India Bombay*, Bombay, 1975, p. 29, fig. 61. It is an element with a hexagonal section (length : 4.5 cm), with a short, slightly narrower cylindrical appendix extending from the upper end and from the lower, a conical tenon (length : 2.2 cm) which could be inserted in an extension or a socle. The lower part of each side of the hexagonal element is decorated with an engraved bust, forming in all three couples in each of which the man and the woman are shown facing each other ; one of the male figures representing a bald old man is astonishingly realistic. The character of the decoration itself indicates that the object was the handle of a mirror. On Indian mirrors (*mukura*) see P.K. Acharya, *Indian architecture according to Mānasāra-Śilpaśāstra*, London, New York, Bombay, 1927, p. 69 ; K. de B. Codrington, "Ancient Indian hand mirrors", *Man*, 1929, pp. 170-171 ; B.S. Upadhyaya, *India in Kālidāsa*, Allahabad, 1947, pp. 207-208 ; J. Marshall, *Taxila*, pp. 658-659 ; J. Naudou, "Symbolisme du miroir en Inde", *Arts Asiatiques*, 13, 1966, pp. 59-82 ; K.K. Murthy, *The Gandhāra sculptures : A cultural Survey*, Delhi, 1977, pp. 69-70, fig. XVI, 20.

196 This measurement is greater than that of the bronze mirror plate **P3-1** (diam. : 10 cm, Cl. Rapin, *Fouilles AKh VIII*, p. 183, pl. 80) discovered on the floor of room *107* ("library") and of other mirrors discovered at Ai Khanum : H.-P. Francfort, *Fouilles AKh III*, p. 53, tableau 18.69 ; O. Guillaume and A. Rougeulle, *Fouilles AKh VII*, n^os 0937-0945, except n° 0943, whose diam. is 22 cm ; O. Guillaume, "Contribution à l'étude d'un artisanat bactrien pré-hellénistique", pp. 261-263 ; in any case it does not contradict the mirror hypothesis ; actually, according to the *Mānasāra-Śilpaśāstra* whose date, though not certain, should be around the 6th-7th cent. A.D. (P.K. Acharya, *Indian architecture*, p. 69), "nine alternative measurements are prescribed for the mirror, namely from 5 (or 6) *aṅgulas* upto 21 (or 22) *aṅgulas*" ; by the size of its reflective plate, the mirror of Ai Khanum, if it is one, would easily fit into this spectrum of 9.5 to 42 cm, *aṅgula* corresponding to about 1.9 cm. Whether we reconstitute it as having a diameter of 16.5 cm or 24.5 cm, it should be noted that its diameter (more than 20 cm) was, in any case, greater than that of Graeco-Bactrian mirrors (see preceding note). It may be however added that in order to be functional these antique mirrors must have had to be polished frequently, an operation which would have had a deteriorating effect on the fragile border if it was situated on the same side as the reflective plate. It is to be remarked also, that according to the same Indian source, mirrors should be circular (*suvṛtta*) with a slightly raised border (the depth is clearly visible in all the Indian representations), their surface should also be absolutely brilliant, the edge

A

B

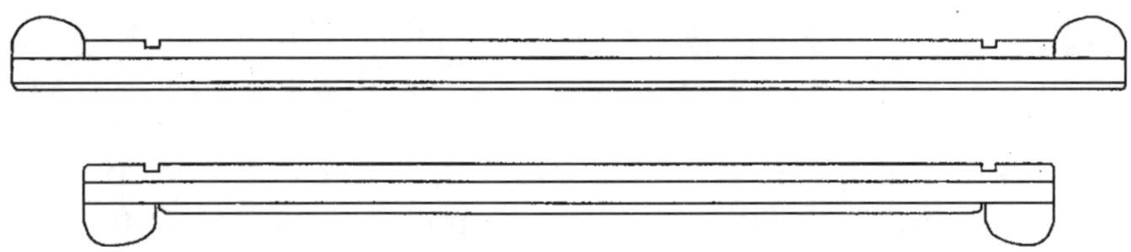

Apart from the glue which was used for sticking the plaquettes, of which no trace remains, small rivets and nails, whose presence is attested by the notches in the corners of some of them, were also used for fixing the plaquettes on the support, which was probably wooden[197]. These notches did not follow any geometrical pattern but were always situated in the hollowed out zones of the plaquettes where the subsequent applications of inlays of molten glass easily permitted the masking of the head of the fastener.

The decoration belongs to the technique of inlay on champlevé, the elements of shells having been previously cut and polished in the form of plaquettes. Inspite of the careful polishing received by each one of these elements, it is possible to distinguish traces of the saw used for cutting the plaquettes, and of the notches for fixing them, as well as of the file used for smoothening them and removing the curvature of the shells, though some parts of the plaquettes still retain a concave surface on the reverse. The alveoles which delimit the outlines of the motifs and in which the inlays with the details of design were done, were hollowed out with the help of gouges in the case of the more voluminous parts. Chisels were used for the lines detailing the paws of animals, the upper part of an umbrella, stems of branches etc.[198] and drills for making holes for fixing the convex part of the border as well as for the small, circular motifs (flowers, ornaments, the lower part of an umbrella and joints in the paws of animals) according to a technique similar to the globolo of Graeco-Persian gems[199]. The various motifs, from the most simple rounds to the most complicated, like the quadriga at the bottom of the composition, are juxtaposed and never overlap each other. The undeniable repetitiveness of their details suggests the utilisation of patterns or models (fig. 34).

Like the figurative decoration which will be analysed later, the material itself reveals the Indian origin of the object. The shells from which the plaquettes have been cut are probably the Xancus pyrum, known also as Turbinella pyrum which are found on the western and eastern coasts of India. Since prehistoric times this has been among the shells which have widely figured in the commercial circuits linking the Indus to Iran and Mesopotamia[200].

should be decorated with a linear design (*rekhā*) and the reverse side with images related to the function of the object such as that of Lakṣmī who incarnated beauty. On the earlist Indian mirrors in metal and, beginning with the period of Kālidāsa, in glass, see also B.S. Upadhyaya, *op. cit.*, pp. 207-208.

197 The elements with protuberant borders were fixed by piercing a hole in the centre of a flower.

198 See below p. 97.

199 See J. Boardman, *Greek gems*, 1970, p. 380 and pl. 932-943; P. Callieri, "La glittica greco-persiana nelle regioni orientali dell'impero achemenide", *Studi di egittologia e di antichità puniche*, a cura di E. Acquaro e S. Pernigotti, 11, 1992, pp. 63-76.

200 *Conchiglie : Il commercio e la lavorazione delle conchiglie marine nel medio oriente dal IV al II millennio a.C.*, Roma, 1981 : origin and trade of *Xancus pyrum* between the Indus and Seistan, pp. 15-17 ; form and usage of the *Fasciolaria trapezium* which resembles it, p. 25 ; J. Marshall, *Taxila*, pp. 667-673. The symbolic importance of the *Xancus pyrum* (conche) in Indian iconography, as the attribute of Viṣṇu, may also be mentioned.

The shaping of shells, particularly for the fabrication of bracelets[201] in oriental jewellery, is well attested from the beginning of ancient times[202]. This material is worked according to a technique related to ivory work and the making of stone vessels where the decoration is often conceived for receiving inlays of semi-precious stones or coloured paste. The plaque of Ai Khanum, however, distinguishes itself by the composite character, probably imposed by its dimensions, of its base of shells which is constituted of numerous plaquettes assembled together according to a process similar to marquetry, and by the diversity of decoration techniques. These latter employ a large variety of engraving processes (which remind one of certain aspects of intaglio work), and inlays with molten glass often combined in the same alveole (fig. 33, pp. 139-142) :

— juxtaposition of monochrome elements (VII-19, 23 to 32, 41, 42) ;

— indication of details on monochrome elements by means of thin strips of gold set in the mass (folds of garments : VII-1 to 12 ; pond : VII-21 and 22 ; harness : VII-37 ; unidentified fragment : VII-38) ;

— technique of *millefiori*[203] in many series of polychrome elements composed of circular pastilles 1.5 to 3 mm in diameter, the mass coloured with points or small sticks (VII-43 à 74), or more complex motifs (VII-38 to 40) ;

— inlays of glass on glass : certain plaquettes of glass are inlaid in their turn with tiny motifs divided by a thin strip or a gold leaf : the eye of the cervidaes VII-33, serpents in the pond (VII-21, 22), spots on the coat of animals (VII-34 to 37), pastilles decorating the pond of the circular frieze and the roofs of edifices with pinnacles (VII-13 to 18)[204].

The range of colours is dominated by bright orange and red with shades going from maroon to brown but white, black, grey, light sea green, pinkish white and light beige are also present.

On Indian shells see also E.H. Warmington, *The commerce*, pp. 172-174 ; J. Hornell, *The sacred Chank of India : A monograph of the Indian conch (Turbinella pyrum)*, Madras Fisheries Bureau, *Bulletin no. 7*, Madras, 1914.

201 On the specimens of *Xancus pyrum* from the excavation of Ai Khanum see H.-P. Francfort, *Fouilles AKh III*, p. 17 and pl. VII (0.2168 and the specimen of rough 0.343), and the bracelet decorated with engraved lines discovered in the treasury (**O34-1**, fig. 23, above p. 37). The accidental discovery made in the region of Ai Khanum of a round fragment of shell, perhaps a button, whose decoration consists of dots arranged around a central orifice (fig. 22) should also be added to this list. This object is identical to a specimen from Taxila and probably comes from the same workshop of North-Western India : see J. Marshall, *Taxila*, pl. 203w, n°44 and p. 669 ; another specimen almost similar to the preceding : pl. 203x, n°45.

202 *BEFEO*, 68, 1980, p. 32, n. 1 ; G. Dales, J.M. Kenoyer, "Shell working at ancient Balakot, Pakistan", *Expedition* 19-2, 1977, pp. 13-19 : Harappan site of Balakot in the Indus delta. See also M.E. Masson, G.A. Pugačenkova, *Parfianskie ritony Nisy*, 1950, pp. 21, 26. For the engraved plaquettes of Shami see R. Ghirshman, *Parthes et Sassanides*, Paris, 1962, fig. 124-125. On a descriptive sketch of the size of the plaquettes from the *Xancus pyrum* see *Conchiglie*, p. 82.

203 See, for example, the beads in molten glass decorated with miniaturised portraits : E.M. Alekseeva, *Antičnye busy Severnogo Pričeřnomor'ja*, tabl. 48-49. See also C.G. Seligman, H.C. Beck, "Far Eastern glass : Some Western origins", *The Museum of Far Eastern Antiquities. Stockholm. Bulletin*, 10, 1938, pl. I-IX.

204 If we exclude inlay techniques used in mosaic and cloisonne in the entire ancient Orient including Egypt, but without the same type of miniaturisation, the most comparable specimen in finesse to the plaquette of Ai Khanum is a vessel in obsidian discovered at Stabiae made in the Egyptising style of the Roman period following the technique of cloisonné, with inlays of enamel and gold : O. Elia in *EAA*, s.v. "Stabiae" (colour pl.) and E. Leospo, "Le coppe di ossidiana", forthcoming.

This glass constitutes a new source of information on a technique which is definitely not of Mediterranean origin. The unfortunate circumstances which so abruptly ended the excavation at Ai Khanum did not permit the collection of specimens for a precise analysis. All that can be said is that these inlays have a consistence which seems, to the touch, much softer than that of traditional glass. This characteristic is probably due to the technique of fabrication, or the ingredients of the molten glass, which was intended for combining in the same mass, strips of gold and a vitreous paste, whereas the compatibility of these materials, particularly at this level of miniaturisation, is difficult. Despite sustained subjection to humid conditions, this material has managed to conserve the brightness of the original colours and to escape the iridescence which has been the cause of the deterioration of most of the glass at Ai Khanum[205].

### 3) Figurative decoration : general description[206]. FIG. 31-32

The decorative motifs are placed in two zones : a circular central area measuring 17 cm in diameter, and a 1.5 cm wide concentric frieze. In the central area, a royal procession, watched by several spectators, advances towards the left across a flowery landscape, figuring animals typical of India, particularly cervidaes and peacocks and an edifice with a pinnacled roof. The frieze of the border illustrates another episode from Indian mythology which is related to the representation in the central area, but where purely decorative considerations override anecdotal ones[207].

The scene in the central area divides itself into three levels, one on top of the other.

— The first, at the bottom of the composition corresponding to the foreground of the scene, is occupied in the centre by a quadriga transporting three personages (II-11 to 13). The personages, of whom only the heads and the lines of the shoulders have survived, are standing under an umbrella. Of the chariot only the guard-rail against which the personage on the right is leaning remains and, on the left, the hoofs of three of the horses can be seen. Three cavalrymen, of whom one wears a helmet and is armed with a lance, escort the vehicle (II-14 to 16).

— In the middle portion of the central area of the plaque, which constitutes the second level, four equidistant columns stand out (IV-5 to IV-8). Behind this set of columns different animals can be seen moving among whom, from right to left, it is possible to recognize a small quadruped (V-12), two peacocks – a male (V-14) and a female (V-13), one or perhaps two cervidaes in the centre of the plaque (V-16) and, to the extreme left, another bird, perhaps a parrot (V-15).

---

205 On various types of polychrome molten glass see B.B. Lal, "Studies in early and mediaeval Indian ceramics - Some glass and glass-like artefacts from Bellary, Kolhapur, Maski, Nasik and Maheshwar", *Bulletin of the Deccan College Research Institute*, 14, 1953, pp. 48-58.

206 Basic bibliography : A. Cunningham, *Mahābodhi, or the great Buddhist temple under the Bodhi Tree at Buddha-Gayā*, London, 1892 ; A.K. Coomaraswamy, *La sculpture de Bodhgayā (Ars Asiatica, 18)*, Paris, 1935 ; A.K. Coomaraswamy, *La sculpture de Bharhut*, Paris, 1956 ; B. Barua, *Barhut*, Calcutta, 1934-1937 ; A. Cunningham, *The Stûpa of Bharhut*, London, 1879 ; J.H. Marshall, A. Foucher, *The monuments of Sāñchī*, Calcutta, London, 1930 ; J. Hackin *et alii*, *Nouvelles recherches archéologiques à Begram (MDAFA, 11)*, Paris, 1954 ; S.J. Czuma, *Kushan sculpture : images from early India*, Cleveland, 1985 ; E.B. Cowell (dir.), *The Jātaka or Stories of the Buddha's Former Births*, Cambridge, 1895-1913.

207 One finds something analogous to Stūpa II of Sanchi, where the medaillons of the balustrade repeat, in a simplified form, the themes developped in greater detail on the toraṇa : *Sāñchī*, pl. 74-91.

— At the upper level, many persons (II-7 to 10) installed on both sides of an edifice with a fully arched roof crowned by pinnacles (II-4) watch the passage of the procession. In the upper curvature of the plaque is placed a flowering tree with animals around it, among whom there are one or two birds.

The spaces between the principal motifs are filled with small decorative elements and flowering stems which suggest a country landscape.

A groove decorated with predominantly orange and white quadrangular inlays separates the central area from the frieze. Only a few of some two hundred inlays which were there originally still adhere to certain plaquettes (I-4, I-12 and I-27 = VII-41 and VII-42).

The frieze of the border of which it is possible to reconstitute at least two-thirds of the area by working out the symmetries, repeats in smaller dimensions, the principal motifs of the central area. The lower part of the circumference is occupied by an axial group comprising, from right to left, a seated couple in conversation (II-2, II-3), an edifice with three pinnacles (IV-2), and a quadrangular pond (IV-9), surmounted by a decorative motif of a floral character (IV-26). Symmetrically, on either side, a pair of cervidaes, a pair of peacocks and a branch of flowers are depicted in succession in an upward movement. An edifice with pinnacles and a seated human being occupy the middle section of the frieze, on the left and the right of the central field. The upper part of the frieze is extremely incomplete. The succession resumes with another flowering stem which, in its inverted representation, is the counterpart of that which precedes the edifice with pinnacles. Beyond this there is a bird followed by another human couple in conversation. The orientation of these different motifs is such that they can be easily comprehended inspite of the curvature of the border : those in the lower half rest against the external border, those of the upper half against the internal border ; the human figures and the edifice with pinnacles which are in the middle are arranged transversally.

### *B) COMPARATIVE RESEARCH*

The above description of the main features of the decor, though it does not explain the subject of the composition, makes it clear, by its complexity, that it has a precise signification. The task before us now is to attempt to identify the central theme of the composition by entering into a finer description of each one of the motifs. Despite the rarity of parallels, this research will help to place the object in its proper context which, pertaining to Indian iconography, is completely devoid of any traces of Greek or Iranian influences. The fragmentary state of the support of shells is a serious obstacle to our enquiry. The remains of the plaque furnish three types of facts : the silhouettes, more or less well conserved, in the plaquettes ; inlays of glass found in isolation for which it is sometimes possible to determine the original place in the plaque ; and inlays still adhering to their alveoles.

Only about half of the motifs still survive and not all lend themselves to any definite interpretation. Among the silhouettes which can be easily identified are the cavalrymen, the members of the group on the upper right hand side, the edifices with pinnacles, the peacocks and the cervidaes and some details such as the bases of columns and the foliage of the frieze. The motif of the quadriga can also be definitely deduced on the basis of the remains. However, the area of our ignorance remains large, whether it is with respect to the exact activity of the dramatic personae in the general context of the legend which itself can be identified, or the type of hair styles and costumes, the nature of the floral motifs and certain animals not be mention the architectural elements – the upper edifice on the right and the small edifices of the frieze, the four independent columns, the four legged object between the two columns on the left and the pond of the frieze – which we will be describing below.

The decoration of the plaque of Ai Khanum presents one of the most complex compositions in ancient Indian art which, as we know, is dominated by the imagery of the large Buddhist sanctuaries, particularly the one of Sanchi. Although the identification of the subject reposes finally on what are acknowledged as "the small objects", we will constantly refer to this rich, sculpture on monuments to throw light on the Indian character of the plaque of Ai Khanum.

The key to the interpretation is provided by the association of three well known themes of Indian iconography. The first theme is the royal procession developed in the lower part, with the indispensable addition of the spectators on the balcony which is placed in the upper right hand side of the central area[208]. The second is that of the cervidaes who are generally present in the hunting scenes linked to the earlier lives of the Buddha as illustrated at Sanchi and at Bharhut[209]. Finally, the geographical background which is that of a hermitage in a forest. The joint representation of cervidaes and hermitages is not rare but no large sculpture combines the three motifs which we have just enumerated in one composition[210]. On the other hand we find them together on a small terracotta plaque discovered at Bhita, whose decor enables it to be identified, with a reasonable amount of certainty, as an illustration of the legend of Śakuntalā. It is with the same legend that we will relate the plaque of Ai Khanum.

Even though several versions of this legend have been transmitted to us from Indian literature, each one differing from the other in the details, this legend has a basic structure which is, in general, compatible with the motifs of the plaque of Ai Khanum. It is with the mention of its principle written sources that we will begin.

The different versions of the legend of Śakuntalā do not contain adequate information which would permit a precise datation of the different stages of its development, because in Sanskrit literature, the weight of traditions and conventions considerably slows down the evolution of

---

208 The two components of the theme which are normally interlinked are here dissociated since the motif of the spectators on the balcony is separated from the procession and integrated with that of the hermitage in the forest. This dissociation of the two motifs has permitted the artist to represent, simultaneously, the image of the balcony which is raditionally linked to the procession and the image of Śakuntalā in the hermitage where the hunter-king meets her.

209 On the theme of hunting see also pp. 79-80, 88-89, 100 and 102.

210 In the illustration of the *jātaka* of Viśvantara (see also n. 285, 289, 290 and 297), at Bharhut and at Sanchi, the three motifs are united but the animals, in this case, the antelopes have only the symbolic function of representing the jungle and are not really integral to the unfolding of the action. It is an elephant which, though not represented, is at the origin of the narrative. Certain poetic descriptions in Indian literature of the visit to the hermitage can be illustrated with the elements present in the plaquette of Ai Khanum : see, for example, Kālidāsa, *Raghuvaṃśa* I, 35 sqq.

literary forms[211]. Even till today, for example, the origins of Indian theatre are difficult to date. Although Kālidāsa, one of the Sanskrit dramatists best known in Europe because of his work *Abhijñānaśakuntala*, belonged to the fourth or the fifth century, it is certain that the theatrical form itself was older, and that it had already been formalised in the period of Patañjali[212]. It is thus possible that the legend of Śakuntalā was part of a theatrical or poetic tradition, even before Kālidāsa, contemporary with its oldest representations such as the one on the disc of Bhita. Painting, to which the plaque of Ai Khanum shows its affinity by its colours, might have been another possible vehicle for the legend of Śakuntalā[213]. In fact the oldest examples of the paintings of Ajanta show the links between theatre and the figurative arts[214].

### *1) Literary sources of the legend of Śakuntalā.*

The seduction of the nymph Śakuntalā by King Duṣyanta, their union from which Bharata, the eponymous ancestor of the Indian nation (*Bhāratavarṣa*), would be born, his abandonment of Śakuntalā and finally the reunion of the lovers, constitutes the common framework of the several literary versions[215].

211 It is also not certain that these versions reflect a chronological evolution as their differences could be due to geographical variants and differences in literary rendering.

212 The oldest dramatists are Aśvaghoṣa and Bhāsa. On the problems relating to the latter see, for example, L. Renou and J. Filliozat, *L'Inde classique, Manuel des études indiennes*, Paris, 1947-1953, t. 2, pp. 265-270.

213 On the Indian foundness for painting, the technique, the portraits and the colours see B.S. Upadhyaya, *India in Kālidāsa*, pp. 230-235. The fact that "dans la séparation, la nostalgie de ceux qui aiment s'exprime en exécutant le portrait de l'absent ou de l'absente" on tablets is a recurrent theme in Indian theatre : Ph. Stern, "Aspects plastiques de l'ancien théâtre indien and peintures murales d'Ajanta (influences réciproques)", in *Les théâtres d'Asie*, Paris, 1961, p. 52. The hypothesis that painted representations of the myth which could have inspired Kālidāsa existed in reality might be suggested by passage VI, 17 of *Śakuntalā* which gives an extremely realistic description of the portrait of the young girl which Duṣyanta is painting (portrait with her two companions, landscape with two antelopes).

214 On the relation between the frescoes of Ajanta and theatre, see Ph. Stern, "Aspects plastiques de l'ancien théâtre indien", pp. 49-68.

215 On Śakuntalā see S. Lévi, *Le théâtre indien (Bibliothèque de l'École des Hautes Études, IVe Section, fasc. 83)*, Paris, 1890, pp. 170-177 ; M. and J. Stutley, *A dictionary of Hinduism*, London, 1977, s.v. "Śakuntalā" ; P. Filliozat in *Encyclopaedia universalis*, s.v. "Kālidāsa" ; *Encyclopaedia Britannica*, s.v. "Kālidāsa ; W. Ruben, *Kālidāsa*, 1956 ; *idem, Die Entwicklung der Dichtung im alten Indien*, 1973, ch. VI ; *Theater of Memory. The plays of Kālidāsa*, ed. by B. S. Miller, New York, 1984.

## The *Saundarananda* of Aśvaghoṣa.

The oldest written reference to the legend in writing is contained in *Saundarananda* of Aśvaghoṣa, dating from the period of Kaniṣka (1st-2nd cent. A.D.) where a simple mention of the names of Śakuntalā and her son Bharata occurs[216] :

"And as Kaṇva did for the son of Śakuntalā, the impetuous Bharata [...]".

## The *Mahābhārata*[217].

Among the developed versions of the legend, the one in the *Mahābhārata* is perhaps the most ancient. Although no evidence allows the precise dating of the final composition of this work – around the fourth or the fifth century A.D. ? – it is possible that some of its parts date to the fourth century B.C. In this work the legend is woven into the history of the origin of the Kuru dynasty and the history of King Duṣyanta. The first part of the narrative, which is of interest here and which we will describe in detail to show the importance accorded to plants and animals in the description of the natural landscape, relates to the King Duṣyanta at hunt and to his discovery of a hermitage in a forest on the banks of the river Mālinī[218], where he expresses his desire to meet the head of this hermitage called Kaṇva Kāśyapa. In the absence of the latter, Duṣyanta makes acquaintance with his adopted daughter Śakuntalā, with whom he falls in love and marries. He then returns alone to his palace after promising Śakuntalā to send for her later. In the second part of the legend, Duṣyanta willingly refuses to recognize Śakuntalā, who has borne him a son, Bharata, before reversing his decision and finally accepting her officially as his wife.

I. 63.1-3 (2816-18) [...] *Vaiśampāyana said* :

Upon a time this strong-armed king rode out, with ample strength of men and mounts, to a dense forest, escorted by hundred of horses and elephants. He progressed surrounded by hundreds of warriors, carrying swords and lances, brandishing clubs and maces, wielding javelins and spears. And the king went on, the lion roars of his warriors, the blasts of conches and drums, the thunder of the chariot rims reinforced by the trumpeting of the grand elephants, the whinnying of the horses, and the growls and arm-slapping of the men rose to a tumultuous noise. From the balconies of their terraced palaces the womenfolk gazed upon the hero, who made his own fame, in all his regal magnificence. [Description of the departure from the royal city]

I. 63.11-12 (2829-30) The overlord of earth filled earth and the heavens with the thunder of his chariot that flew like Fair-Winged Bird [*Garuḍa*]. And as he rode, the alert king chanced to see a wood like Indra's paradise [...].

---

216 Aśvaghoṣa : *The Saundarananda, or Nanda the Fair,* translated from the original Sanskrit of Aśvaghoṣa by E.H. Johnston, Oxford, London, 1932 (edition of the text Lahore, 1928), I, 26 (reference communicated by A. Passi).

217 We give the most, recent English translation here : *The Mahābhārata,* transl. and ed. by J.A.B. Van Buitenen, Chicago, London, 1973-1978, vol. 1, pp. 155-171. Cf. also *The Mahabharata of Krishna-Dwaipayana Vyasa (transl. into English prose from the original Sanskrit text)*3, by P.C. Roy, New Delhi, 1970-1975, vol. 1, *Adi Parva*, pp. 147-163 ; *Le Mahabharata, poème épique*, par H. Fauche, Paris, 1863-1870, vol. 1, pp. 298-330 (old French translation) ; *Storia di Śakuntalā (Śakuntalopākhyāna), Mahābhārata, I, 62-69*, a cura di D. Sagramoso Rossella, Venezia, 1991.

218 River which empties itself into the Ganges and known to Megasthenes as Errenysis : Arrian VIII, 4, 5.

I. 63.13-20 (2832-39) And in this wood, which teemed with herds of deer and beasts of prey that stalk the forest, Duḥṣanta, tiger among men, with retainers, escort, and mounts wrought havoc, killing game of many kinds. Many families of tigers he laid low as they came within range of his arrows ; he shot them with his shafts. Those that were in the distance the bull among men shot down with his arrows ; others that came up close he cut down with his sword ; and antelopes he brought down with his spear, the powerful spearman, who also knew all the points of the circular club swing and whose courage was boundless. He stalked about killing wild game and fowl with javelin, sword, mace, bludgeon, halberd. And when the wondrously valiant king and his warlike warriors raided the great forest, the big game fled it. The herds of deer, their flocks dispersed, their leaders killed, cried out for help everywhere. [...]

I. 64.1-4 (2845-49) Having killed thousands of deer, the king with his plentiful mounts entered into another wood in search of deer. Supremely strong, though hungry and thirsty, he penetrated himself into the depths of the forest till he came to a vast wilderness that was dotted with holy hermitages, a joy to the heart and a feast for the eye. He crossed beyond it and made for still another wood where a cool breeze was blowing, a wood sprinkled with blossoming trees and most prosperous grasslands. It was a wide woodland that echoed with the sweet warblings of birds. [...]

I. 64.15-29 (2861-2879) Looking at the forest with its wildly excited birds, he saw an idyllic and heart-fetching hermitage, covered with all kinds of trees and alight with blazing fires. Ascetics and anchorites peopled it and groups of hermits. Fire halls aplenty were scattered all over, and carpets of flowers. It seemed to shine forth with its large bays of water on the bank of the river Mālinī, holy and gladdening stream, which, O king, bestrewn with flocks of all kinds of fowl, added loveliness to this wilderness of austerities. And on seeing beasts of prey and deer peaceably together, the king was filled with the purest joy.

Thereupon the illustrious warrior drew nigh to the hermitage that most enchanting everywhere, was the image of the world of the Gods. He saw the river that embraced the hermitage with her holy water spreading out like the mother of all creatures, her banks swarming with *cakravāka* birds, her current carrying blossoms and foam – the habitation of *Kiṃnaras* (mythical monsters half man half horse) that was frequented by monkeys and bears. The sound of holy Vedic lessons wafted over the river ; sandbanks strung pearls upon her ; rutting elephants, tigers, and mighty snakes visited her.

When he saw the hermitage and the river that enclosed it, the king set his mind upon entering. And he entered the deep woodland, with its necklace of the Mālinī of the shining isles and lovely banks ; it appeared like the dwelling place of Nara and Nārāyaṇa, adorned by the Ganges, loud with the shriek of madly dancing peacocks. Having drawn near to the hermitage that resembled Citraratha's park, the lord of men, intending to see the great seer and ascetic Kaṇva Kāśyapa, surpassingly virtuous and of undescribable brilliance, halted his escort of chariots with footmen at the gate of the wood and said to his army, "I shall go to see Kāśyapa, that dispassionate hermit of rich austerities. Remain here until my return". And upon entering that wood, like another paradise of Indra, the lord of men shed his hunger and thirst and became overjoyed. Discarding his regalia and accompanied only by councillor and priest, he walked to the grand hermitage to see the seer who had piled up austerities everlasting. [...]

I. 65.1-10 (2894-2904) Thereupon the strong-armed king dismissed his councillors and went on alone. He did not find the seer of strict vows in the hermitage. Failing to find the seer and finding the hermitage empty, he spoke in a loud voice, thundering over the woodland : "Who is here?" Hearing his cry, a young maiden appeared, like Śrī incarnate, and came out of that hermitage, wearing the garb of a female hermit. No sooner had the black-eyed girl seen King Duḥṣanta than she bade him welcome and paid him homage. She honored him with a seat, with water to wash his feet, and a guest gift, and asked, O king, the overlord of men about his health and well-being.

After honoring him properly and inquiring about his health, she said with a faint smile, "What can I do?" The king, seeing that she had a flawless body and having been honored properly, replied to the sweet-spoken girl, "I have come to pay my worship to the venerable seer Kaṇva. Where has the reverend gone, my dear? Tell me, my pretty."

*Śakuntalā said* :

My reverend father has gone out of the hermitage to gather fruit. Wait a while, you will see him return.

*Vaiśampāyana said* :

The king, having failed to find the seer, looked at the girl who had addressed him and saw that she had beautiful hips, a lustrous appearance, and a charming smile. [...].

I. 67.1 (2955) *Duhṣanta said* :

And very clear is that you are the daughter of a king, the way you told it, beautiful girl. Be my wife, buxom woman! [... Duṣyanta marry Śakuntalā according to Gāndharva custom[219]].

I. 67.19-23 (2972-76) *Vaiśampāyana said* :

[...] Having thus spoken, the royal seer took his flawlessly moving bride solemnly by the hand and lay with her. And he comforted her and departed, and said many times, "I shall send an escort for you, with footmen, horses, chariots, and elephants : and with that I shall take you to my castle, sweet-smiling Śakuntalā!"

With such promises, Janamejaya, the king departed, and as he went he worried in his heart about Kāśyapa. "What may the venerable hermit not perpetrate when he hears of it, with all his ascetic power ... ; and with this worry he entered his own capital. Kaṇva himself returned to his hermitage a little while after the king's departure [...]".

## *Rāmacandra of Rajanallur.*

This same *Mahābhārata* is undoubtedly the source of an undated and perhaps modern version, Rāmacandra of Rajanallur whose résumé as given by S. Levi follows[220] :

" [...] Le roi s'est égaré à poursuivre un cerf. Il aperçoit un bosquet qui se mire dans un étang ; il y fixe ses regards. Tout à coup il voit Çakuntalâ, dont la beauté le séduit [...Au moment de son départ] Duṣyanta lui promet d'envoyer la chercher en pompe dès le lendemain. Il s'éloigne, retrouve les chasseurs, et retourne dans sa capitale. [...]".

## The *Purāṇa*.

The *Purāṇa*, texts of ancient origin, but as difficult to date as the *Mahābhārata*, take up the theme of Śakuntalā in brief. The story as reported in the *Bhāgavata-Purāṇa* (IX, 20, 7-22) follows[221] :

8-9 "While on a hunting excursion, (king) Duṣyanta happened to visit the hermitage of Kaṇva. Having seen a beautiful damsel beautifying the surroundings with her effulgence, and enchanting like the Māyā of the Lord, he instantaneously got infatuated. And though surrounded by some of his soldiers, he spoke to that charming lady [...]"

219 On this rite see M. and J. Stutley, *A dictionary of Hinduism*, s.v. Śakuntalā, n. 3.

220 S. Lévi, *Le théâtre indien*, pp. 171-173 ; Râmacandra de Râjanallûr, *Çakuntalâ, drame indien, version tamoule d'un texte sanscrit*, transl. into French by G. Devèze, Paris, 1888.

221 *The Bhāgavata Purāṇā*, transl. and annotated by G.V. Tagare, Delhi, Varanasi, Patna, 1976-1978, vol. 9, pp. 1227-1229. A brief mention in *The Vishńu Puráńa, a system of Hindu mythology and tradition*, transl. by H.H. Wilson, London, 1864-1877, repr. Calcutta, 1972, vol. IV, pp. 132-133 (IV, 19). For the *Padma Purāṇa Svargakhaṇḍa*, text closely related to that of Kālidāsa, see the controversies which tend to date it sometimes before, sometimes after Kālidāsa in L. Rocher, *The Purāṇas, (A history of Indian literature, 2.3)*, Wiesbaden, 1986, p. 84, 209.

## Kālidāsa : *The recognition of Śakuntalā (Abhijñānaśakuntala)*[222].

The play of Kālidāsa[223] which presents the most developed form of the legend dates from the fourth or the fifth century A.D.[224]. Compulsions specific to the theatrical medium led the author to introduce variations with respect to other versions, and particularly to take recourse to the intervention of the supernatural. But the general line followed at the beginning of the affair, which alone concerns us here, is akin to the *Mahābhārata* with the exception of details like the number of cervidaes leading the king towards the hermitage of Kaṇva, or the two companions of Śakuntalā who are absent from the epic poem[225]:

[I.6] (*Then enter king in a chariot, pursuing an antelope, bow and arrow in hand and his charioteer*).
CHARIOTEER (*looking at the king and the antelope*)
O long-lived one,

When I cast my eye on that black antelope and on you with your braced bow, I see (before me) as it were the Pināka-wielder in person, chasing a deer.

[I, 7] KING Charioteer, the antelope has given us a long chase. Even now he from time to time,

Looking back gracefully by the bending of his neck, at the car which follows him ; now, through fear of a descending shaft, by his haunches drawing himself mostly into the forepart of his body, strewing his track with grass, half-chewed, which drops from his mouth, kept open from exhaustion, mark, how by reason of his lofty boundings, he moves much more through the air, and but lightly skims the ground. (7)

[I, 8] (*Wonderingly*). How now the deer is scarce discernible to me though I have been pursuing him ?
CHARIOTEER Long-lived one, seeing that the ground was uneven, I pulled up the reins and slackened the speed of the chariot. But now that you are on level ground, you will not find it difficult to overtake him.
KING Well, then, loosen the reins.
CHARIOTEER As the long-lived one commands. [...] Long-lived one ! look ! look !

the reins being loosed, the chariot-horses run along as if impatient of the speed of the deer, with the fore-part of their bodies well stretched out, with the chowrie-crests motionless, with ears erect and steady, not to be overtaken even by dust that they themselves raise. [...]

[I, 10] (*Behind the scenes*) O king, that is a deer of the hermitage : he must not be slain, he must not be slain.

---

222 On the play of Śakuntalā, see S. Lévi, *Le théâtre indien*, pp. 173-177. L. Renou and J. Filliozat, *L'Inde classique*, t. 2, pp. 275-279. Kālidāsa, *Çakuntalā riconosciuta, Dramma in sette atti*, a cura di M. Morani, Milano, 1982, p. 7 sqq. ; bibliography on Kālidāsa pp. 19-20.

223 The first translation which introduced the West to the myth of Śakuntalā dates to 1789 and was the work of the English orientalist Sir William Jones. This play evoked the admiration of the greatest authors including Goethe : Fr. Wilhelm, H.G. Rawlinson, "India and the modern West", in *A cultural history of India*, Oxford, 1975, p. 475 ; Kālidāsa, *Çakuntalā riconosciuta*, 1982, pp. 14-15. It inspired numerous other works as, for example, the ballet of Théophile Gautier (*L'anneau de Çakountala*), the opera of Franco Alfano in 1921 (*[La leggenda di Sakùntala]. Danza e finale di Sakùntala per orchestra. Partitura*, Milano, 1927 ; *Sakuntala. Partitura d'ochestra*, Milano, 1951), the poems of Guillaume Apollinaire, and several sculptures of Camille Claudel : R.-M. Paris, *Camille Claudel 1864-1943*, Paris, 1984, photographs pp. 244-253.

224 *Encyclopaedia Britannica*, s.v. "Kālidasā" : the hypotheses advanced on the subject of the date of Kālidāsa, between 167 B.C. and 634 A.D. See also M. Morani, in Kālidāsa, *Çakuntalā riconosciuta*, 1982, pp. 10-12.

225 *Works of Kālidāsa*, ed., intr. and transl. C.R. Devadhar, vol. I, 1966 (repr. Delhi, 1985). Cf. also the translation of A. Bergaigne and P. Lehugeur, *Sakuntala, Drame en sept actes mêlé de prose et de vers, [de] Calidasa*, Paris, 1884. See also the Italian translation : Kālidāsa, *Çakuntalā riconosciuta*, 1982.

CHARIOTEER (*Listening and looking*) Long-lived one, here have hermits advanced between you and the antelope that presents a fair mark for your arrows.

KING (*Hastily*) Well, then, rein in the horses.

CHARIOTEER Very well (*Stops the chariot.*) (*Then enter a hermit with two others*)

HERMIT (*Raising his hand*) This is a deer of the hermitage ; this must not be slain, this must not be slain [...]

[I, 13] HERMIT. King, we have set out to collect wood for solemn rites. And this, on the bank of the Mālinī, is, in truth, the religious domicile of the great sage Kaṇva . If no other duty is interfered with, then enter and accept the rights of hospitality. [...]

[I, 14] KING Is the patriarch of the family at home ?

HERMIT Just now, charging his daughter Śakuntalā to perform the rights of hospitality, he is gone to Somatīrtha, in hopes of deprecating her adverse fate. [...]

KING Charioteer, drive on the horses. By visiting the abode of holiness, we shall purify ourselves. [...] even without being told, it may be known indeed that these are the precincts of the sacred grove.

[...] Under (yonder) trees are the grains of wild rice fallen from the openings of the hollow-trunks filled with parrots ; in other places are seen the polished stones which have bruised the fruit of Iṅgoudī ; and the fawns, too, from having acquired confidence bear the sound (of our approach) without varying their course ; [...]

[I, 16] Stop the chariot just here, that I may descend.

[I, 17] (*Behind the scenes*) [*The king hears voices of damsels in a grove of trees*] [...] (*He stands gazing at them.*) (*Then enter Śakuntalā occupied in the manner described and her two friends*)

[I, 18] ŚAKUNTALĀ Come hither, my friends, come hither.

ANASŪYĀ Friend Śakuntalā, I think the trees in the hermitage are dearer to father Kāśyapa than your own self, since he has appointed even you, who are soft like a Navamālikā flower, to fill their basins. [...]

[IV, 11] PRYAṀVADĀ [...] The deer let fall the morsels of Darbha-grass, the peacocks stop their dancing, and the creepers, whose pale leaves fall (to the ground), appear to shed tears. (11) [...]

[Back in his palace, the king remembers of Śakuntalā, and paints her portrait]

[VI, 9] THE CONFIDENT - VIDŪṢAKA Well, have you not told Caturikā, your attendant, that you would be spending this hour in the Mādhavī bower, and that she should bring you there the picture of the lady Śakuntalā which you yourself painted on a tablet ? [...]

[VI, 14] CATURIKĀ Here is our lady in the picture (*She shows the tablet.*). [...]

[VI, 15] VIDŪṢAKA There are to be seen three ladies now, and all are beautiful. Which one is the lady Śakuntalā ? [...]

KING Which one do you think ? [...]

VIDŪṢAKA I think that she who is represented as a little fatigued by the side of the mango-tree whose young leaves are glistening after her watering, with arms drooping in a peculiar manner ; with a face on which drops of perspiration have broken out ; with locks of her hair the flowers of which have dropped down from the loosened braid ; that is Śakuntalā. The others are her friends. [...]

[VI, 17] KING. The stream of Mālinī ought to be drawn with a pair of swans resting on its sands ; and on both sides must appear the sacred hills at the base of the Himālayan ranges, where the deer are squatting ; and I wish to draw, underneath a tree that bears some bark-garments suspended from its boughs, a doe that rubs her left eye on the horn of a black antelope.

## 2) *ICONOGRAPHIC PARALLELS.*

Though frequently found in literary works, the legend of Śakuntalā is almost absent from the Indian figurative arts. The only instance that we can cite with some certainty is a terracotta plaque discovered at Bhita. A relief from the temple of Virūpākṣa at Pattadakal[226] is of a later date and represents the person of Śakuntalā, dissociated from the context of the story. The identification of Śakuntalā on a relief of Udayagiri is doubtful. The engraved decor of a small group of metallic vases from the Punjab and Thailand present a close stylistic resemblance to the plaque of Ai Khanum, although the figures on them have no connection with the legend of Śakuntalā[227].

### Terracotta disc of Bhita.

Fig. 38

Discovered at Bhita, near Allahabad in North India, this object is a circular terracotta plaque with an approximate diameter of 7.5 cm, which is dated to the second or first century B.C.[228]. The decor, identical on both sides, consists of a central area in bas-relief formed by moulding[229], with furrow like slanting incisions on the border[230].

---

226 The theme of Śakuntalā and Duṣyanta was proposed for a relief on a pillar inside the temple of Virūpākṣa of Pattadakal dating to about 740 A.D. Not having personally seen this representation, we do not know if the motif uses the same elements as the plaque of Ai Khanum : H. Zimmer, *The art of Indian Asia, its mythology and transformations*, New York, 1968, p. 413, pl. 306. For the temple see J.C. Harle, *The art and architecture of the Indian Sub-Continent*, London, 1986, pp. 178-180.

227 Mention must also be made here of the illustrations of the manuscript of the play of Kālidāsa which Prof. G. M. Bongard-Levin was kind enough to show to us even though they present the heroine as an ordinary woman in a garden. One of these miniatures in a Rajasthani manuscript of Śakuntalā dating from about 1800 is cited but not illustrated in the catalogue of an exhibition held in London about forty years ago : *The art of India and Pakistan : A commemorative catalogue of the exhibition held at the Royal Academy of Arts, London 1947-48*, London, 1950 : loaned by Raja Pratap Singh, Rhao Bhonsale of Nagpur : [p. 125], n° 496 (595). This same tradition has perpetuated itself in modern Indian art, as witnessed, for example, in a painting of Ravi Varma illustrating the theme of Śakuntalā writing a love letter, around 1880-1885 : J.C. Harle, *Indian art in the Ashmolean Museum*, Oxford, 1987, pp. 85-86, n° 96, fig. 21.

228 First publication by J.H. Marshall, *Excavations at Bhītā (ASIAR 1911-12)*, Calcutta, 1915, pp. 29-94, particularly 35-36 and p. 73, photograph pl. XXIII, design pl. XXIV, n° 17. Photograph only in J.H. Marshall, "The monuments of ancient India", in *Cambridge history of India*, I, 1922, p. 583, pl. XXIX, 81 ; design in G. Combaz, *L'Inde et l'Orient classique*, Paris, 1937, pl. 33, pp. 83, 90, 91, 94 ; A.L. Basham, *The wonder that was India*[3], London, 1969, p. 193, fig. xiii, where it is identified simply as a "country scene" and dated to the 1st cent. B.C. ; photograph in R. Mukerjee, *The flowering of Indian art, the growth and spread of a civilization*, London, 1964, pl. 50 and pp. 285-286 : identification with the legend of Śakuntalā, "Narrative sculpture, religious or secular, is met with in Indian art from its early stages of development. This terracotta medallion in its sensitiveness and delicacy of modelling reaches the standard of excellence of Sanchi reliefs". S.I. Tjuljaev, *Iskusstvo Indii*, Moscow, 1988, pp. 82-83, fig. 57, without any identification of the subject, with an inexact location of the discovery of the find at Pāṭaliputra and with an incorrect dating to the 4th cent. B.C. We are extremely grateful to Ch. Fabrègues for having attracted our attention to this object.

229 J.H. Marshall, *Excavations at Bhītā*, pp. 35-36, suggests that the original matrix was perhaps ivory, a material with which numerous seals discovered at Bhita were made. According to him, stone or marble could not have permitted the same meticulousness and finesse in the rendering of details ; J.H.M. considers that this object is

The central area is occupied by a narrative scene without any particular religious connotation, but the representation has a very close stylistic relation to Buddhist iconography at Bharhut, and specially at Sanchi. The action in which at least seven persons participate, takes place in a rustic or forest landscape suggested by the diverse plants among which there is a flowering shrub and a palm tree, and by the depiction of the waves of a river or a pond, as well as rocks. The foreground, at the bottom of the scene, is occupied by two female deer and a dancing peacock. In the water, in the middle of floating lotuses, a person in a half-squatting position is apparently either filling water in a vessel, or plucking the flowers[231]. Against the border on the left, at the middle level, is a small structure which, in its general appearance, resembles the huts of hermits in Indian art, with an arched roof crowned with two pinnacles and an arched door. The construction is surrounded by a barrier which descends towards the water in a steep slope[232]. A woman standing before the hut seems to be lifting with difficulty a large vessel in her arms, perhaps a wicker basket or a bucket made with strips of wood. On the right side of the scene, a chariot harnessed with four horses and transporting two persons advances towards the right, while a third person stands before the harness yolk and appears to be seizing it by the reins, as if to stop it. In the upper part of the scene, in the background, a barrier extends, against which two persons are leaning in conversation, with only the upper half of their bodies visible. This barrier seems to extend further plunging towards the right amidst large rocks.

The identification of this representation as the legend of Śakuntalā by J.M. Marshall, on a suggestion from J.Ph. Vogel, upon its first publication, has every possibility of being exact. Although the author is silent on the question of the correspondence between textual sources and its iconographic transcription, there is no doubt that the common features are sufficiently clear. The hut could be of Śakuntalā or of the hermit Kaṇva who, as in the *Mahābhārata* and Kālidāsa's play, is absent at the time of the meeting between his adopted daughter and Duṣyanta. The water would represent "the Mālinī with its glittering isles and charming banks" celebrated by the Indian dramatist. The quadriga would be of King Duṣyanta, accompanied by his charioteer or by one of his companions in arms. As for the person standing in front of the harness, it could be one of the anchorites who, in Kālidāsa – the *Mahābhārata* follows a different tradition –, asks the king to halt the deer hunt. The role assigned to the other persons is not clear. It seems, however, that this composition is characterized by a narrative structure with multiple scenes, in which the same actors figure many times. The person seen in the upper part of the composition, on the extreme left, could be Duṣyanta himself : this is deduced on the basis of similarity between his gesture of a raised right arm, and the gesture of the person standing in the chariot next to of the charioteer who is

contemporary with the art of Sanchi and with the ivory workers who worked in Ujjain. On the relationship between ivory work and sculpture see further pp. 91, 93 and 100.

230 For a border with an analogous but moulded decoration, see a terracotta disc from Mathurā dating to the 2nd cent. A.D. which represents an amorous couple (*mithuna*) : S.J. Czuma, *Kushan sculpture*, p. 128, n° 55.

231 If we refer to the narrative of Kālidāsa (*Śakuntalā*, I, 16), Śakuntalā goes into the hermitage to water the trees with water containers which she empties into irrigation channels. Cf. B.S. Upadhyaya, *India in Kālidāsa*, p. 336.

232 J.H. Marshall, *Excavations at Bhītā*, p. 73 : "shrine with chaitya doorway and rail around. In front and below shrine, tank with lotuses and figure drawing water".

probably the king[233]. The person who is standing with Duṣyanta behind the barrier could be Śakuntalā. It is possible that the female figures represented in the pond and in front of the hut are also Śakuntalā, unless they happen to be the two companions of the heroine, presented in the drama of Kālidāsa.

The two female deer represented in the lower part of the area who seem to have no direct relationship with the subject are, in fact, the animals whom Duṣyanta was chasing when he encountered Śakuntalā. They contribute thus in giving a precise signification to the scene, just as it is the discreet presence of a deer lying in a nook, in a representation on ivory from Begram, which enables it to be identified as the *Jātaka* of the birth of the Buddha in the form of an antelope or a unicorn[234]. The peacock represents birds living in the forest "... echoing the cries of peacocks who were dancing madly"[235]. The plaque of Bhita might thus be combining three scenes of the legend : on the left, the life of Śakuntalā in the hermitage and her relationship with the plants and the animals ; on the right, the arrival of Duṣyanta and the intervention of the hermit, and on top, the meeting of the couple. It may be emphasized that the presence of the anchorite seems to establish special links with Kālidāsa's version of the legend as opposed to the tradition followed by the *Mahābhārata* which does not mention such a person.

### Bas-relief of Udayagiri.

This bas-relief[236] combines two episodes of the same story in a single panel : on the left, near a horse held by an attendant, a royal person armed with a bow and arrows hunts a winged antelope, recognisable as such by its rectilinear horns ; on the right, the same person, standing with a bow in hand, is in conversation with a woman perched on the branch of a tree. Although one identifies in this double scene a hunter-king and his encounter with a woman, it departs too much from the narrative of Kālidāsa to remind us of the legend of Śakuntalā. It should rather be seen as an example of unidentified Jain legends with an educative purpose, which are often not easy to differentiate from the Buddhist *jātakas*.

---

233 Mention may be made of the slightly different interpretation of R. Mukerjee, *The flowering of Indian art*, who sees a group of three persons behind the barrier at the top of the scene : "From the top Dusyanta, with a companion on each side, spies Sakuntala". As for us, we are able to distinguish only two persons. If it is not the couple Duṣyanta-Śakuntalā after their encounter, hypothesis which we prefer, one could think of Duṣyanta with his confidant : for the theme of the King and his confidant who in a love affair conceal themselves in order to spy on the beloved, see Ph. Stern, "Aspects plastiques de l'ancien théâtre indien", p. 55.

234 See below p. 88-89.

235 *Mahābhārata*, 2872.

236 Khandagiri-Udayagiri, Rani-Gumpha, upper gallery : H. Zimmer, *The art of Indian Asia*, fig. 57, pp. 223-224 : 1st cent. A.D. (n. 70) ; A.K. Coomaraswamy, *History of Indian and Indonesian art*, London, Leipzig, New York, 1927, fig. 36, p. 38 : middle of the 2nd-middle of the 1st cent. B.C. ; N. Ray, *Maurya and Post-Maurya art : a study in social and formal contrasts*, New Delhi, 1975, fig. 59-60, p. 118 : middle of the 2nd cent. A.D. ; V.S. Agrawala, "Vāsavadattā and Śakuntalā scenes in the Raṇīgumphā cave in Orissa", *Journal of the Indian Society of Oriental art*, 14, 1946, pp. 102-109 ; D. Mitra, "East India", in *Jaina art and architecture*, t. 1, 1974, pl. 32 and p. 83.

**Vase from Gundla.** Fig. 39 and 59

This vase for libation (*loṭa*) was discovered in 1857 in eastern Punjab, near Gundla (Kulu Hills, Kangra district) and is exhibited these days at the British Museum[237]. We will give a detailed description of this vase which, except for the author responsible for its first publication, has never received the attention that it merits inspite of its great iconographic and artistic interest. The vessel is in yellowish copper (or an alloy) and the technique used for its fabrication is probably not hammering, but lost wax[238]. Its diameter measures about 13.5 cm (5 1/4 inches) with a height of 16 cm (6 1/4 inches). and it is comprised of an almost spherical belly, with an elongated neck on top which is extended by a wide horizontal lip, of which only a segment of 2 cm remains[239]. The walls are very thin (1.5 cm). The top of the lip is decorated with radiating bands, alternately with and without hachures. A lotus with long overlapping petals is engraved under the base. A crack mounts from the base upto the ankles of the first walking person of the scene.

The vessel is decorated around its belly with a continuous frieze about 42 cm long and 7.3 cm wide, bordered with two series of decorative bands, of which six are placed above and three below it. Starting from the top, their geometrical motifs are as follows :

---

237 Inv. B.M. 1880-22. For the most recent publication see *The crossroads of Asia*, Cambridge, 1992, pp. 162-164 (by E.A. Errington). For the bibliography see also Ch. Horne, "Notes on an ancient Indian vase with an account on engraving thereupon", *JRAS*, 1871, pp. 367-375 ; the article is accompanied with two engravings representing the vase and the decorative frieze ; G.C.M. Birdwood, *The industrial arts of India*, London, 1880, pp. 154-155, pl. 12 : "discovered by Major Hay, in 1857, at Kundlah in Kulu, where a landslip had exposed the ancient Buddhist cell in which it had been lying for 1,500 years ; for it is attributed by oriental scholars to the date AD 200-300. It is exactly of the shape now made, and is enchased all round with a representation of Gautama Buddha, as Prince Siddhārtha, before his conversion, going on some high procession. An officer of state, on an elephant, goes before ; the minstrels, two damsels, one playing on a *vina* and the other on a flute, follow after ; in the midst is the prince Siddhārtha, in his charriot drawn by four prancing horses, and guarded by two horsemen behind it ; all rendered with that gala air of dainty pride, and enjoyment in the fleeting pleasures of the hour, which is characteristic of the Hindus to the present day" ; J.A.S. Burgess, *Report on the Buddhist cave temples and their inscriptions*, London, 1883, p. 6, fig. 4 (vase) and fig. 5 (design of the frieze based on the work of Birdwood) ; J.H. Marshall, "The monuments of ancient India", p. 583, pl. XXIX, 82 ; R.-J.-E.-C. Lefebvre des Noëttes, *L'attelage, le cheval de selle à travers les âges : contribution à l'histoire de l'esclavage*, Paris, 1931, fig. 263 ; B. Rowland, *The art and architecture of India*, 1967, p. 65, pl. 193.A ; P.K. Agrawala, *Early Indian bronzes*, Varanasi, 1977, pp. 59-60, ill. 127 ; I.C. Glover, *Early trade between India and Southeast Asia*, 1989, fig. 27. On a stone reliquary with an analogous form see H. Härtel, J. Auboyer, *Indien und Südostasien (Propyläen Kunstgeschichte, 16)*, 1971, p. 245, pl. 189 and B. Rowland, *The art and architecture*, p. 65, pl. 193.B : Sonari, near Bhilsa, vers 200 av. J.-C., around 200 B.C., engraved decoration consisting of a stylised lotus flower at the base and an animal represented in each panel on the body.

238 The technique of melting, which renders vessels extremely fragile, was observed in India by Nearchus : Strabo XV, 1, 67 : "the use of vessels made of cast brass, that when they fall to the ground, they break into pieces like pottery" (transl. by H.L. Jones, *The geography of Strabo*, 1966). On the metallic composition and the origin of this type of vessel see also below p. 71.

239 The adherence of this remain of the rim to the neck is rendered fragile because of a crack in the metal.

| **Above** | | **Below** | |
|---|---|---|---|
| 1 | latticing | 1 | latticing |
| 2 | concentric lines | 2 | losanges |
| 3 | triangles | 3 | triangles and dotted circles |
| 4 | dotted circles | | |
| 5 | concentric lines | | |
| 6 | interlocked triangles with hachures | | |

The frieze represents a royal procession comprising three of the four traditional wings of the Indian army (elephant, chariot, cavalry) and advancing to the right towards a flowery landscape, but it is not possible to say whether the scene alludes to a story or to any precise event[240]. The object can be dated to the end of the Mauryan period or the Śuṅga period (second century B.C.)[241], because a close parallel to this scene is furnished by one of the oldest Indian bas-reliefs, at the *vihāra* of Bhaja[242].

The relationship of this object with the plaque of Ai Khanum is apparent because of the similarity of certain motifs and particularly, the complex nature of the scene, its style and the miniaturisation of details, which is possible in the technique used for metal engraving.

Ten persons are represented in a row at the same level. They are, from right to left, two cavaliers, two men mounted on an elephant, three persons on foot, among whom two are female musicians and, finally a group consisting of a royal personage on a chariot, with a woman on each side, which marks the end of the procession[243].

The mount of the first cavalier advances in a slow trot, its left leg is folded and its hindquarter is lowered. Its coat is spotted, unlike the coats of the four horses harnessed to the chariot. On top of its head, which is cross-strapped, there is a tuft tied below with a ribbon, with the ends flowing backwards. The very short mane is indicated by small parallel incisions. The tail, on the contrary,

---

240 On Indian royal processions as described in Western literature see Strabo XV, 1, 69.

241 According to the inventory of the British Museum ; Ch. Horne, "Notes on an ancient Indian vase" : 1st-2nd cent. A.D. ; J.A.S. Burgess, *Report on the Buddhist cave temples* : end of 2nd-3rd cent. A.D. ; B. Rowland, *The art and architecture*, p. 65 : Śuṅga period.

242 This rupestrian relief which probably dates between the 2nd-1st cent. B.C. is sculpted on both sides of the gate of a cell cut in a rock. The left side represents a male figure in royal costume under an umbrella, probably Sūrya, standing between two women in a quadriga harnessed with plumed horses and trampling a Rākshasa, with his foot ; the woman on the right holds a fly whisk ; two accompanying cavaliers of smaller dimension are represented on both the upper corners of this scene, the one on the left appears to be holding a lance ; on the right side of the gate of the cell, two persons on an elephant are represented as on the vase of Gundla, the elephant driver with a garland around his neck (possibly Indra) and a passenger who holds a flag. Bibliography : J.A.S. Burgess, *Report on the Buddhist cave temples*, pl. VI, fig. 1 ; A.K. Coomaraswamy, *History of Indian and Indonesian art*, fig. 24 and 27, pp. 24-25 ; G. Combaz, *L'Inde et l'Orient classique*, pl. 129 ; Ph. Stern, "Les ivoires et os découverts à Begram", in J. Hackin *et alii*, *Nouvelles recherches*, p. 46 ; H.G. Franz, *Buddhistische Kunst Indiens*, Leipzig, 1965, fig. 24 and 26 ; B. Rowland, *The art and architecture*, pl. 18 : beginning of 1st cent B.C. ; C. Sivaramamurti, *L'art en Inde*, Paris, 1974, fig. 396, p. 364 : 2nd cent. B.C. ; N. Ray, *Maurya and Post-Maurya art*, fig. 39-40, pp. 113-114 : 1st half of the 1st cent. B.C.

243 We begin our description with the two cavaliers because we consider that, in this continuous frieze where one end meets the other, it is these two persons who open the procession and the royal chariot which closes it (Cl. Rapin, *Fouilles Akh VIII*, p. 201, n. 711 ; the photograph taken by the British Museum [fig. 59] and the recent drawing published in *The crossroads of Asia*, p. 164, propose the same subdivision).

has long hair. The saddle consists of a rug with triangular fringes, decorated with a lattice-like motif. The feet of the cavalier are inside primitive stirrups formed by the loop of a cord or strap placed on the spine of the mount[244]. The cavalier is armed with a sort of halberd : below the triangular point of the lance, a blade stands out in the form of an axe, as also a long hooked appendage ; the base is provided with a lance head. His clothes, like the clothes of the other male figures in the composition, are of a traditional type, a *dhoṭī* held by a fold on the waist and a shawl (*chaddar*) whose ends flow behind his back. He wears earrings and his hair, held tight under a turban, are knotted in a large bun on the left side of the head.

The mount of the second cavalier moves in a half reared up position. It shares the same characteristics as the preceding horse, with the exception that the untied tuft of hair fans out on its forehead. The cavalier himself is like the first, but his hair is not knotted in an asymmetrical bun and is held in a net.

The elephant, whose saddle rug is similar to that of the horses, is extremely small as compared to the two passengers it is carrying. The tail of the animal is made to pass between its legs and is connected with the end of its trunk with a rope[245]. The person seated in front, in the place usually occupied by the elephant driver, and under an umbrella held by his companion who grips an elephant hook (*Aṅkuśa*) with his right hand, is undoubtedly a royal personage. He is adorned with a necklace and his hair is dressed in a bun, like the first cavalier. The umbrella bearer, who is seen balanced precariously on the croup of the animal, with a fly whisk in his right hand, and with an asymmetrical hairstyle, is probably an attendant.

The elephant is followed by three persons on foot dressed in transparent fabric. The first is a young man wearing a *dhoṭī*, with a wide, flowing scarf on his shoulders, and with his hair dressed in a side bun. He looks backwards, his arms gracefully spread out in the pose of a dancer. A slightly elongated and curved object is held by him in the left hand (castanets or a small branch ?). Behind him are two female musicians, in long, transparent loin cloths. Their ornaments, like those of the women in the chariot, comprise of asymmetrical earrings, the one in the right ear being discoidal and the one in the left, conical. Their hair puff up above the forehead. A strip of fabric which goes down their backs has decorative motifs in a broad band, and appears to be fixed in front on the left shoulder, from where the end flows down[246]. Under their long transparent *dhoṭī* the impression of large round plaques with incised hachures can be seen on their thighs probably

---

244 On stirrups see A.D.H. Bivar, "The stirrup and its origins", *Oriental art*, 1-2, 1955, pp. 61-65 ; *idem*, "Cavalry equipment and tactics on the Euphrates Frontier", *Dumbarton Oaks Papers*, 26, 1972, pp. 273-291 ; J.M. Rosenfield, *The dynastic arts of the Kushans*, Berkeley, Los Angeles, 1967, pp. 101-102, pl. XVI, seal 1, 2nd cent. A.D. : cavalier on Kushana gem ; D. Metzler, "Das Pferd auf den Münzen des Labienus – ein Mithras-Symbol?", in *Studien zur Religion und Kultur Kleinasiens*, Leiden, 1978, p. 622. n. 20 ; L. White, *Technologie médiévale et transformations sociales*, Paris, La Haye, 1969, pp. 10-19, particularly n. 72 and fig. 1. See also P. Vigneron, *Le cheval dans l'antiquité gréco-romaine*, Nancy, 1968, pp. 86-88, 327 (non-existence of stirrups in antiquity). For a Central Asiatic origin in antiquity : A. Leroi-Gourhan, *L'homme et la matière*, Paris, 1971, pp. 129-130.

245 Although rare, there is evidence of this system at Bharhut : A.K. Coomaraswamy, *La sculpture de Bharhut*, pl. XXX, fig. 76. See also the elephants on the silver plaques from the Oxus treasure : O.M. Dalton, *The treasure of the Oxus*[3], London, 1964, pp. 52-53, pl. XXVIII, 199 ; B. Rowland, *The art and architecture*, pl. 192.c and d. *The crossroads of Asia*, Cambridge, 1992, pp. 160-161 (Ch. Fabrègues, M.A. Claringbull).

246 On this ponderous hair style see Ph. Stern, "Les ivoires et os découverts à Begram", p. 44.

representing, tattoo marks. The first musician is shown playing a harp with six chords ; she is wearing a necklace and bracelets on her wrists and ankles ; the second musician is playing a transversal flute. Three containers, a narrow-necked round bottle, a pear shaped vase and a plate decorated with food stuffs or fruits are arranged on the floor on both sides of the harpist.

Only a three-quarter view of the quadriga and its three occupants, for whom the procession opens the way, is represented. Pointed tufts can be seen on the heads of the animals. The tail of the horse in the foreground is brought forward to the front, as already observed in the case of the elephant, to prevent it from getting entangled in the wheels of the chariot : the hair are brought across the right flank towards the front by a string attached to the back of the chariot. Two bells or pompons are visible on its ear and its right shoulder. The body of the chariot which, as shown by the small parallel incisions[247], is of wickerwork, is enclosed by a rounded guard-rail forming three foils – a typical form in Indian chariots. The chief passenger standing in front with both his hands on the guard-rail is a young man with his hair dressed in a bun on the left side of his head[248], a shawl draped on his shoulders and a necklace. On each side is a richly dressed woman, wearing bracelets like all the other female figures in the composition : the first, on the left serves as the driver[249] and holds four reins in each and a spur in the left ; the second holds the umbrella shading the prince in the left hand and a fly whisk in the right.

The empty spaces in the area are sprinkled with plant motifs (flowers and leafy stems) suggesting both the presence of nature and a festive atmosphere.

This vase, like the plaque of Ai Khanum, employs a technical device in common use, consisting of using models or patterns for drawing the silhouettes of the principal figures. Although no figure is superimposable on the other, it should be noted that all of them present almost identical curves, indicating that they were composed either by modifying the curves of the same pattern or by combining different patterns. We have been able to distinguish six groups in these patterns :

**1** — Chest and hindquarters of the elephant have the same curves as the second mounted horse. This similarity indicates, perhaps, the existence of a proto-type meant for all mounts.

**2** — Horses of the quadriga : left tibia in front (with a difference of inclination).

**3** — Mounted horses = at least three different patterns : hind legs along with the rump, neck and head.

**4** — Cavaliers and persons behind the elephant : left shoulder and right flank.

**5** — The legs and hips of the two musicians are identical (in spite of differences in the design of their dress).

**6** — The faces of persons, irrespective of their sex, divide themselves in two groups according to the difference in size : **a**) those of persons on a mount (elephant, horse or quadriga), with the exception of the passenger behind the elephant, are almost identical though the inclination of their heads and their hairstyles are different. The head of the occupant on the left of the quadriga is turned towards the royal personage, but its details are identical with those of the passenger on the

247 In form and technique it is identical to the chariot of Bhaja : see above n. 242.

248 This hair style is similar to the hair styles of the passengers of the quadriga of Bhaja.

249 This order is different from that of the quadriga of Bhaja in that, here it seems that the driver is the prince himself.

right, and were surely reproduced by inverting the model. **b**) The faces of persons on foot are slightly bigger than the preceding and form a second group which is quite distinct from the first.

Although there is no doubt that the iconography of the vase of Gundla is of Indian origin, it is not possible to determine its place of fabrication with precision. As in some other Indian finds, the vessel is probably made of an alloy of bronze with 23-28% tin which confers on it a yellow shine evocative of gold. But there is no evidence of this type of alloy in India because tin was not mined here[250].

### Vases in bronze from Thailand.

Fig. 40-45

There is however evidence of the type of alloy of bronze and tin of which, supposedly, the vase of Gundla is made, in the funerary vessels of Thai necropolises in the west of the country, in Ban Don Ta Phet and near the Burmese frontier, at Khao Jamook ("Nose Mountain"), where a tin mine is situated. Among the finds there are many vessels which are analogous to the specimen of Gundla, with a similar engraved decoration of scenes in which buildings, human beings, animals (elephants, horses and cattle), and floral motifs are represented, along with the stylised motif of the lotus flower under the base[251]. Finds consisting of Indo-Roman vessels in Indonesia, near Jakarta and on the northern coast of Bali, and Indian pearls from Thai necropolises are evidence of the existence of a flow of Indian commercial goods towards South-East Asia. However, according to Ian C. Glover who bases himself on the metallic composition of these bronze vases found in Thailand, they were fabricated locally and were not directly related with this commerce. In addition, they should date from the first half of the fourth century B.C.[252]. If these hypotheses are confirmed, the origin of the vase of Gundla itself would be open to question. But wherever be the workshop of its fabrication, the subject and the style of the imagery indicates that they were made by artisans from India and, more exactly, perhaps from the valley of the Ganges.

## *C) DETAILED COMMENTARY ON THE PLAQUE OF AI KHANUM*

### 1) Human figures.

Fig. 87, 88, 92

A *Couples in the frieze :*

The motif of a couple sitting cross-legged, with the right hand of each partner raised in a conversational gesture, is repeated at least three times in the frieze. The partners are represented side by side in the lower portion (II-2 and II-3) and upper left portion (II-5 and II-6) of the frieze

---

250 I.C. Glover, *Early trade between India and Southeast Asia*, 1989, pp. 31 and 42. Regarding the text of Strabo XV, 1, 67 see above n. 238.

251 I.C. Glover, *op.cit.*, pp. 31, 38-42. On the lotus : *ibidem*, fig. 26 (Ban Don Ta Phet), and fig. 28 (Khao Jamook, and not Chombung, according to a recent correction by the author). These vessels are fragmentary because they are ritually broken at the time of inhumation.

252 This dating – furnished by a series of analyses done in the archaeological context – is much earlier than that proposed initially for Ban Don Ta Phet by the first excavator Chin You-di (*ibidem*, p. 18 : between the middle of the 1st cent. B.C. and the middle of the 3rd cent. A.D.).

but in the middle zone they are shown facing each other on either side of the central area (II-1 and II-4).

In each of these couples, the person on the right is shown frontally (II-1, II-2 and II-6), the frontal position being recognisable from the silhouette of the figure. The heads are framed by four small round inlays which represent respectively earrings[253] and ornamental plates, as observed in the hairstyles of women in Indian art from the beginning of the Mauryan[254], at Mathurā[255], Patna[256] or Kauśāmbī[257]. Their right hands are raised.

---

[253] *Kuṇḍala* or *patrakuṇḍala* if it relates to discoidal rings. See also the terminology of ornaments in B.S. Upadhyaya, *India in Kālidāsa*, pp. 202-204. Cf. A.-M. Loth, *La vie publique et privée dans l'Inde ancienne. Les bijoux*, Paris, 1972.

[254] These figurines might represent the goddesses of fertility, whose model goes back to the proto-historic figure types from the Indus Valley ; the rich and heavy ornaments, which begin to be depicted in detail particularly with the arrival of the technique of moulding are symbols of abundance (general presentation : D.H. Gordon, "Early Indian terracottas", *Journal of the Indian Society of Oriental art*, 11, 1943, pp. 136-195 ; S.P. Gupta, *The roots of Indian art*, 1980, pp. 137-185 ; A.G. Poster, *From Indian earth. 4,000 years of terracotta art*, New York, 1986). But there is a terracotta discovered at Barikot (Pakistan) belonging to the Hellenistic period and style with symmetrical ornaments resembling those found in the plaque of Ai Khanum : P. Callieri, "Bīr-Koṭ-Ghwaṇḍai 1990-1992. A preliminary report on the excavations of the Italian Archaeological Mission, IsMEO", in *Istituto Univ. Orientale*, 52, 1992 (*Annali*, Suppl. n. 73, fasc. 4), pp. 1-48 (pl. XVI.3). In the iconography of Sanchi and Bharhut, the female coiffure is lighter with hair pulled back and separated by a central parting, giving the head usually a more spherical shape, adorned sometimes by a big lateral bun (see also the hair style of the soldiers of the king who ordered the killing of the Boddhisattva in his incarnation as the king of monkeys in the *Mahākapi-jātaka* [E.B. Cowell, *The Jātaka*, 3, n° 407] : A.K. Coomaraswamy, *Bharhut*, fig. 68 = Cunningham, *Bharhut*, pl. XXXIII, 4. On hairstyles see also K.K. Murthy, *Hair Styles in ancient Indian art*, Delhi, 1981 ; K.K. Murthy, *The Gandhāra sculptures*, p. 52 sqq.

[255] The figurine of a goddess (height : approx. 20 cm) dated between the 3rd and the 1st cent. B.C. presents ornaments consisting of a necklace, a pair of heavy earrings composed of dual discs and three discs with the impression of rosettes (similar to the "flowers" forming the earrings in the plaque of Ai Khanum) on both sides of the forehead and on top of the head ; they combine the following techniques of fabrication : shaping of the body by hand, moulding of the face and the decorative appliques of the ornaments of the head (Museum of Fine Arts of Boston) : H. Zimmer, *The art of Indian Asia*, fig. after p. 246 : B3, c ; a similar one : S.P. Gupta, *The roots of Indian art*, pl. 78a. Another figurine with the head similarly adorned with different and asymmetrical earrings, with a large mass of hair arranged on both sides of the head in a roll instead and in the place of heavy earrings, and a disc representing a flower or a turban fixed on the head above the forehead : A.K. Coomaraswamy, *History of Indian and Indonesian art*, fig. 23, pp. 20-21.

[256] A figurine of Bulandibag (Museum of Patna) wears large double earrings as well as side ornaments in the shape of rosettes of which only the one on the left has survived : N. Ray, *Maurya and Post-Maurya art*, pp. 108-110, fig. 20 ; specimen of the same type : earrings, two thick plaits of hair falling on both sides of the nape, large rosette shaped disc on the sides of the forehead : fig. 21 ; specimen of the same type : garment with pleats, finely detailed by incisions and decorated with rosette motifs in applique, hair dressed in a large bun : fig. 23. See also S.P. Gupta, *The roots of Indian art*, p. 164, fig. 24 ; also *The art of India and Pakistan*, n° 39 [p. 24], pl. 4 : specimen clothed in a "pannier" skirt (the puffed out form is an effect of a dance movement), h. : 28.5 cm, 200 B.C.

[257] S.C. Kala, *Terracotta figurines from Kauśāmbī*, Allahabad, 1950, particularly pl. VIIIB : draped feminine figurine dated by the author to 200 A.D. ; apart from two earrings crowned by an ornament consisting of a stem between two *nāga*, two small discs decorated with a chequered impression symmetrically adorn the two upper sides of the head. See also *The art of India and Pakistan*, n° 153, [p. 42], pl. 4 : 1st cent. A.D.

The persons on the left also have their right hands raised (II-3, II-4 and II-5). Two buns, one bigger than the other are visible on top of each head[257b]. Only one earring, of the size of a dot, can be seen. It is the disproportion in the contours of the silhouettes which enables one to state that a three quarter view of the heads has been represented. The bodies are presented frontally (II-3 and II-5) or in profile (II-4). Among these couples, the person on the right seems to be a female figure and the person on the left a male. The ornaments of the heads of the persons on the right are bulkier than those of their partners, and perfectly paired on both sides, as in the case of the three persons in the kiosk in the upper right side of the central area, who probably represent Śakuntalā and her two companions (on their identity, see below pp. 99-102). The heads of the persons on the left with their asymmetric buns may, on the other hand, be associated with the chief occupant of the chariot in the composition, who could be none other than Duṣyanta.

The clothes of the figures forming the couples can, in particular, be reconstituted on the basis of the form of the alveoles and some fragments of inlay which are still in place. This is the case of the female figure on the right side of the frieze II-I which still retains a group of three glass inlays (fig. 33.1-3). The garment in two pieces covers the whole body[258]. The upper garment with large pleated sleeves is orange in colour. The legs are covered with a brownish red fabric. A narrow gap at the waist between these two pieces probably marks the place for a belt[259].

The clothes worn by the men and the women appear to be similar, as suggested by the similarity in their silhouettes. The fullness and the opacity of the fabric[260] contrasts sharply with the lightness and the transparency of those seen in Indian art. This type of garment which has nothing in common with the clothes traditionally shown in Indian art (*dhotī* for women and men and *chaddar* or veil, particularly for the men)[261], is the most singular and surprising element in a

---

[257b] It is not certain that this bun was worn on the front of the head, as at Sanchi I : *Sāñchī*, pl. 18a/2 (southern toraṇa, king in his chariot), pl. 26/2, 34a/1, 35a/2, 36a-b (northern toraṇa). For a type of male bun projecting at the back of the head at Sanchi I : *Sāñchī*, pl. 45/7 (eastern toraṇa, two persons adorned with a diadem). There is sufficient evidence of the puffed up style (hair or turban) worn on the side in the princely figures of Bharhut, Sanchi I, (*Sāñchī*, pl. 18a/3, southern toraṇa, king on an elephant), Karli (D. Barret, *A guide to the Karla caves*, Bombay, 1957), Kondane, Junnar, Begram, Mathura. See also the first cavalier of the vase of Gundla. On the evolution of male hair styles from the side towards the front from Sanchi I : Ph. Stern, "Les ivoires et os découverts à Bégram", p. 44.

[258] We can cite certain example of a very ample *dhotī* leaving only the chest uncovered ; see, for example S.C. Kala, *Terracotta figurines from Kauśāmbī*, pl. XXVA : female torso in a *dhotī* with extremely marked close parallel pleats and pl. VIII B : figurine with the *dhotī* or *chaddar* wrapped around the stomach and the arms like a coat with sleeves but leaving the chest uncovered (dating from 200 A.D.).

[259] In Kālidāsa the belt worn by hermits is called *muñjī (mauñjī)*, because it was made with a cord fabricated with the plant *muñja* (Kālidāsa, *Kumārasaṃbhava*, V, 10).

[260] In figures in the old style, the fabrics are characterised by pleats which also give an impression of opacity but, from the beginning of the 1st cent., at Sanchi, Mathurā and Begram, the fabrics are light and transparent.

[261] On Indian costume see Strabo XV, 1, 71 ; Arrian VIII, 16, 2 ; Curtius VIII, 9, 20 ; G.S. Ghurye, *Indian costume*, Bombay, 1951, pp. 68-113. On costumes at Bharhut see A. Cunningham, *Bharhut*, pp. 31-34. For a costume closely resembling the costumes represented on the plaque of Ai Khanum : H.-P. Francfort, *Les palettes du Gandhara (MDAFA, 23)*, Paris, 1979, pl. VIII, fig. 15. See also M. Chandra, *Costumes and textiles, cosmetics and*

work which is otherwise typically Indian. It is not possible to say whether they reflect a regional costume[262] or the characteristic dress of a certain social category[263].

The colours of the garments worn by the persons, mainly red and orange, are also at variance with what we know of the ancient Indian custom, in which it was white which was the predominant[264] colour in fabrics of cotton and flax, relieved sometimes by coloured motifs (braids of golden thread, embroidery, precious stones[265]). It is true that Kālidāsa mentions red in connection with the clothes of hermits. Is it possible that the use of this colour for some garments in the plaque of Ai Khanum was related to the fact that the scene in question takes place in a hermitage[266]?

Several observations from the point of view of iconography may be made regarding the motif of the seated couple. The manner of representing the cross-legged position with the legs folded horizontally, while the toes point downwards vertically is hardly natural and is no doubt a compulsion of the engraving technique. The relief sculpture of Bharhut[267] and Sanchi[268] does furnish some parallels, but the tradition later would represent the legs asymmetrically crossed, as seen for example, at Begram[269] and Mathurā[270]. The general stiffness of bearing of the couples contrasts sharply with the posture of seated couples in Indian art where, even in the religious art of Bharhut[271] and Sanchi[272], the partners are shown embracing each other tenderly in compositions which relate not so much to edifying scenes as to genre paintings.

*coiffures in ancient and medieval India*, New Delhi, 1973 ; A.-M. Loth, *La vie publique et privée dans l'Inde ancienne. Les costumes*, Paris, 1979, p. 9 sqq.

262 A. Foucher, "Deux Jātaka sur ivoires", in J. Hackin *et alii*, *Nouvelles recherches*, p. 84, fig. 96 ; A.-M. Loth, *Les costumes*, 31-35 ; P. Bernard, *BEFEO*, 68, 1980, p. 35.

263 For military costumes see J. Auboyer, "La vie privée dans l'Inde ancienne d'après les ivoires de Begram", in J. Hackin *et alii*, *Nouvelles recherches*, p. 63 ; see also A.K. Coomaraswamy, *Bharhut*, fig. 43 = A. Cunningham, *Bharhut*, pl. XXXII, 1 and pp. 32-33 ; A.-M. Loth, *Les costumes*, pl. V, 7 and p. 32 ; as well as certain costumes of Ajanta : A. Ghosh *et alii, Ajaṇṭā Murals*, New Delhi, 1967.

264 Strabo XV, 1, 71 reports that Indians were clothed in white and refutes the view that they wore brightly coloured clothes. See also A.-M. Loth, *Les costumes*, pp. 14-15.

265 Strabo XV, 1, 69 ; Curtius VIII, 9, 24. At Begram the fabrics are rarely decorated : Ph. Stern, "Les ivoires et os découverts à Begram", p. 24.

266 On red fabric, *kāsāya*, see Kālidāsa, *Mālavikāgnimitra*, p. 99 (B.S. Upadhyaya, *India in Kālidāsa*, pp. 201 and 333). The costume of a more modest hermit is made of bark : Kālidāsa, *Śakuntalā*, VI, 17 (see also Kauṭilīya, *Arthaśāstra* II, 23, on the weaving of bark).

267 Medaillon : A.K. Coomaraswamy, *Bharhut*, fig. 81 and 124 = A. Cunningham, *Bharhut*, pl. XXX, 4 and XXXVI, 1.

268 Māyā seated on a big lotus in a scene of the Nativity : Stūpa I, southern toraṇa (*Sāñchī*, pl. 13/5, pp. 183, 197) and northern toraṇa (pl. 25/2 and 30/3), but in the eastern toraṇa (pl. 41/3 ; 44/2), as well as in Stūpa III (pl. 102/4), her legs are placed asymmetrically, one folded in front of the body, the other stretched towards the floor.

269 Ph. Stern, "Les ivoires et os découverts à Begram", p. 24, fig. 476 and 483.

270 *Ibidem*, p. 24, fig. 477 and 478.

271 Amorous couples (*Gandharva)* who abound in the initial period of Buddhist art : A.K. Coomaraswamy, *Bharhut*, p. 59, pl. XV, fig. 37 (frontal view of standing couple in royal costume in which the man takes the

**B** *Central area*

The human figures in the central area are divided into two groups : those in the upper level are in the hermitage (II-7 and 8 to 10) and those in the lower level participate in the procession represented in front of the hermitage (cavaliers II-14 to 16 and occupants of the quadriga II-11 to 13).

*Human figures in the hermitage*

A side or three quarters profile of a seated person facing the right is represented on the extreme left. The line of the back is markedly rounded, as of the cavalier II-15, its lower end terminating in a horizontal line which probably represented a seat without a backrest[273]. Only the ornaments at the back and the top of the head have survived. These comprise at least one earring and two other quadrangular ornaments of the type worn by the group of persons represented on the upper right side (see below). The first ornament projects horizontally on the left side or the back of the head[274] and the second is placed on top of the head. The silhouette is too fragmented to permit the identification of the sex of this person. The hairstyle differentiates itself from the hairstyles of the other actors of the scene and belongs to another category. If we adopt the hypothesis that the plaque illustrates the legend of Śakuntalā, this could be a representation of a hermit – perhaps not Kaṇva himself because according to the sources he was absent at the time of Duṣyanta's visit to the hermitage, but to one of those who received him[275]. If we accept that the building towards which the person's face is turned is the artist's own representation of the refuge of a hermit (see below), it is possible to conclude that this image pertains to a hermit in front of his hut, a theme which is well attested in Indian art[276].

woman in his arms). See also K. Fischer, "How were love scenes on Gandhāran stūpas understood by contemporary worshippers", in *South Asian archaeology 1983*, Naples, 1985, II, pp. 629-639.

272 Seated couples of *yakṣa* and *yakṣī*, whose amorous pose is very different from that of the couples of Ai Khanum : Stūpa I : *Sāñchī*, pl. 13/2, 19a (southern toraṇa), pl. 44/1 (eastern toraṇa, couple between two peacocks). In the context of representations of celestial life see also seated couples in paradise : pl. 64c/1, pp. 228-229 (western toraṇa).

273 Among the numerous examples of seats see at Sanchi I the scene of *Ṛṣya-śṛṅga* (n. 340) in which a brahmin hermit is seated on a throne of stone similar to the throne of the Buddha : *Sāñchī*, pl. 27/1 (northern toraṇa). On the most elementary form of the altar-throne of the Buddha derived from the seats of hermits, see J. Auboyer, *Le trône et son symbolisme dans l'Inde ancienne*, Paris, 1949, p. 10 sqq.

274 We opt for the hypothesis of an ornament rather than of a bun worn by the hermits on the nape : A.K. Coomaraswamy, *Bharhut*, fig. 170 and 231 = A. Cunningham, *Bharhut*, pl. XLVIII, 2 and XLVI, 2.

275 It is quite unlikely that it is either Śakuntalā or Duṣyanta for that would imply a composition consisting of multiple scenes in which the same actors would appear many times.

276 See, for example, at Sanchi I : *Sāñchī*, pl. 27/1, 29/3a (northern toraṇa) ; pl. 52a/2 (eastern toraṇa) ; Bharhut : A.K. Coomaraswamy, *Bharhut*, fig. 233 ; 176 = A. Cunningham, *Bharhut*, pl. XLVI, 4 ; XLVIII, 7 ; p. 122 ; Bodh-Gaya : A.K. Coomaraswamy, *Bodhgayā*, pl. XI and XLVII, 4 ; Mathurā : J. Ph. Vogel, *La sculpture de Mathurâ (Ars Asiatica, 15)*, Paris, Bruxelles, 1930, pl. XVIa and p. 63 (hermit in front of his hut with a deer, two birds and a serpent ; edifying story of four animals discussing which is the worst form of suffering in the presence of the hermit ; on this representation see also in this document n. 273 and 340) ; pl. LXa.

Three female spectators, seen frontally, are placed in a row, side by side under an umbrella, to the right of the pinnacled edifice. The portrayal of the figure standing on the extreme left (II-8) gives an idea of the pose in which they are represented. Her left arm, folded at right angles in front of her chest, rests on a horizontal line which could only belong to a balustrade. The slope of the canopy which overhangs it is visible on the left. Unlike the figures in the frieze this group is thus not represented in a squatting position but rather leaning on the elbows, from a balcony or a kiosk, a little like the spectators on the disc of Bhita and still others in Indian sculpture, in which this appears as one of the favourite motifs. It is almost certain that the two persons standing beside the first are represented in a similar pose. In addition, each of the two figures on the sides has two "flagpoles" slanting towards it from both sides, whose shaft has the rudimentary figure of a goat at the top end[277]. We do not know the importance and the function of these objects, which could well be fans rather than flagpoles[278].

The two persons on the sides are adorned with four ornaments which frame the silhouettes of their heads : two in a round shape, corresponding to earrings and two quadrangular, which seem to be ornaments for the hair. These ornaments, of which only three have survived, were represented by pastilles of red molten glass with black dots. The appearance of these ornaments is quite similar to the ones worn by the female figures on the right among the couples of the frieze. We can thus infer that three women in a kiosk are represented here[279].

The central figure distinguishes herself from the others by her much richer adornment : on the right side of the hair, the usual round or quadrangular ornament is replaced by an egret with three balls. There is no doubt that this central personage is also a woman and like the other two, represented frontally (or three quarters). Here also the umbrella indicates that the personage is of royal blood like the personage who occupies the central place in the quadriga[280]. Her proposed identification as Śakuntalā is in accordance with the royal dignity conferred on her by this symbolic attribute since, even though in this scene she is not yet married to the King, the heroine is of royal

---

277 Because of their oblique position, these shafts certainly do not serve as a support for an animal as one might surmise from one of the ivories of Begram representing a vertical support on which a bird, perhaps a peacock of the feminine residential quarters, is perched : Ph. Stern, "Les ivoires et os découverts à Begram", pp. 37-38, fig. 30 bis.

278 See the flagpoles in the representations of Indian armies at Bharhut : Cuningham *Bharhut*, pl. 32, 4 ; Sanchi I : *Sāñchī*, pl. 11/2, 15/3, 16/1 and 3, 17/3 (southern toraṇa) ; pl. 42/4, 44/3 (eastern toraṇa) ; pl. 63/1 (western toraṇa) ; these numerous examples consist of flags formed of shafts with a *triratna* on one end over which the flag is placed. See also a symbol which is very similar but also unidentified on Indian punch-marked coins : J. Allan, *BMC. Ancient India*, pp. xxxiv and 308.

279 For this theme in written sources see, for example, the scene depicting Duṣyanta's departure from his royal city as contained in the *Mahābhārata* (2818) : p. 59.

280 On the parasol or umbrella (*chattra*) as symbols of royalty and power see Arrian VIII, 16, 5 and Strabo XV, 1, 52 ; K.K. Murthy, *The Gandhāra sculptures*, pp. 113-114 ; K.K. Murthy, *Nagārjunakoṇḍā : A cultural study*, Delhi, 1977, pp. 232-235 ; M.M. Spagnoli, "The symbolic meaning of the club in the iconography of Kuṣāṇa kings", *EW*, 17, 1967, pp. 248-267, particularly p. 251. This motif, whose origin goes back to the most ancient times, occupies a special place in the royal imagery of the oriental world as proved, for example, by the numerous representations in Mycenian, Phoenician, Assyrian and Persian art. On the umbrella in Achaemehid art see M.C. Root, *The King and Kingship in Achaemenid art*, 1979, p. 287 ; for the remains of the iron framework of a specimen of this period see R. Ghirshman, "L'art animalier aulique achéménide", *Monuments Piot*, 60, 1976, p. 12.

descent from her father[281]. The umbrella confers the same social status on the group which she forms with her companions as the occupants of the quadriga. It is to be noted that the representation of the two companions beside her refers to the tradition as portrayed by Kālidāsa where Duṣyanta paints his loved one surrounded by two young women[282]. We will subsequently see that the episode of the arrival of the hunter-king at the hermitage also makes it possible to relate the disc of Bhita and the plaque of Ai Khanum to that version of the legend which is close to the one found in Kālidāsa and different from the version transmitted by the *Mahābhārata*.

*Persons outside the hermitage*

*Quadriga* : Only the heads of the three occupants standing in the box of the carriage[283], along with the shoulder of the figure on the right and the umbrella which shades the group, have survived. The central figure is turned three quarters towards the left and his adornment is on the whole similar to that of the male figures on the left in the couples of the frieze. Two earrings are visible on both sides of his neck and his hair, puffed up on the right side of the head, is arranged in the form of a bun on the left side. The figure on the right who holds a fly whisk[284] in his left hand, wears earrings and a heavy ornament consisting of two clusters of three small discs. The adornment of the figure on the left is of the same type but the two clusters of small discs are linked by a sort of diadem. This same person functions as the charioteer, as suggested by the section of a pole in the lower right corner of the plaquette which probably belonged to a spur.

If the umbrella is indicative of a royal presence, then which figure in this group is the king ? Given that the figures on the two sides wear the same kind of ornaments it is logical to infer that the

---

281 *Mahābhārata*, IX, 39, 11.

282 See above p. 58, n. 213 and p. 63.

283 On the chariot and its importance in Indian armies : P. Bernard, "Le monnayage d'Eudamos, satrape grec du Pandjab et «maître des éléphants»", *Orientalia Iosephi Tucci Memoriae Dicata*, Roma, 1985, pp. 65-94, particularly pp. 75-76 (literary sources : Strabo XV, 1.52 ; Arrian VIII, 12, 3, Curtius VIII, 14.3) : the chariot represented on the tetradrachma of Babylon pl. I, 4 dated by P. Bernard to 317/316 B.C. may be one of the most ancient representations of the Indian war chariot ; the representation of the guardrail is straight here but iconographic parallels are too few to date the appearance of the guardrail with three foils in Indian chariots. See also R.-J.-E.-C. Lefèbvre des Noëttes, *La force motrice animale à travers les âges*, Paris, 1924, pp. 78-79 and fig. 112-116 ; E. Popplow, *Pferd und Wagen im alten Orient*, Berlin, 1934 ; D. Faccenna, *Sculptures from the Sacred Area of Butkara I (Swat, W. Pakistan), Catalogue*, by M. Taddei, Roma, 1962-1964, pl. 418-421 ; S.D. Singh, *Ancient warfare with special reference to the Vedic period*, Leyde, 1965, p. 23 sqq. ; K.K. Murthy, *The Gandhāra sculptures*, pp. 100, 102-103 ; J. Spruytte, *Etudes expérimentales sur l'attelage*, Paris, 1977 ; K. Fischer, "Eine Reitergruppe in Vorderansicht aus Swāt nach dem Vorbild von Quadriga-Darstellungen", in *Orientalia Iosephi Tucci ...*, pp. 355-370, frontal view of quadriga ; M. Sparreboom, *Chariots in the Veda*, diss., Leiden, 1983 ; W. Rau, *Zur vedischen Altertumskunde, (Abhandlungen der geistes- und sozialwissenschaftlichen Klasse, 1983.1)*, Wiesbaden, 1983.

284 On fly whisks see M. Stutley, *The illustrated dictionary of Hindu iconography*, London, Boston, Melbourne, 1985, s.v. : *camara* ; K.K. Murthy, *Nagārjunakoṇḍā*, pp. 45-46 ; K.K. Murthy, *The Gandhāra sculptures*, pp. 114-115. ; K.K. Murthy, *Nagārjunakoṇḍā*, pp. 235-237. The bearers of fly whisks, particularly in chariot scenes, are generally women but the one represented on the vase of Gundla is a man.

central figure represents the king[285]. Although, unlike his two associates, his hair is not loaded with ornaments, his hair style is very similar to the figures on the left in the couples of the frieze who, we think, it would not be a mistake to identify as Duṣyanta in conversation with Śakuntalā (see pp. 65-66, 71-74)[286]. We have no definite clues to decide whether the two other figures are male or female. However the sumptuousness of the ornaments which deck their hair could be regarded as an indication that they are women.

Since the prince is also the chief of the army, the royal procession is, in Indian art, an occasion for a military parade in which the prince is represented on a chariot (*ratha*), the most prestigious section of the army, flanked by a variable number of companions, both men and women[287]. The three other arms of the military force namely, the cavalry, the infantry and the elephants could also be present in these royal parades. On the plaque of Ai Khanum, the artist chose to represent the cavalry along with the royal chariot whereas on the vase of Gundla an elephant is also represented with the cavalry.

Ancient representations of the vehicle of the sun-god, Sūrya, present two principle models : at Bodhgaya, Sūrya, under an umbrella, is represented frontally while the horses in pairs, thrusting upwards and diverging to the left and to the right are seen in profile[288] ; at Bhaja, a three quarter view of the quadriga is shown, which, later becomes the more common form of representation. The royal chariot constitutes the central element in numerous representations on the monumental

285 On the king's place among the other occupants of the chariot in Indian iconography : Sanchi I, southern toraṇa : *Sāñchī*, pl. 15/3 : among the occupants, the king stands in the front of the chariot, with the driver to his left ; pl. 11/2 : here also the king stands in the front of the chariot, the driver to his left, the carrier of the fly-whisk to his right, but there is no umbrella. A.K. Coomaraswamy, *Bharhut*, fig. 25 upper. [= fig. 28], pp. 47-48 = A. Cunningham, *Bharhut*, pl. XIII, 3, pp. 90-91 : Bharhut, visit of king Prasenajit : on his visit to the Buddha, this king arrives in a quadriga accompanied by three assistants ; the first holds the fly-whisk, the second the royal umbrella and the third is the driver ; two cavaliers and two elephants accompany the chariot. Sometimes the king himself is the chariot driver : Sanchi I, northern toraṇa, story of Viśvantara (see n. 210, 289, 290 and 297) : the prince himself holds the reins in the absence of assistants, and it is the princess who holds the fly whisk. In the relief of Bhaja also, Sūrya himself seems to be the chariot driver. In the vase of Gundla, the king is in the front of the chariot between two women but not as the chariot driver (see above p. 70). On elephants the king is generally seated in front and the flag bearer behind him : *Sāñchī*, pl. 16/7, 17/6, Sanchi I, southern toraṇa ; pl. 59a, western toraṇa ; see also the archer installed between the king and the flag bearer : pl. 16/3, 17/3, southern torana. Cf. P. Bernard, "Le monnayage d'Eudamos", pp. 76-79.

286 For the side bun very similar in appearance to the hair style of the central figure of the quadriga on the plaque of Ai Khanum, see also the relief of Sanchi I, southern toraṇa : *Sāñchī*, pl. 18a/3 (above n. 257b).

287 On the vase of Gundla and the relief of Bhaja (on the latter see n. 242) it is the women who accompany the king on his chariot. According to Strabo XV, 1, 52, in addition to the driver, Indian war chariots carried two soldiers. Cf. Arrian VIII, 12, 3 and Curtius VIII, 14, 3.

288 A.K. Coomaraswamy, *Bodhgayā*, pl. XXXIII, northern side and LIII, 2 ; Ph. Stern, "Les ivoires et os découverts à Begram", p. 46, fig. 608 ; C. Sivaramamurti, fig. 247 and p. 340 (Śuṅga, 1st cent. B.C.) ; M. Hallade, *Arts de l'Asie ancienne, I, l'Inde (Publications du Musée Guimet, 5)*, Paris, 1954, pl. XIV, n° 153 : later than the 1st cent ? See also M. Bussagli, "The "frontal" representation of the Divine Chariot", *EW*, 6, 1955, pp. 9-25, particularly p. 2, n. 14-15.

complexes of Bharhut[289], Stūpas I[290] and II[291] of Sanchi (two horse chariots of the royal processions), of Mathurā[292], and of Amaravati[293], etc.

Mention must also be made of a bronze seal from the Houghton collection, dated around the beginning of the Christian era, which represents the image of a royal quadriga (fig. 60)[294]. The chariot has a lightly constructed box with three foils in wickerwork and is being pulled towards the right by four horses who have a double egret on top of their heads. The three passengers are

---

289 A.K. Coomaraswamy, *Bharhut*, fig. 83, p. 75 = A. Cunningham, *Bharhut*, pl. XXV, 4 : quadrigas of the *jātaka* of Temiya. On the theme itself of *Mūga-pakkha-jātaka* see E.B. Cowell, *The Jātaka*, 6, n°538 : previous life in which the Bodhisattva as Temiya becomes a hermit while still a child. To be particularly noted in the scene represented in this relief is the palace (the Bodhisattva is the son of a king) and the quadriga, two motifs whose presence symbolises the royal status of Temiya. On the visit of king Prasenajit of Kosala : see n. 285 and 310. A.K. Coomaraswamy, *Bharhut*, fig. 39, pp. 60-61 : gift of the chariot in the departure of prince Viśvantara. This *jātaka* illustrates the first rebirth of the Buddha under the name Viśvantara, the prince of charity : E.B. Cowell, *The Jātaka*, 6, n°547 ; this prince who was exiled for having given the magic elephant to the brahmins on whom the prosperity of Jettatura depended, left the city for the forest with his family in a quadriga. See also n. 210, 285, 290 and 297.

290 *Sāñchī*, pl. 16/3 and 17/3 (southern toraṇa) : two horse chariot ; pl. 61/2 (western toraṇa) : two horse chariot, horse and elephant ; pl. 35a/1 (northern toraṇa) : two horse chariot without passenger in an aniconical representation of the Buddha ; pl. 61/3 (western toraṇa) : two horse chariot of the vanquished in the Great Miracle of the Sambodhi, that is, the victory on Māra ; pl. 35b/2 (northern toraṇa) : royal chariot leaving the town in a procession ; pl. 51b, p. 217 (eastern toraṇa) and pl. 62/2 (western toraṇa) : chariot in a royal visit ; pl. 50a/1 (eastern toraṇa) : two horse chariot in the return of the Buddha to Kapilavastu ; pl. 15/3, pp. 214-215 (southern toraṇa) : in the siege of a town during the war of the relics, Aśoka stands in a two horse chariot with two other occupants of whom one is the driver and the other, the bearer of the fly whisk ; pl. 18a/2 (southern toraṇa) : Aśoka in a two horse chariot in the visit to the Bodhi tree; pl. 11/2, pp. 215-216 (southern toraṇa) : in the Stūpa of Rāmagrāma, Aśoka stands in a two horse chariot preceded by a cavalier and followed by three elephants : the driver stands on his left while the bearer of the fly whisk stands in front of the king. For a representation of the quadriga see pl. 23a/1, pp. 225-226 (northern toraṇa) : in this *jātaka* of Viśvantara, a large number of motifs related to the plaque of Ai Khanum and the disc of Bhita figure (on the reproduction of the same theme at Bharhut see above n. 289) ; this relief first illustrates the departure of the king with his family. The king stands in a quadriga holding the reins and a very long spur in his hands ; his spouse holds the fly whisk ; the umbrella is apparently fixed in a socle ; the rest of the story appears in pl. 33/1 with the representation of the prince and his family at the entry of the forest at the beginning of the trees and in proximity of wild animals among whom we recognize the antelopes by their tapering horns ; in the relief of pl. 29 the couple is seated in front of the hut of an anchorite, similar in type to the one represented in the disc of Bhita, situated in a landscape with trees and animals among whom the deer are recognisable by their antlers ; the pond in which lotuses float can also be compared to the motif of the pond in the plaque of Ai Khanum.

291 *Sāñchī*, pl. 79, 27b.

292 Chariot of Surya seen frontally : J. Ph. Vogel, *La sculpture de Mathurâ*, pl. XXXVIIIa, p. 46 ; A.K. Coomaraswamy, *History of Indian and Indonesian art*, fig. 103.

293 C. Sivaramamurti, *Amarāvatī sculptures in the Madras Government Museum (Bulletin of the Madras Govt. Museum, N.S., 4)*, 1956, pl. X, 13.

294 P. Callieri, *I sigilli e le cretule del Nord-Ovest del Sub-continente Indiano e dell'Afghanistan (4° secolo A.C. - 1° secolo D.C.)*, Napoli, 1987 (unpublished thesis) : inv. VAM, IS, 15, 1948, ref. 15981/35, n° 8 : round form ; diam. : 2.9 cm. Mention may also be made of a medaillon in terracotta from Patna with the representation of the chariot of Sūrya : B. Rowland, *The art and architecture*, p. 66 and pl. 195.a.

shaded by an umbrella. The driver is standing towards the front, holding the reins with his left hand while his right arm, tending forward, seems to be holding a spur. The right hand of the passenger in the centre is raised towards the pole of the umbrella, probably fixed to the box of the chariot, as if he were holding on to it. The third person who stands behind holds the fly whisk. A floral motif and a swastika occupy the space above the composition. Inspite of the greatly reduced dimensions and the resulting simplification of detail, this image is a particularly successful representation of the Indian style royal quadriga. The design of horses with slender legs, which shows a finesse in contrast to the generally thick silhouettes of horses in large sculpture, is definitely linked to the technique of incision in intaglio itself. This sharpness of lines can also be found, technique notwithstanding, in other miniaturised representations of horses, whether in the excised motifs of the plaque of Ai Khanum, in the moulded disc of Bhita or in the vase of Gundla.

The association of the quadriga of Ai Khanum with the legend of Śakuntalā as developed by Kālidāsa is not forced. According to him it is precisely the chase of a game animal which leads Duṣyanta in his chariot to the gate of the hermitage where Śakuntalā lives[295]. It is this same version which is reflected in the disc of Bhita with the almost negligible difference in the number of persons occupying the chariot : two – the king and his coachman – in the disc of Bhita is also the number found in Kālidāsa, and three on the plaque of Ai Khanum which, in this respect, is closer to the version in the *Mahābhārata*[296].

It is to be noted that the plaque of Ai Khanum and the disc of Bhita are the only available representations of a royal hunt in a chariot which conform to certain literary narratives[297]. Other scenes of a royal hunt where the king hunts with a bow, are also relatively rare in Indian art : see for example, the reliefs of Udayagiri[298], Bharhut[299] or the ivories of Begram[300].

*Cavaliers* : The quadriga is escorted by three cavaliers represented in profile. Only the head and a foot, probably the left one, suspended in air[301], remain of the first cavalier, represented in

---

295 In the version found in the *Mahābhārata*, 2845 and 2862, the role of deer appears more anecdotal : see above pp. 59-60.

296 (2879) "Discarding his regalia and accompanied only by councillor and priest, he walked to the grand hermitage".

297 Though the king is associated with antelopes in the *jātaka* of Viśvantara at Sanchi, the context is not of a hunting scene : see also n. 210, 285, 289 and 290. The theme of the royal hunt is abundantly utilised in the oriental arts, but outside Indian art, representations of the king hunting in a chariot are few : Achaemenido-Persian cylinder : P. Zazoff, *Jagddarstellungen auf antiken Gemmen*, Hamburg, Berlin, 1970, fig. 6 and *idem*, *Die antiken Gemmen*, München, 1983, p. 169, pl. 38.1 ; Graeco-Persian gem : J. Boardman, *Greek gems*, London, 1976, fig. 928. See also M.A. Littauer, J.H. Crouwel, *Wheeled vehicles and ridden animals in the ancient Near East*, Leiden, Köln, 1979, pp. 63, 133, etc.

298 See n. 306 and 339. See also the image of the hunter-king holding a bow and conversing with two young women at Kondane 1 : D.D. Kosambi, *The culture and civilisation of ancient India in historical outline*, Delhi, Bombay, 1966, fig. 93. Also the mention of the Indian king hunting animals enclosed in a park with a bow in Curtius VIII, 9, 28.

299 See n. 306 and 339 (*Ruru-jātaka*).

300 J. Auboyer, "La vie privée dans l'Inde ancienne", pp. 71-72.

301 The evidence of stirrups in Indian iconography is rare : see above p. 69.

front of the chariot. The mount has completely disappeared. The relatively restricted space which it occupied between the frieze and the first of the four horses of the quadriga leads us to suppose that the forelegs intersected by the border were never represented. The second cavalier is not better preserved than the first, except for his horse whose forequarters are missing. Like the first cavalier it is possible to identify him by his left leg, which stands out under the belly of the animal, and by the tail of a scarf which flows down his back[302]. The third cavalier placed above the preceding presents the only almost intact silhouette of this series (fig. 37). He wears a helmet and is armed like a warrior with a lance[303] and a shield[304]. One of his earrings is visible.

The weapons of a cavalier in Indian iconography are, in general, the same as those of an infantryman, that is, a lance or a bow[305]. Sometimes the bow may be utilised in a hunt of cervidaes and gazelles[306], but it is usually employed against elephants and felines[307]. The lance, the pike or the hunting spear are also traditional weapons employed in the hunt of deer, gazelles and other game animals like lions and wild boars[308]. The crest of the helmet worn by this cavalier can be clearly distinguished. The head of the first cavalier on the left is too damaged to enable us to say whether he was also wearing a helmet.

---

302 *Sāñchī*, pl. 56/6 and 58/5, Sanchi I, western toraṇa : shawl or scarf (*uttarīya*) flows down the backs of cavaliers. This fabric should not be confused with a shield. This defensive weapon of cavaliers is elongated in form, rectilinear below and rounded at the top, and is held vertically. See also the vase of Gundla.

303 The clearly triangular form of the tip of this lance can be found on the vase of Gundla and on a bas-relief of Sanchi I (western toraṇa) : *Sāñchī*, pl. 62/3.

304 It is in this manner that we interpret the line behind the silhouette which defines a large section of the arch behind the neck and prolongs itself towards the back in a straight vertical line : on the form of Indian shields see also n. 753 and 756. If we regard it as the line of the back we would have to imagine a person in an extremely arched position which does not conform to the position of a cavalier in saddle. Examples of an arched back seen in profile are extremely rare : Sanchi I : *Sāñchī*, pl. 62/3 (western toraṇa) ; Bharhut : A.K. Coomaraswamy, *Bharhut*, fig. 67, p. 69 = A. Cunningham, *Bharhut*, pl. LVII.

305 Arrian VIII, 16, 10 : "Their horsemen have two javelins, like lances (*saunia*), and a small shield, smaller than the infantry".

306 Udayagiri, Bharhut (*Ruru-jātaka*), Sanchi (*Śyāma-jātaka)*, account of Kālidāsa, etc.

307 On Indian bows see above n. 298 sqq. and P. Bernard, "Le monnayage d'Eudamos", pp. 74-75. Graeco-Persian gems portraying bow hunting: J. Boardman, *Greek gems*, n° 904, 924, 928, 929 (lion) ; 927 (goat). A lion hunt with a bow and a wild boar hunt with a lance : P. Zazoff, *Jagddarstellungen auf antiken Gemmen*, fig. 16 and *idem*, *Die antiken Gemmen*, p. 182, pl. 42.4. On Sassanid hunting scenes : D. Thompson, *Stucco from Chal Tarkhan-Eshqabad near Rayy*, Warminster, 1976, pp. 9-18, pl. XX.1–XXI.1 and 3-4.

308 On hunting weapons in Begram see, for example, J. Auboyer, "La vie privée dans l'Inde ancienne", pp. 71-72 ; antelope hunt on horseback with lance : fig. 117 ; see also fig. 160. Graeco-Persian gems representing hunting with lance : J. Boardman, *Greek gems*, n° 863, 888, 965 (cervidae) ; 885, 889, 905, 924, 925, 926 (wild boar, hunter on foot or on horse back). P. Zazoff, *Jagddarstellungen auf antiken Gemmen*, fig. 14-16 and *idem*, *Die antiken Gemmen*, pl. 42.

## 2) Animals.

### *a- Horses*

Horses constitute the only animal motif in the lower section of the plaque. Out of a total of seven horses in the scene, only the two mounts of the cavaliers marching behind the quadriga are relatively well preserved (V-22 and V-23 ; fig. 34.4-5 and 37). Apart from certain differences of detail concerning the position of the legs, the outlines of these two horses present an undeniable similarity in their dimensions, the design of their bodies and the curves of their bellies and hindquarters, confirming the thesis that several set patterns (body, legs etc.) were used interchangeably by the artisan who associated one to the other depending on the movement to be shown. The surviving hoofs and the hocks of the horses of the quadriga (plaquettes I-27 and I-28) also reflect the use of the same pattern. In succession, from right to left, there are three regularly spaced pairs of hoofs corresponding to the hindlegs of three of the four horses. The hindlegs of the fourth which would have been on the right side of the yoke were not represented because of lack of space. In addition, the similarity which exists between the outlines of the bellies of the cervidae in the centre of the plaque (V-16) and the horse V-22 shows that the same pattern could be used for different species and that, in these cases the tendency was to ignore the respective proportions of different types of animals.

Whereas in the domain of iconography on coins, the image of the horse is known mainly on coins of Greek origin in India[309], it is abundantly represented in Indian monumental sculpture with all the details of its harness. The animal is usually presented in profile or in a slightly three-quarter view but there are also instances of the frontal view (quadriga of Sūrya) or back view[310], in the trotting, galloping[311] or reclining position[312]. The most common image is of a mounted horse, as for example at Bharhut[313] and Sanchi[314], but it is also found without a rider on the same monuments in scenes of the Great Departure, as the aniconic representation of the Buddha[315]. It is

309 O. Bopearachchi, "Roi-cavalier ou Reine-amazone ?", *Bull.Soc.fr.Num.* 1988, pp. 453-456 ; J.M. Rosenfield, *The dynastic arts*, n° 270 (coin of Azes).

310 A.K. Coomaraswamy, *Bharhut*, fig. 25 upper and fig. 28 = A. Cunningham, *Bharhut*, pl. XIII, 3 : back view of cavalier, with a shortened perspective (Prasenajit's visit to the Buddha).

311 A.K. Coomaraswamy, *Bharhut*, fig. 35 centre = A. Cunningham, *Bharhut*, pl. XVIII, 2 and pp. 79-82 : flying horse of Puṇṇaka in a trotting position, richly harnessed but clumsily represented, with very short forelegs (*Vidhurapaṇḍita-jātaka* : E.B. Cowell, *The Jātaka*, t, n°545). Mauryan capital from Sarnath : leaping horse with forelegs thrust forward ; the form of the animal is much finer and the movement more lively than in representations from ancient Indian art : V. Smith, *A History of fine art in India and Ceylon*, 3rd ed. rev. by K. Khandalawala., repr. Bombay, 1969, pl. V. Cf. also the Babylonian decadrachmas of the Indian type : W.B. Kaiser, "Ein Meister der Glyptik aus dem Umkreis Alexanders des Grossen", *JDAI*, 77, 1962, p. 229 ; P. Bernard, "Le monnayage d'Eudamos", pl. I, 1 and 2.

312 Two mounted and richly harnessed horses reclining back to back : Sanchi I : *Sāñchī*, pl. 12/6, 13/6 (southern toraṇa) ; pl. 31/2, 33/2 (northern toraṇa) ; Sanchi III : pl. 97/6, 98/7.

313 Cavalier : A.K. Coomaraswamy, *Bharhut*, fig. 16 = A. Cunningham, *Bharhut*, pl. XXXII, 6.

314 Sanchi I : *Sāñchī*, pl. 11/2, 15/3, 18a/3, 29/3d (southern toraṇa) ; pl. 34b/1 (northern toraṇa) ; pl. 61/1, 62/3 (western toraṇa).

315 Bharhut : on the horses see A. Cunningham, *Bharhut*, pp. 42-43. A.K. Coomaraswamy, *Bharhut*, fig. 38, pp. 59-60 = A. Cunningham, *Bharhut*, pl. XXa : horse under an umbrella associated with two fly whisks.

to be noted that even when the horses are presented in profile, a three-quarter view of the cavaliers is more common[316].

In the most ancient Indian art, particularly at Bharhut, the silhouette of these animals is stocky and their movement is often quite unnatural. The rendering of the animal is more realistic at Sanchi but it remains heavy.

The horses in our plaque wore plumes on the head as apparent from the fragmentary decoration on top of the head of horse V-23 of the second cavalier. This accessory whose form varies according to the artistic school is a well known element of the harness of horses as testified by the plaque of Bhita, the vase of Gundla, the bronze seal described above p. 79, the reliefs of Sanchi and Bharhut[317].

Only one horse has conserved, engraved on a shell, the bridle of the cavalier suspended between his mouth and the front of the chest (V-23). But the most revealing detail regarding harness is contained in two fragments of brown molten glass inlays encrusted with minute decoration and encircled with gold wire which were found detached from their support of shells but which seem to us to have been related. The left profile of the head of a horse is preserved on the first, broken at the neck and above the eyes (fig. 33.36-37 and 47). A cluster of four small orange pastilles represent the decorative plates of the bit[318]. The headstall which passes behind the nape and is indispensable for the maintenance of the harness of the head in place is not represented[319]. It is clear that the artist has simplified the details. Two strokes of inlays, one white and the other orange are all that remains of the mane. The orientation of these strokes with the point turned

Sanchi I : *Sāñchī*, pl. 16/1 ; 17/1 (southern toraṇa) and pl. 35a/1 (northern toraṇa) : an unmounted but entirely harnessed horse, in association with the umbrella and the fly whisk during the Great Departure from the gate of Kapilavastu, the rider Chandaka holding the umbrella ; pl. 40/2 (eastern toraṇa) : same horse associated with the Foot Print and the sacred vessel. Sanchi II : pl. 88, 74b ; see also the overlapping examples of the Bodhisattva : pl. 82/40b, 86/63b, 90/84b, pp. 187-188.

316 See also p. 77 sq.

317 A.K. Coomaraswamy, *Bharhut*, fig. 25 sup. (= fig. 28), 35 centre and 83 = A. Cunningham, *Bharhut*, pl. XIII, 3, XVIII, 2 and XXV, 4.

318 The bit under which the reins generally hang is not part of the harness of the face (*Sāñchī*, pl. 12/6, etc. : see also n. 343).

319 The text of Arrian VIII, 16, 10-12 describes the difference between the Indian and the Greek bit : "Their horses are not saddled nor do they use bits like the Greek or Celtic, but a band of stitched rawhide is fitted round the muzzle of the horse, with bronze or iron goads, not very sharp, turned inwards. The rich use goads of ivory. Inside their mouths their horses have a piece of iron like a spit, to which the reins are attached. And so when the rein is pulled, the spit controls the horse and, since the goads are attached to it, they prick the horse and compel him to obey the rein" (transl. of P.A. Brunt, *Arrian*, vol. II, 1983, p. 355) ; it is not a complete description of the bridle. The fact that the headstall has not been mentioned does not signify that it was absent from the system by which the bit was suspended. On the different elements of the bridle see, for example, the edition of *L'art équestre* de Xénophon by Ed. Delebecque, Paris, 1958, pp. 173-177. See also E.W. Hopkins, "Notes from India. 1. Bridles in sculpture and painting", *JAOS*, 19/2, 1898, pp. 29-36 ; A. Cunningham, *Bharhut*, pp. 42-43 ; for Begram : J. Auboyer, "La vie privée dans l'Inde ancienne", p. 65, fig. 117, 118, 121, 123, 125.

towards the head indicate that the strands of the mane had been turned down on the neck[320]. The place of the eye is marked by a minute perforation which has not conserved its inlay.

The second fragment which is a plaque of brown molten glass similar to the one observed on the preceding fragment represents the colour of the coat of a horse. Three rows of inlays arranged in arcs of concentric circles form the design on this base (fig. 33.37 and 37). The first, comprising of a succession of small orange pastilles from one end to the other may represent the rein with a decoration of appliques, falling from the bit and mounting up towards the left hand of the cavalier. The three orange coloured pastilles in the form of teardrops arranged under the rein may represent a decoration of small bells or phalera[321]. Nothing remains of the third row of decorative elements except what appears to be a part of the inlay in the form of teardrops.

Whatever be the hypothesis for the interpretation of these two fragments, it is possible to be certain of one thing, which is that, given the similarity of their base, they belong to the same type of representation. A comparison with other remains of fragments helps to ascertain that they could belong neither to representations of buildings or human beings, nor to those of animals other than mounted horses.

*Animals specific to India*

The other animals in the composition, birds or quadrupeds who occupy the area above the zone occupied by the horses, are typical of the gardens and forests of India. The peacocks and the cervidaes are the only animals common to both the circular frieze and the central field. The other species appear to be restricted to the latter, judging from the available evidence. Whether still or in movement, all these animals are represented in profile, in contrast with the representation of human beings and edifices in the frieze. We get an idea of their appearance from the several inlays preserved in their alveoles or detached from their support.

***b- Birds : The peacocks***

Along with the cervidae, peacocks are the only animals systematically represented in pairs[322]. Four of these birds (V-3, V-4, V-7, V-8), are placed in the lower part of the frieze. They ascend in pairs, the male following the female, flying on either side of the central field, towards the top of the plaque. Their ovoid body prolongs itself in the form of a long curved neck leaning forward and ending in a round head with an egret and a long beak. Three tapering claws project out at the end of slender feet. The form of the tail which helps to differentiate their sex is broad and rounded for the females (V-8), and thin and long for the males, with two minute round projections representing plumes sticking out (fig. 33.31-32). The similarity of the curves of their bodies and

---

320 This type of a brushed down mane is rare in the early ancient period ; however see on the column of Sarnath (above n. 311) and at Bharhut A.K. Coomaraswamy, *Bharhut*, fig. 25 upper (= fig. 28) and 35 centre = A. Cunningham, *Bharhut*, pl. XIII, 3 and XVIII, 2. Same motif for the lions : A.K. Coomaraswamy, fig. 5 = A. Cunningham, pl. VIII.

321 On phaleras see, for example, J. Auboyer, "La vie privée dans l'Inde ancienne", p. 65.

322 The representation of animal pairs in hunting scenes is a convention in oriental art : see hunting scenes in Iranian art mentioned above n. 297 and 307-308.

heads is a proof of the use of two sets of common patterns, one for the central area and the other for the frieze (fig. 34.9-10). With respect to the tails of the males, one observes that the same pattern has been used both for the birds in the central area (V-14) and in the frieze (V-3).

The few inlays which are still in place in their alveoles reveal the appearance of the plumage of the females (V-4 and V-8). In the first, three circular pastilles, each one different from the other (types VII-65, VII-58 and VII-54), stuck on a white background constitute the dorsal plumage ; beneath it the wing is formed by a rod with polychrome bands (orange-brown-white). In the other female peacock V-8, the colours of the tail are less bright and consist of four small white and grey sticks, juxtaposed alternately.

The peacock is, among exotic animals, one of the most popular in Indian art[323], be it in scenes of domestic life, as depicted in the ivories of Begram[324], or of religious life[325], illustrated in the sculpture of Bharhut[326], Sanchi[327], or Gandhāra[328]. The examples can be multiplied[329].

---

323 K.K. Murthy, *Nagārjunakoṇḍā*, p. 248 ; M. Hallade, *Arts de l'Asie ancienne, I,* pl. XV. On peacocks and China E.H. Schafer, *The golden peaches of Samarcand*, pp. 96-99 ; on the peacock's tendency to dance at the sound of music observed both in China and in India, p. 98.

324 Ph. Stern, "Les ivoires et os découverts à Begram", pp. 37-38, fig. 203 : solitary peacock ; fig. 30 bis : peacock perched on a column. J. Hackin *et alii*, *Recherches à Bégram*, pl. XLII, fig. 94 and p. 69 : plaquette in bone. J. Auboyer, "La vie privée dans l'Inde ancienne", p. 65, n. 4, reminds that the image of domestic peacock perched on a pillar in the middle of the garden is often evoked by Kālidāsa. See also B.S. Upadhyaya, *India in Kālidāsa*, p. 47.

325 On its function as sacred animal see J.N. Banerjea, *The development of Hindu iconography*, Calcutta, 1956, pp. 140-146 ; P. Bernard, *BEFEO*, 68, 1980, p. 33, n. 16.

326 A.K. Coomaraswamy, *Bharhut*, fig. 121, pp. 82-83 : medaillon with a frontal representation of a peacock between two female peacocks (probably the *Mora-jātaka* : E.B. Cowell, *The Jātaka*, 2, n°159 ; see also 4, n°491 : life of the Bodhisattva as a peacock where he is caught in a trap after having been tempted by a female peacock). See also A. Cunningham, *Bharhut*, pl. XVII, 11 ; B. Barua, *Barhut*, III, pl. LXXI, fig. 91 : two ducks on both sides of a peacock fanning its tail, on an entablature that we know only on the basis of a design.

327 Sanchi I : *Sāñchī*, pl. 13/3 (southern toraṇa) ; pl. 30 and 32 (northern toraṇa) ; 42 and 44 (eastern toraṇa). On the hypothesis of the peacock being a symbol of the Mauryan dynasty see p. 231. Peacock fanning its tail at Sanchi II : *Sāñchī*, pl. 76/10b.

328 H. Ingholt, *Gandhāran art in Pakistan*, New York, 1957, pl. XVIII, 3 and fig. 460 and 461 (Gandhāra relief from Sahri Bahlol at the Museum of Peshawar) : animated foliage. Cf. K.K. Murthy, *The Gandhāra sculptures*, p. 121.

329 Coin reproductions : P. Bernard, *BEFEO*, 68, 1980, p. 33 ; *RN*, 15, 1973, p. 249, fig. 4, n° 7 ; J. Allan, *BMC. Ancient India*, pp. xxv and 298 : peacock on a hill on punch-marked coins. *Ibidem*, pp. cl-cli, pl. XL, 1-9 : Kārttikeya with a peacock on his side on coins of the Yaudheyas, 3rd-4th cent. A.D. On the importance of birds in Indian parks see Aelian XIII, 18. This bird, about which the Greeks came to know thorough Persia from the beginning of the 5th cent. B.C., begins to be widely represented in Graeco-Roman iconography after the intensification of commercial relations between India and the Mediterranean world : J.W. McCrindle, *The invasion of India by Alexander the Great*, 1898, pp. 362-363 ; O. Keller, *Die antike Tierwelt*, Leipzig, 1909-1913, t. 2, p. 148 sqq. ; D'Arcy W. Thompson, *A glossary of Greek birds*, Oxford, London, 1936², pp. 277-281 ; W.W. Tarn, *The Greeks in Bactria and India*, p. 366 ; E.H. Warmington, *The commerce*, pp. 105, 147, 156 ; J. Pollard, *Birds in Greek life and myth*, London, 1977, pp. 91-93. For the representation of a peacock on an engraved bone at Dal'verzintepe see G.A. Pugačenkova, *Dal'verzintepe*, fig. 36 ; on a tomb painting at Kertsch : N. Kondakoff, J. Tolstoï, S. Reinach, *Antiquités de la Russie meridionale*, Paris, 1891, p. 34, fig. 32.

Born from the feathers dropped by the mythical bird Garuḍa, the peacock was considered, simultaneously, the symbol of immortality as the killer of serpents who symbolise time, the symbol of war because of its association with Durgā and Kārttikeya, gods of war for whom it serves as the mount, and also the symbol of love[330]. It is thus possible that the presence of peacocks, along with the deer which are associated with the legend of Śakuntalā, has amorous connotations. The disc of Bhita, in which we again find a peacock among the deer in the context of the same legend, reinforces this interpretation.

*Other birds*

In the upper left part of the frieze, we find the head and the legs of another bird which undoubtedly had its counterpart on the right side of the frieze. With its egret, its slightly hooked beak and its long arched neck, this bird resembles a peacock. But a "crest" dangling below its head renders its identification difficult. It is possible that this was a mistake on the part of the craftsman who had wanted to represent a peacock.

The central area has at least five different types of birds, with silhouettes which are disproportionate with respect to the cervidaes and the human figures. A pair of peacocks occupy the space between the third and the fourth column, behind a pair of cervidaes in the middle portion of the central area. Another pair of birds is to be found on either side of a tree with three branches at the top of the central area. Only the front portion of the bird on the left survives (V-11). The right profile of the bird is shown but its head is turned towards the left. In the lower right corner of the plaquette I-2, above the pinnacle (see below p. 90-93), two grooves which cut the border on the right can be perceived which, by way of a simple hypothesis, can be regarded as the end of the tail of this same bird. We are hesitant to regard this bird as a peacock[331] because the characteristic egret is missing from the head and the neck is much shorter. It cannot be compared with a parrot either. The general silhouette suggests a goose (*haṃsa*), which is a common bird in Indian gardens and is often represented in pairs[332]. Finally, towards the right side of the first column, there are the extremely fragmentary remains, of the last bird – a long tail descending vertically. It is not possible to identify this bird also.

---

330 Kārttikeya or Skanda, Hindu god of war and of the planet Mars is represented on the peacock Paravāṇi, holding a bow in one hand and an arrow in the other : see S.J. Czuma, *Kushan sculpture*, pp. 114-115. For a painting of Dil'berdžin in which probably Skanda is sitting astride on a peacock see I.T. Kruglikova, *Drevnjaja Baktrija 2*, 1979, fig. 13, 14, 24, 27 : 5th-6th cent. The peacock is sometimes held by the God : R.C. Agrawala, M. Taddei, "An interesting relief from the Swat Valley", *EW*, 16, 1966, pp. 82-88 (with bibliography). Cf. also B.S. Upadhyaya, *India in Kālidāsa*, p. 239.

331 Sanchi I : *Sāñchī*, pl. 47/2 (eastern toraṇa). On parrots see E.H. Schafer, *The golden peaches of Samarcand*, pp. 99-102 ; Cf. Aelian XIII, 18.

332 Begram : J. Hackin *et alii*, *Nouvelles recherches*, fig. 46, 49, 144, 201-205, etc. ; Sanchi II : *Sāñchī*, pl. 84/55b, 86/66c, 90/86a ; Sanchi I : *Sāñchī*, pl. 11/1 (southern toraṇa), pl. 51b (eastern toraṇa) ; Bharhut : A. Cunningham, *Bharhut*, pl. XXVII, 11.

### *c- Cervidaes*

Along with horses and birds, the cervidae are the most frequently represented on the plaque.

The only almost completely preserved cervidae are the two pairs who ascend symmetrically on either side of the central area behind the peacocks in the lower part of the frieze. The branched antlers of the male in the pair on the left allow them to be identified as a deer and a doe (fig. 33.33-34)[333].

The head of the female V-5 is made of a dark brown ovoid plaquette of molten glass which is itself inlaid with an eye made of gold wire comprising two small black and white discs stuck to each other. The body of the male V-6 is also constituted by marron plaquette sprinkled alternately with small round white and orange spots in imitation of the spots found on the coats of male and female deer.

The form of the antlers with only two twists, and the representation of the coat make it possible to identify it more precisely within the genus of cervidaes[334]. The sub-type *dama* is characterized by a fawn coloured coat with white spots in the adults as well as in the young and by a fairly long tail ; the sub-type *pseudaxis* in the Asiatic region includes six or seven types of antlers with simplified forms and a coat with lighter spots which disappear in winter ; the sub-type *axis* consists of only one variety – the spotted axis (*axis maculatus*), which has a bright auburn coat with white spots and the type of antlers which we have described above. The place of origin of the last mentioned is mainly India, South China and Ceylon where it lives in fairly large bands. It is probably this type which is represented on our plaque[335].

Although the position of the body and particularly the angle at which the head is inclined is perceptibly different in the four silhouettes of the frieze, it is clear that the design of the legs is based on two patterns representing the forelegs and the hindlegs respectively which the artist has inversed in the left and the right sections of the frieze (fig. 33.7-8).

A second pair of deer occupies the middle of the central area. The remains of only one of the two animals are left, These can be distinguished under the umbrella of the princely chariot. Although the animal is extremely mutilated – only the legs and the lower part of the belly having survived (plaquettes I-15 and I-16) –, there can be no doubt whatsoever with respect to its identity. If we start with the hypothesis that the frieze reproduces a miniaturised version of the same motifs which are to be found in the central scene, a hypothesis which is corroborated by the

---

333 The horns of antelopes are hard and without any ramifications. These animals belong to a genre which also includes gazelles whose horns are spiral in shape.

334 E. Trouessart, in *La grande encyclopédie, inventaire raisonné des sciences, des lettres et des arts*, Paris [1886-1902, 31 vol.], s.v. "Cerf". S. Frechkop, R. Lavocat, "Sous-ordre des Sélénodontes ou Ruminants", in *Traité de zoologie*, dir. P.-P. Grassé, t. 17, fasc. 1, Paris, 1955, pp. 609-614.

335 *Traité de zoologie (op.cit.)*, p. 610 : *axis* called *chital* or *chitra* in India, *spotted-deer* in English. The other sub-genres of stags are further removed from the animals on the plaquette ; a type of *rucervus*, the stag of Duvancel (*cervus Duvancelii*), is found in India (Assam and Bhutan). It is bright red in colour and has antlers with two twists, curving backwards and with the ends spreading out in the shape of a palm with several tips. The sub-type *rusa* comprises about ten types with a heavier form and shorter legs. Their antlers are analogous in form with those of our cervidae, but thicker. We also find the stag of Aristotle (*cervus Aristotelis*), dark brown in colour and the hippelaph stag (*cervus equinus*).

pinnacled edifices, the peacocks in pairs and the human personages, it would be legitimate to consider the deer represented in the centre of the plaque as an analogue of the animal represented in the frieze. At first sight this animal does not appear to be a deer. In fact, the flexion of its legs, the form of its hoofs and the curve of its belly do not allow it to be distinguished from the horses in the same scene (particularly from the horse V-23), and it is likely that it was designed with the help of the same pattern. However, the fact that it has no mount and that it is placed in the precincts of the hermitage, at a distance from the group of cavaliers and the quadriga, amidst other wild animals is a strong argument in favour of its identification as a deer. In addition the rump is shorter and more flattened at the back than in the case of the horses. The tail, which is shorter and descends vertically without undulations, is also different. Finally, it is not improbable that the two fragments of an orange inlay of molten glass sprinkled with small, alternately maroon and white pastilles encircled with gold wire which we have recovered, belong to the spotted skin of this animal or, what amounts to the same, to its partner whom we situate just above him (fig. 33.35). The orange colour of this plaquette distinguishes it both from the brown base of the coat of the deer in the frieze and the brown or white background of the roofs of the pinnacled edifices.

The representation of the peacocks in pairs in the frieze and the central area justifies the hypothesis of a similar arrangement of the deer. The pair of deer in the middle of the central area thus corresponded to the pair of deer in the frieze. There is in fact place for a second deer above the one mentioned, in the space which is below the edifice with seven pinnacles IV-4 and the group of three female spectators in the balcony II-8 to 10. The presence of a pair of deer in the very centre of the composition adds weight to the hypothesis that the subject of the plaque was inspired by the legend of Śakuntalā for, even if it is true that at the beginning of the drama of Kālidāsa, there is only a single animal being hunted by Duṣyanta, later, in another passage of the same work (VI, 17 and above on p. 58, n. 213), the portrait which the king paints represents the heroine in a landscape in which there are two gazelles : "I wish to draw, underneath a tree that bears some bark-garments suspended from its boughs, a doe that rubs her left eye on the horn of a black antelope".

Deer, naturally associated to gazelles and antelopes by a close physical resemblance[336], constitute, along with peacocks, the preferred animals in hermitages, forests and gardens in India[337]. It is therefore not surprising that they occupy an important place in Indian iconography in which they are not simply limited to being decorative elements but often appear as principal actors in scenes which their presence helps to identify. It is thus in the third Great Miracle or the First

---

336 M. Stutley, *The illustrated dictionary*, s.v. "Antelope, black" : *Kṛṣṇamṛga* ; "Deer" ; "Gazelle" : *Hariṇa, Mṛga.*

337 B.S. Upadhyaya, *India in Kālidāsa*, pp. 335-336.

Sermon[338], in the Birth of the deer[339] or antelope[340], in the sacrifice of the hermit Śyāma[341], in *Migapotaka-jātaka*[342], and in other scenes in which religious imagery is adapted to the representation of lay-scenes of hunting or domestic life[343].

---

338 Sanchi I : *Sāñchī*, pl. 18a/1 (southern toraṇa) : does and deer (or antelopes?) symbolising the garden of gazelles (*Mṛgadāva*) in Benares; pl. 55/2 (western toraṇa). Sanchi II : pl. 74/5a.

339 Bharhut : A.K. Coomaraswamy, *Bharhut*, fig. 73, p. 72 = A. Cunningham, *Bharhut*, pl. XXV, 1 : Reincarnated in the form of a deer, the Bodhisattva saves a man from drowning but this man betrays him and the deer is pursued by the king of Benares ; the deer then obtains security for himself and for the other animals ; the same deer, whose antlers resemble the antlers of the deer in the plaquette of Ai Khanum, appears atleast twice in the same painting which illustrates the *Ruru-jātaka* ; on this see E.B. Cowell, *The Jātaka*, 4, n°482.

340 Bharhut : A.K. Coomaraswamy, *Bharhut*, fig. 74 and pp. 72-73 = A. Cunningham, *Bharhut*, pl. XXVII, 9 and pp. 67-68 : landscape with animals in the context of the *Kuruṅga-miga-jātaka*, in which the Bodhisattva, reincarnated as an Antelope (*Ṛṣya-śṛṅga*, or Son of the Antelope, *Isi-siṅga* in pāli), is trapped by a hunter and liberated by a tortoise : E.B. Cowell, *The Jātaka*, 2, n°206. Begram : A. Foucher, "Deux Jātaka sur ivoires", p. 85 and fig. 97, b : reclining deer in an *āśrama* ; the representation of the animal, though discreet is not intended as a decorative motif ; it probably refers to the same *jātaka* to the one about the love of the Unicorn (*Ekaśṛṅga*) or the Horn of an antelope (*Isi-siṅga*) and princess Nālinī. Sanchi I : *Sāñchī*, p. 225, pl. 27/1 (northern toraṇa) : same type of scene in a hermitage with a seated brahmin. Gandhāra : A. Foucher, "Représentations de Jâtaka dans l'art bouddhique", in *Mémoires concernant l'Asie orientale*, Paris, 1919, III, pp. 1-52, particularly pp. 20-23 and pl. IV, 3 : same scene representing a paysage with antelopes ; pl. II, 3 : Bharhut ; II, 4 : Sanchi.

341 Sanchi I : *Sāñchī*, p. 225, pl. 65a/1 (western toraṇa) : illustration of *Śyāma-jātaka* (E.B. Cowell, *The Jātaka*, 6, n° 540), theme of the filial devotion of the young hermit Śyāma, struck with an arrow by the King in the pond where he bathes. The scene has all the features of a hermitage : huts, trees, beasts.

342 Bharhut : A.K. Coomaraswamy, *Bharhut*, fig. 157, p. 87 = A. Cunningham, *Bharhut*, pl. XLIII, 8 (but Cunningham, p. 101, gives a different interpretation). In this *jātaka* illustrated by the relief (E.B. Cowell, *The Jātaka*, 3, n°372) the Bodhisattva, reincarnated in human form as Sakka, descends from the sky and sermonises to a hermit who is lamenting the death of his doe : it is of no consequence that instead of a doe, the artist has represented an antelope.

343 Bharhut : A. Cunningham, *Bharhut*, pl. XXXVI, 3 : demi-medaillon presenting two deer back to back. Coomaraswamy, *Bharhut*, fig. 207, p. 92 = A. Cunningham, *Bharhut*, pl. XLIV, 8, p. 102 : scene in a foliage with a *rukkha-cetiya* and six spotted deer, three male and three female ; the coat is sprinkled with small dots arranged in parallel lines like those of the deer in the plaquette of Ai Khanum. A.K. Coomaraswamy, fig. 151 = A. Cunningham, pl. XLIII, 2 and p. 75 : antelope in the Birth of the deer-hermit (*Isi-Miga-jātaka*). A.K. Coomaraswamy, fig. 153 = A. Cunningham, pl. XLIII, 4 : antelopes, deers and lions. Sanchi II : *Sāñchī*, pl. 80/31b : demi-medaillons with two leaping antelopes represented back to back under a fig tree ; pl. 82/40b : two antelopes squatting back to back under a fig tree. Sanchi I : *Sāñchī*, pl. 12/6 and 13/6 (southern toraṇa) : two mounted stage shown back to back with reins but without the harness of the head, which brings them closer to our reconstitution of the harnessed horse of the plaquette of Ai Khanum ; pl. 66b (western toraṇa) : supernatural animals made with the antlers of deer ; pl. 46/2 (eastern toraṇa) : *Aśvattha* of Śākyamuni surrounded with animals among whom there are antelopes recognisable by their slender horns ; pl. 47/2, 48/2 (eastern toraṇa) ; pl. 52a/2 : hermitage in the context of the miraculous victory over the *Nāga* with, among other animals, two antelopes. Mathurā : Ph. Vogel, *La sculpture de Mathurâ*, pl. LXa : frieze representing three unidentified *jātaka* scenes of which one has two antelopes running between two huts. Hunting scenes at Begram : J. Hackin *et alii*, *Nouvelles recherches*, fig. 117, 183 and 186.

*d- Other quadrupeds*

In the zone to the right of the central area, on the right edge of the plaquette I-11, the head and the hind legs of a quadruped are represented which do not seem to have a counterpart in what remains of the decor of the circular frieze. On the upper left edge of the plaquette I-12, the ends of the hind legs are represented in the form of two minuscule notches. The animal was shown running or leaping, with the legs stretched out above the column on the right IV-8 but unrelated to it. The dimensions of its head and the extension of its legs precludes the possibility of its being part of a capital with protoma. It should be noted that, of all the quadrupeds which are preserved, this is the only one to have been represented with the body stretched out in movement. This representation was perhaps dictated by the lack of space between the capital of the column and the group of spectators in the balcony.

### 3) Buildings and objects.

*a- Palace* Fig. 31.19, 35

The natural backdrop of vegetation and flowers in which animals and human beings live side by side also comprises, both in the frieze and the central area, of a certain number of buildings, some wide open (*b, c, d*) and others enclosed (a) with a typical Indian arched roof crowned with pinnacles. Among the last mentioned, the most important one is situated in the upper left side of the central area (plaquettes I-2 and I-3). A large brown plaquette inlaid with black and orange dots encircled with gold wire (I-2 = VII-13/14) represents the profile of the roof over the left wing of the building[344]. It definitely had its counterpart on the right, the two wings framing the main building in the centre which was represented frontally. Details regarding the facade of the building, whose foundation was, no doubt, situated at the same level as the human figure II-7, and to which probably the fragment of the shell I-6 is related, remain unknown. The summit of the roof of these three buildings was decorated with moulded pinnacles which should be visualized in terracotta identical to specimens contemporary with our plaque which the excavation has brought to light[345]. One of these pinnacles can be seen in the lower right corner of the plaquette of the shell I-2 ; it was located on the extreme left of the left wing which the glass plaquette VII-13/14 has helped us to reconstitute. Three other pinnacles belonging to the right wing have been reconstituted with the lower part of the shell plaquette I-3. Following the logic of symmetry we have reconstituted the same number of pinnacles for the left wing.

---

344 The right edge of this glass plaquette which is preserved marked the joint of this left wing with another part of the building. The proof is furnished by the curve in the adjacent row of small inlaid intended pastilles to fit into the curve traced by it ; if the roof had been prolonged towards the right without any break, the alignment of the small pastilles would have remained rectilinear, like the others more to the left, encroaching on the contiguous plaquette.

345 For real specimens see H. Härtel, "Some results of the excavations at Sonkh. A preliminary report", *German scholars in India*, New Delhi, 1976, 2, pp. 69-99, particularly fig. 6. Temple 18 of Sanchi : *Sāñchī*, p. 55, pl. 111d : specimens dating from the Mauryan period. These pinnacles must have certainly coincided initially with the supporting pillars of the roof : see E.B. Havell, *The ancient and medieval architecture of India*, London, 1915, pl. II.

The circular frieze also contained edifices with pinnacles, probably four in number, situated at cardinal points. They provide a miniaturised and unicellular version of the preceding edifices[346]. The two which were situated in the lower and the middle section of the right side of the frieze (IV-2 and IV-1) have partially retained their glass inlay decoration. Of the third, situated on the left below the human figure II-4, only the base of the facade has survived. No trace whatsoever remains of the fourth which was placed in the upper part of the frieze. The building IV-1 on the right, which is the most complete among them, presents a three-quarter view from the left. Its arched roof with three pinnacles on top was coloured with whitish pink molten glass sprinkled with orange dots. The position of the roof of the building at the bottom IV-2 indicates that it is oriented three-quarters to the right in the direction of the two human figures seated on its side. The colour of its roof is brown with white and orange dots.

We have very little information about the roofs of buildings in ancient India. The documents show the huts of hermits covered with foliage and stūpas with domes decorated with plant motifs[347]. The only real parallel available of the decorative covering of the roofs of our buildings is in a relief of Stūpa I of Sanchi which represents a building with a plan similar to the plan of the building in the central area of our plaque and an arched roof decorated in a similar manner with a sprinkling of small engraved circles[348]. The parallel is all the more significant because this relief, according to an inscription of the first century B.C., was offered and perhaps sculpted by the guild of ivory workers of Vidiśā, capital of the region in which Sanchi is situated. Such a decoration is only possible on a facing of ceramic tiles. Tiles have in fact been discovered in various Indian sites[349]. The oldest, from the excavation at Sonkh[350], go back to the Śuṅga period and are thus, more or less, contemporary to our plaque. Some specimens are decorated exactly in the same manner with hollow circular motifs, although this is not the most common form of decoration[351].

The pediment of our edifices is arched with no trace of the decoration which might have been there[352]. The building on the right side of the frieze has retained all the decoration of the facade

---

346 For monocellular edifices with pinnacles see the punch-marked coins : J. Allan, *BMC. Ancient India*, pp. xxxv and 302.

347 A.K. Coomaraswamy, *Bharhut*, fig. 24 upper and 65 = A. Cunningham, *Bharhut*, pl. XIII, 2 and XXXI, 1. For huts see also J. Auboyer, J.-Fr. Enault, *La vie publique et privée dans l'Inde ancienne. L'architecture civile et religieuse*, Paris, 1969, pp. 49-50. For roofs : pp. 30-31.

348 *Sāñchī*, pl. 18b/3 lower (southern toraṇa) = J.M. Rosenfield, *The dynastic arts*, fig. 155 : scene representing the thirty three gods (*Trayastriṃśa*). The text of the inscription reads "Sculpture made by the ivory workers of Vidiśā" (*Sāñchī*, inscription n° 400, p. 342). It is possible that the execution was left to stone sculptors – the style is not different from that of the other reliefs –, but it is logical to think that it was the ivory workers who conceived atleast the sketch of the scene.

349 O. Nalesini in G. Verardi *et alii*, *Harigaon Satya Nārāyaṇa, Kathmandu*, Rome, 1988, pp. 72-75, with bibliography.

350 H. Härtel, "Some results of the excavations at Sonkh", p. 74, fig. 6.

351 H. Härtel, "Some results of the excavations at Sonkh", fig. 6 left and right.

352 We are hesitant to attribute the fragments of a small, black, semi-circular inlay (fig. 33, 39 and 40 and fig. 35) decorated with a red star shaped motif reminiscent of the pediments with radiating beams found in certain rupestrian *vihāra* to a type of pediment which, in sculpture, has the form of iron niches straddling it (*kūḍu*) (J.A.S. Burgess, *Report on the Buddhist cave temples*, p. 7, n° 7 : Bhaja ; pl. opposite p. 49 : Nasik ; pl. IX : Bedsa ; etc.). The star of this inlay might also represent the flames of a hearth, a motif that is quite common in

below the pediment (IV-1, fig. 33.19). The doorway is richly framed with elements in molten glass which cover the entire facade. We can distinguish, from inside to outside : a) the frame of the door consisting of two uprights and a lintel slightly curved downwards in orange molten glass ; b) a brown band c) a white frame which is curved at the top in the form of a pendant in which a semi-circular disc constituting a floral motif with round orange petals on a brown background (type VII-50) is lodged. These different panels should be visualised as in rock architecture, varying in depth. It should be noted that evidence of lintels curved in pendants, though relatively rare is, nevertheless, definitely available in archaic architecture in India[353] and apparently also in Thailand as seen in the representation of a door on one of the vases of Ban Don Ta Phet (fig. 40)[354]. One wonders whether there is any relationship between the "sagging lintels" known from figurative documents in bronze age architecture of Southern and South-Eastern Iran and the zones in contact with India[355].The edifices with barrel vaulted roofs or fully-arched vaults with pinnacles on top and slightly extending beyond the walls belong to early antiquity in India and Iran have no doubt originated in civil and religious buildings in wood[356]. The plan and the general appearance of these

representations of hermitages (Ph. Stern, M. Bénisti, *Evolution du style indien d'Amarāvatī,* Paris, 1961, pp. 46-48) or the design of a shield carried by the cavaliers of the royal procession.

353 Sanchi I : *Sāñchī*, pl. 34a/2 (northern toraṇa) : two pinnacled edifices with a central door which is very close in appearance to the upper right edifice of the plaquette of Ai Khanum and a hut (scene of the gift of the *Jetavana*). Bharhut : A.K. Coomaraswamy, *Bharhut*, fig. 221 = A. Cunningham, *Bharhut*, pl. XLV, 7 : door. See also A.K. Coomaraswamy, fig. 36, 81, 196, 182, 221 = A. Cunningham, pl. XIX ; XXX, 4 ; XLI, 5 ; XLII, 7 ; XLV, 7 : openings on the curves of four sides. Bodh-Gaya : A. Cunningham, *Mahabodhi*, pl. 8, 8. Mathurā : J. Ph. Vogel, *La sculpture de Mathurâ*, pl. VIIIc. Gandhāra : H. Ingholt, *Gandhāran art*, fig. 15, 33, 76, etc.

354 I.C. Glover, *Early trade between India and Southeast Asia*, 1989, fig. 26. I.C. Glover is of the opinion that the edifices represented on these bronzes could be the wooden houses of the local type or granaries for rice.

355 P. Baudot, "'Steatite' Vessels in the third Millennium in the ancient Orient", in *India and the ancient world*, 1987, pp. 1-32, pl. I-IV ; P. de Miroschedji, "Vases et objets en stéatite susiens du Musée du Louvre", *Cahiers de la DAFI*, 3, 1973, pp. 9-79, particularly pp. 15-19 ; L. Al-Ghailani, "'Steatite' stone vessels from Mesopotamia and elsewhere", *Sumer*, 31, 1975, pp. 41-48 ; P. Amiet, *L'âge des échanges inter-iraniens 3500-1700 avant J.-C.*, Paris, 1986, fig. 64, 70, 96, 125 ; A. Hakemi, in *South Asian Archaeology 1987*, Rome, 1990, pp. 459-473. According to P. de Miroschedji, the curve of the lintel was due to the weight of the unbaked bricks which made the wood sag as opposed to the hypothesis of an architecture of reeds proposed by P. Delougaz, "Architectural reproductions on steatite vases", *Iraq*, 24, 1962, pp. 90-95. Regarding the Indian domain, F.A. Durrani, "Stone vases as evidence of connection between Mesopotamia and the Indus Valley", *Ancient Pakistan*, 1, 1964, pp. 51-96, challenges the evidence of the finds of Mohenjo-daro (3rd millenium B.C.) because he considers that the specimens discovered at this site were imported from Baluchistan. The revival of this curious architectural detail in north-western India in the middle of the historical period makes one wonder whether, even if is admitted that the stone vases of Mohenjo-daro were imported from outside, the "sagging lintel" was not known to this region from the beginning of the bronze age.

356 S.P. Gupta, *The roots of Indian art*, pp. 257-263 and pl. 105a : foundations of the temple of Yasudeva at Vidiśā with an ellipsoidal plan with the porch placed on one of the longer sides. *Sāñchī*, pl. 2 : edifices with an apsidal form : first stage (Śuṅga) of the temple 18, pl. 111-112, pp. 52-56 and first stage (Maurya) of the temple 40, pl. 109-110, pp. 64-68. See also P. Brown, *Indian architecture (Buddhist and Hindu periods)*[2], Bombay, 1942, particularly pp. 6-38, pl. X 2, XII, XIII. : reconstitutions of temples. *Indian Archaeology 1958-59 – A Review*, New Delhi, 1959, p. 13, n° 9, fig. 6 : "Excavation at Rajgir, District Patna". *Indian Archaeology 1961-62 – A Review*, New Delhi, 1964, pp. 26-27, n° 42 and pl. XLVII B : "Exploration in District Thanjavur", Kilaiyur :

buildings are known mainly by monasteries and rock sanctuaries[357] like those of Ajanta[358], Bhaja[359], Bedsa[360], Guntupalli[361], Lomas Rishi[362], which are reproductions in rock of traditional open air architecture. But it must be stated that if there is anything which distinguishes figurative sculpture of religious buildings, from that of palatial building it is the character of the scenes for which they serve as a background[363]. The modest dimensions of the monocellular buildings of the frieze on the plaque of Ai Khanum correspond to the huts of anchorites typical in Indian religious art even if their rich decor contrasts with the simplicity which we expect in monastic abodes. The edifice in the central area distinguishes itself by a much more monumental appearance and a more complex plan with the central portion in relief and the elongated sides ending in rounded apses. It has a close resemblance with two edifices related to Vidiśā : the abode of the gods who figure on the relief of Stūpa I of Sanchi which was offered by the ivory workers of this town and the temple whose foundations have been discovered by excavators near the column of Heliodorus at Besnagar. In the context of the legend of Śakuntalā and the forest in which this construction is situated, it is tempting to see it as an idealised representation of the hermitage of the adoptive father of the heroine, raised to the dignity of prestigious architecture. In a similar fashion, Christian artists were led to paint and sculpt the Virgin and the Child against sumptuous backdrops which had nothing to do with the poor crèche of Bethlehem.

brick building from the beginning of the Christian era. Cf. also *Indian archaeology, new perspectives,* ed. R.K. Sharma, Delhi, 1982, pl. 25/8, 26/11. On figurative representations see J. Auboyer, J.-Fr. Enault, *L'architecture civile et religieuse*, pp. 30-31. For the relationship between the *vihāra* and the round hut see A. Foucher, *Art gréco-bouddhique du Gandhâra*, I, 1905, pp. 128-129. The barrel vaulted roofs corresponded to climatic requirements : E.B. Havell, *The ancient and medieval architecture of India*, London, 1915, pp. 21-22.

357 In general see J. Auboyer, J.-Fr. Enault, *L'architecture civile et religieuse*, pp. 10-13, and S. Nagaraju, *Buddhist architecture of Western India (c.250 B.C.-c.A.D. 300)*, Delhi, 1981.

358 S. Nagaraju, *Buddhist architecture*, pl. 11-12 : Cave 10, end of 3rd cent. B.C.

359 S. Nagaraju, *Buddhist architecture*, pl. 38-39 : Cave 12, end of 3rd-beginning of 2nd cent. B.C. ; V. Dehejia, *Early Buddhist rock temples (Studies in art and archaeology)*, London, 1972, fig. 8 ; B. Rowland, *The art and architecture*, pp. 68-69 (Sātavāhana period) ; A.K. Coomaraswamy, *History of Indian and Indonesian art*, pp. 24-28, 2nd century B.C.

360 S. Nagaraju, *Buddhist architecture*, pl. 23-27, Cave 7, beginning of 1st cent. B.C. ; C. Sivaramamurti, *L'art en Inde*, p. 472, approximately contemporary to Bhaja and Kondane.

361 V. Dehejia, *Early Buddhist rock temples*, fig. 4.

362 V. Dehejia, *Early Buddhist rock temples*, fig. 2 ; A.K. Coomaraswamy, *History of Indian and Indonesian art*, p. 18 (Maurya).

363 a) Sanchi I : *Sāñchī*, pl. 18b/1 (southern toraṇa) ; pl. 34a/2 (northern toraṇa) ; pl. 40/3 (eastern toraṇa) ; pl. 61/3 (western toraṇa). Palace : pl. 49a (eastern toraṇa). City : pl. 15/3 (southern toraṇa) ; pl. 35a/1, 35b/2 (northern toraṇa) ; pl. 50a/1, 51b, 52a (eastern toraṇa). b) Bharhut : A. Cunningham, *Bharhut*, pp. 122-124. A.K. Coomaraswamy, *Bharhut*, fig. 83, p. 75 = A. Cunningham, *Bharhut*, pl. XXV, 4 : palace in the upper part of the scene slanting on two columns (medaillon of the *Mūga-pakkha-jātaka* : the Bodhistattva as prince Temiya who refuses the throne of his father). A.K. Coomaraswamy, fig. 86 (on the *bodhi* : pp. 19-20) = A. Cunningham, XXXI, 3 : *Bodhi-gara*. On the plan of the *caityagṛha* see A.K. Coomaraswamy, p. 99. See also A.K. Coomaraswamy, fig. 27, 28, 32, 36, 66, 67, 69, 81, 87 = A. Cunningham, pl. XIII, 1 and 3 ; XVI, 1 ; XIX ; XXVI, 2 ; XXVIII, 3 ; XXX, 4 ; XXXI, 2 and 4.

### *b- Kiosk*

Too little survives of the kiosk in which the three female spectators were placed to permit the reconstitution of its appearance. The upright on the left must have had its counterpart on the right, the two serving to uphold the roof. The representation of the kiosk in the upper right section of the composition conforms to the traditional representation of procession scenes in which the artist included female spectators, often installing them in balconies[364].

### *c- Columns*

The four big, equidistant columns (IV-5 to IV-8) with representations of the animals of the forest in the intervening spaces constitute the dominant element in the middle section of the central area. These columns have a base in the form of a lotus vase (*loṭa*)[365] on a socle with two levels of the type utilised in the so-called Indo-Persian columns in India[366] and in Gandhāra where the most

---

364 Sanchi I : *Sāñchī*, pl. 12/2 and 15/3 (southern toraṇa). For types of palanquins see J. Auboyer, J.-Fr. Enault, *L'architecture civile et religieuse*, p. 43, pl. 35.

365 E.L. Burnouf, *Le vase sacré et ce qu'il contient dans l'Inde, la Perse, la Grèce et dans l'Eglise chrétienne*, Paris, 1896 ; Ph. Stern and J. Auboyer, in J. Hackin *et alii*, *Nouvelles recherches*, pp. 32-33 and 70-71. Begram : *ibidem*, fig. 530 and 533 ; Mathurā : *ibidem*, fig. 531 ; Amaravati : *ibidem*, fig. 532 and 534. Sanchi I : *Sāñchī*, pl. 16/4 (southern toraṇa) and pl. 30/3 (northern toraṇa) : scenes of the Nativity. The similarity between the form of the vase of Gundla and the vessels engraved on the frieze is also to be noted.

366 For columns see J. Auboyer, J.-Fr. Enault, *L'architecture civile et religieuse*, pp. 19-23, 34-35. Ambikā : V. Dehejia, *Early Buddhist rock temples*, fig. 61 (*caitya*). Bedsa : J.A.S. Burgess, *Report on the Buddhist cave temples*, pl. XI ; C. Sivaramamurti, *L'art en Inde*, p. 472 ; *idem*, *The art of India*, New York, 1977, fig. 794 ; S. Nagaraju, *Buddhist architecture*, pl. 23 (Cave 7 : beginning of the 1st cent. B.C.) ; A.K. Coomaraswamy, *History of Indian and Indonesian art*, fig. 32-33 (beginning of the 2nd cent. B.C.). Bhaja : S. Nagaraju, pl. 36 (Cave 12 : end of 3rd - beginning of 2nd cent. B.C., base of column). Bharhut : the columns have bulbous base in levels but they are extremely decorated and differ in their silhouettes : A.K. Coomaraswamy, *Bharhut*, p. 39, fig. 11 ; p. 59, fig. 38 and 66 with plinth at two levels, etc.) ; P. Brown, *Indian architecture*, pl. XIII, 3. Bima Shankar : V. Dehejia, fig. 57 (cavern). Bodh-Gaya : Ph. Stern, "Les ivoires et os découverts à Begram", fig. 601, 608 (p. 46 : style later than Sanchi I) ; N. Ray, *Maurya and Post-Maurya art*, pp. 112-113, fig. 35-36 (dating from the middle of the 1st cent. B.C). Ganesh Pahar (Junnar) : S. Nagaraju, pl. 71-72 (Cave 6 : beginning of the 2nd cent. A.D.). Jaggayapeta : J. Hackin *et alii*, *Nouvelles recherches*, fig. 581-582 ; Ph. Stern, *ibidem*, p. 45 (dated between Sanchi I and Mathurā) ; A.K. Coomaraswamy (1st-2nd cent. B.C.) ; B. Rowland, *The art and architecture*, p. 55 (same date as Sanchi II). Kandagiri : J. Auboyer, J. Fr. Enault, *L'architecture civile et religieuse*, 1, pl. 13, 1. Kanheri : S. Nagaraju, pl. 95-96 (Cave 3 : end of 2nd cent. B.C. - beginning of 2nd cent. A.D.). Karli : J.A.S. Burgess, pl. XIII, fig. 1 ; S. Nagaraju, pl. 129, 131 (Cave 8 : end of 1st cent. B.C.) ; C. Sivaramamurti, *L'art en Inde*, p. 482 (middle of the 1st cent. A.D.) ; A.K. Coomaraswamy, *History of Indian and Indonesian art*, fig. 34 (1st cent. B.C.). Kuda : V. Dehejia, fig. 72 (Cave 9) ; S. Nagaraju, pl. 157 (Cave 9 : 2nd cent. A.D.). Lenyadri : V. Dehejia, fig. 62, 64 (*caitya* 6). Manmodi (Junnar) : S. Nagaraju, pl. 65-66 (Caves 1-3, 26 : 1st - 2nd cent. A.D.). Mathurā : J. Ph. Vogel, *La sculpture de Mathurâ*, pl. VI, XVIIc, XXIId, Lb, LIVa ; A.K. Coomaraswamy, *History of Indian and Indonesian art*, fig. 71-72 (end of the 1st cent. B.C.). Nasik : V. Dehejia, fig. 47, (Cave 10), 48 (Cave 3), 49 (*caitya*) ; C. Sivaramamurti, *L'art en Inde,* p. 483 ; G. Combaz, *L'Inde et l'Orient classique*, pl. 12 ; A.K. Coomaraswamy, *History of Indian and Indonesian art*, fig. 31 (middle of the 1st cent. B.C.) ; B. Rowland, *The art and architecture* (1st cent. B.C.) ; S. Nagaraju, pl. 181, 184, 185, 190, 193, 197 (Caves 4, 10, 17, 18, 20 : 2nd cent. A.D.). Sanchi I : The following elements are not combined in Sanchi in any column : a plinth in levels, a

common type is of Western origin possessing the base of a Corinthian column with two torus and scotia[367].

The height of these pillars, excluding the crown, is given by the bases of IV-5, IV-7 and IV-9 and by the notch carved in the upper right edge of plaquette I-10 which indicates the lower edge of the crown of the column IV-6. A simple capital, preferably in the shape of an inverted bell, may be proposed for the reconstitution of the top of the column, as it is the habitual form in this region. The presence of the leaping quadruped in the area just above the column on the right precludes the possibility of this bell shaped capital being topped with other elements like the tablets with animals leaning on their backs for the columns under the architrave[368] or various other symbolic representations in the form of round protuberances (wheel, animal) for the columns which are free[369]. It also excludes the possibility of the columns with their crowns rising up to the height of the buildings (kiosk and hermitage) represented in the upper section of the central area. The row of columns is thus not linked to these buildings. It does not also appear that they were linked to each other by an architrave. What then is the function of this row of isolated columns grouped together ? It should be remarked at the outset that there is absolutely nothing of a similar nature in Indian architecture. Inspite of the absence of any parallel, it is possible to imagine that this row of columns marks the entry to a sacred area, in this case the forest and the hermitage[370] though another interpretation related to the preceding is also possible. On a reliquary from Gandhāra, the stūpa is flanked by four columns, each bearing an animal, which are supposed to delimit the sacred precinct at the four cardinal points[371]. It is possible that the columns in the plaque of Ai Khanum

bulbous base and a capital : *Sāñchī*, pl. 18a/1 (southern toraṇa) : only column with a wheel instead of protomas of animals, capital with base in four levels ; pl. 51a (eastern toraṇa) : column with bulbous base without levels ; pl. 22, 3 (northern toraṇa) and 49 (eastern toraṇa) : column without base. Sivaneri (Junnar) : S. Nagaraju, pl. 82, 85 (Caves 2, 43 : end of 3rd cent. A.D.).

367 H. Ingholt, *Gandhāran art*, fig. 10 (relief combining the two styles), 39, etc. ; J. Marshall, *Taxila*, pl. 215, n° 37.

368 *Sāñchī*, pl. 51a, etc. See also the capitals of the Aśokan pillars of Sanchi and Sarnath, pl. 107. J.A.S. Burgess, *Report on the Buddhist cave temples*, pl. XVIII, 2 : leaping lions. J. Hackin *et alii*, *Nouvelles recherches*, fig. 601, 608 ; A.K. Coomaraswamy, *Bodhgayā*, pp. 17-18, pl. XVII ; XVIII ; XXVI ; XXXIII ; LIII, 1 ; LIV ; LV : columns on vase and plinth in levels. A. Cunningham, *Bharhut*, pl. VIII ; same column but without the animals : A.K. Coomaraswamy, *Bharhut*, fig. 66 = A. Cunningham, *Bharhut*, pl. IX and XXXI, 2 : octagonal column with an bulbous base in three level and bell shaped capital crowned with animals represented back to back ; A.K. Coomaraswamy, fig. 23-25, 30-31, 34-36, 87 = A. Cunningham, pl. XIV-XIX ; XXXI, 4 : columns without base.

369 On the Aśokan columns, for example, see n. 370 below.

370 Compare the isolated columns standing at the entry of Indian sanctuaries as in Bharhut : A.K. Coomaraswamy, *Bharhut*, fig. 23, 27, 86 = A. Cunningham, *Bharhut*, pp. 121-122, pl. XIII ; XXX, 3 ; XXXI, 3 : isolated pillars with bell-shaped capital crowned with an elephant, and Karli : S. Nagaraju, *Buddhist architecture*, fig. 45 and pl. 128 : Cave 8 : column with four lions on the capital at the entry of one of the grottos, 1st cent. B.C., as well as the pillars erected by Aśoka whose symbolic importance was brought to the fore by the study of J. Irwin : "'Asokan' pillars : The mystery of foundation and collapse", in *India and the ancient world*, 1987, pp. 87-93 ; cf. also the interpretation of A. Ghosh, "The pillars of Aśoka, their purpose", *EW*, 17, 1967, pp. 273-275.

371 M. Taddei, "Neue Forschungbelege zur Gandhāra-Ikonographie", in *Aus dem Osten des Alexanderreiches*, 1984, pp. 154-175, particularly p. 164, fig. 14. It may also be mentioned that isolated columns stood near the three

served a similar purpose of demarcating the boundary around the sacred precincts of the park and the hermitage even though they were represented at the same level because of certain artistic compulsions.

*d- Diverse*

Various decorative motifs figured in the space between the first two columns, whose near total disparition renders the interpretation of the few that remain extremely difficult. Between the bird with a long tail near the column on the left and the column on the right, it is possible to distinguish the upper right corner, seen from a bird's-eye view (plaquette I-10, fig. 36), of an object or of a construction which is in the form of a horizontal surface resting on four slender supports which have a bulge towards the upper part suggestive of moulding. The horizontal surface had an inlaid decoration consisting of a wide border with circular motifs in the centre. The idea that this was a covered passage which marked the entry to the park where the hermit lived is not acceptable because, in Indian iconography, entries were usually presented in the form of toraṇa. Instead, the hypothesis that it was a dais or canopy installed in the park or that it was a piece of low furniture, table or conch is proposed[372].

Under the tree with three branches, located at the top of the composition, a quadrangular motif can be perceived in the upper left corner. Its proximity to the tree suggests some kind of a relation between the two motifs. We are tempted to associate it with a motif common since the Mauryan period of a throne under the sacred tree[373] but we have no supportive evidence to establish it as such.

Apart from the small buildings with three pinnacles, the frieze comprised of another architectural motif at the bottom of the composition. This is an element in parallelepiped form which is a simplified representation of a pond seen in perspective (fig. 33.21-22). The sea-green inlay of molten glass which is still there was itself inlaid with several small, round brownish orange dots and two minuscule serpentine motifs. These last mentioned consist of a spear-like head with two small white dots outlined with gold wire and an extension at the back in the form of a

toraṇa of Stūpa I of Sanchi : A. Cunningham, *The Bhilsa Topes ; or, Buddhist monuments of Central India*, repr. Varanasi, 1966, pl. VIII. On the symbolism of the precincts and the gates at the four cardinal points see also E.B. Havell, *The ancient and medieval architecture of India*, London, 1915, p. 9 sqq., 28, 57-58. See also J. Auboyer, J.-Fr. Enault, *L'architecture civile et religieuse*, pp. 6-7.

372 For kiosks or pavilions with slender pillars and flat roofs seen in Indian court painting from Ajanta to the Moghul period see E.B. Havell, *ibidem*, pl. IV, B. See also J. Auboyer, J.-Fr. Enault, *L'architecture civile et religieuse*, p. 43, pl. 35. On the identification of some of these pavilions as theatre halls see Ph. Stern, "Aspects plastiques de l'ancien théâtre indien", p. 54. It must be mentioned however, that the figurative documents of the ancient period do not present similar examples with the exception of a relief representing a small boat : Sanchi I : *Sāñchī*, pl. 65a/3 (western toraṇa) : river in which a small boat in the shape of a winged griffin with an entertainer aboard navigates, probably while the relics of the Buddha were being carried across. A more complete version of the design published by F.C. Maisey, *Sanchi and its remains*, London, 1892, pl. 21, fig. 2.

373 See below p. 98 and 100.

long, undulating tail made also of gold wire. The motif is evocative of lotuses[374] or serpents[375] in a pond.

#### 4) Floral decor.

Apart from their decorative value, the different floral motifs, trees, flowering stems and flowers which fill all the spaces are there to create an impression of the countryside in which the scene is set[376]. In the central area the most common floral motif consists of polychrome inlays, either isolated in small round alveoles or grouped in twos, threes or fours in bigger, more unevenly shaped alveoles (fig. 34.14). The other floral motifs are more complex, like the four petalled flowers or short stems which are seen in a more or less stylised form in friezes or decorative bands at Bharhut[377], Sanchi, Amaravati, Jaggayapeta, Begram[378].

Inspite of the profusion of decorative elements in Indian art, the use of floral motifs as fillers in the depiction of a scene is relatively rare : the bronze vases of Gundla (fig. 39) and Thailand (fig. 40-45) or the section to the left of the fresco in grotto X of Ajanta[379] may be mentioned here. In fact, plant motifs other than trees are rarely utilised as a decor in compositions, except for the lotus, the flower par excellence. At Sanchi, for example, plant and animal motifs are dominant only in the decoration of the balustrade of Stūpa II, the oldest, whereas the representation of the story prevails clearly in Stūpa I. The same can be observed at Bharhut[380], Bodh-Gaya[381], Mathurā[382].

The most complete plant motif in the plaque of Ai Khanum namely, the branch with round flowers is found in all the three areas of the plaque, the central area, the circular frieze and the border. It is usually represented as an isolated branch in a curved or undulating shape bearing about

---

374 As, for example, at Sanchi I : *Sāñchī*, pl. 65a/1 (western toraṇa) ; Bodhgaya : A.K. Coomaraswamy, *Bodhgayā*, pl. XLVIII. On the lotus : E.H. Schafer, *The golden peaches of Samarcand*, pp. 127-131.

375 J. Allan, *BMC. Ancient India*, pp. lxxxi, clvii, 120, 282 and 307 ; P.L. Gupta, *The Amaravati hoard of silver punch-marked coins*, Hyderabad, 1963, pl. III, 245. For the motif on Indian coins : P. Bernard, *BEFEO*, 68, 1980, p. 34, n. 1-3. On the *nāgas* see also Sanchi I : *Sāñchī*, pl. 52a/2 (eastern toraṇa).

376 These isolated round flowers are quite widespread. See, for example, circular pastilles on the bronze vase of Gundla ; the rosettes on a terracotta plaque from Kauśāmbī : S.C. Kala, *Terracotta figurines from Kauśāmbī*, pl. XXX and XXXIA representing the escape of Udayana and Vāsavadatta from the territories of Avantī on an elephant ; the floral motifs on punch-marked coins : J. Marshall, *Taxila*, pl. 232, n°47b, etc.

377 A.K. Coomaraswamy, *Bharhut*, fig. 10 = A. Cunningham, *Bharhut*, pl. X.

378 Ph. Stern and J. Auboyer, in J. Hackin *et alii*, *Nouvelles recherches*, pp. 36-37, 76 ; Begram : fig. 8, 9, 25, 60-90, 113, 114, 117-151, 157, 220, 222, 225, 232 etc. See also the same type of decoration on a band on the upper part of the shell handle of a mirror : *Dawn of civilization in Maharashtra*, fig. 61 (above n. 195).

379 J.A.S. Burgess, *Report on the Buddhist cave temples*, pl. XVI : group of elephants in a landscape of trees and lotuses with a scene of palatial life juxtaposed on the right.

380 See, for example, the rare lotuses inserted in the scenes on the lintels of the stūpa : A.K. Coomaraswamy, *Bharhut*, fig. 5 = A. Cunningham, *Bharhut*, pl. VIII, or on the pillars : pl. XIII. Medaillons : A.K. Coomaraswamy, fig. 1, 2, etc. = A. Cunningham, pl. XI, XII, etc.

381 A.K. Coomaraswamy, *Bodhgayā*, pl. IV, etc.

382 J. Ph. Vogel, *La sculpture de Mathurā*, pl. XIIIa.

a dozen round red flowers but without any leaves[383]. The floral motif at the top of the central area in which three such branches are grouped together should probably be interpreted as a tree. Even though it is not possible to indicate the exact species[384], given the conventional character of the representation, which uses the same motif for plants which are clearly dissimilar, one does not miss being struck by its resemblance to a frequent image in Indian art of the sacred tree rising above a throne[385]. Familiar to the artist, this image unconsciously imposed itself on him. The semi-cylindrical border of the plaque is decorated with foliage whose undulating stalk breaks into flowering branches with small round balls as described above (fig. 30.1). Foliage, associated with different plants or with small scenes constitutes, with the garland one of the favourite decorative motifs of Indian art[386].

The motif with two symmetrical coils found at the bottom of the frieze above the pond is definitely a floral motif. It occurs in a more complete form on the annulet of sacred stones from the Mauryan period[387]. It is difficult to identify it exactly. Perhaps it is a lotus with petals opened out

---

383 We find an analogous stylisation of trees in certain representations on punch-marked coins : J. Marshall, *Taxila*, pl. 230, n° 39.

384 The only trees which come to mind on the basis of the representation of trees on monuments are the pipal, the fig tree, the banian tree, the Aśoka tree, the mango tree and the bignonia tree : *Sâñchi*, p. 200. For pipal (*aśvattha : Ficus religiosa*, tree of Śākyamuni and also in the very ancient pre-Buddhist cults) see Sanchi I : *Sâñchi*, pl. 18b/1 (southern toraṇa) ; pl. 40/3, 46/2, 51a (eastern toraṇa) ; pl. 58/4, 61/3 (western toraṇa) ; *aśvattha* on the throne : 65b/1 (western toraṇa). For the banian (*nyagrodha : Ficus Indica*, tree of Kāśyapa) see Sanchi I : *Sâñchi*, pl. 15/2 (southern toraṇa) ; pl. 50a/1 (eastern toraṇa) ; pl. 58/2 (western toraṇa). For the tree with leafy stems attached to a trunk (*udumbara : Ficus glomerata*, tree of Kanakamuni) see pl. 58/1 (western toraṇa). For the mango tree (*Āmra? : Mangifera Indica* Linn. or *Puṇḍarīka*, a type of mango tree belonging to an unknown species, tree of Śikhin) : J. Hackin *et alii*, *Nouvelles recherches*, fig. 22-23, (=660-661) : see also fig. 199, 200, 233. For the bignonia (*pāṭalī : Bignonia suaveolens*, tree in which the flowers and the leaves are intermixed, tree of Vipāśin) : see Sanchi I : *Sâñchi*, pl. 12/4 ; 24/1 (southern toraṇa) ; A.K. Coomaraswamy, *Bharhut*, fig. 48, 56 = A. Cunningham, *Bharhut*, pl. XXIII, 3 ; XXIX, 1, pp. 46-47, "trumpet jasmine". On the cults see O. Viennot, *Le culte de l'arbre dans l'Inde ancienne (Annales du Musée Guimet, 59)*, Paris, 1954, particularly pp. 120-125 ; B.N. Sinha, *Tree worship in ancient India (Worship in India Series, 1)*, New Delhi, 1979.

385 On thrones under trees see p. 96.

386 Sanchi I : *Sāñchī*, p. 231, pl. 11/3 and 19a and b (southern toraṇa) : scenes inserted in the spirals of foliage formed by an undulating stem of the lotus ; pl. 37 (northern toraṇa) and pl. 50b and c (eastern toraṇa) : foliage and flowers of lotus ; Sanchi II : pl. 78/22a and 23a : foliage of lotus framing a panel of Māyā ; Sanchi III, pl. 96, 1 ; 100, 3 (toraṇa) : foliage with undulations occupied by grotesque images. Cf. M. Hallade, *Arts de l'Asie ancienne, I*, pp. 74-75 : n° 177. Bharhut : A.K. Coomaraswamy, *Bharhut*, fig. 127-251 = A. Cunningham, *Bharhut*, pl. XXXIX-XLVIII. Mathurā : J. Ph. Vogel, *La sculpture de Mathurâ*, pl. xxx. Bégram : Ph. Stern and O. Kurz, in J. Hackin *et alii*, *Nouvelles recherches*, pp. 33-35 and 55-57, fig. 180 to 182, 211, 218, 219, 233, etc. ; O. Kurz, "Le rinceau d'acanthe de la plaque d'ivoire n° 329", pp. 55-57. Amaravati : *ibidem*, pl. 540-544, 551. Gandhāra : B. Rowland, "The vine-scroll in Gandhara", *Artibus Asiae*, 19, 1956, pp. 353-361. Cf. M. Hallade, *Arts de l'Asie ancienne, I*, pp. 74-75, pl. XVI.178. On the origin of garlands and on foliages see Ph. Stern, M. Bénisti, *Evolution du style*, pp. 26-33.

387 S.P. Gupta, *The roots of Indian art*, pp. 53-77, pl. 17a ; 18a.

or a simplified representation of the decorative motif in the shape of a palm leaf or the *śrīvatsa*[388] (shield), a well known motif in Indian art.

## *D) CONCLUSION*

The lacunae that remain in our reconstitution only add to the problems posed by this object. These problems are too numerous and too complex and it would be pretentious to claim that we have resolved them all here. The importance of this object for the history of Central Asia and India is, however, evident. Although it probably originated in a workshop in North India, our present knowledge of early Indian art and the extent of Greek conquest in this region does not help us either in locating its origin exactly nor in explaining the events which brought it to Ai Khanum. The site at which it was found is itself one of the interests of this plaque as it is an evidence of the relations that Bactria had begun to establish with India through the military campaigns of Eucratides at a time when the cultural and religious influence of India and of Buddhism had not gone beyond the Hindu Kush. As for its origin, the only thing that can be said with certainty is that it was part of a booty collected by the Greeks but we do not know whether it was from one of the neighbouring regions of Bactria like Arachosia or Paropamisadae or from a more distant region like Taxila whose links with Ai Khanum are established on the basis of the coin finds made in or near the treasury. (see above p. 14).

Although it is not possible to exactly locate the workshop, this work is undoubtedly Indian inspite of a few isolated features which are foreign to Indian art like the extremely classical silhouette of the horses or the engraving technique which is close to Achaemenid glyptic. These particularities certainly cannot be explained in terms of direct borrowing.

The plaque is also a testimony of a great mastery of the most complex techniques of goldsmithery, the richness and variety of which is suggested by the figurines loaded with ornaments from the Mauryan and the Śuṅga periods[389].

Over and above the rarity of technical and iconographic parallels, the importance of the plaque of Ai Khanum resides in the fact that it is represents one of the most ancient examples of figurative art in India, its date being certainly anterior to 145 B.C.[390]. Such an early date might appear surprising for an object which we have been led to compare mainly with the reliefs of Bharhut[391] and Sanchi I, the last mentioned being later by at least one century to the find of Ai

---

388 P.K. Agrawala, *Early Indian bronzes*, Varanasi, 1977, p. 38, fig. 86-92. This motif, whose origin remains an enigma, is common in Jaina art : S.J. Czuma, *Kushan sculpture*, pp. 52-53, n°3, and in Buddhist art, as in Bodh-Gaya : J. Hackin *et alii*, *Nouvelles recherches*, fig. 609 ; at Begram : fig. 221, 222, 226, etc. ; for Sanchi see *Sāñchī*, p. 172 ("Symbols").

389 Only eight ornaments in Taxila pre-date the Śaka period : J. Marshall, *Taxila*, fig. on p. 622, one of which belongs to the Mauryan period : n°1, pp. 621-623, pl. 190a. Cf. P. Bernard, *BEFEO*, 68, 1980, p. 36 and n. 2.

390 The pillage of the treasury around 145 B.C. gives a *terminus ante quem* for this object. On this date and on the campaigns of Eucratides in India, see pp. 108-110.

391 Apart from differences in style, the rarity of motifs of the cavaliers, quadrigas and peacocks is also to be noted.

Khanum which is also the case of the majority of the Northern Indian schools of sculpture[392]. The three-quarter view that we find in figures and buildings in the plaque of Ai Khanum was, however, already current in ancient Indian art. Excluding some sculptures of Bharhut, the Indian style of representation was, right from the very beginning, far removed from frontality, making use of the depth of the field by presenting the back view of human figures in the foreground who were shown facing the background, or the three-quarter view.

Apart from a few motifs whose meaning is ambiguous, such as the tree with three branches at the top of the composition, or the foliage resembling in form the motif of *śrīvatsa*, the subject of the plaque of Ai Khanum is manifestly secular. Since most of Indian art is of a religious character, it is not surprising that the theme of Śakuntalā figures in it but rarely. Most of the individual motifs used in the representation of the scene, however, are well known in the sculpture of the large stūpas and *vihāras* which are prior to the Christian era, and exhibit the close association between the secular and the religious in Indian religious art – Buddhist, Hindu or Jain[393].

One of the most important features, particularly significant from the point of view of its link with India, is the similarity of our pinnacled edifices with those which figure on the bas-relief made by the ivory craftsmen of Vidiśā at Sanchi I. The engraved circles which decorate the roof of the edifice of this relief are identical to those of the edifices on the plaque of Ai Khanum. These are not found in any other architectural representation in the sculpture on monuments. Since the style of this relief is identical to the style of its neighbouring reliefs, it is possible to suppose that the addition of this decoration on the edifice of Sanchi was done at the instance of those who had commissioned this work or that this motif, common in the miniaturising work of ivory, was put here by the ivory craftsmen who were, in fact, as competent in carving stone as the official sculptors. We have naturally no argument in support of the view that the plaque of Ai Khanum is the work of a sculptor of mother of pearl or shell whose workshop was close to Sanchi or Vidiśā rather than of an ivory worker, because the sculptures of this site are of a much later date than those of Ai Khanum and the century which separates them was a period which witnessed an artistic evolution which was marked by the constantly shifting and reciprocal influences of numerous artistic schools which are difficult to define with any precision.

Each of the two decorative areas of the plaque of Ai Khanum, the central area and the frieze, in which the motifs duplicate themselves from one area to the other, illustrates a different episode of the same story. If we accept the hypothesis of the legend of Śakuntalā, these scenes represent respectively, the arrival of Duṣyanta and his hunting companions at the hermitage or his departure after marrying Śakuntalā (central area) and the pair, Duṣyanta and Śakuntalā (frieze). The persons

392 The sites of Ajanta IX and X, Bedsa, Karli, Kondane, Junnar, Jaggayapeta, Bodh-Gaya, Amaravati are located, from the chronological point of view, between Sanchi and Mathurā, that is during the course of the 1st cent. A.D. : Ph. Stern, "Les ivoires et os découverts à Begram", pp. 20-22. On the bas-relief of the ivory workers of Vidiśa see above pp. 91 and 93.

393 It should be noted that sculptures related to many different religions were executed by the same artists at Mathurā and at Ellora : *Sāñchī*, pp. 179-180. On the absence of Buddhist themes in the sculpture of Sanchi II at the beginning of the 2nd cent. B.C. see M. Bénisti, "Observations concernant le stūpa n° 2 de Sāñcī", *Bulletin d'études indiennes*, 4, 1986, pp. 165-170.

in the first scene, in which there is action, appear only once[394]. The second scene, on the contrary, is characterised by purely decorative or rather symbolic repetition of the same motifs. The one which is repeated the most frequently, at least four or five times, is that of a seated couple in conversation which, no doubt, symbolises Duṣyanta and Śakuntalā. This is followed by the motifs of the hermitage and the pairs of cervidaes and peacocks. Because the same action is represented, this object does not use the method of multiplying episodes in the same painting common in Indian art, contrary to the disc of Bhita where the representation includes simultaneously, the arrival of Duṣyanta in the hermitage, scenes from Śakuntalā's past life and the reunion of the couple on the balcony.

If most of the motifs have been well identified, it seems, on the contrary, that the representation on the plaque of Ai Khanum takes certain liberties with the theme of Śakuntalā as found in the texts. Inspite of this and, notwithstanding the fact that we have tended to link the plaque to texts which are later in date by many centuries, the identification of Śakuntalā does not seem to be in doubt. Like the textual sources, the plaque combines the theme of a chariot hunt with that of an amorous encounter[395]. The umbrella in the upper part of the composition is a royal attribute and permits the identification of Śakuntalā. However, it does not enable us to know whether she is already married to the king as she is entitled to this attribute by her royal descent. We thus do not know, in the context of the legend, whether the scene represents the arrival of Duṣyanta in the hermitage or his departure from it[396].

The identification of the other actors of the legend, on the other hand, is not certain. It is difficult to tell whether the human figure with an ornate hairstyle which is represented on the left in the upper section is a man or a woman. Perhaps it is not a royal personage because it is not shaded by an umbrella and it is improbable that it represents Śakuntalā, or her adoptive father, Kaṇva because the latter was absent at the time of the arrival of the king. The most plausible hypothesis seems to be that it is the hermit who entreats Duṣyanta not to hunt animals in the precincts of the hermitage whom we find again as the person who stands in front of the quadriga on the plaque of Bhita.

The interpretation of the motifs is also not free from incertitude. As a case in point, there are the four independent columns, which we propose to interpret as marking the boundary of the hermitage, as well as the canopy. Though water is present everywhere in written sources as well as

394 The ancient art of India is characterized by detail and a flood of images : the same background serves sometimes for the depiction of many episodes of the same narrative according to the technique of continous narration. Rich in human figures, whose extremely detailed features reflect their psychological states, the images fit into a narrative style which, adopted undoubtedly because of pressure from the financiers, strongly contrasts with the traditional religious style which must have been fundamentally aniconic.

395 On hunting scenes see also pp. 77-81, 89.

396 In support of the initial hypothesis, it is possible to imagine that the cavalier partially represented on the left side of the composition who opens the procession is preparing to leave the scene instead of being about to enter the hermitage. On the architecture of Indian theatre see L. Renou and J. Filliozat, *L'Inde classique*, t. 2, pp. 263-264.

in iconographic documents[397] because hermitages are traditionally situated on river banks, it is nowhere visible on the plaque of Ai Khanum except in the frieze in the form of a pond in which either serpents or lotuses float. Is it possible to explain its absence by the very lacunary state of the plaque ? Similarly, as compared with traditional huts made with branches, the edifices of the plaque with their medley of colours are certainly much more sumptuous. Perhaps this was done in anticipation of the royal palace of Śakuntalā or simply, because of the taste of those who had commissioned the work.

Independently of the differences resulting from the incomplete state of the plaque, how can we explain the discrepancies between this version and versions of literary sources and iconographic parallels ? The most probable reason is that this representation does not reflect the form that the legend assumes in the play of Kālidāsa or the *Mahābhārata*, both later in date than the plaque, but that it either corresponds to an older version of it or a local variant. Although this textual source remains unknown to us, the plaque of Ai Khanum and the disc of Bhita help to confirm the oldness of the legend and the belief that the *Mahābhārata* does not necessarily constitute the only source of Kālidāsa and that both originate in older versions. It is not totally unlikely that the legend was given a theatrical form even before Kālidāsa specially if we accept that a poetic version had already existed along with figurative representations in the second century B.C. Finally we can pose the question whether, as an object of feminine ornament, which the plaque of Ai Khanum probably is, the story of Śakuntalā was not chosen as an allegory of an amorous encounter[398], in this case in the context of a hunt.

Inspite of its fragmentary state, the scintillating character of the object shows the social status of its owners, rich and luxury loving, residing in a sumptuous palace amidst gardens adorned with all sorts of flowers and abounding in peacocks and pheasants, with pools filled with fish, as Megasthenes had seen when he sojourned in Pāṭaliputra[399], an Indian version of the Iranian paradise, greatly appreciated by the Achaemenid sovereigns[400]. Very few of the luxury objects from Indian courts have come down to us and, by a historical paradox, almost all this rare evidence has been found in foreign lands : after the ivories of Begram and Pompeii[401], we have now the plaque of Ai Khanum.

397 Attention should be drawn, for example, to the illustration on the disc of Bhita and Duṣyanta's description of a portrait of Śakuntalā, bathed by the Mālinī in the hermitage : above p. 58, n. 213.

398 On the relation of this plaquette with Indian mirrors see above pp. 51-53. The association between the hunt and the seduction is well established in Greek imagery and is illustrated in the amorous encounter of Aeneas and Dido : Virgil, *Aeneid* IV, 129-172.

399 Arrian VIII, 10 ; Diodorus II, 39 ; Aelian XIII, 18 ; the description of Megasthenes uses the same stereotype as Indian literature (N.S. Kalota, *India as described by Megasthenes*, Delhi, 1978, pp. 61-70 : see, for example, Kauṭilīya, *Arthaśāstra* II, 2-4). Also Curtius VIII, 9, 26 sqq. and the *Milindapañha* below p. 111. On gardens see E.B. Moynihan, *Paradise as a Garden in Persia and Mughal India*, New York, 1979. On scenes of paradise see *Sāñchī*, pp. 228-230 and, for example, the Stūpa III, pl. 96/3.

400 M. Wheeler, *Flames over Persepolis*, p. 131.

401 See p. 48, n. 187. For the recent discovery of Takht-i Sangin see the appendix p. 50 and fig. 29b.

CHAPTER VII

# CONCLUSION

## TREASURIES IN THE GRAECO-ORIENTAL WORLD

The treasury represents one of the major discoveries of the excavation of Ai Khanum. Despite their small number, the economic inscriptions found on the remains of the jars not only constitute the side evidence we possess today about Graeco-Bactrian political administration, but they also form an invaluable supplement for the study of Greek financial institutions. The contents of this treasury also make it possible to reconstruct, in part, the history of the Greeks in Eastern Bactria under Eucratides. The remains of the spoils of war or tribute, in particular, provide evidence of the distant expeditions of this sovereign in the south of the Hindu Kush, probably against Menander. The architecture of the building, its location in the plan of the palace, and the administrative organisation which it represents, show the same synthesis between Hellenistic and oriental influences as has been observed in the other buildings of the city.

The treasury of Ai Khanum also represented a synthesis of Greek financial practices with those imposed in the East by the Achaemenids. Though the language is different, the administrative terminology utilised by the State and by the sanctuaries was generally the same as employed by earlier institutions, and was later to be adopted by the successors of the Greeks. This is proved by the numerous similarities which exist between Greek documents on the one hand, and the tablets of Persepolis under Darius and Xerxes from the beginning of the fifth century, the Parthian ostracons of Nisa from the first century B.C., or the Greek cuneiform tablets of Uruk, on the other. It is, in fact, from the Persian vocabulary in use in Achaemenid administration, *ganza* (treasury), and ganzabara (treasurer), that the Seleucids borrowed the most important terms for their financial institutions: γάζα, γαζοφυλάκιον and γαζοφύλαξ. It is probable that the corps of officials in the treasury of Ai Khanum was not very different from other treasuries – Persepolis for example – with a treasurer general, scribes, accountants, inspectors of the currencies and officials in charge of supervision over the coins.

The architectural units of the southern part of the palace are aligned according to an extremely strict orthogonal plan, representative of the architectural heritage of the East, of which many examples can be found in Mesopotamia and Iran[402].

The layout of the palace of Ai Khanum consists of an arrangement of units with very distinct functions into a whole. These different units – administrative, political, economic, residential – are juxtaposed and linked with each other by a network of corridors. As an architectural conception, this is foreign to the politico-economic structure of a Greek city. Although the plan of the palace of Ai Khanum, as we know it, dates from the middle of the second century B.C., the organisation of its inner units follows a scheme in which a certain Mesopotamian influence is visible. This relationship can only be understood in the light of the continued existence of

402 On palace architecture see P. Bernard, "Les traditions orientales", pp. 252-257, fig. 2-3.

Achaemenid complexes even after the Hellenistic period was well under way. However, the palatial architecture of Persepolis, the native land of the Achaemenids, reveals a tradition which is quite distinct from the Mesopotamian. It is thus in those regions of the empire which were the least influenced by Iran – Babylonia and the border provinces, where the influence of Achaemenid architecture does not seem to have challenged ancient palatial plans – that we ought to look for the roots of the tradition which we find in the palace of Ai Khanum. The palace of Nebuchadnezzar in the southern chateau of the acropolis of Babylon and that of Darius at Susa, with which it shares many common traits, may have served as its prototypes. Both of these escaped destruction and pillage during the Greek conquest and seem to have survived for sufficiently long to make it possible for Seleucid architects to use them as their source of inspiration[403].

The treasury of Ai Khanum thus represents a confluence of two oriental trends : its location in the palace complex may be attributed to the influence of Mesopotamia or Susiana, but Iranian and probably even Central Asiatic influences are discernible in the internal organisation of the treasury, as apparent from the architectural parallels of Dahan-i Ghulaman, Altyn 10 and Nisa[404]. The architectural plan adopted at Ai Khanum thus depends on the function of each building. But although each building has its own particularity, the gymnasium[405] and the theatre[406] are, on the whole, influenced by the Greek tradition, as they were built to provide for activities which were unknown in Bactria before the Greeks. Similarly, the treasury borrows its plan from Iran since no prototype which corresponded to the economic administration of Greek-Bactria existed either in Mesopotamia or Greece. This economy itself was also probably largely modelled on a system which already existed in Central Asia.

Like all oriental palaces, the layout of the palace of Ai Khanum was also guided by considerations of grandeur and prestige and, from the general conception of the building, it is possible to have an idea of the opulence of the court during important official ceremonies. The presentation of tribute and gifts to the King is one of the major themes of Near and Middle – Eastern art of the ancient period[407]. The procession of Ptolemy II Philadelphus in Alexandria described by Callixenus of Rhodes is evidence of the practice of exhibiting treasures in Hellenistic courts[408]. This practice influenced, in its turn, Roman triumphal processions, as testified by the procession of Paullus Aemilius after his victory against Perseus[409], and the parading of the treasures of Mithridates of Pontus, (see above p. 47) organised by Pompey. India also provides

403 For a general introduction to the palace of Babylon in the context of Mesopotamian palaces see E. Heinrich, *Die Paläste im alten Mesopotamien*, Berlin, 1984, pp. 198-221 ; P. Bernard, "Les traditions orientales", pp. 254-257. For the post-Achaemenid period in Susa see R. Boucharlat, "Les niveaux post-achéménides à Suse, secteur nord. Fouilles de l'Apadana-Est et de la Ville Royale-Ouest (1973-1978)", *Cahiers de la DAFI*, 15, 1987, pp. 145-311.

404 Cl. Rapin, *Fouilles AKh VIII*, pp. 276-277, pl. 46-48.

405 S. Veuve, *Fouilles AKh VI.*

406 On theatre see P. Bernard, *CRAI* 1978, pp. 429-441.

407 On tributes carried in procession see, for example, M.C. Root, *The King and kingship in Achaemenid art*, 1979, pp. 227-284. See also P. Briant, "Le nomadisme du Grand Roi", *Iranica Antiqua*, 23, 1988 (*Mélanges P. Amiet*, t. 1), pp. 253-273.

408 Athenaeus V, 197c-203b ; E.E. Rice, *The Grand Procession of Ptolemy Philadelphus*, Oxford, 1983.

409 Plutarch, *Vita Aemilii Paulli* 32-35.

examples of the ceremonial presentation of gifts to the King[410]. It is thus possible to imagine that the large court I of the palace of Ai Khanum also witnessed similar occasions when the spoils of war or tribute were displayed, before being put away in the treasury adjacent to it.

## EUCRATIDES I : THE CONQUEST OF INDIA

The history of Greek kingdoms in the East around the third century B.C., from the time when Bactria separated itself from the Seleucid Empire and upto the disappearance of the last Greek sovereign in India, a little after the beginning of the Christian era, is not to be found in classical sources. However, an examination of the coins of this period reveals that at least 42 Graeco-Bactrian and Indo-Greek sovereigns ruled in these regions during this period[411]. This large number of kings – almost double of the number of Seleucids over the same period – indicates a history troubled by wars and incessant rivalries, which resulted in the breakdown of power in the principalities. During the course of the third century B.C., Bactria, with its capital of the same name, was still the centre of a unified Greek kingdom. From the beginning of the second century, a policy of territorial expansion towards the south, dictated by the lure of Indian riches, was started. Demetrius I, son of Euthydemus I, was the first Graeco-Bactrian sovereign who succeeded in establishing himself in the south of the Hindu Kush, in the extreme western territories of the Mauryan empire. After him, Agathocles and Pantaleon embarked on the conquest of North-West India and succeeded not only in restoring Greek domination over all the territories traversed by Alexander, but also in extending it further. The Seleucid kings, Seleucus I at the end of the fourth century, and Antiochus III in 205[412] had attempted to reconquer these territories earlier, but without success. This empire became so extensive that the successors of Demetrius I were obliged to partition it into two, with Hindu Kush as the line of division. The accession of Eucratides I inaugurated one of the most outstanding, as also one of the most violent, periods in the history of these Greek kingdoms.

The reign of Eucratides represents one of the important turning points in the history of Greek Central Asia, witnessing both the expansion of his kingdom towards the south, and the advent of the nomads in Greek territories in the north. Till recently the knowledge of the existence of these two opposing forces in the kingdom of Eucratides was based only on a passage of Trogus-Pompey abridged by Justin[413] and an account of the Chinese ambassador Chang Kien. The

410 On royal gifts in India see B.S. Upadhyaya, *India in Kālidāsa*, p. 154. On treasuries *ibidem*, pp. 155-156 ; see also Kauṭilīya, *Arthaśāstra* II, 5.

411 For the development of the arguments of the conclusions in the numismatic context see O. Bopearachchi, *Monnaies gréco-bactriennes et indo-grecques*, 1991, pp. 66-88 ; *idem*, "Ménandre Sôter, un roi indo-grec", *Studia Iranica*, 19, 1990, pp. 39-85 and his attempt to give the chronology see below p. 144.

412 Polybius XI, 39.

413 Justinus XLI, 6 : "A peu près en même temps (*eodem ferme tempore*) deux hommes supérieurs, Mithridate (I dit le Grand : 171-139/8) chez les Parthes, Eucratide (I : 171-145) chez les Bactriens montent sur le trône. Mais alors que sous la direction du premier la fortune plus favorable amena les Parthes à l'apogée de leur puissance, les Bactriens, ballotés de guerre en guerre, perdirent non seulement leur royaume mais même leur liberté : usés par des guerres contre les Sogdiens, les Arachosiens, les Drangiens, les Ariens et les Indiens, et devenus comme exsangues, ils furent finalement écrasés par les Parthes plus faibles qu'eux. Eucratide déploya cependant une grande

excavation of the treasury of Ai Khanum enables us to observe, in the same monuments, the simultaneous occurrence of these two developments in the reign of Eucratides.

It was by a decisive victory over the legitimate king Demetrius II (about 175-165 B.C.) that Eucratides acquired a firm hold over Bactria[414]. His coins, struck according to the Graeco-Bactrian standard on the one hand, and the Indo-Greek on the other[415], provide evidence of the extent of his kingdom on both sides of the Hindu Kush[416].

Indian products form the majority of the finds in warehouse *109* of the treasury of Ai Khanum. They comprise objects of great value such as the disc of shells and the throne, and a series of other precious objects of lesser importance, among which figure particularly, the vessels in agate and rock crystal and beads in hard stones. The similarity between these finds and objects found in India provides a clear evidence of the relations which the last Graeco-Bactrian kings begun to establish with North-West India, and confirm that Eucratides' conquests extended to Taxila[417], though he did not stay there for long. The mention of deliveries of Indian punch-marked

valeur dans de nombreuses guerres. Alors que, épuisé par celles-ci, il était assiégé par Démétrios, le roi des Indes, il vint à bout, avec 300 soldats, de 60.000 ennemis par des sorties répétées. Ayant au bout de quatre mois forcé le blocus, il conquit l'Inde. Comme il en revenait il fut assassiné sur le chemin du retour par son fils qu'il avait associé au trône. Celui-ci, loin de dissimuler son parricide et comme s'il avait tué non pas son père mais un ennemi, fit passer son char dans son sang et fit jeter le corps sans sépulture" (translation of P. Bernard in O. Bopearachchi, *Monnaies gréco-bactriennes et indo-grecques*, p. 66, n. 1). We do not know which of the sons of Eucratides, Heliocles or Plato is the parricide : see A.K. Narain, *The Indo-Greeks*, pp. 70-72 ; O. Bopearachchi, "Ménandre Sôter ...", p. 62.

414 Perhaps the account of Justin suggests that Eucratides assumed the title of King when Demetrius was sojourning in the south of the Hindu Kush (in 171 B.C.). We do not know the details of the rivalry between these two kings but it is possible that the victory of Eucratides against Demetrius who had besieged him was slightly later in date (around 170-165, for example) and that it was after this that Demetrius finally lost control over Bactria : see O. Bopearachchi, *Monnaies gréco-bactriennes et indo-grecques*, pp. 65-66. On the problem of the "era" of Eucratides see P. Bernard, *Les monnaies hors trésors*, pp. 97-105 and particularly references to the study of G. Fussman and A.D.H. Bivar, p. 100, n. 4. For the historical context see also R.N. Frye, *The history of ancient Iran*, pp. 177-204. Mention must also be made of the hypotheses of A.K. Narain who, inspite of the global information furnished by the excavation, decreases by several decades the different phases of the chronology of Ai Khanum (see p. 16, n. 21) : "The earliest Brāhmī inscription outside India", *JAOS*, 106, 1986, pp. 797-801 ; *idem*, "On the foundation and chronology of Ai-Khanum : A Greek-Bactrian city", in *India and the ancient world*, Leuven, 1987, pp. 115-130 ; *idem*, "On some Greek inscription from Afghanistan", *Annali dell'Istituto Universitario Orientale di Napoli*, 47, 1987, pp. 269-392 ; *idem*, "Notes on some inscriptions from Ai Khanum (Afghanistan)", *Zeitschrift für Papyrologie und Epigraphik*, 69, 1987, pp. 277-282.

415 Agathocles, whose reign extended from the valley of Kabul to North-West India (Gandhāra and Taxila) between c.190-180, was the first among the Indo-Greeks to strike square, bilingual coins : see the find of six Indo-Greek bilingual drachmas of Agathocles in Greek and Brahmi at Ai Khanum (workshop of Taxila) : R. Audouin, P. Bernard, *RNum*, VI-16, 1974, pp. 6-41 ; P. Bernard, *Les monnaies hors trésors*, pp. 65-66. See also the bilingual coins of Apollodotus in Greek and Kharoṣṭhī found in the gymnasium and the treasury (**B2-170**) : P. Bernard, *Les monnaies hors trésors*, pp. 66-67.

416 The presence of Eucratides in India is attested by Justinus XLI, 6 and Strabo XV, 1, 3.

417 On the chronology of Sirkap, which was perhaps founded at the time of the destruction of Ai Khanum : G. Erdosy, "Taxila, Political history and urban structure", in *South Asian Archaeology 1987*, ed. M. Taddei, Rome,

coins on the vessels of the treasury, and the specimens collected during the excavation, provide better evidence than any other find that the city of Taxila or another neighbouring region contributed a part of the booty hoarded in the palace of Ai Khanum[418].

The finds of Ai Khanum which are related to India form two distinct groups : the first consists of the remains of the goods from India stored in the treasury; the second, of some objects found in the city outside the palace (terracotta or bronze ink-pots, *decapitator*, etc.), which are all in Greek style and identical to the specimens discovered at Taxila. With the ivory[419] and grey schist utilised in the manufacture of stone vessels, this second group represents the meagre remains of what might have constituted the commercial intercourse between Bactria and the territories south of the Hindu Kush (Paropamisadae, Arachosia, North-West India). It should be noted that Eucratides seems to have attempted to unify the two parts of his empire into an economic whole. His silver coins were struck only according to the Attic standard of Bactria, but almost all his bronze coins are of a much lighter standard and present a bilingual legend on them, characteristic of Indo-Greek coinage[420]. Except the objects in the treasury, which were found dispersed in the rest of the palace and in the sanctuary of the temple à redans, we do not find Indian or Indo-Greek type objects among the things used in everyday life. Nor do we find any trace of Indian influence in architecture or sculpture. Thus, the coins and other purely Indian products which, during the Greek period, were found exclusively in the treasury, were not the outcome of regular commercial traffic but were probably brought in war booty or tribute which was hoarded. They throw light on the military operations conducted by Eucratides towards the end of his life, from about 150 B.C. onwards, in North-Western India, even beyond Gandhāra[421].

1990, pp. 657-674; G. Fussman, "Taxila: the Central Asian connection", in *Urban form and meaning in South Asia: the shaping of cities from Prehistoric to Precolonial times*, ed. by H. Spodek and D. Meth Srinivasan *(Studies in the history of art, 31, Center for advanced study in the visual arts, Symposium papers XV, National Gallery of Art*, Washington, Hanover, London, 1993, pp. 83-100.

418 See also the role of gifts in the relations between Greek kings and the cities in their area of influence : P. Briant, *Iranica Antiqua*, 23, 1988, pp. 253-273.

419 On Graeco-Bactrian artisanal products in ivory see P. Bernard, "Sièges et lits en ivoire d'époque hellénistique en Asie Centrale", *Syria*, 47, 1970, pp. 327-343 ; H.-P. Francfort, *Fouilles AKh III*, pp. 7-18. For ivory in Achaemenid Arachosia see W. Vogelsang, "Early historical Arachosia in South-East Afghanistan, Meeting-place between East and West", *Iranica Antiqua*, 20, 1985, pp. 55-99.

420 Hypotheses of P. Bernard, *Les monnaies hors trésors*, pp. 69-70, 101 ; it should be remarked that the Indian finds in the treasury of Ai Khanum can not be explained in terms of trade relations because they probably represent the spoils of war ; we cannot however entirely deny the existence of such relations after Heliocles, as indicated by the Indo- Greek coins struck according to the Attic standard attested by the treasure of Qunduz (R. Curiel, G. Fussman, *Le trésor monétaire de Qunduz*, Paris, 1965) buried around 70 B.C. : *idem*, pp. 103-105 ; see also O. Bopearachchi, *Monnaies gréco-bactriennes et indo-grecques*, pp. 74-76 and the hypothesis of G. Le Rider according to whom the issue of these coins might have been intended as tribute to the nomads of the North : *ibidem*, pp. 76 n. 1.

421 The label on the oldest vase mentioning Indian coin deposits (κασαπανα ταξαηνά) is of Timodemus (inscription 4b), dates, according to our chronology, to the year 149, which supposes an expedition to India in the preceding year, but this dating is purely indicative. On the chronology of Indian coins see P. Bernard, *Les monnaies hors trésors*, pp. 75-78.

The success of these distant expeditions could not have been possible if the intermediate provinces – Paropamisadae and Arachosia – had not been first conquered and firmly held[422]. The exact details of territorial expansion and the chronology of the Greek kingdoms in the south of the Hindu Kush still elude us to a large extent[423]. Before the accession of Eucratides I, Apollodotus I (about 180-160 B.C.), Antimachus I (about 185-170 B.C.) and Demetrius II (about 175-165 B.C.) ruled around the same time in the Greek territories, which extended then from Bactria to Gandhāra. The fall of Demetrius II left Eucratides free to cross the Hindu Kush for the first time and to take possession of Paropamisadae. In the second stage he pushed towards Arachosia[424] and subsequently towards India. This is indicated by the deposits of Indian coins mentioned on the vases of the treasury, which must have been current in the most Indianised regions, principally North-West India, where, if Eucratides ruled at all, he did so for a very short period only. It is thus probable that his relations with the Greek rulers of these regions were hostile and were marked by armed conflicts.

The principal rival who came in conflict with Eucratides, from the time he began to push towards Paropamisadae, was probably Menander[425]. This king, whose fame was such that the title of one of the great works of Buddhism, the *Milindapañha*, was named after him, lived around the middle of the second century B.C.[426]. His biography – almost as incomplete as that of Eucratides – is based mainly on the *Milindapañha* and on some allusions in Greek sources, such as Strabo who presents him as the greatest Greek conqueror of India (XI, 11, 1). The spread of the mints of Menander is the only means of evaluating the extension of his domains between the Hindu Kush and North-West India. In historical reconstruction relating to Menander, his name is never found in association with that of Eucratides. The excavation of Ai Khanum enables us to contribute some new information with respect to these two rulers.

An Indian source informs us that around 155-150 B.C., that is a little before the Indian expeditions of Eucratides, Greek armies had invaded the Ganges valley, which was then under

422 For the routes across the Hindu Kush, see P. Bernard, "Diodore XVII, 83, 1 : Alexandrie du Caucase ou Alexandrie de l'Oxus?", *Journal des Savants* 1982, pp. 227-233.

423 The historical hypotheses developed by us here are based on the work of P. Bernard, *Les monnaies hors trésors*, and on the work of O.Bopearachchi cited above. The chronology of the kings proposed by O.B. modifies significantly those proposed in the reference works on Graeco-Bactrian and Indo-Greek coins : W.W. Tarn, *The Greeks in Bactria and India* ; A.K. Narain, *The Indo-Greeks* ; M. Mitchiner, *The early coinage of central Asia*, London, 1973 ; *idem, Indo-Greek and Indo-Scythian coinage*, London, 1975 ; etc.

424 W. Vogelsang, "Early historical Arachosia", pp. 55-99 ; on Hellenism in Arachosia see P. Bernard, *Les monnaies hors trésors*, pp. 25-26, 85-9.

425 Apollodotus I, predecessor of Menander in Arachosia had, no doubt, already ceased to rule. Although only Indo-Greek coins of Agathocles and Apollodotus figure in the coins found at Ai Khanum, it was probably at the cost of Menander that Eucratides extended his empire in Paropamisadae - Menander might have had a workshop for minting coins in the city of Begram before the one of Eucratides. According to the *Milindapañha* (see below) he was in fact a native of Kapisi-Begram.

426 The *Milindapañha* has been translated by numerous authors among whom T.W. Rhys Davids, I.B. Horner in English, L. Finot in French (based on an old version in Pali : see the bibliography under *Milinda–*). For a more complete history of this text and on Menander see O. Bopearachchi, "Ménandre Sôter ...", pp. 39-85. See the criticism of G. Fussmann, "L'Indo-Grec Ménandre ou Paul Demiéville revisité", *JA*, 281, 1993, pp. 61-138.

Puṣyamitra, the founder of the Śuṅga dynasty (c. 184-148 B.C.). They reached Pāṭaliputra (Patna), capital of Magadha, but they had to beat a hasty retreat due to internal quarrels[427]. In all probability, this expedition was headed by Menander[428], who had been deprived of his possessions south of the Hindu Kush by Eucratides, and who was no doubt trying to compensate his losses by the conquest of the rest of the Śuṅga empire. One wonders whether the account of the *Yuga-Purāṇa*, relating to a civil war in the very homeland of the Greeks, was not referring to the victories of Eucratides in Gandhāra hard at the heels of Menander : "Ayant conquis Sāketa [Ayodhyā], les Pañcāla [Doāb] et Mathurā, les Yavana méchants et vaillants atteindront Kusumadhvaja [Pāṭaliputra].... Mais les Yavana, ivres de batailles, ne demeureront pas au Madhyadeśa. Une guerre civile éclatera chez eux : sur leur propre territoire, aura lieu une terrible bataille, extrêmement meurtrière : il en résultera la destruction complète des Yavana ..."[429]. The dates recording the arrival of Indian coins on the vases in the treasury are perhaps only a fortuitous coincidence, but in case they are related to the march of Eucratides towards Taxila, the date of the latter would be after 150 B.C. It is possible that Eucratides made use of a period of disorder in the Indo-Greek armies of Pāṭaliputra, or simply of their absence, to make a direct attack on the last possessions of Menander in the Gandhāra region and in the western part of the Punjab. The *Milindapañha* and numismatic evidence also seem to confirm that Menander's kingdom extended in the east beyond Gandhāra and that his capital was Śākala (Sialkot)[430], which would imply that Puṣkalāvatī (Charsada), the old capital of the Indo-Greeks, had been abandoned. If we accept the hypothesis based on the finds of the treasury, the shifting of the old capital might well be linked to

427 The *Yuga-Purāṇa* is the Indian source for the invasion of Pāṭaliputra by the *Yavanas* (Greeks) : H. Kern, *The Bṛhat-Saṃhitā of Varaha-Mihira*, vol LXVII, Calcutta, 1865 ; K.P. Jayaswal, "Historical data in the Gārgī-Saṃhitā and the Brahmin Empire", *JBORS*, 14, 1928, pp. 397-421 and 15, 1929, pp. 129-135 ; D.R. Mankad, "Yuga Purāṇa : A critically edited text of the Yuga-Purāṇa", *Journal of the Uttarpradesh Historical Society*, 1947, pp. 32-64. For documentation on Menander and the expedition of Pāṭaliputra see A.K. Narain, *The Indo-Greeks*, p. 74 sqq. and 174-179, and the work of G.R. Sharma, *Reh inscription of Menander and the Indo-Greek invasion of the Gaṅgā Valley*, Allahabad, 1980 : however, the incorrect reading of the name of Menander and the failure to synchronise with Eucratides invalidate the general conclusions of the work : see the commentary of B.N. Mukherjee, "The problem of attribution of the Reh inscription", *UNESCO, International Association for the Study of the Culture of Central Asia, Information Bulletin*, 11, Moscow, 1988, pp. 43-48. For Indian sources see G.R. Sharma, *op. cit.*

428 Strabo XI, 11, 1 : "The Greeks ... became masters, not only of Ariana, but also of India, as Apollodorus of Artemita says : and more tribes were subdued by them than by Alexander – by Menander in particular (at least if he actually crossed the Hypanis towards the east and advanced as far as the Imaüs), for some were subdued by him personally and others by Demetrius, the son of Euthydemus the king of the Bactrians". The allusion of Strabo XV, 1, 27 is probably to these events : "Of the eastern parts of India, then, there have become known to us all those parts which lie this side of the Hypanis, and also any parts beyond the Hypanis, as far as the Ganges and Palibothra" (*The geography of Strabo*, transl. of A.L. Jones, 1966, vol. VII, p. 47).

429 Translation of A. Tardieu in E. Lamotte, *Histoire du bouddhisme indien, des origines à l'ère Saka*, Louvain, 1958, pp. 411-412. See also O. Bopearachchi, "Ménandre Sôter ...", pp. 49-51.

430 Saṅgala in classical sources : for example Arrian V, 22-24. On Śākala see B.C. Law, "Śākala, an ancient Indian city", *EW*, 19, 1969, pp. 401-409 and O. Bopearachchi, "Ménandre Sôter ...", pp. 45-47, 52 ; *idem*, *Monnaies gréco-bactriennes et indo-grecques*, pp. 79-81 ; see also G. Fussman, "L'Indo-Grec Ménandre...", pp. 82-84.

the vicissitudes at the beginning of Menander's reign. The expeditions of Eucratides to Arachosia and his incursions in the territories of North-West India may have progressively obliged the Indo-Greek sovereign to install himself beyond the Jhelum. After sojourning for some time at Mathurā[431], it seems that Menander succeeded in finding refuge in Śākala until the premature death of his rival Eucratides permitted him to re-establish his authority on a long term basis in the West[432].

The account of Justin is too brief to reveal the real cause of the violent circumstances leading to the assassination of Eucratides on his return from India[433]. Gifted with a strong personality, this sovereign certainly played a crucial role in the history of the period. His entire career is an expression of an unusual lust for power and an ambition without scruples, reflected in his military successes against Demetrius and Menander and the proclamation of his triumphs. It should be noted that the appearance on his coins of the title of Great King, Βασιλέως Μεγάλου, perhaps the literal translation of the Sanskrit genitive *mahārājasa*, and the issue of the largest gold coins known to antiquity[434], are innovations which probably commemorate the main stages of his progression in the south of the Hindu Kush and in North-West India. His ostentatious program of reconstructing the palace and other large buildings in Ai Khanum should also be noted in this context.

Apart from their coins, there is no other material evidence to indicate the presence of the Greeks in the southern regions of their kingdoms in the second century. However, the peculiarities of the regions in the north and the south of the Hindu Kush dictated the policies of all the Indo-Greek sovereigns. From the time of Agathocles, for example, the necessity of adapting Greek money to the economic conditions of the Indianised provinces became evident. The benevolence which Greek sovereigns showed towards Indian cults, whether Hindu or Buddhist, which had implanted themselves in Arachosia under the aegis of the Mauryas, was perhaps the key to their hold on these areas[435]. Menander, famous because of his sympathy towards Buddhism as attested

431 On Mathurā, eastern limit of Greek territories see W.W. Tarn, *The Greeks in Bactria and India*, pp. 227-228.

432 Thus it was not to control the Jamna, tributary of the Ganges, against the Śuṅga in the East that Menander installed himself at Śākala, but to save himself from Eucratides who menaced him from the West. For a recent bibliography on India see G. Erdösy, "Early historic cities of Northern India", *South Asia Studies*, 3, 1987, pp. 1-23.

433 Cf. G. Woodcock, *The Greeks in India*, London, 1966, pp. 80 sqq.

434 Regarding this coin of 20 staters – exhibited in the Cabinet des Médailles – see the bibliographic references in P. Bernard, *Les monnaies hors trésors*, pp. 101, n. 2 and pp. 102 (impact of Eucratides on the tradition) ; O. Bopearachchi, "Ménandre Sôter ...", pp. 55-56. Like other large coins such as the decadrachmas of Agathocles and Amyntas, the purpose of this coin is not clearly established. According to a suggestion of G. Le Rider, these pieces might correspond to the special issues intended for the nomadic peoples in return for peace. They might thus have served as propoganda in which the volume and weight of precious metals was proportionate to the desire for prestige among the Greek sovereigns.

435 Evidence of the importance of Buddhism in Arachosia during the reign of Aśoka is available in the form of multingual inscriptions – including Greek – proclaiming the Buddhist precepts of this King. The six Indo-Greek drachmas of Agathocles found at Ai Khanum bear the representation of the god Vāsudeva-Krishna : ref. Cl. Rapin,

by the *Milindapañha*, was the principal Greek figure to support this policy. It is he, undoubtedly, who encouraged the expansion of this religion in the Indo-Greek kingdoms extending upto the foot of the Hindu Kush, after Eucratides had disappeared from the political and military scene. The description of the funeral ceremony of Menander, as reported by Plutarch, clearly presents evidence of a religious connotation, which seems directly influenced by the account of the *War of Relics* of the Buddha[436]. On the contrary, no such Indian or Indo-Greek influence is perceptible in the regions north of the Hindu Kush, inspite of the conquests of Demetrius and Eucratides on the southern side of the chain. The verdict of Ai Khanum in this regard is negative (see above p. 107).

It is to be noted that certain finds in the treasury of Ai Khanum, like the vessels in rock crystal (**N15-4** à **8**, fig. 11, p. 24 and 124) and some of the specimens of beads and rough and worked semi-precious stones could well have come, on the basis of their appearance, from the depots of Buddhist stūpas. Is it possible to conclude on this basis that Eucratides indulged in the pillage of Buddhist sanctuaries ? It would be imprudent to do so in the absence of any other evidence[437]. The poetic description of Śākala in the *Milindapañha* belongs to a style of stereotype narratives which is typically Indian, and the disc of shells in the treasury is definitely a product of this type of imagery[438]:

> "There was a city called Sāgala, a centre of all kinds of merchandise for the Greek Bactrians, graced with rivers and mountain-slopes, having delightful districts and regions, possessed of parks, pleasure-grounds, woods, lakes and lotus-pools – a lovely scene of rivers, mountain-slopes and woods, it was laid out by knowledgeable men. Enemies and adversaries had been destroyed, it was without oppression ; divers, varied and strong were its watch-towers and ramparts, its splendid and noble arches curving over the city-gates ; the palace was surrounded by a deep moat and pale encircling walls ; well laid out were its carriage-roads, cross-roads, squares and the places where three or four roads met ; the bazaar shops were filled inside with innumerable varieties of well-displayed goods ; it was richly adorned with a hundred varieties of halls where gifts (were given) ; it was splendid with hundred of thousands of magnificent dwellings like crests of snowy mountains ; it was filled with elephants, horses, chariots and pedestrians, with groups of handsome men and women ; it was crowded with ordinary people, warriors, nobles, Brahmans, merchants and workers ; resounding with a variety of salutations to ascetics and Brahmans, it was the resort of skilled men knowing a great variety (of things). It had divers and varied shops for cloths : Benares muslin, Koṭumbara stuffs and so on. It was sweet-smelling with the great variety of shops for flowers and perfumes, well and tastefully displayed. It was filled with an abundance of alluring jewels. Its shops, well-displayed and facing (all directions), were frequented by crowds of elegant merchants. Full of *Kahāpaṇas*, silver, bronze and

*Fouilles AKh VIII*, pp. 106, n. 233 and above p. 50. On Menander see O. Bopearachchi, "Ménandre Sôter ..." ; *idem*, *Monnaies gréco-bactriennes et indo-grecques*, p. 66 sqq. and 76-88.

436 Plutarch, *Moralia* 821e. : "But when a certain man named Menander, who had been a good king of the Bactrians, died in camp, the cities celebrated his funeral as usual in other respects, but in respect to his remains they put forth rival claims and only with difficulty came to terms, agreeing that they should divide the ashes equally and go away and should erect monuments to him in all their cities" (*Plutarch's Moralia*, transl. of H.N. Fowler, Cambridge, London, 1969, vol. X, pp. 277-279).

437 Our supposition that the Indian merchandise in the treasure of Eucratides was the result of forcible appropriation is however only a hypothesis. It is also possible that this merchandise represented the tributes and gifts which the Oriental cities had given at the time of their surrender to the Great King : regarding the Indian expedition of Alexander see P. Briant, *Iranica Antiqua*, 23, 1988, pp. 253-273.

438 *Milinda's questions*, transl. from the Pali by I.B. Horner (*Sacred books of the Buddhists*, 22), London, 1963, pp. 1-3.

stone-ware, it was the abode of shining treasure. The warehouses were full of an abundance of riches and corn and wealth ; there were many foods, sweets, beverages and savouries as in Uttarakuru. Its harvests were heavy as in Aḷakamandā, the city of devas."

The closest iconography parallels, the bronze vase of Gundla and the terracotta disc of Bhīta, are both from a region adjacent to the one which led from Śākala-Sialkot to Pāṭaliputra. The disc of Ai Khanum itself might well belong to the Ganges valley which the *Yavanas* of Menander had traversed before the incursions of their rival, Eucratides, in North-West India.

## EUCRATIDES I : THE TWO NOMADIC INVASIONS

As reported by Justin, the assassination of Eucratides took place on his return from an expedition to India[439]. This sovereign was probably the last Greek king to rule over Ai Khanum, because its excavation has not yielded any numismatic evidence of his successors, Heliocles, Plato or Eucratides II[440]. The last evidence of the treasury's administrative activity dates from 146 B.C. The death of Eucratides thus might have occurred in 145 B.C.

– *Identification of the nomads* : It is not possible to reconstitute the frontiers of Greek Central Asia (around 145 B.C.) with certainty, as also for the frontiers between the different nomadic peoples. The distinction between the different nomadic tribes in the period immediately following the Greek period is still the subject of numerous controversies[441]. The most precise information in this regard comes not from classical texts but from a Chinese source. We are alluding to the memoirs of the historian Sse-Ma Ts'ien, which gives a description of the state of Bactria a little after 130 B.C. :

"The Great Yüeh-chih live some two or three thousand li west of Ta-yüan {Ferghana}, north of the Kuei (Oxus) River. They are bordered on the south by Ta-hsia {Bactria}, on the west by An-hsi (Parthia), and on the north by K'ang-chü. They are a nation of nomads, moving from place to place

439 The climatic conditions in Central Asia and India tend to attain extrems : very cold and humid winters in the first case and torrid summers in the second. They might have controlled a seasonal movement between the regions in the north and the south of the Hindu Kush. The return of Eucratides towards Central Asia might thus have occurred in spring, at the beginning of the hot season in India : on the political importance of the trips of Oriental kings, both Achaemenid and Greek, to the cities of their empires see P. Briant, *Iranica Antiqua*, 23, 1988, pp. 253-273.

440 P. Bernard, *Les monnaies hors trésors*, pp. 97-98. The reign of Heliocles ends around 130, date indirectly attested by Chinese sources.

441 Strabo XI, 8, 2. We will not repeat the details of the problems relating to the invaders of Bactria with their implications concerning the origins of the Kushan empire ; we will limit ourselves to mentioning the syntheses – sometimes outdated, with respect to the chronology – of W.W. Tarn, *The Greeks in Bactria and India*, pp. 270-311 and 513-514 ; R.N. Frye, *The history of ancient Iran*, pp. 191-197 ; B.Ja. Staviskij, *La Bactriane sous les Kushans*, p. 32 : Chinese sources ; p. 48, n. 2 : Classical sources ; pp. 31-43 : Kushan chronology ; 47-55 ; 113-126 : hypotheses on the identification of nomadic peoples and chronology of Bactrian invasion ; O. Bopearachchi, *Monnaies gréco-bactriennes et indo-grecques* and, particularly, P. Bernard, "Les nomades conquérants...", *CRAI* 1987, pp. 758-768 ; on the geography of Bactria and Sogdiana from the Achaemenid to the Islamic period and the identification of their frontiers see particularly P. Bernard in *Etudes de géographie historique*, pp. 3-15 and pp. 45-48. A recent bibliography on these problems is presented by G. Fussman, "Chronique des études kouchanes (1978-1987)", *JA*, 275, 1987, pp. 340-342.

> with their herds, and their customs are like those of the Hsiung-nu. (...) Ta-hsia is situated over two thousand li south-west of Ta-yüan, south of the Kuei River. Its people cultivate the land and have cities and houses. Their customs are like those of Ta-yüan. It has no great ruler but only a number of petty chiefs ruling the various cities. The people are poor in the use of arms and afraid of battle, but they are clever at commerce. After the Great Yüeh-chih moved west and attacked and conquered Ta-hsia, the entire country came under their sway. The population of the country is large, numbering some million or more persons. The capital is called the city of Lan-shih (Bactra) and has a market where all sorts of goods are bought and sold"[442].

This text makes it possible to situate one of the groups of invaders, the Yueh-chi, about whom the ambassador Chang Kien reports that at the time of his passage in 128 B.C., they were installed on the right bank of the Oxus, and that they had already extended their control on the left bank of the river, where they had allowed local potentates to remain[443].

Archaeological discoveries made in Central Asia in recent years may, however, throw light on some of the important stages in the progression of nomadic tribes, for example, the Śakas, or the Yueh-chi, founders of the future Kushan empire[444]. Although the hypothesis that we are formulating is subject to caution, we tend to identify the Yueh-chi as the nomads who took over Eastern Bactria for a long time. But did this correspond exactly with the fall of Ai Khanum ? If the metallurgical activities noted in the treasury correspond indeed to the first phase of occupation by the nomads[445] and if the burial of the ingots of precious metal (pp. 10-11) corresponds to the

442 B. Watson, *Records of the Grand Historian of China, translated from the Shih chi of Ssu-Ma Chien*, 2, London, 1961, pp. 267-269. O. Bopearachchi, *Monnaies gréco-bactriennes et indo-grecques*, p. 74, n. 2, with a translation of Fr. Thierry. On Chang Kien see E. Chavannes, *Les Mémoires historiques de Se-Ma Ts'ien*, Paris 1895-1905, pp. LXXI-LXXII ; L. Boulnois, *La route de la Soie*, Paris, 1986, p. 33 sqq. ; M.A. Levi, *I nomadi alla frontiera*, Roma, 1989, p. 67 sqq.

443 The Kuei river mentioned by Sse-Ma Ts'ien is the Oxus-Amu-darya, including its upstream course at Ai Khanum. Basing himself on the geography of Ptolemy, P. Bernard, in *Etudes de géographie historique*, pp. 5-9, is of the opinion that the region of Ai Khanum may have belonged to Sogdiana and that the frontier between Bactria and Sogdiana was constituted by one of the tributaries on the left bank of the Amu-darya which, according to recent hypotheses (*infra* n. 454), may be near the river of Qunduz. The term "Ta-hsia" which corresponds in Sse-Ma Ts'ien to the south of Amu-darya reflects a very different historical situation from the one known to the Greeks and would constitute a general name for the whole of Bactria and ex-Greek Sogdiana in the south of Amu-darya. The amalgam between the peoples of these two regions is possible since they belonged to the same cultural zone.

444 On the hypotheses concerning the expansion of the Yueh-chi and the Śakas in Bactria upto the 1st cent. A.D. see P. Bernard, "Les nomades conquérants ...", who bases his argument on the decor of the palace of Khalčayan, the necropolis of Tilia-tepe which he attributes to Śaka princes and the iconography of Indo-Parthian coins. On Khalčayan see the references in G. Fussman, "Chronique des études kouchanes (1978-1987)", *JA* 1987, p. 341 ; on Tilia-tepe see also G.A. Pugačenkova, L.I. Rempel', "O "zolote bezymjannyx carej" iz Tilja-Tepe. K probleme stilja i svjazej", in *Iz Istorii kul'turnyx svjazej narodov Srednej Azii i Indii*, Taškent, 1986, pp. 5-24 ; V. Sarianidi, *Bactrian Gold*. Bibliography in G. Fussman, *loc. cit.*, p. 342. For the most recent hypotheses see B. Lyonnet, *Prospection archéologique de la "Bactriane orientale" (Afghanistan du N.E.)*, Paris, 1995 (forthcoming).

445 On the identification of a group of ceramic poles which might date from the first post-Greek phase see B. Lyonnet, "Les nomades et la chute du royaume gréco-bactrien : quelques nouveaux indices en provenance de l'Asie centrale orientale. Vers l'identification des Tokhares – Yueh-Chi ?", in *Histoire et cultes de l'Asie centrale préislamique*, 1991, pp. 153-161 ; *eadem, Prospection archéologique*.

departure of the new masters of the city (period IIIb), followed by the installation of indigenous inhabitants in the same buildings (period IIIc), then these observations are not necessarily applicable to the account of Chang Kien mentioned above. In fact, if we consider the final pillage, whose traces have been observed particularly in the treasury and the sanctuary (period III d), it appears that two distinct waves of nomads succeeded each other in the city. The second, which came many years after the first, was unable to collect anything but the debris left behind by the latter. That this final pillage was made by a nomadic people is indicated by the discovery of very typical ceramic objects from the last Greek level which was disturbed by the pillage. The forms and the technique of these ceramics are in no way influenced by the Greek tradition, which the natives continued to follow even after the departure of the Greeks, but are akin to the type of vases which are found in nomadic tombs in the region of Dangara in the north of Ai Khanum[446]. If we accept that this pillage took place shortly before the passage of the Chinese ambassador, it is to the Yueh-chi and not to the Śakas that the ultimate destruction must be attributed. As for the identification of the nomads who captured the city, and are the authors of the inscription on silver ingot, and whom a type of ceramic pole identified by B. Lyonnet distinguishes from their successors, could they not be the Śakas ?

— *Conclusion :* The facts furnished by the construction and the pillage of the treasury, coupled with the study of the post-Greek occupation of the city, provide invaluable evidence concerning the rapid decline of Greek power in this province from 145 B.C. which constituted a turning point in the history of Bactria. They lead to the formulation of the following propositions : a) The Greek city of Ai Khanum was abandoned suddenly without passing through a preceding period of decline ; b) The destruction of the palace occurred immediately, in the same year as the abandonment. The haste displayed by the invaders in destroying this building seems to be motivated less by a desire to recover building material and more by the will to efface all traces of the power it symbolised[447].

One must look for the causes of the fall of the city in the disturbances which preceded the death of Eucratides. The suddenness of the disintegration of Graeco-Bactrian power, which has been duly noted, becomes explicable only if the nomads, whose pressure on Bactria had begun to be felt as early as the third century B.C[448], had already come close to the Amu-darya. It is not certain if the Greeks were fully conscious of the extent of this menace. The involvement of

446 B. Lyonnet, *ibid.*

447 Along with the palace, all the structures of Greek life in the city have also probably disappeared as, for example, the cults of the central sanctuary. The excavation of the sanctuary of Takht-i Sangin, only about a hundred kilometres from Ai Khanum, leads to very different observations. It seems that this sanctuary continued to function even after the Hellenistic period uninterruptedly. The will of the nomads to destroy Ai Khanum is thereby reaffirmed.

448 The nomadic peoples on the periphery played an important economic and political role, as much under the Greeks as under the Achaemenids, partly because of the menace of invasion that they represented for sedentary populations and partly because of the trade which they developed. Their incursion into Greek territories took place in stages : the menacing neighbourhood is already invoked by Euthydemus I to convince Antiochus III to sign a treaty with him after the unfruitful siege of Bactria (Polybius XI, 39, Ed. Will, *Histoire politique du monde hellénistique*, II, pp. 58-61) and one observes, towards the end of the reign of Euthydemus or slightly later, the appearance of first imitations of coins in the territories annexed by the nomads. On the relations between sedentary and nomadic populations see the work of P. Briant, *Rois, tributs et paysans.*

Eucratides with his Indian conquests does not betray any real anxiety on his part on this account. Even the loss of Bactria's western satrapies mentioned by Justin, which has often led to the suspicion that the Parthians were the cause of the death of the sovereign, does not seem to have turned Eucratides away from this course[449].

When the city was founded towards the end of the fourth or the beginning of the third century B.C.[450], its establishment at the eastern extremity of the plain of Amu-darya, as in the case of all other Greek colonies, was dictated by economic[451] and strategic[452] considerations. The program of enlarging the palace and the reorganisation of the monuments of the city launched by Eucratides a little before 150 B.C. might well have been conceived to mark the completion of the conquest of the territories in the south of the Hindu Kush, at the cost of Menander. The mines of Pandshir which had come into his possession would provide the sovereign with the means to execute his project. The Indian material collected in the treasury marked the expansion of his conquests towards India in the subsequent period. Thus, in 146 B.C., Ai Khanum was no longer an ordinary Greek city but a veritable capital, a counterpart of Bactria in the east which was the traditional capital of the kingdom. The centralisation of the power of Eucratides in this region, away from the traditional route of India, served two purposes : first, by closing the access to eastern Bactria, bordered by menacing nomads, it ensured the protection of the hinterland of Greek power and imposed the spectacle of a powerful and flourishing city, and second, it helped to develop a policy of southward expansion. From the beginning of his reign Eucratides had perhaps recognised the military and strategic importance of this city, and it is quite possible that the fortress in which he entrenched himself during his revolt against Demetrius, was the one which stood in the south-western extremity of the acropolis of Ai Khanum. After his victory, he might have wanted to re-establish the city and make it the northern capital of his State, naming it Eucratideia after himself (Strabo XI, 11, 2)[453].

Assuming that Ai Khanum had acquired the status of a capital, it seems hardly probable that it would also share administrative and political power of the same satrapy with Bactria. P. Bernard's hypothesis that Ai Khanum was associated to Sogdiana – although its geographical

449 The satrapies of Turiva and Aspiones (Strabo XI, 11, 2 : N.C. Debevoise, *A political history of Parthia*, Chicago, 1958, pp. 19-20, 57) were conquered by Mithridates I after 148, perhaps at the same time as the disorders which followed the death of Eucratides ; see the analysis of P. Bernard, *Les monnaies hors trésors*, pp. 98-99 and 110 : Alexander Balas was still in control in Media in 148. On the reference to the defeat of Eucratides at the hands of the Parthians see also Strabo XI, 9, 2. See also G. Le Rider, *Suse*, p. 345.

450 P. Bernard, "Alexandre et Aï Khanoum", *Journal des Savants* 1982, pp. 125-138.

451 On the agricultural importance of the plain of Ai Khanum and the adjacent regions see J.-Cl. Gardin, P. Gentelle, "Irrigation et peuplement dans la plaine d'Aï Khanoum de l'époque achéménide à l'époque musulmane", *BEFEO*, 63, 1976, pp. 59-99 ; P. Gentelle, *Données paléogéographiques et fondements de l'irrigation*, Paris, 1989. On the mineral resources on which the palace had a monopoly see P. Bernard, "Problèmes d'histoire coloniale", pp. 108-120.

452 P. Leriche, *Fouilles AKh V*.

453 Ptolemy XI, 8 situates Eucratideia in Bactria ; however this location can not be regarded as absolutely certain knowing that this Alexandrian geographer had attributed Maracanda-Samarkand to the same province (XI, 9), See P. Bernard in *BEFEO*, 68, 1980, p. 38, n. 2 ; *idem*, *Les monnaies hors trésors*, pp. 100-101.

context was Bactria – might help to solve this difficulty[454]. The development of Ai Khanum and its region would have compensated, in a certain sense, the loss of Sogdiana proper in the north of the Amu-darya and the fall of her old capital Samarkand[455]. Nomadic invasions were temporarily stopped in the west of Ai Khanum. Heliocles, one of the three sons and successor of Eucratides, had the time to rule for another fifteen odd years in Bactria before the permanent abandonment of Greek territories in the north of the Hindu Kush.

The finds of the treasury concern not only the history of the city, but they also throw a different light on the history of Central Asia and of North India. The events which we have tried to reconstruct occurred in a very small time frame, between 150 and 145 B.C. This was a period when the confidence of Eucratides was such that the menace of nomads near his northern frontier did not prevent him from pursuing an active policy of conquest towards India. The territories which became victims of the expansionist policies of Eucratides had already been conquered by other Greeks, particularly Menander. The rivalry between these two rulers is now capable of being represented with a certain amount of precision. The year 145 B.C. thus constitutes a landmark which witnessed a historical event of far reaching importance : the interruption of the conquest of India by Eucratides, and the opening up of the northern frontiers of the rich kingdom of Bactria to the invasion of the nomads. But this date does not simply represent the end of the rivalry between the two rulers, with the defeat or death of one of them. It also does not merely signal the end of Greek power in Bactria. Over and above all this, it represents a veritable watershed in the civilisations of Central Asia and India, for the fall of Ai Khanum paved the way for the end of Graeco-Bactrian Hellenism, a Hellenism which was desirous of maintaining its purity and of remaining solidly anchored to its Mediterranean roots, even if a certain syncretism with oriental religions, similar to what existed in other Greek kingdoms in the Near East, could be noted. However, this fall favoured the flowering of a new Hellenism under the aegis of Menander, the Indo-Greek rival of Eucratides, which developed in a close symbiosis with Indian civilisation, avoiding nevertheless, in contrast with other centres of the Hellenic world, the creation of a fusion between the Greek and the Indian pantheons.

One of the examples of the outcome of this Hellenism is the Graeco-Buddhist art of Gandhāra, which developed during the Kushana empire and which appeared in North-Western India already in the course of the first century B.C. Many of the traits of this civilisation may thus have resulted from the confrontation of two types of Hellenism, personified according to us, by

454 Description of Bactria and Sogdiana by Ptolemy XI, 1 to XII, 6 in I. Ronca, *Ptolemaios, Geographie, 6,9-2,1, Ostiran und Zentralasien, Teil I (Reports and Memoirs 15,1)*, Rom, 1971, pp. 24-36. The present state of our information does not enable us to say whether the Oxus – the river or its plain – constituted the frontier between Bactria and Sogdiana along its entire course. According to B. Lyonnet, who develops this argument in her forthcoming work, the nomadic incursions directed against the Bactria of Heliocles – reconstituted on the basis of a study of post-Greek ceramics identified in Ai Khanum – might have reached the valley of Qunduz. The frontier between Sogdiana and Bactria might thus have been situated between the river of Qunduz and the confluence of the Wakhsh where the sanctuary of the Oxus of Takht-i Sangin is located. It should be remembered that Ptolemy situates the cities of Oxeiana (XII, 5) and Alexandria of the Oxus (XII, 6) in Sogdiana.

455 The date of the ultimate fall of Samarkand is not certain but the coins of Eucratides found in the valley of Zerafsan suggest a date later than is usually given : P. Bernard, *Les monnaies hors trésors*, pp. 138-140.

Eucratides and Menander. The consequences of the ambitious policies of Eucratides, and of his assassination, for the history of Central Asia and the whole of North India are obvious.

## HELLENISM AND RELATIONS WITH THE WEST

Stratigraphically, the finds of the treasury of Ai Khanum fit into a very narrow chronological spectrum of less than five years. This relatively small period represents the life of Ai Khanum in a very limited way, not permitting us to view its historical evolution in the *longue durée*. They are also among the most fragmentary finds of Ai Khanum. However, as pointed out by P. Bernard and attested by the literary and economic texts of the treasury, as well as by the overall discoveries made at the site, the material and intellectual culture of the Greeks in Bactria reflects a will to reproduce, in the words of Diodorus, the ἑλληνικὴ ἀγωγὴ καὶ δίαιτα, in their society[456]. The buildings which correspond to institutions which are totally Greek, like the theatre and the gymnasium, remain, on the whole, faithful to western models and even though the Orient has left a profound mark on the plan of numerous buildings, the architectural decor (columns, antefixes) make an attempt to remain Greek, sometimes maladroitly. Similarly the *instrumentum* of everyday life is predominantly Greek (writing material, stone of the fulling mill, mill stone, ironwork), even though these objects were locally manufactured[457]. As for intellectual life, be it language, education, love of theatre or artistic tastes, almost all the evidence that has come down to us manifests an ardent desire to keep Greek values alive.

It is important to emphasise that the vehicle of these influences of the Mediterranean world and the Hellenized Near-East was not trade. In fact, objects made in the West are rare in Ai Khanum[458] and consist essentially of what can be regarded as luxury or semi-luxury goods in the central Asiatic context like olive oil, or wine, incense, cinnamon, plaster mouldings on metallic vases[459], and also an intaglio in garnet (portrait of a queen ?). As for the disc of Cybel which was initially considered to be of Syrian origin, the discovery in the sanctuary of Takht-i-Sangin of the fragments of an analogous disc made of the same material and illustrating, it appears, the same subject, opens up the possibility that it was of local origin[460]. The case of ceramics is particularly

456 L. Robert, *CRAI* 1968, p. 421 ; P. Bernard, *Les monnaies hors trésors*, pp. 127-128.

457 The synthesis between Greek and Oriental cultures occurred mainly after the Hellenistic period : G.A. Košelenko, "Les traditions de la Bactriane ancienne et les étalons culturels du monde hellénistique", in *L'archéologie de la Bactriane ancienne*, pp. 269-272.

458 For a similar observation of B. Ja Staviskij regarding the early Kushans in Bactria see P. Bernard, "La Bactriane à l'époque Kushane d'après une nouvelle publication soviétique", *Journal des Savants* 1979, p. 246. It should be remembered that even a material like coral which was traditionally imported from the Mediterranean, was worked in India - see the pendant cut in the form of *nandipāda* – before arriving in Ai Khanum. The coral which we find in Ai Khanum, even in the form of rough, has every chance of being from India.

459 P. Bernard, *CRAI*, 1971, pp. 432-435 ; H.-P. Francfort, *Fouilles AKh III*, pp. 35-37, pl. XVI and 18 ; see also the impression on unbaked clay : *ibidem*, pp. 45-46, pl. XVII and 18.

460 H.-P. Francfort, *Fouilles AKh III*, pp. 93-104, pl. XLI ; for the specimen from Takht-i Sangin see I. Pičikjan, *Kul'tura Baktrii. Axemenidskij i ellinističeskij periody*, Moscow, 1991, fig. 19. See also Fr. Grenet, "Mithra au temple principal d'Aï Khanoum?", in *Histoire et cultes de l'Asie centrale préislamique*, pp. 147-151. M. Boyce, Fr. Grenet, *A history of Zoroastrianism*, 1991, pp. 160-193.

significant. There is a surprising contrast between an almost total absence of ceramic importation, and the tenacious fidelity with which Mediterranean forms and techniques were emulated. Thus no more than the small objects, the ceramics do not indicate intensive commercial relations with the Mediterranean West. It would of course be absurd to deny any commercial relations whatsoever. For example, the importation of vases to be used as models is duly attested by the few finds of amphora, which were used for the transportation of Mediterranean or Near Eastern products, or the small splinters of vases with black paint[461].

Of the four categories of marketable products which Greek Cèntral Asia had at its disposal, namely : precious metals (gold definitely more than silver), ivory of Indian origin, semi-precious stones[462], and agricultural produce – mainly cereals – only the first two could be exported to distant lands. Agricultural produce naturally could only be exported to neighbouring regions[463]. As for jewellery, the Mediterranean world was not yet ready for the fashion of inlays in semi-precious stones (lapis-lazuli, turquoise etc.) which Bactria could have supplied in the international market[464]. We know that imports from India were mainly limited to ivory and most of the finds in the treasury are linked to the military expeditions of Eucratides and not to trade[465].

The land route of silk, which was to procure substantial benefits to the successors of the Greeks as middlemen, had not yet been opened up in the middle of the second century B.C. Inspite of the presence of the Greeks in Bactria and the two conquests of North-Western India, at the end of the fourth century and in the first half of the second century B.C. respectively, and inspite of the special relations of Egypt with the regions bordering on the Indian Ocean, it appears that the Mediterranean peoples were not aware of the true origin of the most beautiful precious stones (the best agates and carnelians, pearls, beryls, sapphires or lapis-lazuli sold in the Indian

461 The imports of Mediterranean ceramics with black coating are comparatively more numerous in the south of the Hindu Kush, at Kandahar in spite of the rarity of probes conducted on this site : D. Whitehouse, "Excavations at Kandahar, 1974, First interim report", *Afghan Studies*, 1, 1978, p. 15, pl. IVa and fig. 5. On the exports to Ceylon see J. Bouzek, S.U. Deraniyagala, "Tessons de vases hellénistiques trouvés en Sri Lanka", *BCH*, 109, 1985, pp. 589-596.

462 In contrast with most of the remains of Hellenism (sculpture, objects of everyday life), of which parallels are, quite often not available in Central Asia, articles of jewellery constitute a rich material exemplified by the very numerous finds in India and the Mediterranean. These show the generalised taste for ornaments in antiquity and it is probably unnecessary to review the inventory of each site here. The conclusions that we wish to present concern mainly the general understanding that these finds can provide of the transport of merchandise between the West and India and the role that Bactria might have played during the last years of the Greek Kingdoms.

463 This trade relates as much to Greek territories as those of the nomads : P. Briant, *Etats et pasteurs*, 1982, p. 214 sqq.

464 On the finds of Graeco-Bactrian coins in the Near East and in the Mediterranean region see P. Bernard, *Les monnaies hors trésors*, pp. 107-113 and tableau p. 158. We are not in a position to explain the importance of the finds of rough stone stored in the treasury, particularly lapis-lazuli, of which Ai Khanum had assumed the monopoly during the reign of Eucratides. The finds of ornaments made of this stone in the jewellery of Central Asia, India and the Mediterranean are very few.

465 The finds of Graeco-Bactrian coins in the treasure of Mir-Zakah, near Gardez (on one of the routes between Arachosia and India) is unimportant as compared to Indo-Greek coins of the 2nd-1st cent. : R. Curiel, D. Schlumberger, *Trésors monétaires d'Afghanistan (MDAFA,14)*, Paris, 1953 : "Le trésor de Mir Zakah près de Gardēz", pp. 65-100, particularly p. 91.

ports), as well as of spices and perfumes like cinnamon and incense, produced in the south of the Arabian peninsula, for a very long time. It should be noted that these middle men did their best to keep it a closely guarded secret.

The earliest imports of precious stones reached the Mediterranean world following the expedition of Alexander to Asia. Subsequently these imports were made via the Ptolemaic[466] and the Seleucid[467] kingdoms. But the great discovery of riches of the Orient came for the Romans when Pompey celebrated his triumph over Mithridates VI Eupator in 61 B.C. (Pliny XXXVII, 11-14, above, p. 47) and when, after the victory of Actium, Augustus seized the treasures of the Ptolemies (Suetonius, *Augustus*, 71). We know how much these initial contacts impressed the Romans who immediately developed a taste for oriental luxury goods, silk, gems[468], beads, mother of pearl, ivory, furniture items and vessels in hard stones[469]. The earliest accurate information about the origin of these stones arrived in Rome only during the period when the *Periplus* was being written (around the middle of the first cent. A.D.)[470]. From the time of Augustus[471], trade, taking over from war, flooded Rome with oriental goods to an extent that, according to certain authors, the import of silk became a serious threat to the economy of the

466 On the basis of the sources on the Erythraean sea such as Agatharchides cited by Diodorus and Photius, and Artemidorus utilised by Strabo, it is possible to say that India and the Mediterranean world were linked mainly by the Red sea and the Indian Ocean in the Ptolemaic period : G. Le Rider, *Suse*, pp. 347-349 ; L. Mooren, "The date of *SB* V 8036 and the development of the Ptolemaic maritime trade with India", *Ancient Society*, 3, 1972, pp. 127-133 ; J. Rougé, "La navigation en Mer Erythrée dans l'Antiquité", *L'Arabie et ses mers bordières I*, Lyon, Paris, 1988, pp. 59-74, particularly pp. 65-68. In his procession, Ptolemy II Philadelphus had paraded his Indian captives : Athenaeus V, 201a : γυναῖκες Ἰνδαὶ ... ὡς αἰχμάλωτοι, and Indian animals : V, 201b-c. A papyrus of Oxyrhynchus mentions a wife or daughter of a merchant who had returned from India : M.G. Raschke, "New studies in Roman commerce", p. 660, n. 1265. On Greek traders and artisans in India before the Roman empire see E.H. Warmington, *The commerce*, pp. 61-62.

467 It does not seem that the Seleucids tried to open a southern maritime route for their trade with India because they controlled the land routes : J. Rougé, "La navigation en Mer Erythrée dans l'Antiquité", pp. 64-65 ; M. Cary, E. Warmington, *Les explorateurs de l'Antiquité*, Paris, 1932, pp. 107-108 (commercial expeditions towards the Indus at the beginning of the Seleucid period). Coin finds are evidence of the fact that Failaka – which was a stopover between India and Seleuceia on the Tigris – nevertheless played a certain role in the maritime trade at the beginning of the Hellenistic period, and subsequently under Antiochus III and Antiochus IV, perhaps during the periods when the land route of Central Asia was closed. See also G. Le Rider, *Suse*, pp. 309-310. G.L.R., p. 407, imagines the existence of a Silk route through Indian ports and Spasinou Charax from the end of the 2nd cent. B.C.

468 The diminution of the volume of glass gems in the second half of the 1st cent. is an indirect evidence of the increase in the imports of Oriental stones : E.H. Warmington, *The commerce*, p. 82.

469 The extent to which this afflux modified the mentality of the people is known to us by the complaints of the moralists which have been transmitted to us by Seneca and Pliny. Numerous authors including Petron, referred to the taste for Indian beads, emeralds, crystals and rubies.

470 On the date of this text and its relation with the discovery of the monsoon see E.H. Warmington, *The commerce*, p. 43 sqq. ; M.G. Raschke, "New studies in Roman commerce", pp. 660-665 ; A. Dihle, "Die entdeckungsgeschichtlichen Voraussetzungen des Indienhandels...", pp. 547-551 ; Chr. Robin, "L'Arabie du Sud et la date du *Périple de la Mer Érythrée* (Nouvelles données)", *JA*, 279, 1991, pp. 1-30 ; G. Fussman, "Le *Périple* et l'histoire politique de l'Inde", *JA*, 279, 1991, pp. 31-38.

471 E.H. Warmington, *The commerce*, pp. 35-41.

Empire[472]. The merchandise arrived in Rome by stages, first passing through Syria or Alexandria where a portion of stones was worked, then Pozzuoli and Ostia where the large depots to stock this merchandise were located. This trade reached a culmination in the first century B.C. due to the development of the important commercial routes : the silk route by land which, through the medium of the nomads, brought Rome in contact with China[473], and the direct sea route via the Indian Ocean, which was opened when it was possible to master the monsoons.

If trade relations existed between Bactria and the Mediterranean Hellenistic world[474], their extent was yet not as large as it would be between the Roman and the Kushan Empire (Begram, Taxila). It is thus more by men than by trade that the influences from the West penetrated into Greek Central Asia – initially when the first colonies were established by Alexander, then under the hegemony of the Seleucids (305-250 B.C.), who brought a new and powerful flow of colonisers with them and finally, during the long campaign of Antiochus III in Bactria in the last years of the third century. It is certain that apart from periods when the migratory flux accelerated, the Parthian empire never sealed itself hermetically or opposed the free movement of men-artists, intellectuals, artisans and adventurers figured as much, if not more than merchants[475].

472 See nevertheless the nuances of M.G. Raschke, "New studies in Roman commerce", pp. 622-637, particularly his criticism of Pliny pp. 634-635.

473 The historian of Alexander, Aristobulus (cited by Strabo II, 1, 15 et XI, 7, 3) writes that the Oxus made it possible to transport Indian merchandise upto the Caspian Sea and that once this was crossed they were directed upto to Euxine-Sea again by the maritime route. This assertion which is based on the supposition that a part of the water of the Oxus had again begun to flow towards the Caspian by the dried up channel of the Uzboi : W.W. Tarn, pp. 488-493. X. Jusupov, *Drevnosti Uzboja*, Aškhabad, 1986. The supposition that the waters of the Uzboi were sufficiently abundant to permit a veritable river traffic is not necessary to explain either the tombs of the nomadic pasteurs from the 5th cent. B.C. or the fortresses of Igdy-Kala dated of the Parthian or Sassanian period [P. Bernard]. For trade in animals like tigers or parrots and in animal materials, like ivory, tortoise shell, beads, see E.H. Warmington, *The commerce*, p. 89. See also L. Boulnois, *La route de la Soie*, Paris, 1986 ; J. Ferguson, "China and Rome", in *ANRW*, II, Principat, 9,2, pp. 581-603 ; M.G. Raschke, "New studies in Roman commerce", pp. 606-622. Apart from ivory, the merchandise in Nisa which might have been related to Central Asia was small : an object in rock crystal, some fragments in lapiz lazuli among which there is a block of rough stone and shells from the Indian Ocean may be cited M.E. Masson, G.A. Pugačenkova, *The Parthian rhytons of Nisa*, pp. 16-17. On the trade from the Mediterranean towards Central Asia during the Kushan period see, for example, T. Sherkova, "The nature of contacts between the Kushan kingdom and the Eastern Mediterranean (on the basis of archaeological evidence from Bactria)", *The International Association for the Study of the Cultures of Central Asia. Information Bulletin, Issue 1*, Moscow, 1982, pp. 47-55.

474 On the Graeco-Bactrian coins found in the Near East and in the Mediterranean region see P. Bernard, *Les monnaies hors trésors*, pp. 107-113 and tableau p. 158.

475 Evidence of individual voyages between the West and Central Asia in the Hellenistic period is rare but there is : passage of Clearchus in Ai Khanum ; mention of the despatch of Buddhist emissaries by Aśoka to Hellenistic courts (XIIIth edict) : V.A. Smith, *Asoka, the Buddhist emperor of India*, Oxford, 1910, p. 172 ; J.W. Sedlar, *India and the Greek world*, Totowa, 1980, p. 14, 80, 277 ; mention of a Bactrian by the name of Hyspasines in an inscription of Delos : *ID* 442 B, l. 109 ; 443 Bb, l. 33 ; 1432 Aa, col. II, l. 27 : Fr. Grenet, *BCH*, 107, 1983, pp. 378 and 381, and P. Bernard, *Les monnaies hors trésors*, pp. 135-136. See also P. Briant, "Colonisation hellénistique et populations indigènes", in P. Briant, *Rois, tributs et paysans*, pp. 227-279 ; M.G. Raschke, "New studies in Roman commerce", p. 658, n. 1190. For the cultural contribution of Greek emigrants see also L. Robert, in *JA*, 246, 1958, pp. 12-13 and *CRAI* 1964, pp. 138-139.

The relative isolation of Greek Bactria, as revealed by an examination of its trade relations, is also reflected in the scarcity of information on its history, geography, and its populations in the classical sources, in the post-Alexandrian era. This signifies the marginal place given by Western authors to this distant Greek kingdom. When certain episodes of its history are referred to by them, it is because they are directly linked with the destinies of the Seleucid or the Parthian empires[476], the only ones which, along with the kingdom of the Ptolemies and the Roman empire, really count in the histories of the Mediterranean and the Near-Eastern world for a Polybius, a Strabo, a Trogus-Pompey or an Arrian[477]. The silence of the *Lives* of Plutarch on the great men of the Greek empire in Central Asia like Eucratides and Menander, has, in a certain manner, the same significance. Lack of information or of real interest ? The two are related. It is not surprising, in these circumstances, that the study of Graeco- Bactrian and Indo-Greek coins continues to play such an important role in the reconstruction of Bactrian and Indo-Greek history. The present work will show, we hope, that archaeology has its word to add.

476 Source : Isidore of Charax, Apollodorus of Artemita, Arrian, Justin, Strabo and Ptolemy ; on this observation see A. Dihle, "Die entdeckungsgeschichtlichen Voraussetzungen des Indienhandels", p. 552 ; Ed. Will, *Histoire politique du monde hellénistique*, I, pp. 279-290 ; see also D. Schlumberger, "Aï Khanoum, une ville hellénistique en Afghanistan", *CRAI* 1965, pp. 36-39. On the absence of Achaemenido-Bactrian documents see P. Briant, *L'Asie Centrale et les royaumes proche-orientaux du premier millénaire*, Paris, 1984, pp. 57-62.

477 Polybius XI, 39 : expedition of Antiochus III to the upper satrapies : Ed. Will, *Histoire politique du monde hellénistique*, II, pp. 61-62. Strabo, *Geography* XI, 9, 2 and XV, 1, 3 : revolt of Bactria ; XI, 9, 2 and XI, 11, 2 : fall of the satrapies of Aspiones and Turiva under Eucratides. Justin XLI, 6 : Parallel between Mithridates and Eucratides. Arrian, *Parthica*, Fr. 30, in *Die Fragmente der Griechischen Historiker (FGH)*, n° 156, p. 858 : the founder brothers of the Parthian empire driven away from Bactria ; N.C. Debevoise, *A political history of Parthia*, pp. 9-10.

# CATALOGUE OF FINDS

## LIST OF ABBREVIATIONS

— c. court, corridor
— canal. canalisation
— cm centimetre
— d. diameter
— dim. dimensions
— E east
— ext. external
— fgt. fragment
— f. floor
— h. height
— g gramme
— inv. inventory
— l. length
— m meter
— max. maximum
— N north
— NE north-east
— NW north-west
— r. room
— rect. rectangular
— S south
— SE south-east
— SW south-west
— t. type
— tabl. tableau
— th. thickness
— W west
— wi. width

The dimensions are expressed in millimetres and the weights in grammes except where otherwise stated.

### D3 - INK-POT: bronze (Cl. Rapin, *Fouilles d'AKh VIII*, p. 306)

Fig. 6 and p. 17

| N° | Location | Form | Dim. | Observations |
|---|---|---|---|---|
| 1 | c. *128*–r. *129* | handle | wi.: 80; h.: 60 | ink-pot handle with loop for suspension |

### E17 - WEIGHT: agate (Cl. Rapin, *Fouilles d'AKh VIII*, p. 307)

Fig. 7, p. 18 and 30

| N° | Location | Object | Form | Dim. | Observations |
|---|---|---|---|---|---|
| 1 | r. *108* SE | weight | stylised duck | l.: 27; h.: 23 | perforation (utilisation as pendant); 27 g |

### I17 - IMPLEMENT IN AGATE (Cl. Rapin, *Fouilles d'AKh VIII*, p. 314)

Fig. 8 and p. 38

| N° | Location | Object | Dim. | Observations |
|---|---|---|---|---|
| 1 | r. *115–116* | polisher | l.: 60; d.: 7 | slender, polished tip in dark brown agate; polished heel |

## M17 - ROUGH AND WORKED AGATE (Cl. Rapin, *Fouilles d'AKh VIII*, p. 322) Fig. 9-10 and p. 43

| N° | Location | Dim. | Observations |
|---|---|---|---|
| 2 | c. *105* / r. *107*<br>r. *109* | th.: 7-8 | 3 interlocking fgts. of the same type; traces of the saw; smoothened and partially polished surface with the mark of horizontal cutting |

## N15 - VESSELS IN ROCK CRYSTAL (Cl. Rapin, *Fouilles d'AKh VIII*, p. 332) Fig. 11 and p. 24-26

| N° | Location | Object | Dim. | Observations |
|---|---|---|---|---|
| 1 | r. *109* NW<br>c. *105* / r. *109* | bowl (rim) | d.: 132; h.: >75 | some broken pieces with cracks; polished by turning; interlocking pieces |
| 2 | r. *110* NE | bowl (base) | d. of base: 50 | annular base |
| 3 | r. *108* fireplace | lid? | 60 x 40 | rounded; engraved star-shaped decoration |
| 4 | c. *105* / r. *110*<br>r. *123* SW | lid | d.: 55; h.: >16 | internal groove in spiral form; variable thickness; 2 fgts. of interlocking pieces |
| 5 | c. *105* / r. *118* | vase ? | d.: 81; th.: 2 - 3<br>h.: >15 | polished; internal edge threaded; crack at the level of a moulding |
| 7 | r. *108* | vase ? | d.: ~70; h.: >48 | inner section unpolished |

## N17 - VESSEL IN AGATE (Cl. Rapin, *Fouilles d'AKh VIII*, p. 332) Fig. 12 and p. 24-27

| N° | Location | Object | Dim. | Observations |
|---|---|---|---|---|
| 1 | c. *105* / r. *109*<br>c. *105* / c. *113* | cup | broken piece:<br>55 x 32;<br>th.: 1.5-2.5 | brown agate with white veins; fgt. of conical body; 3 fgts. of interlocking pieces |

## O3 - ORNAMENTS IN BRONZE (Cl. Rapin, *Fouilles d'AKh VIII*, p. 334) Fig. 13 and p. 37

| N° | Location | Object | Form | Dim. | Observations |
|---|---|---|---|---|---|
| 3 | r. *117* W | pendant | anthropomorphic | 19 x 15; th.: 0.5 | small loop found near by |

## O15 - ORNAMENTS IN ROCK CRYSTAL (Cl. Rapin, *Fouilles d'AKh VIII*, p. 336) Fig. 14 and p. 30

| N° | Location | Object | Form | Dim. | Observations |
|---|---|---|---|---|---|
| 1 | c. *115* / r. *109*<br>r. *127* S | bead | round with facets | d.: 26; h.: 22<br>d. of the hole: 9 | 2 fgts. of interlocking pieces |
| 2 | c. *113* / r. *123* | bead | disc | d.: 24; h.: 8;<br>d. of the hole: 7.5 | |
| 3 | r. *109*, pit | bead | faceted | l. of the fgt.: 14 | diagonal crack; heptagonal |
| 4 | r. *119* E | bead | spherical | d.: 5;<br>d. of the hole: 1 | slightly conical perforation |

## O17 - ORNAMENTS IN AGATE (see also S17-94 to 105)

Fig. 15 and pp. 30-31
(Cl. Rapin, *Fouilles d'AKh VIII*, pp. 336-337)

| Nº | Location | Object | Form | Dim. | Observations |
|---|---|---|---|---|---|
| 1 | r. *111* N | bead | plano-convex | l.: 22; wi.: 18 th.: 12 | beige and brown agate; white veins only visible on the convex side |
| 2 | r. *107* SE | bead | lens | d.: 24; th.: 5 | brown agate; white veins; perforation on decorated side |
| 3 | c. *105* / r. *109* / r. *106 - 107* | pierced cylinder | | l.: 43; d.: 9 | brown agate; white veins; perfectly cylindrical hole; 2 interlocking fgts.; see p. 38 |
| 5 | c. *105* / r. *115 - 117* | bead | barrel | d.: 3; l.: 5 | light brown agate; white vein; uneven perforation from the two ends |
| 6 | r. *111* door | bead | barrel | d.: 5; l.: 11.5 | brown agate; white vein |
| 7 | c. *113* / r. *123* | bead | barrel | d.: 11; h.: 7 | agate with two layers of dark and light brown separated by a white vein |
| 8 | r. *108* S | pendant bead | drop | max. d.: 7 h.: 16 | agate with parallel veins |
| 16 | c. *105* / r. *115 - 117* | bead | lotus flower with six petals | d.: 6 | bead in translucent stone with red extremity, perhaps a variety of agate; fgt. |
| 17 | c. *105* / r. *115 - 117* | bead | lotus flower with six petals | d.: 6 | bead in opaque white stone grey at the extremity, perhaps a variety of agate (burnt or baked?) |

## O19 - ORNAMENTS IN CARNELIAN (Cl. Rapin, *Fouilles d'AKh VIII*, pp. 337-339)

Fig. 16, pp. 31-32

| Nº | Location | Object | Form | Dim. | Observations (stone generally translucent) |
|---|---|---|---|---|---|
| 1 | c. *105* SW | bead | parallelepiped | 12.5 x 6.5 x 5.5 | orange |
| 2 | c. *105* N | bead | cube with corners cut | sides of the cube: 4 | red |
| 3 | r. *116* N | bead | biconical | | orange |
| 5 | r. *104* NE | bead | disc | max. d.: 4.2 h.: 2 | orange; identical specimen in garnet O23-15 |
| 9 | r. *104* NW | incrustation / fgt. of bead | unidentified figure | l.: 8; th.: 1 | red |
| 10 | r. *117* S | inlay or fgt. of bead | bird | h.: 6; l.: 7.5; th.: 1 | red |
| 11 | c. *105* / r. *116 - 117* | inlay | leaf | l.: 8; wi.: 6 th.: 1 | orange |
| 13 | r. *123* W | inlay | | 22 x 15 x 2.5 | brown |
| 14 | r. *108* | intaglio | oval | th.: 2 | brownish orange; decorated fgt. (fold of a garment falling to the ground ?) |
| 16 | r. *111* NE | mounted stone | oval | 31 x 24 x 4 | reddish orange; slightly concave on the reverse |

## O20 - ORNAMENTS IN LAPIS-LAZULI (Cl. Rapin, *Fouilles d'AKh VIII*, p. 339) Fig. 17, p. 33

| N° | Location | Object | Form | Dim. | Observations |
|---|---|---|---|---|---|
| 1 | r. *119* S against the wall | bead | lotus flower | wi.: 4 | 2 petals; rounded inside |
| 2 | r. *115* | bead | pentagonal | h.: 6 | unpierced |
| 3 | r. *116* SE | bead | hexagonal | d.: 6.5; d. hole: 1.5 | stone of inferior quality |
| 4 | r. *117* W | bead | demi-sphere | d.: 11; h.: 5 | appears to be pierced after having been cut in two; fine stone, homogeneous blue |

## O23 - ORNAMENTS IN GARNET (Cl. Rapin, *Fouilles d'AKh VIII*, p. 340) Fig. 18, p. 34

| N° | Location | Object | Form | Dim. | Observations |
|---|---|---|---|---|---|
| 1 | r. *115* S | intaglio | oval | th.: > 6.5 | fgt., trace of decoration |
| 2 | r. *118* E | mounted stone | plano-convex | 11 x 9 x 4 | violet, polished surface with some finishing defects |

## O24 - ORNAMENT IN TRANSPARENT BLUE STONE: sapphire ? (Cl. Rapin, *Fouilles d'AKh VIII*, p. 340) Fig. 19, p. 35

| N° | Location | Object | Form | Dim. | Observations |
|---|---|---|---|---|---|
| 1 | r. *116* SE | inlay | leaf | l.: 9<br>th.: 2.5 | transparent blue stone comparable to certain sapphires; broken tip |

## O25 - ORNAMENT IN TRANSPARENT GREEN STONE (Cl. Rapin, *Fouilles d'AKh VIII*, p. 341) Fig. 20

| N° | Location | Object | Form | Dim. | Observations |
|---|---|---|---|---|---|
| 1 | r. *120* N | bead | oval | d.: ~6 | olive green transparent stone resembling certain emeralds or peridots; 5 small holes arranged around the perforation which itself has a twisted gold thread inside it; imitation of fruit |

## O33 - ORNAMENTS IN CORAL (Cl. Rapin, *Fouilles d'AKh VIII*, pp. 341-342) Fig. 21, pp. 20, 35-36

| N° | Location | Object | Form | Dim. | Observations |
|---|---|---|---|---|---|
| 1 | c. *113* / r. *126* | pendant-bead | *nandipāda* | h.: 12 | rough coral surface partly grooved and pierced under the head |
| 2 | c. *105* / r. *116 - 117* | bead | biconical | d.: 5<br>l.: 13 | orange; polished surface, with unevenness; ends decorated with a groove |
| 16 | r. *104* NE | bead | rough coral | l.: 15 | perforated |

| | | | | | |
|---|---|---|---|---|---|
| 18 | r. *104* NE | bead | rough coral | l.: 28 | perforated |
| 21 | r. *117* fireplace 1 | bead | rough coral | l.: 26 | unperforated |

## O34 - ORNAMENTS IN MOTHER OF PEARL AND SHELLS

Fig. 22 and 23, p. 37 and 54
(Cl. Rapin, *Fouilles d'AKh VIII*, p. 342)

| Nº | Location | Object | Form | Dim. | Observations |
|---|---|---|---|---|---|
| x | found outside the treasury | round | | d.: approx. 60 | fgt. (fig. 22, p. 54, n. 201) |
| 1 | c. *128 S* | bracelet | | d.: ~80 | conch; incised decoration; fgt. |
| 2 | r. *120* | mother of pearl bead | uneven sphere | d.: 4.5 - 5 | small uneven perforation |

## P3 - SURGICAL IMPLEMENTS: bronze (Cl. Rapin, *Fouilles d'AKh VIII*, p. 343)

Fig. 24, p. 37

| Nº | Location | Object | Dim. | Observations |
|---|---|---|---|---|
| 4 | r. *107* NE | *decapitator* ? | l.: 58; wi.: 5-6 | hole for fixing; fragmentary and twisted stem (applique ?) |

## R35 - FURNITURE: inlays in bone - ivory

Fig. 25, p. 38
(Cl. Rapin, *Fouilles d'AKh VIII*, pp. 345-346)

| Nº | Location | Object | Dim. | Observations |
|---|---|---|---|---|
| 2 | r. *129* S | monkey ? | h.: 24 | ivory; of 4 mm diameter hole for fixing runs through the entire depth |
| 3 | r. *129* SW | lid of a square box | wi.: 73<br>h.: 28 | ivory; section of the lid of a square box of which the figurine of the monkey mentioned above probably constituted the knob for holding; edge decorated with incised crossed lines |

## S - FURNITURE inlaid with semi-precious stones: throne

Fig. 26 to 29, pp. 41-49

## S3 - ELEMENTS IN BRONZE: rivets and nails (Cl. Rapin, *Fouilles d'AKh VIII*, pp. 346-347)

Fig. 26

| Nº | Location | Object | tot. h. | wi. head | th. | Observations |
|---|---|---|---|---|---|---|
| 1 | r. *109* SW | rivet | 13 | 10 | | wire folded in H shape |
| 2 | r. *109* NW | rivet | 13 | 10 | | |
| 7 | r. *109* | rivet | 9 | 10 | | |
| 28 | c. *105* / r. *108-109* | rivet in T shape | 25 | 9 | | nail with T shaped head |

## S14 - ELEMENTS IN SCHIST (points for fixing) (Cl. Rapin, *Fouilles d'AKh VIII*, pp. 347-348)

| N° | Location | Observations |
|---|---|---|
| 1-6 | c. *105* / r. *109*<br>r. *109* | 42 points |

## S15 - ELEMENTS IN ROCK CRYSTAL (approx. 37 fgts.) (Cl. Rapin, *Fouilles d'AKh VIII*, pp. 348-349)

Fig. 27

| N° | Location | Form | Type | Dim. | Observations |
|---|---|---|---|---|---|
| 1 | c. *105* / r. *109* | disc | thinned edge<br>t. A | d.: 113<br>th.: ~1.8 | polished on both sides; rim cut and mat; fragmentary |
| 2 | c. *113* / r. *123* | disc | thinned edge<br>t. A | d.: 32<br>th.: 2.5 - 3 | polished on both sides; rim mat; surface of the two sides not parallel |
| 3 | r. *111*, fosse | disc | thinned edge<br>t. A | d.: 18<br>th.: 3 | polished; side with small d. slightly scratched |
| 4 | r. *109* NW | disc | thinned edge<br>t. A | d.: ~150<br>th.: 2 | polished, small fgt. of edge |
| 5 | r. *104* NE | disc | t. B | d.: ~60<br>th.: 2.5 | polished, edge cut with pincers and then rounded by polishing but slightly irregular |
| 6 | r. *104* NE | disc | t. B | d.: ~60 | polished, edge cut with pincers and then touched up by turning but some irregularities remain |
| 8 | c. *105* /<br>r. *109 - 110* | tube-sheath | conical;<br>hexagonal; t. C | max. d.: 22<br>d. hole: 4-15 | upper end broken (h.: >19) |
| 9 | r. *112* SW | tube-sheath | octagonal;<br>t. D | int. d.: 22<br>ext. d.: 34 | "button" in relief on the edge (h.: >50) |
| 10 | <br>r. *127* SE<br>c. *105* N | tube-sheath | octagonal;<br>t. D | int. d.: 23.5<br>ext. d.: 32<br>h.: >52 | wall slightly rounded; 3 fgts.; a fragment of the end of the tube with two holes for fixing at 2 mm from the edge on 2 opposite facettes |
| 11 | r. *126* S | tube-sheath | octagonal ?<br>arched; t.: D | int. d.: ~1<br>h.: >42 | same form (but bigger) as the preceding |
| 16<br>17 | c. *105* N | tube-sheath | octagonal ?<br>arched; t. E | int. d.: 10<br>ext. d.: 14 | 2 fgts. non interlocking, but probably belonging to the same object (h.: >14) |
| 18 | r. *119* W | tube-sheath | cylinder; t. F | int. d.: 13<br>ext. d.: 25 | decorative demi "button" on one end of the fgt.; (h.:>26) |
| 19 | r. *109* S | tube-sheath | cylinder; t. G | int. d.: 23<br>ext. d.: 34 | end with oblique cut towards the inside of the tube; fgt. |
| 24<br>to<br>26 | r. *119* E<br>r. *119* W<br>c. *105* / r. *109* | tube-sheath | cylinder; t. H | int. d.: 18<br>ext. d.: 22 | thickness of the wall: between 1.5 and 3 mm; hole for fixing near the end; edge unpolished |

## S17 - INLAYS IN BANDED AGATE (approx. 520 fgts.)

Fig. 28.1-3, p. 24, 30-31, 41 sqq.
(Cl. Rapin, *Fouilles d'AKh VIII*, pp. 349-355)

| Nº | Location | Form | Type | Dim. | Th. | Observations (fragmentary, intact signalised) |
|---|---|---|---|---|---|---|
| 1 | r. *109* SW against the wall | trapezoid | A | h.: 126 min. wi.: 65 max. wi.: 157 | 4-5 | brown agate |
| 2 | r. *119* W | trapezoid | A | h.: ~130 min. wi.: 59 max. wi.: 95 approx. | 1-3 | brown agate |
| 3 | c. *105* / r. 118 | trapezoid? | A | | 2.2 -3 | light beige agate; obverse polished, reverse tarnished with fine parallel saw marks |
| 4 | r. *109* NW | trapezoid? | A | | 5 | black agate |
| 5 | r. *109* W | triangle | B | | 4.5 | black agate, colourless crystalline veins |
| 6 | c. *105* / r. *108 - 109* | triangle | B | | 4.5 | black agate |
| 7 | r. *109* SW | triangle | B | | 5 | agate: burnt fgt. (grey) |
| 8 | r. *109* NW | triangle | B | | 3.5 | black agate |
| 10 | r. *118* E door | oval | C | l.: >20 | 3 | light brown agate; obverse polished, reverse mat; edge filed |
| 11 | r. *119* W against the wall | triangle | D | 28 x 28 | 6 | light brown agate; complete triangle rectangle, with perforation on one side; obverse polished; reverse and 2 edges unpolished; 1 edge with saw marks |
| 12 | r. *109* NW | triangle | D | 9 x 12 x 12 | 4 | light brown agate; polished triangle, chamfered edge (surface mat; crack accidental ?) |
| 13 | c. *105* / r. *104* | disc | E | d.: 56 | 5 ? | brown agate; obverse rounded and polished, reverse mat with cutting fault; complete |
| 14 | r. *109* NW c. *105* / r. *109* | disc | E | d.: ~58 | 2 | black agate with thin while veins; 2 interlocking fgts. |
| 15 | r. *109* NW | disc | E | d.: 60 | 5 | black agate |
| 16 | c. *105* / r. *110* door | disc | E | d.: 28 | ? | brown agate |
| 17 | r. *109* W | disc ? | E | d.: 160 ? | 4-5 | black agate; see also the following shape |
| 18 | r. *118* SE | section of disc | F | wi.: 52 | ? | brown agate; obverse polished disc |
| 19 | r. *109* SW | rectangle | G | 38 x >21 | 3 | black agate with white veins; obverse polished; partially flattened edges; veins as in numerous other plaquettes from the same block |
| 20 | r. *109* NW | rectangle | G | >28 x 22-23 | 2.5 | black agate, white vein, edge flattened with cutting marks of the pincers |
| 21 | r. *109* SW | rectangle | G | >39 x 18-19 | 3 | black agate with crystalline vein, obverse polished, edge out with pincers |
| 23 | r. *109* W | rectangle | G | >23 x 23-24 | 3 | brown agate, edge cut with pincers |
| 24 | r. *109* NW | rectangle | G | >24 x 23 | 3 | edge cut with pincers |
| 25 | r. *109* SW | rectangle | G | >20 x 22-24 | 3 | brown agate - flattened edges with cutting marks of the pincers |

| | | | | | | |
|---|---|---|---|---|---|---|
| 26 | r. *109* NW | rectangle | G | >20 x 23-24 | 2-3 | brown agate |
| 27 | r. *109* NW | rectangle | G | >33 x >43 | 4 | black agate with white veins; obverse polished and damaged, reverse mat |
| 28 | r. *109* W | trapeze ? | ? | >12 x >22 | 5 | black agate with white veins; flattened edge with rim on the reverse side resulting from cutting with the saw |
| 29 | r. *109* NW | rectangle | G | >21 x >30 | | black agate with white veins; flattened edge |
| 30 | r. *109* NW | rectangle | G | >21 x >18 | 1 | black agate with white veins |
| 32 | r. *109* NW | rectangle ? | G | >23 x >11 | 2 | brown agate with white veins |
| 34 | r. *109* W | rectangle | G | >23 x >9 | 3 | brown agate |
| 36 | r. *109* SW, NW | rectangle | G | >49 x 29 | 2-4 | agate (greenish?) light coloured; obverse polished, reverse mat with rim resulting from cutting with saw; 2 fgts interlocking |
| 39 | r. *118* W | "demi-disc" | H | 48 x 27 | 3.5-5 | complete specimen; brown agate with white veins cut from the same block as n° 54; edge cut with pincers; work: cutting with a smooth saw, reverse mat |
| 40 | r. *109* W<br>pit | "demi-disc" | H | 68 x 38 | 2-7 | *idem*; work: obverse partially polished and rim due to cutting with jagged saw, reverse mat |
| 41 | c. *105* / r. *109* | "demi-disc" | H | 78 x 35 | 3-4.5 | *idem*; work: sides mat |
| 42 | c. *105* / r. *110*<br>door | "demi-disc" | H | 61 x 32 | 2-4 | *idem*; work: sides mat, obverse iridescent with saw marks on the lower part |
| 43 | r. *118*<br>SE, W | "demi-disc" | H | 58 x 35 | 1-4.5 | *idem*, but broken in 3 fgts.; work: obverse mat with traces of polishing, reverse with fault due to cutting with saw |
| 44 | r. *109* W | "demi-disc" | H | >34 x 31 | 5 | fgt. of agate from the same block as the preceding, but black with white veins (colour obtained by heating) with marks of fire |
| 48 | r. *109* NW | "demi-disc" | H | >37 x 33 | 2-6 | *idem*, but black colour; work: *idem* |
| 51 | r. *119* W | "demi-disc" | H | >40 x 33 | 1-4.5 | *idem*, with crystalline upper edge; work: *idem*, rim due to severance flattened |
| 56 | c. *105* / r. *107*<br>c. *105* / r. *109*<br>r. *118* S | cylindrical tube-sheath | K | int. d.: 100<br>ext. d. 110<br>h.: 36 | 4<br>4<br>3 | 3 fgts. of agate with the same veins; 2 interlocking |
| 58 | r. *109*<br>NW, W | tube-sheath | L | int. d.: 36<br>h.: >21 | | black agate with white veins, polished; inner wall furrowed due to turning; external section triangular or square with rounded corners; 3 fgts. |
| 59 | r. *111* NW | tube-sheath | L | int. d.: 36<br>h.: 20-24 | | dark brown and grey agate; external section triangular or square with rounded corners; 2 fgts. |
| 62 | r. *109* W | cylindrical tube-sheath | M | int. d.: 29<br>ext. d.: 43<br>h.: >22 | 7 | light beige agate with white veins |
| 64 | c. *105* / r. *109* | cylindrical tube-sheath | M | int. d.: 25<br>ext. d.: 39<br>h.: >30 | 6 | black agate with crystalline and white veins, polished exterior, interior mat |
| 65 | r. *109* SW | cylindrical tube-sheath | M | int. d.: 28<br>ext. d.: 40<br>h.: >23 | 6 | beige agate with whitish veins; external surface polished |
| 67 | r. *109* NW | cylindrical tube-sheath | M | int. d.: 27<br>ext. d.: 39 | 6 | black agate with white veins; inner wall has fine furrows resulting from turning |

| | | | | | | |
|---|---|---|---|---|---|---|
| 68 | c. *105* / r. *110* / r. *109* | cylindrical tube-sheath | M | int. d.: 30<br>ext. d.: 44 ?<br>h.: >46 | 7 ? | black agate with white and crystalline spots on the outer wall only; inner wall marked by fine furrows resulting from turning; 2 interlocking fgts. |
| 94 | c. *105* / r. *109* S | bracelet | t. A | d.: ~70 | | agate |
| 95 | c. *105* / r. *109* | bracelet | t. A | d.: ~84<br>h.: >35 | 2.5-<br>3.5 | brown agate, white vein; 3 fgts, of the same object (?) |
| 101 | r. *109* W | bracelet | t. B | d.: ~80 | 3 - 5 | black agate, parallel veins on the edge; fgts. of the same object |
| 103 | r. *109* | bracelet | t. C | | | |
| 104 | c. *105* / r. *109* | bracelet | t. D | d.: ~66 | 2 - 3 | brown agate; 2 fgts |
| 105 | c. *105* / r. *107* | bracelet | t. D | d.: ~75 | | brown agate; inner traces of turning visible |

## S18 - INLAYS IN WHITE AGATE (Cl. Rapin, *Fouilles d'AKh VIII*, pp. 355-356) Fig. 29, p. 46

| N° | Location | l. | wi. | th. | Observations |
|---|---|---|---|---|---|
| 1 | r. *109* W pit | 55 | 9 | 3.2 | complete; 1 edge polished; chamfered ends; sides mat |
| 2 | r. *110* W | 64 | 9 | 4 | almost complete; burnt |
| 3 | r. *109* SW | 37 | 7.5 | 3.4 | fgt.; burnt; thin saw mark on one side, 1 edge polished |
| 6 | r. *109* NW | 31 | 7.8 | 3.8 | 1 edge cut with pincers; 1 edge and one side polished |
| 11 | c. *105* / r. *110* | 46 | 9.9 | 3.2 | 1 edge and one side polished; burnt ? |
| 13 | r. *109* SW | 9 | 9 | 2.8 | losange, 1 edge and 1 side polished |

## S36 - ELEMENTS IN WOOD (Cl. Rapin, *Fouilles d'AKh VIII*, p. 356)

| N° | Location | Object | Dim. | Observations |
|---|---|---|---|---|
| 1 | r. *109* NE | gilt cylindrical wood | d.: ~26 | probably belongs to the same article as the tubes in rock crystal and the plaquettes in agate; some fgts. |
| 5 | r. *109* | | | burnt wood: pear tree (*Pirus sp.*) |

# Q - INDIAN DISC

See pp. 51-102; fig. 30-60

## Catalogue of the fragments and inventory of the motifs.

— Place of discovery: Ai Khanum, Treasury of the palace, court *105* West, except the plaquette I-10 discovered in room *111* (inv. O77, 196).

— Plaquettes: 33 specimens, of which 4 are restuck (N[os] 23, 26, 27, 32) and 7 are broken and incomplete (N[os] 1, 6, 10, 14, 17, 24, 28). N°5 is an inlay and is not counted.

Technique of making the plaquettes: saw, rasp, drill, chisel, patterns.

The veins of the shells of the plaquettes are generally oriented vertically in relation to the image, with the exception of elongated fragments arranged horizontally like the plaquettes N° 27, 31, 32, 33, and probably also the plaquettes N° 7 and 8.

— Inlays: 67 specimens, complete or fragmentary, fixed on 14 plaquettes (N[os] 1, 3, 4, 7, 8, 11, 12, 13, 15, 19, 20, 21, 27, 32); 134 isolated specimens, complete or fragmentary.

Colours of the inlays: light orange, wine brown to brown, black, white, green, light green, light rosy beige (whitish).

The term "centre" under the column "Location" designates the central area of the plaque; the term "frieze" designates the flat circular edge with smaller motifs; the term "border" designates the convex border decorated with foliage.

### I) Catalogue of the plaquettes in mother of pearl

Fig. 30

| N° | Location | h. mm | wi. mm | max. th. mm | th. base mm | General description | Fixing details |
|---|---|---|---|---|---|---|---|
| 1 | convex border | | 20 | 8.5 | | fgt. | hole for fixing inside a flower |
| 2 | frieze-upper left centre | 28 | 19 | 2.8-3 | 1.1-1.8 | | |
| 3 | centre above | 26 | 25 | 2.4-2.5 | 0.8-2.3 | upper right corner cut | |
| 4 | centre-upper left edge | 31 | 10 | 2.6-3 | 1-1.3 | | |
| 5 | centre-upper left | - | - | - | - | glass inlay | |
| 6 | centre-upper left? | 24 | >10 | - | ? | fgt. of inlaid base | |
| 7 | centre-upper right | 27 | 22 | 3-3.1 | 1-1.9 | lower right corner cut | = notch for adjusting or fixing? |
| 8 | centre-upper right | 27 | 16.5 | 1.5-2-2 | 1.5 | notch on lower right corner | |
| 9 | frieze-left | 18 | 21.5 | 2.1-2.6 | 0.8-1 | | |
| 10 | centre left | 17 | <17 | 3-3.2 | 1.5-2 | fgt. | |
| 11 | centre right | 33 | 28 | 2.2-2.7 | 0.9-1.8 | notch on upper right corner | = notch for adjusting or fixing? |
| 12 | frieze-right | 33 | 20 | 2.3-2.9 | 1 | upper left corner chipped | |
| 13 | frieze-left | 33 | 21 | 2.2 | 2.9 | notch on lower left edge | = notch for fixing? |

| Nº | Location | h. mm | wi. mm | max. th. mm | th. base mm | General description | Fixing details |
|---|---|---|---|---|---|---|---|
| 14 | centre left | 29.5 | 18 | 2.2-2.7 | 1 | fgt.; notch or chip on the upper left corner | |
| 15 | centre | 26 | 18.5 | 2.1-3 | 0.7-1 | | |
| 16 | centre | 25 | 23 | 2.9-3 | 1.2-1.8 | upper right corner cut | |
| 17 | centre right | >18 | >7 | 2.5 | 1 | fgt. | |
| 18 | centre right | 28 | 16 | 3 | 1.5-1.8 | lower left corner chipped | corners of the pl. 18, 19 and 25: chipping due to an earlier fixing? |
| 19 | centre right | 31 | 21 | 2.3-2.9 | 0.9-1.1 | lower left corner chipped | |
| 20 | frieze-right | 32 | 19 | 2.2-3 | 0.9-2 | | |
| 21 | frieze-left | 28 | 21.5 | 1.9-2.8 | 0.9-1.2 | left corner cut | |
| 22 | frieze-lower left-centre | 27 | 7 | 1.5-2.3 | 0.7-1.3 | lower right corner chipped | = chipping or notch for fixing? |
| 23 | centre below | 23 | 21 | 2-2.9 | 0.8-2 | restuck, but a fgt. of the head of the human figure is missing | |
| 24 | centre below | >17 | 21 | 1.9-2.7 | 1 | fgt. | |
| 25 | centre-lower right | 31 | 23 | ? | ? | upper edge, upper right corner chipped, lower corners cut | |
| 26 | frieze-lower left | 18.5 | 16.5 | 1.5-1.9 | 0.3-0.6 | upper corners chipped; restuck | chipping or notch for fixing on the upper right corner? |
| 27 | frieze-lower left centre | 17 | 34 | 1.9-2.6 | 0.4-0.8 | upper left corner chipped; restuck | |
| 28 | centre below | >7 | 18 | 1.9-2.8 | - | fgt. | |
| 29 | frieze-lower centre | 30 | 23 | 2.7-3.3 | 1.5-1.7 | | |
| 30 | frieze-lower right | 17 | 16 | 2 | 0.8 | upper left corner chipped | = chipping or notch for fixing? |
| 31 | frieze-lower | 9 | 19 | 1.4-2.3 | 1.1 | lower right corner chipped | |
| 32 | frieze-lower | 15.5 | 33 | 2.2-2.5 | 0.8-1.2 | restuck; left and lower edge, upper right corner chipped;<br>notch at the bottom of the right edge;<br>notch on the lower edge; cut perpendicular to the veins of the mother of pearl | <br><br>= notch for fixing<br><br>= notch for fixing? |
| 33 | frieze-lower | ~5 | ~26 | 2 | 0.2 | | |
| 34 | frieze-lower | 17 | 19.5 | 2.8-3 | 1-1.5 | | |

## Inventory of motifs

Fig. 32

### II) Human figures (16 in number)

| N° | Description (Dim. in mm) | Preserved inlays | Plaquettes | Location |
|---|---|---|---|---|
| 1 | female figure seated with raised hand, front view; h.: ~16.5 | folds of the garment of the arms and the legs | 12 | frieze right |
| 2 | female figure seated with raised hand, front view; h.: 13 | | 34, 29 | frieze lower |
| 3 | male figure seated with raised hand, right profile; h.: 14 | | 34 | frieze lower |
| 4 | male figure seated with raised hand, right profile; h.: 18 | | 9 | frieze left |
| 5 | male figure seated with raised hand, right profile; h.: 13 | | 2 | frieze upper left |
| 6 | female figure, seated with raised hand, front view; h.: ~13 | | 2 | frieze upper left |
| 7 | seated figure, right profile | earring | 4 | centre upper left |
| 8 | female figure, first among the three figures under an umbrella and probably on a balcony, front view | folds of the garment of the left arm and decoration on the head | | centre upper right |
| 9 | female figure, front view, face turned three quarters to the left (?), in the centre of the same group | | 7, 8 | centre upper right |
| 10 | female figure, front view, third of the same group | earring | 8 | centre upper right |
| 11 | figure holding a spur, front view, first of the group of three persons in the quadriga under an umbrella | | 15 | centre below |
| 12 | male figure in the centre of the same group, face turned three quarters to the left (?) | | 15, 16, 23 | centre below |
| 13 | figure holding a fly whisk on the right shoulder, third of the same group, frontal view | | 16, 23 | centre below |
| 14 | figure of cavalier advancing to the left | | 14, 22 | centre lower left |
| 15 | figure of cavalier armed with a lance (?) and advancing to the left | | 17, 18, 19, 25 | centre lower right |
| 16 | figure of cavalier advancing to the left | | 23, 24, 25, 29 | centre lower right |

### III) Ornaments, attributes and costumes of the 16 persons listed in table II

| N° | Ornaments of persons | Attributes | Costume |
|---|---|---|---|
| 1 | pair of earrings and double ornament on the head | | folds of orange garment on the arm and brown garment on the legs |
| 2 | pair of earrings and double ornament framing the head | | |
| 3 | bun in front and at the back of the head and earring | | |
| 4 | bun in front and at the back of the head and earring | | |

| N° | Ornaments of persons | Attributes | Costume |
|---|---|---|---|
| 5 | bun in front and at the back of the head | | |
| 6 | pair of earrings and double ornament framing the head | | |
| 7 | earring and buns | | |
| 8 | pair of earrings and double ornament framing the head | shaft on either side of the body, umbrella (IV-13) | folds of orange garment on the left arm |
| 9 | earring of the left side, bun on the forehead and a group of three curls on the side of the head | umbrella (IV-13) | |
| 10 | pair of earrings and double ornament framing the head | shaft on either side of the body, umbrella (IV-13) | |
| 11 | pair of earrings and double ornament consisting of two groups of three small discs on the sides linked by a band | spur of the driver (IV-22), umbrella (IV-14) | |
| 12 | pair of earrings and bun on the right side | umbrella (IV-14) | |
| 13 | pair of earrings and double ornament consisting of two groups of three small discs on the sides | fly-whisk (IV-18), umbrella (IV-14) | |
| 14 | fgt. | head wearing a helmet (?) | |
| 15 | earring, lance or arrow (IV-19) | helmet with crest (IV-20), lance or arrow (IV-19) | |
| 16 | fgt. | scarf flowing down the back (IV-22) | |

## IV) Architecture and objects

Fig. 32, 35-36

| N° | Type | Description (Dim. in mm) | Preserved inlays | Plaquettes | Location |
|---|---|---|---|---|---|
| 1 | edifice | roof with three pinnacles, three-quarter orientation towards the left; h.: 17; h. door: 7.5 | door on the facade and section of the roof | 12 | frieze-right |
| 2 | edifice | roof with three pinnacles, three quarter orientation to the right;h. 13; h. door: ~5.5 | section of the roof | 32, 34 | frieze-lower |
| 3 | edifice | identified only by the line of its base | | 13 | frieze-left |
| 4 | edifice | roof with 6-7 pinnacles; two sections of the roof arranged symmetrically on either side of the central facade (?) | 4 fgts. of the roof | 2, 3, 5, 6 | centre-upper left |
| 5 | column | first of a series of four equidistant columns | | 14 | centre left |
| 6 | column | second of the same series of columns | | 10 (?) | centre left |
| 7 | column | third of the same series of columns | | 16 | centre right |
| 8 | column | fourth of the same series of columns | | 19 | centre right |
| 9 | balcony? | architectural structure below and to the left of the group of three spectators II-8, 9, 10 | | 7, 8 | centre-upper right |
| 10 | pond? | parallelepiped form (three-quarter view); h.: 7.5 | 2 blue fgts. | 32, 33 | frieze-lower |
| 11 | canopy or table | three-quarter view of the structure | | 10 | centre left |

| N° | Type | Description (Dim. in mm) | Preserved inlays | Plaquettes | Location |
|---|---|---|---|---|---|
| 12 | throne? | unidentified structure under a tree | | 3 | centre above |
| 13 | chariot | guard-rail (tot. h. of the quadriga: 47) | VII-38? | 23 | centre below |
| 14 | umbrella | edge represented by a groove; l.:36 (see III-8, 9, 10) | | 7, 8 | centre-upper right |
| 15 | umbrella | grainy edge; l.: 27 (see III-11.12.13) | | 15, 16 | centre below |
| 16 | shafts | four shafts arranged obliquely in pairs (see III-10) | | 7, 8 | centre-upper right |
| 17 | spur | held in slanting position by the driver (II-11) | | 15 | |
| 18 | fly-whisks | held over the shoulder by the third occupant of the quadriga (II-13) | | 23 | |
| 19 | lance or arrow | held by the cavalier II-15 | | 18 | |
| 20 | helmet? | cavalier II-14 | | 14 | |
| 21 | helmet | cavalier II-15 | | 18 | |
| 22 | shield? | cavalier II-15 | | 18 | |
| 23 | reins | cavalier II-16 | | 23 | |
| 24 | panache | head of the horse V-23 | | 23 | |
| 25 | foliage | related to floral motifs | | 1 | convex border right |
| 26 | unidentified | decorative motif; l.: 19 | | 32 | frieze-lower |

## V) Animals (the description of the frieze is done from below to above)

Fig. 32, 37

| N° | Animal | Description (Dim. in mm) | Preserved inlays | Plaquettes | Location |
|---|---|---|---|---|---|
| 1 | deer | advancing to the right, head lowered; h.: 12 | | 29 | frieze-lower right |
| 2 | doe | advancing to the right | | 25, 30 | frieze-lower right |
| 3 | peacock | turned to the right | | 20, 30 | frieze-lower right |
| 4 | female peacock | turned to the right; h.: 10 | on the back and on the lower edge of the wing | 20 | frieze-lower right |
| 5 | doe | advancing to the left; l.: 25 | head | 27, 31, 32, 33 | frieze-lower left |
| 6 | deer | advancing to the left; l.: 23 | hindquarters | 26, 27, 31 | frieze-lower left |
| 7 | peacock | turned to the left; l.: 36 | | 21, 22, 26 | frieze-lower left |
| 8 | female peacock | turned to the left; l.: 27 | tail | 13, 21 | frieze-lower left |
| 9 | bird | turned to the right; egret on the head and under the chin (peacock designed erroneously or an undetermined species of bird | | 2, 4 | frieze-upper left |

| N° | Animal | Description (Dim. in mm) | Preserved inlays | Plaquettes | Location |
|---|---|---|---|---|---|
| 10 | ? | forelegs of a quadruped or tail of bird V-11 | | 2 | centre upper left |
| 11 | bird | bird without a crest on the head (duck?); body turned to the right and head looking at the left | | 3 | centre above |
| 12 | quadruped | running to the left; hindlegs or tail on plaquette N°12; model of the deer in the frieze | | 11, 12 | centre right |
| 13 | female peacock | above a male peacock; turned to the left | | 11 | centre right |
| 14 | peacock | turned to the left | | 11, 18, 19 | centre right |
| 15 | bird? | end of the tail falling vertically (parrot?) | | 14 | centre left |
| 16 | deer | middle of the central area; advancing to the left | | 15, 16 | centre |
| 17 | horse | first horse (right side) of the quadriga (disappeared) | | | centre below |
| 18 | horse | second horse of the quadriga | | 27, 28 | centre below |
| 19 | horse | third horse of the quadriga | | 27, 28 | centre below |
| 20 | horse | fourth horse (left side) of the quadriga | | 27, 28 | centre below |
| 21 | horse | mounted by the cavalier II-14; advancing to the left | | 14, 22 | centre-lower left |
| 22 | horse | mounted by the cavalier II-15; advancing to the left, foreleg folded high; tot. h.: 35 | | 17, 18, 19, 25 | centre-lower right |
| 23 | horse | mounted by the cavalier II-16, equipped with reins and a panache on the head | | 23, 24, 25, 29 | centre-lower right |

## VI) Plants and floral decor

Fig. 32

| N° | Type | Description | Preserved inlays | Plaquettes | Location |
|---|---|---|---|---|---|
| 1 | flowering shrub | linked to the foliage (IV-25) | 1 flower (type VII-47) | 1 | convex border |
| 2 | flowering shrub | l.: 18 mm | 3 flowers (type VII-47) | 20 | frieze-lower right |
| 3 | flowering shrub | l.: 22 mm | 5 flowers (type VII-47) | 13 | frieze-lower |
| 4 | flowering shrub | stalk bent down? | | 4 (?), 9 | frieze-upper left |
| 5 | flowering shrub | three branches fanning out | 4 flowers (type VII-47) | 3 | centre above |
| 6 | flowering shrub | | | 9, 13, 14 | centre left |
| 7 | flowering shrub | | 5 flowers (type VII-47) | 15 | centre |
| 8 | flowering shrub | | 3 flowers (type VII-47) | 12, 19 | centre right |
| 9 | flowering shrub | placed apparently under the chariot | | 29 | centre below |

| Nº | Type | Description | Preserved inlays | Plaquettes | Location |
|---|---|---|---|---|---|
| 10 | flowering shrub | l.: 21 mm | | 25 | centre lower right |
| 11 | decorative motif? | | | 27, 28 | centre below |
| 12 | 4 petalled flower | | | 21 | frieze-below left |
| 13 | 4 petalled flower | | | 13 | frieze-below left |
| 14 | 4 petalled flower | | | 11 | centre right |
| 15 | 4 petalled flower | | | 18 | centre right |
| 16 | 4 petalled flower | | | 19 | centre lower right |
| 17 | 4 petalled flower | behind the hoof of the last horse | | 28 | centre below |
| 18 | quadruple floral motif | 6 x 8 mm; same pattern as VI-19 and 34(?) | flowers (type VII-63) | 11 (top) | centre-upper right |
| 19 | quadruple floral motif? | | | 27 | centre-lower left |
| 20 | triple floral motif | same pattern as VI-24, 27 and probably 22, 25, 32, 33 | | 3 (bottom) | centre above |
| 21 | triple floral motif | same pattern as VI-28 | | 3 (centre) | centre above |
| 22 | triple floral motif | 6 x 7 mm | flowers (type VII-68) | 11 (bottom) | centre-upper right |
| 23 | triple floral motif | | | 11 (right) | centre-upper right |
| 24 | triple floral motif | | flower (type VII-52) | 15 | centre |
| 25 | triple floral motif | | | 16 (centre) | centre |
| 26 | triple floral motif | | | 16, 23 | centre below |
| 27 | triple floral motif | | | 25 (right) | centre-lower right |
| 28 | triple floral motif | | | 25 | centre-lower right |
| 29 | triple floral motif | | | 29 | centre-lower right |
| 30 | double floral motif | | | 2 | frieze-upper left |
| 31 | double floral motif | | | 19 | centre right |
| 32 | multiple floral motif | perhaps triple (same edges VI-20) | | 3 (top) | centre above |
| 33 | multiple floral motif | perhaps triple (same edges VI-20) | | 27 | centre-lower left |
| 34 | multiple floral motif | | | 25 (right) | centre-lower right |
| 35 | isolated flower | | (type VII-47) | 1 | convex border |
| 36 | 9 isolated flowers | | | 1 | convex border |
| 37 | 5 isolated flowers | | (type VII-47) | 20, 32, 21 13, 4 | frieze |
| 38 | 51 isolated flowers | | | diverse | frieze |
| 39 | isolated flower | | (type VII-53) | 19 | centre |
| 40 | 3 isolated flowers | | (type VII-47) | 3, 7, 19 | centre |
| 41 | 54 isolated flowers | | | diverse | centre |

## VII) Inlays of molten glass

Fig. 33

(those plaquettes are signalled on which the inlays were still in place)

| N° | Type | Plaquettes | Description |
|---|---|---|---|
| 1 | feminine figure (II-1) | 12 | orange garment of the left arm in molten glass inlaid with gold wire |
| 2 | *idem* (II-1) | 12 | orange garment of the right arm in molten glass inlaid with gold wire |
| 3 | *idem* (II-1) | 12 | brown garment of the legs in molten glass inlaid with gold wire |
| 4 | feminine figure (II-8) | 7 | orange garment of the left arm in molten glass inlaid with gold wire |
| 5 | draped figure | | fgt.; orange garment of arms (?) in molten glass inlaid with gold wire |
| 6 | draped figure | | fgt.; orange garment of arms (?) in molten glass inlaid with gold wire; belonging to a figure in the central area (passenger of the quadriga?) |
| 7 | draped figure | | fgt.; orange garment of arms (?) in molten glass inlaid with gold wire; probably interlocking with preceding fragment |
| 8 | draped figure | | fgt.; orange garment of arm (?) in molten glass inlaid with gold wire |
| 9 | draped figure | | fgt.; orange garment in molten glass inlaid with gold wire |
| 10 | draped figure | 23? | brown garment of the left arm in molten glass inlaid with gold wire; belonging perhaps to one of the passengers of the quadriga |
| 11 | draped figure | | brown garment of the left arm in molten glass inlaid with gold wire |
| 12 | draped figure | | fgt.; brown garment of arm (?) in molten glass inlaid with gold wire; belonging probably to a figure in the central area |
| 13 | edifice with 7 pinnacles (IV-4) | 2, 3 | brownish red fgt. of the left section of the roof; molten glass inlaid with small discs arranged alternately white and orange in a chequered pattern and encircled with a gold leaf; h.: 11 mm |
| 14 | *idem* (IV-4) | 2, 3 | fgt. of the left section of the roof stuck to the preceding fgt. |
| 15 | *idem* (IV-4) | 2, 3 | fgt. of the right section of the roof, appearance similar to the preceding fgt. |
| 16 | *idem* (IV-4) | 2, 3 | fgt. of the right section of the roof; same as the preceding fgt. |
| 17 | edifice with 3 pinnacles (IV-2) | 32, 34 | right section of the roof; brown molten glass inlaid with small orange discs arranged in a chequered pattern and probably encircled by a gold leaf; h.:6 |
| 18 | edifice with 3 pinnacles (IV-1) | 12 | right section of the roof; white molten glass inlaid with small orange discs arranged in a chequered pattern and apparently encircled by a gold leaf; h.: 6 |
| 19 | *idem* (IV-1) | 12 | door composed of a rectangular element in black molten glass and framed by a polychrome border in orange, brown and white crowned by a small demi disc of type VII-47; h.: 7.5 mm; wi.: 6 mm |
| 20 | edifice with 3 pinnacles | | rectangular element in black molten glass of the door of an edifice which has a border of the same type as the preceding |
| 21 | pond (?) (IV-9) | 32, 33 | left fgt. of a plaquette of green molten glass probably depicting water and inlaid with two orange or brown spots encircled with a gold leaf and a fragmentary motif with a lance-like form (see below) |
| 22 | *idem* (IV-9) | 32, 33 | right fgt. of the same inlay; 4 orange or brown pastilles; same motif encircled by a gold leaf and with a lance-like form, of which the black tip precedes two white "eyes" and which has an undulating tail designed with gold wire at the other end: serpent or lotus leaf? |
| 23 | edifice? | | fgt. of an assemblage of three sticks coloured white-brown-white in that order; 6x 2.5 mm |
| 24 | edifice? | | fgt. of an assemblage of three sticks coloured black-orange-black in that order (total: 4 isolated fgts.) |

| N° | Type | Plaquettes | Description |
|---|---|---|---|
| 25 | edifice? | | fgt. of an assemblage of 2 sticks coloured orange and brown (total: 5 isolated fgts.) |
| 26 | edifice? | | fgt. of an assemblage of four undulating sticks coloured orange-brown-white-white in that order and pertaining probably to the upper element of the frame of a door (comparable to the lintel of the door VII-19) |
| 27 | edifice? | | fgt. of an assemblage of 3 sticks coloured orange-brown-white in that order; (total: 6 isolated fgts.): same observations as for the preceding: they belong either to doors or to animals (see the wing of the peacock in VII-31) |
| 28 | edifice? | | fgt. of an assemblage of 3 curved sticks coloured brown-orange-white in that order |
| 29 | edifice? | | fgt. of an assemblage of 3 sticks coloured orange-brown-white in that order; two square orange and brown fgts. stuck side by side on the white stick (total: 2 isolated fgts.) |
| 30 | edifice? | | fgt. of an assemblage of 4 curved sticks coloured white-orange-brown-white in that order |
| [31 | female peacock (V-4) | 20 | inlay of the body comprising of the assemblage of several pastilles: the black is composed, from front to back, of pastilles of type VII-54, VII-58, VII-65; the lower edge of the wing consists of two fgts. with an assemblage of sticks coloured, from top to bottom, white-brown-orange in that order (see VII-27) |
| 32 | female peacock (V-8) | 13, 21 | inlay of the tail composed of an assemblage of sticks coloured, from top to bottom, grey-white-grey-white in that order |
| 33 | doe (V-5) | 27 | inlay of the head in brown molten glass, itself inlaid with an eye circled with a gold leaf, the eyes are designed with two juxtaposed black and white pastilles; dim.: 5x2.5 mm |
| 34 | deer (V-6) | 27 | fgt. of the inlay of the hindquarters in brown molten glass itself inlaid with small pastilles arranged in a chequered design, alternately white and orange encircled with a gold leaf following the same technique as the roofs above; h.: 4.5 mm |
| 35 | animal | | 2 fgts. of a plaquette of orange molten glass inlaid with small alternating white and brown pastilles arranged in a chequered design and encircled with gold leaf; they probably belong to a deer in the central area (V-16) rather than a horse; h.: 7 mm |
| 36 | animal? | | fgt. of a plaquette of brownish-red molten glass inlaid with two motifs divided by gold leaf; the first consists of two slightly arched points, one black and the other brownish-orange; the second motif is composed of 4 brownish-orange agglutinated pastilles; a hole separates the two motifs, we do not know if it is the result of deliberate design or an accident; perhaps this fgt. belonged to a horse in the central area and it is possible that it forms part of a head looking to the left, the points representing the mane brushed forward on the side of the neck and the 4 pastilles, the decoration of the bit; 10x4.5 mm |
| 37 | animal? | | fgt. of a plaquette of brownish red molten glass similar to the preceding; inlay of small brownish orange pastilles encircled with gold leaf and forming 3 curved lines arranged as arcs of concentric circles, that is, a group of 5 pastilles followed by 3 pastilles in the form of drops arranged in radiating lines pointing inside, followed, in turn by a third line which is similar but very fragmentary; 8x6.5 mm |

| Nº | Type | Plaquettes | Description |
|---|---|---|---|
| 38 | ? | | circular rim (?) of a fgt. of plaquette coloured beige and inlaid with undulating gold wire and a slightly curved alignment of at least 5 points extended by undulating gold wire arranged in a fan shape perpendicular to the edge (element from the central area of the plaque: quadriga, deer in the centre or cavalier?); 6x5.5 mm. See IV-13 |
| 39 | ? | | fgt. with an oval edge belonging to a black plaquette decorated with star-shaped brownish red lines |
| 40 | ? | | fgt. of the rectilinear edge of the same plaquette decorated with radiating lines; the association of the two plaquettes makes it possible to reconstitute a plaquette of a semi-oval shape: cornice of the pinnacled edifice of the border (h.: 5-7 mm)? |
| 41 | concentric grooves | | small plaquette of white molten glass forming part of an alignment of orange or white (perhaps also black and green) generally square or slightly rectangular inlays which filled the groove separating the central area from the border;there are 33 specimens (17 in place and 16 isolated) of the 200-220 which this groove originally had; 2 x 3 mm |
| 42 | concentric grooves | | plaquette of orange molten glass of the same type; 3 x 3 mm |
| 43 | pastille | | small discoidal inlay of molten glass formed of two colours arranged in a concentric design; with an orange centre and a brown border; technique of fabrication identical to that of millefiori; diam.: 1.5 mm |
| 44 | edifice? (assemblage) | | alignment of pastilles of the type VII-43 enclosed between two small brown and orange sticks (total: 2 isolated fgts.) |
| 45 | pastille | | small discoidal inlay of the same type of molten glass as VII-43 but with the colours inversed;centre brown-border orange |
| 46 | edifice? (assembl.) | | pastille of type VII-45 stuck to two small brown and orange sticks |
| 47 | pastille | | small disc of molten glass fabricated according to the technique of millefiori; orange base sprinkled with 7 minuscule brown points forming a polygonal shape imitating the petals of a flower (total; 22 isolated specimens, 31 in place); diam.: 2.5 mm |
| 48 | pastille | | *idem* |
| 49 | pastille | | *idem*, but surface cut obliquely with respect to the tigella forming the inlay (with enlargement) |
| 50 | pastille | | same type as VII-47 but with colours inversed (orange, generally circular points on a brown base) (total; 9 isolated specimens) |
| 51 | pastilles (assemblage) | | 3 specimens with an assemblage of a whole and a demi pastille of the type VII-50 (the demi-pastilles are also utilised with other types: see the door VII-19) |
| 52 | pastille (VI-24) | 15 | same design as VII-50 but oval in form, utilised in association with other types particularly in the inlay VII-74 |
| 53 | pastille (VI-39) | 19 | similar to the preceding but larger |
| 54 | pastille | | discoidal pastille fabricated according to the same technique: Y shaped motif, with brown centre (total: 17 isolated specimens; see also the wing of the peacock V-4 / VII-31) |
| 55 | (assemblage) | | 3 pastilles of the same type, interstices masked by white putty |
| 56 | (assemblage) | | 2 (pastilles of the same type, interstices masked by white putty) |
| 57 | (assemblage) | | a full and a demi pastille of the type VII-54; interstices masked by white putty |
| 58 | pastille | | similar to type VII-54, but with the colours inversed (Y in the centre is orange) (total: 4 isolated specimens; see also the wing of the peacock V-4 / VII-31) |

| N° | Type | Plaquettes | Description |
|---|---|---|---|
| 59 | pastille | | discoidal pastille: orange Y motif on brown base (total: 1 isolated specimen; see also VII-70, 71, 72, 74) |
| 60 | pastille | | discoidal pastille: brown base punctuated by 4 orange drops |
| 61 | pastille | | similar |
| 62 | pastille | | similar, 3 parallel droplets |
| 63 | pastille (VI-18) | 11 | similar, 3 droplets arranged in fan shape: 3 associated specimens (VII-69) |
| 64 | pastille | | similar, 2 big droplets elongated and parallel |
| 65 | pastille (VII-31) | 20 | similar, 2 droplets (body of the peacock V-4 / VII-31) |
| 66 | pastille | | similar, a thick droplet (associated with others in the inlays VII-70, 71, 73) |
| 67 | pastille | | same technique, 6 radiating lines from the centre of the pastille |
| 68 | floral motif (VI-22) | 11 | assemblage in place of several unidentified pastilles stuck with white putty |
| 69 | floral motif (VI-18) | 11 | assemblage in place of 3 pastilles of the type VII-63 stuck with white putty |
| 70 | (assemblage) | | fragmentary assemblage of 2 pastilles (VII-59 and VII-66) stuck with white putty |
| 71 | (assemblage) | | 3 pastilles of the types VII-59 and VII-66 stuck with white putty |
| 72 | (assemblage) | | 2 pastilles of the types VII-59 and VII-63 |
| 73 | (assemblage) | | 2 broken pastilles of the types VII-66 and VII-64 |
| [74] | (assemblage) | | pastilles of the types VII-52 and VII-59 |

## VIII) Repetitive motifs

Fig. 34

| N° | Type | Description |
|---|---|---|
| 1 | human figures | right silhouette of II-5 similar to left silhouette of II-6 (inversion) |
| 2 | human figures | right silhouette of II-4 similar to left silhouette of II-1 (inversion) |
| 3 | human figures | silhouettes of the heads and shoulders of II-8, 9 and 10 similar |
| 4 | horses | silhouettes of the belly and hindquarters of horses V-22 and V-23 similar |
| 5 | horse and deer | position of the forelegs and silhouette of the belly of V-22 (horse) and V-16 (deer) similar; the differences in the length of the hindquarters and the tail make it possible to identify the animal |
| 6 | horses and deer | position of hoofs |
| 7 | deers | similar flexion of the forelegs of the deer V-1 and V-6 (inversion) |
| 8 | does | similar flexion of the forelegs of the does V-2 and V-5 (inversion) |
| 9 | peacocks | same form of the body of V-4, 7 and 8 but the position of the tail and the head varies in each |
| 10 | peacocks | head and neck of the peacocks on the border (V-4, 7 and 8) have the same form but their positions in relation to the body vary |
| 11 | peacocks | tail of the male peacock V-14 in the central area is of the same size as that of the peacock V-3 of the border |
| 12 | birds | inversion of the body of the bird V-11 and the peacock V-13 |
| 13 | columns | same profile |
| 14 | floral motifs | repetition of quadruple and triple floral motifs (eg. VI-18 and VI-20, VI-21 respectively) |
| 15 | four petalled flowers | dimensions and proportions of VI-11 to VI-16 are identical |
| 16 | flowering stalks | same curve of the upper section of VI-2 and VI-3; the lower section of VI-3 which is additional as compared to VI-2 distinguishes itself from the rest of the stem by a different orientation |

## APPENDIX I : Chronology of events in Bactria and India in the 2nd century B.C.

According to hypotheses based on the remains of the treasury and numismatic study

| Date | Inscriptions of the treasury of Ai Khanum | North India and the Ganges valley | North-West India and the Indus valley | Paropamisadae and Arachosia (Alexandria of the Caucasus) | Western Bactria (Bactra) | Eastern Bactria (Ai Khanum) | North of the Oxus and Sogdiana |
|---|---|---|---|---|---|---|---|
| 205 | | | | | | | agreement between Euthydemus I and Antiochus III in view of the threat from the nomads |
| 200-190 | | | Demetrius I | Demetrius I | Demetrius I | Demetrius I | Demetrius I |
| 190-180 | | 185: end of the Mauryan, beginning of the Śunga period | Agathocles (190-180), Founding of Taxila-Sirkap | Pantaleon (190-185), Agathocles | Euthydemus II (190-185), Antimachus I (185-170) | Euthydemus II, Antimachus I | Euthydemus II |
| 180 | | | Apollodotus I (180-160) | | | | |
| 175 | | | *idem* | | accession of Demetrius II | | |
| 171 | | | *idem* | Demetrius II in the south of the Hindu Kush | | accession of Eucratides I | |
| 165 ? | | | *idem* | | Eucratides I | siege and death of Demetrius in Ai Khanum ? (Eucratidia) | fall of Sogdiana (Samarkand), non dated |
| 155 | | | accession of Menander | accession of Menander | | | |
| ~153-151 ? | | expeditions of Menander | Menander | Eucratides in Paropamisadae and Arachosia, double decastater of Eucratides (*Basileus Megas*) | | reconstruction of the great monuments of Ai Khanum | Ai Khanum capital of the last Greek Territories north of the Oxus ? |
| 150 | Zeno (drachmas) | Menander in Pataliputra | attack on Taxila by Eucratides | | Heliocles I associated with power | | |
| 149 | Timodemus (*kasapana*) | Menander in Mathura then at Sakala | campaigns of Eucratides | | | | |
| 148 | Strato (*kasapana*) Ἔτους κδ' | Menander in Sakala | *idem* | | | construction of the treasury | |
| 147 | Philiskos (*kasapana*) | *idem* | *idem* | | | *idem* | |
| 146 | Nikeratos | *idem* | last campaign of Eucratides (Justinus) | | | incompletion of the construction of the treasury | first nomads (Sakas or Yueh-chi ?) on the Oxus |
| 145 | Nomadic inscription | | return of Menander to Taxila | assassination of Eucratides I by one of his three sons | Heliocles I, Plato or Eucratides II in Bactria | first nomadic invasion, destruction of Ai Khanum | passage of the first nomads to the south of the Oxus |
| ~144 ?> | | | Menander in Begram | | | departure of the first nomads and indigenous occupation of the site | |
| ~138/135 ? | | | | | | second nomadic invasion: abandonment of the site | |
| 130 | | | death of Menander, accession of Agathocleia | | death of Heliocles I and fall of Bactria | Bactrians | |
| 128 | | | | | Bactrians (Chang Kien) | Bactrians (Chang Kien) | Yueh-chi in the north of the Oxus (Chang Kien) |

# APPENDIX II

## Chronology of Graeco-Bactrian and Indo-Greek sovereigns

According to O. Bopearachchi, *Monnaies gréco-bactriennes et indo-grecques*, 1991, Tableau 5
and J.R. Rea, R.C. Senior, A.S. Hollis, *Zeitschrift für Papyrologie und Epigraphik*, 1994, p. 261-280.

| Eastern Bactria | Western Bactria | Paropamisadae | Arachosia | Gandhara | Western Punjab | Eastern Punjab |
|---|---|---|---|---|---|---|
| <———— | Diodotus I and II (250 - 230 B.C.) | | | | | |
| <———— | Euthydemus I (230 - 200 B.C.) | | | | | |
| <———— | Demetrius I (200 - 180 B.C.) | ———— | ————> | | | |
| <— Euthydemus II (180 - 174 B.C.) | ————> <———— | Agathocles <-> (180 - 174 B.C.) | Pantaleon (180 - 175 B.C.) | ———— | ————> | |
| Demetrius II (175 - 170 B.C.) | ———— | ———— | ————> | | | |
| <———— | Antimachus I (174 - 165 B.C.) | ———— | —> | | | |
| | | Apollodotus I (174 - 160 B.C.) | ———— | ———— | ————> | |
| Eucratides I (171 - 145 B.C.) | ———— | ———— | ———— | ———— | ————> | |
| | | Antimachus II (160-155 B.C.) | ———— | ———— | ————> | |
| | Eucratides II —> (145-140 B.C.) | Menander I (155 - 130 B.C.) | ———— | ———— | ———— | ————> |
| | Plato ———> (145 -140 B.C.) | | | | | |
| | Heliocles I ——> (145 -130 B.C.) | | | | | |
| | | Zoilus I (130 - 120 B.C.) | ————> | Agathocleia (130 - 125 ~ B.C.) | ————> | |
| | | Lysias (120 - 110 ~ B.C.) | ————> | Strato I (125 - 110 B.C.) | ————> | |
| | | Antialcidas (115 - 95 B.C.) | ————> | Heliocles II (110-100 B.C.) | ————> | |
| | | Polyxenus (100 B.C.) | ————> | Demetrios III (100 B.C.) | | |
| | | Philoxenus (100 - 95 B.C.) | ———— | ———— | ————> | |
| | | Diomedes (95 - 90 B.C.) | ———> <——— | Amyntas —> (95 - 90 B.C.) | Epander (95 - 90 B.C.) | |
| | | Theophilus (90 B.C.) | ———> <——— | Peucolaos —> (90 B.C.) | Thrason (90 B.C.) | |
| | | Nicias (90 - 85 B.C.) | ———> <——— | Menander II (90 - 85 B.C.) | Artemidorus (85 B.C.) | |
| | | Hermaios (90 - 70 B.C.) | ———> <——— | Archebius (90 - 80 B.C.) | ————> | |
| | | | | Maues (Indo-Scythian) | ————> | |
| | | | | Telephus (75 - 70 B.C.) | Apollodotus II (80 - 65 B.C.) | ————> |
| | | | | | Hippostratus (65 - 55 B.C.) | Dionysius (65 - 55 B.C.) |
| | | | | | Azes I (Indo-Scythian) | Zoilus II (55 - 35 B.C.) |
| | | | | | | Apollophanes (35 - 25 B.C.) |
| | | | | | | Strato II (25 B.C.-10 A.D.) |
| | | | | | | Rajuvula (Indo-Scythian) |

# BIBLIOGRAPHY

## Abbreviations

| | |
|---|---|
| — *ANRW* | *Aufstieg und Niedergang der römischen Welt.* |
| — *ASIAR* | *Archaeological Survey of India. Annual Reports.* |
| — *BCH* | *Bulletin de Correspondance Hellénique.* |
| — *BEFEO* | *Bulletin de l'École française d'Extrême-Orient.* |
| — *Cahiers de la DAFI* | *Cahiers de la Délégation archéologique française en Iran.* |
| — *CRAI* | *Comptes rendus de l'Académie des Inscriptions et Belles Lettres.* |
| — *DAGR* | C. Daremberg and E. Saglio, *Dictionnaire des antiquités grecques et romaines, d'après les textes et les monuments*, Paris, 1896-1919. |
| — *EW* | *East and West.* |
| — *Fouilles AKh* | *Fouilles d'Aï Khanoum.* |
| — *JA* | *Journal Asiatique.* |
| — *JAOS* | *Journal of the American Oriental Society.* |
| — *JBORS* | *Journal of the Bihar and Orissa Research Society.* |
| — *JDAI* | *Jahrbuch des deutschen archäologischen Institut.* |
| — *JRAS* | *Journal of the Royal Asiatic Society.* |
| — *MASI* | *Archaeological Survey of India. Memoirs.* |
| — *MDAFA* | *Mémoires de la Délégation archéologique française en Afghanistan.* |
| — *MDP* | *Mémoires de la Délégation en Perse.* |
| — *MMAP* | *Mémoires de la Mission archéologique en Perse.* |
| — *OIP* | *Oriental Institute Publications.* |
| — *ONU* | *Obščestvennye nauki v Uzbekistane.* |
| — *RA* | *Revue Archéologique.* |
| — *RE* | *Realencyclopädie der classischen Altertumswissenschaft.* |
| — *RNum* | *Revue Numismatique.* |
| — *TrJuTAKE* | *Trudy Južno-Turkmenistanskoj Arxeologičeskoj Kompleksnoj Èkspedicii.* |
| — *WVDOG* | *Wissenschaftliche Veröffentlichungen der deutschen Orient-Gesellschaft.* |
| — *ZDMG* | *Zeitschrift der deutschen Morgenländischen Gesellschaft.* |

### Titles

*150 Jahre. Deutsches Archäologisches Institut 1829-1979. Festveranstaltungen und internationales Kolloquium 17.-22. April 1979 in Berlin*, Mainz, 1981.

Abdurazakov, A.A., "Ximičeskie sostavy srevnix i srednevekovyx stekol Afganistana" ("Chemical composition of ancient and medieval glass of Afghanistan"), *ONU*, 1986-11, pp. 36-39.

Acharya, P.K., *Indian architecture according to Mānasāra-Śilpaśatra (Mānasāra Series, 2)*, London, New York, Bombay, ca. 1927.

Agrawala, P.K., *Early Indian bronzes*, Varanasi, 1977.

Agrawala, R.C., M. Taddei, "An interesting relief from the Swat Valley", *EW*, 16, 1966, pp. 82-88.

Agrawala, V.S., "Vāsavadattā and Śakuntalā scenes in the Raṇīgumphā cave in Orissa", *Journal of the Indian Society of Oriental art*, 14, 1946.

Al-Ghailani, L., "'Steatite' stone vessels from Mesopotamia and elsewhere", *Sumer*, 31, 1975, pp. 41-48.

Alekseeva, E.M., "Antičnye busy Severnogo Pričernomor'ja" ("Antique pearls from the Northern Black Sea") (*Arxeologija SSSR, 1-12*), Moscow, 1982.

Alfano, Franco, *[La leggenda di Sakùntala]. Danza e finale di Sakùntala per orchestra. Partitura*, Milano, 1927 ; *Sakuntala. Partitura d'orchestra*, Milano, 1951.

Allan, J., *BMC. Ancient India : A catalogue of the Indian coins in the British Museum. Ancient India = Catalogue of the coins of ancient India*, J. Allan, London, 1936 (repr. 1967).

Amiet, P., *L'âge des échanges inter-iraniens 3500-1700 avant J.-C. (Notes et documents des musées de France, 11)*, Paris, 1986.

*Appian's Roman history*, ed. and transl. by H. White (*The Loeb classical library*), London, Cambridge, 1955-1958.

*L'Arabie et ses mers bordières. I. Itinéraires et voisinages, séminaire de recherche 1985-1986* edited by J.-Fr. Salles *(Travaux de la Maison de l'Orient, 16)*, Lyon, Paris, 1988.

*L'Archéologie de la Bactriane ancienne, Actes du Colloque franco-soviétique, Dushanbe (U.R.S.S.), 27 octobre - 3 novembre 1982*, Paris, 1985.

*L'Archéologie de l'Iraq du début de l'époque néolithique à 333 avant notre ère. Perspectives et limites de l'interprétation anthropologique des documents, Paris, 13-15 juin 1978 (Colloques internationaux du C.N.R.S., N° 580)*, Paris, 1980.

Arnaud, D., Y. Calvet, J.L. Huot, "Ilšu-Ibnišu, orfèvre de l'*E.Babbar* de Larsa. La jarre L.76.77 et son contenu", *Syria*, 56, 1979, pp. 1-64.

Arrian, *Anabasis Alexandri*, ed. and transl. by P.A. Brunt *(The Loeb Classical library)*, Cambridge, London, 1976>.

*The art of India and Pakistan : a commemorative catalogue of the exhibition held at the Royal Academy of Arts, London 1947-48*, London, 1950.

Aśvaghōsa : *The Saundarananda, or Nanda the Fair*, translated from the original Sanskrit of Aśvaghōsa by E.H. Johnston, Oxford, London, 1932 (edition of the text, Lahore, 1928 ; repr. Delhi, Patna, Varanasi, 1975).

Auboyer, J., *Le trône et son symbolisme dans l'Inde ancienne*, Paris, 1949.

Auboyer, J., "La vie privée dans l'Inde ancienne d'après les ivoires de Begram", in J. Hackin and others, *Nouvelles recherches*, 1954, pp. 59-82.

Auboyer, J., J.-Fr. Enault, *La vie publique et privée dans l'Inde ancienne (IIe siècle av. J.-C. - VIIIe siècle environ), 1, L'architecture civile et religieuse*, Paris, 1969>.

Audouin, R., P. Bernard, "Trésor de monnaies indiennes et indo-grecques d'Aï Khanoum (Afghanistan)", *RNum* 1973, pp. 238-289 (Indian coins) and *RNum* 1974, pp. 6-41 (Indo-Greek coins).

*Aus dem Osten des Alexanderreiches : Völker und Kulturen zwischen Orient und Okzident Iran, Afghanistan, Pakistan, Indien*, J. Ozols, V. Thewalt ed., Köln, 1984.

Ball, V., "A geologist's contribution to the history of ancient India (Early notices of metals and gems in India)", *The Indian Antiquary*, 13, 1884, pp. 228-248.

Banerjea, J.N., *The development of Hindu iconography*, Calcutta, 1956.

Bariand, P., J.-F. Poullen, "The pegmatites of Laghman, Nuristan, Afghanistan", *The Mineralogical Record*, sept.-oct. 1978, pp. 301-308.

Barrett, D., *A guide to Karla caves*, Bombay, 1957.

Barua, B., *Barhut*, Calcutta, 1934-1937 (3 vol., repr. 1979).

Basham, A.L., *The wonder that was India : a survey of the culture of the Indian Sub-Continent before the coming of the Muslims,* London, 1954.

Basham, A.L. (ed.), see *A Cultural history of India.*

Baudot, P., "'Steatite' vessels in the third millennium in the ancient Orient", in *India and the ancient world*, Leuven, 1987, pp. 1-32, pl. I-IV.

Beck, H.C., *The beads from Taxila (MASI, 65)*, Delhi, 1941.

Belaiew, N.T., "Examen des documents pondéraux", in *MMAP, 25*, Paris, 1934, p. 135, fig. I.

Bénisti, M., "A propos du triratna", *BEFEO*, 64, 1977, pp. 43-81.

Bénisti, M., "Observations concernant le stūpa n° 2 de Sāñcī", *Bulletin d'études indiennes*, 4, 1986, pp. 165-170.

Bernard, P., "Première campagne de fouilles d'Aï Khanoum", *CRAI* 1966, pp. 127-133.

Bernard, P., "Deuxième campagne de fouilles d'Aï Khanoum en Bactriane", *CRAI* 1967, pp. 306-324.

Bernard, P., "Troisième campagne de fouilles à Aï Khanoum en Bactriane", *CRAI* 1968, pp. 263-457.

Bernard, P., "Quatrième campagne de fouilles à Aï Khanoum (Bactriane)", *CRAI* 1969, pp. 313-355.

Bernard, P., "Campagne de fouilles 1969 à Aï Khanoum en Afghanistan", *CRAI* 1970, pp. 301-349.

Bernard, P., "La Campagne de fouilles de 1970 à Aï Khanoum (Afghanistan)", *CRAI* 1971, pp. 385-452.

Bernard, P., "Campagne de fouilles à Aï Khanoum (Afghanistan)", *CRAI* 1972, pp. 605-632.

Bernard, P., "Fouilles de Aï Khanoum (Afghanistan), campagnes de 1972 et 1973", *CRAI* 1974, pp. 280-309.

Bernard, P., "Campagne de fouilles 1974 à Aï Khanoum (Afghanistan)", *CRAI* 1975, pp. 167-197.

Bernard, P., "Campagne de fouilles 1975 à Aï Khanoum (Afghanistan)", *CRAI* 1976, pp. 287-322.

Bernard, P., "Campagne de fouilles 1976-1977 à Aï Khanoum (Afghanistan)", *CRAI* 1978, pp. 421-463.

Bernard, P., "Campagne de fouilles 1978 à Aï Khanoum (Afghanistan)", *CRAI* 1980, pp. 435-459.

Bernard, P. and others, "Campagne de fouille 1978 à Aï Khanoum (Afghanistan)", *BEFEO*, 68, 1980, pp. 1-103, pl. XXIX-XL.

Bernard, P., "Chapiteaux corinthiens hellénistiques d'Asie Centrale découverts à Aï Khanoum", *Syria*, 45, 1968, pp. 111-151.

Bernard, P., "Sièges et lits en ivoire d'époque hellénistique en Asie Centrale", *Syria*, 47, 1970, pp. 327-343.

Bernard, P., "Les traditions orientales dans l'architecture gréco-bactrienne", *JA* 1976, pp. 245-275.

Bernard, P., "La Bactriane à l'époque kushane d'après une nouvelle publication soviétique", *Journal des Savants*, 1979, pp. 237-256.

Bernard, P., "Pratiques financières grecques dans la Bactriane hellénisée", *Bulletin de la Société Française de Numismatique* 1979, pp. 517-520.

Bernard, P., "Problèmes d'histoire coloniale grecque à travers l'urbanisme d'une cité hellénistique d'Asie Centrale", in *150 Jahre. Deutsches Archäologisches Institut 1829-1979. Festveranstaltungen und internationales Kolloquium 17.-22. April 1979 in Berlin*, Mainz, 1981.

Bernard, P., "Diodore XVII, 83, 1 : Alexandrie du Caucase ou Alexandrie de l'Oxus?", *Journal des Savants*, 1982, pp. 217-242.

Bernard, P., "Alexandre et Aï Khanoum", *Journal des Savants* 1982, pp. 125-138.

Bernard, P., *Fouilles d'Aï Khanoum IV. Les monnaies hors trésors. Questions d'histoire gréco-bactrienne (MDAFA, 28)*, Paris, 1985.

Bernard, P., "Le monnayage d'Eudamos, satrape grec du Pandjab et "maître des éléphants"", *Orientalia Iosephi Tucci Memoriae Dicata*, Roma, 1985, pp. 65-94.

Bernard, P., "Les nomades conquérants de l'empire gréco-bactrien. Réflexions sur leur identité ethnique et culturelle", *CRAI* 1987, pp. 758-768.

Bernard, P., "Le temple de Takht-i Sangin en Bactriane : Temple du feu ou pas ?", *Studia Iranica*, 23, 1994, pp. 112-113.

Bernard, P., "Gimnasij v Ajxanum", in *Gorodskaja kul'tura*, 1987, pp. 22-31.

Bernard, P. and others, "Fouilles d'Aï Khanoum (Aghanistan) : Campagne de 1974", *BEFEO*, 63, 1976, pp. 5-51.

Bernard P., M. Le Berre, "Architecture. Le quartier administratif : l'ensemble nord", in *Fouilles d'Aï Khanoum I*, pp. 17-61.

Bernard, P., H.-P. Francfort, *Études de géographie historique sur la plaine d'Aï Khanoum (Afghanistan) (Mémoires CNRS URA 10, N° 1)*, Paris, 1978.

Bernard, P., Cl. Rapin, "Campagne de fouilles 1978 à Aï Khanoum : III. Le palais. La trésorerie", *BEFEO*, 68, 1980, pp. 10-38, pl. 6-10, 29-31.

Bernard, P., D. Schlumberger, "Aï Khanoum", *BCH*, 89, 1965, pp. 590-657.

*The Bhāgavata Purāṇā,* transl. and annotated by G.V. Tagare, Delhi, Varanasi, Patna, 1976-1978.

Birdwood, G.C.M., *The industrial arts of India*, London, 1880.

Bivar, A.D.H., "The stirrup and its origins", *Oriental art*, 1-2, 1955, pp. 61-65.

Bivar, A.D.H., "Cavalry equipment and tactics on the Euphrates Frontier", *Dumbarton Oaks Papers*, 26, 1972, pp. 273-291.

Blümner, H., *Die Römischen Privataltertümer*, München, 1911.

Blümner, H., *Technologie und Terminologie der Gewerbe und Künste bei Griechen und Römern*, Leipzig, Berlin, 1879-1912.

Boardman, J., *Greek gems and finger rings. Early bronze age to late classical*, London, 1976.

Bopearachchi, O., "Roi-cavalier ou Reine-amazone ?", *Bulletin de la Société Française de Numismatique* 1988, pp. 453-456.

Bopearachchi, O., "Ménandre Sôter, un roi indo-grec. Observations chronologiques et géographiques", *Studia Iranica*, 19, 1990, pp. 39-85.

Bopearachchi, O., *Monnaies gréco-bactriennes et indo-grecques. Catalogue raisonnné*, Paris, 1991.

Borriello, M.R., "Gli avori e gli ossi lavorati", in *Le collezioni del Museo Nazionale di Napoli*, Roma, 1989, pp. 111-113.

Boucharlat, R., "Les niveaux post-achéménides à Suse, secteur nord. Fouilles de l'Apadana-Est et de la Ville Royale-Ouest (1973-1978)", *Cahiers de la DAFI*, 15, 1987, pp. 145-311.

Boulnois, L., *La route de la Soie*², Paris, 1986.

Bouzek, J., S.U. Deraniyagala, "Tessons de vases hellénistiques trouvés en Sri Lanka", *BCH*, 109, 1985, pp. 589-596.

Boyce, M., Fr. Grenet, *A history of Zoroastrianism, III, Zoroastrianism under Macedonian and Roman rule (Handbuch der Orientalistik, 1. Abt., Der nahe und der mittlere Osten, 8/1/2/2)*, Leiden, New York, 1991.

Brein, F., "Ear studs for Greek ladies", *Anatolian Studies*, 32, 1982, pp. 89-92.

Briant, P., *États et pasteurs au Moyen-Orient ancien*, Cambridge, Paris, 1982.

Briant, P., *Rois, tributs et paysans. Études sur les formations tributaires du Moyen-Orient ancien*, Paris, 1982. "Colonisation hellénistique et populations indigènes", pp. 227-279.

Briant, P., *L'Asie Centrale et les royaumes proche-orientaux du premier millénaire (c. VIIIe-IVe siècles avant notre ère (Éditions Recherches sur les civilisations, Mémoire n° 42)*, Paris, 1984.

Briant, P., "Le nomadisme du Grand Roi", *Iranica Antiqua*, 23, 1988 (*Mélanges P. Amiet*, t. 1), pp. 253-273.

Brown, P., *Indian architecture (Buddhist and Hindu periods)*², Bombay, 1942.

Bruneau, Ph., Cl. Vatin and others, *L'îlot de la Maison des Comédiens (École française d'Athènes, Exploration archéologique de Délos, 27)*, Paris, 1970.

Bühler, H.-P., *Antike Gefässe aus Edelsteinen*, Mainz, 1973.

Bulgarelli, G.M., "Tepe Hisar. Preliminary report on a surface survey, August, 1972", *EW*, 24, 1974, pp. 15-27.

Burgess, J., *Report on the Buddhist cave temples and their inscriptions. Being part of the results of the fourth, fifth and sixth seasons' operations of the*

*Archaeological Survey of Western India 1876-77, 1877-78, 1878-79. Supplementary to the volume on "The cave temples of India" (Archaeological Survey of Western India, 4)*, London, 1883 (repr. Varanasi, 1964).

Burnouf, E.L., *Le vase sacré et ce qu'il contient dans l'Inde, la Perse, la Grèce et dans l'Église chrétienne*, Paris, 1896.

Bussagli, M., "The "Frontal" representation of the Divine Chariot. Similarities between the figurative arts in the East and West", *EW*, 6, 1955, pp. 9-25.

Callieri, P., *I sigilli e le cretule del Nord-Ovest del Subcontinente Indiano e dell'Afghanistan (4° secolo A.C. - 1° secolo D.C.)*, Napoli, 1987 (unpublished thesis).

Callieri, P., "La glittica greco-persiana nelle regioni orientali dell'impero achemenide", *Studi di egittologia e di antichità puniche*, a cura di E. Acquaro e S. Pernigotti, 11, 1992, pp. 63-76.

Callieri, P., "Bīr-Koṭ-Ghwaṇḍai 1990-1992. A preliminary report on the excavations of the Italian Archaeological Mission, IsMEO", in *Istituto Univ. Orientale*, 52, 1992 (*Annali*, Suppl. n. 73, fasc. 4), pp. 1-48.

*Cambridge History of India*, ed. E.J. Rapson, I, 1922.

Carl, J., "Le Bazar de Begram (chantier I, 1936)", in J. Hackin, J. Carl, J. Meunié, *Diverses recherches*, 1959, pp. 85-102.

Cary, M., E. Warmington, *Les explorateurs de l'Antiquité*, Paris, 1932.

Casson, L., *Periplus Maris Erythraei*, ed., transl. and comment., Princeton, 1989.

Caubet, A., J.-Fr. Salles, "Le sanctuaire hellénistique (B6)", in *Faïlaka. Fouilles françaises 1983*, Lyon, 1984, pp. 73-156.

Chandra, M., *Costumes and textiles, cosmetics and coiffures in ancient and medieval India*, New Delhi, 1973.

Chandra, R.G., *Indo-Greek Jewellery*, New Delhi, 1979.

Chavannes, E., *Les Mémoires historiques de Se-Ma Ts'ien*, Paris 1895-1905 (reed. with supplements and index, Leiden, 1967-1969.

Christensen, A., *L'Iran sous les Sassanides*, Copenhague, 1944 (repr. Osnabrück, 1971).

Cima, M., "Il "prezioso arredo" degli Horti Lamiani", in *Le tranquille dimore degli dei*, 1986, pp. 105-144.

Codrington, K. de B., "Ancient Indian hand-mirrors", *Man*, 1929, pp. 170-171.

Colledge, M.A.R., *Parthian art*, Ithaca, New York, 1977.

*Le collezioni del Museo Nazionale di Napoli*, Roma, 1989.

*Colloquiums, congresses*: see *150 Jahre. Deutsches Archäologisches Institut 1829-1979 ; L'Arabie et ses mers bordières ; L'archéologie de la Bactriane ancienne ; Gorodskaja kul'tura ; Histoire et cultes de l'Asie centrale préislamique ; South Asian Archaeology.*

Combaz, G., *L'Inde et l'Orient classique*, Paris, 1937 (2 vol.).

*Conchiglie : Il commercio e la lavorazione delle conchiglie marine nel medio oriente dal IV al II millennio a.C., Roma, Palazzo Brancaccio 14 maggio - 19 luglio 1981*, Roma, 1981.

Coomaraswamy, A.K., *History of Indian and Indonesian art*, London, Leipzig, New York, 1927.

Coomaraswamy, A.K., *La sculpture de Bodhgayā (Ars Asiatica, 18)*, Paris, 1935.

Coomaraswamy, A.K., *La sculpture de Bharhut (Annales du Musée Guimet, n.s., 6)*, Paris, 1956.

Cowell, E. B. (dir.), *The Jātaka or Stories of the Buddha's Former Births*, Cambridge, 1895-1913 (6 vol.).

*The crossroads of Asia, Transformation in image and symbol (in the art of ancient Afghanistan and Pakistan). An exhibition at the Fitzwilliam Museum, Cambridge, 6 october-13 december 1992 supported by the Ancient India and Iran Trust*, ed. E. Errington and J. Cribb, Cambridge, 1992.

*A Cultural history of India*, A.L. Basham ed., Oxford, 1975.

Cunningham, A., *The Bhilsa topes ; or, Buddhist monuments of Central India : comprising a brief historical sketch of the rise, progress, and decline of Buddhism ; with an account of the opening and examination of the various groups of topes around Bhilsa*, London, 1854 (repr. Varanasi, 1966).

Cunningham, A., *The Stûpa of Bharhut : a Buddhist monument ornamented with numerous sculptures illustrative of Buddhist Legend and history in the third century B.C.*, London, 1879 (repr. Varanasi, 1962).

Cunningham, A., *Mahābodhi, or the Great Buddhist Temple under the Bodhi Tree at Buddha-Gayā*, London, 1892.

Curiel, R., D. Schlumberger, *Trésors monétaires d'Afghanistan (MDAFA,14)*, Paris, 1953.

Curiel, R., G. Fussman, *Le trésor monétaire de Qunduz (MDAFA, 20)*, Paris, 1965.

Czuma, S.J., *Kushan sculpture : images from Early India*, Cleveland, Cleveland Museum of Art, 1985.

Dales, G., J.M. Kenoyer, "Shell working at ancient Balakot, Pakistan", *Expedition* 19-2, 1977, pp. 13-19.

Dalton, O.M., *The treasure of the Oxus*[3], London, 1964.

*Dawn of civilization in Maharashtra - Prince of Wales Museum of Western India Bombay*, Bombay, 1975.

*De l'Indus aux Balkans, Recueil à la mémoire de Jean Deshayes*, Paris, 1985.

Debevoise, N.C., *A political history of Parthia*, Chicago, 1958.

Dehejia, V., *Early Buddhist rock temples (Studies in art and archaeology)*, London, 1972.

Delmas, A.B., M. Casanova, "The lapis-lazuli sources in the Ancient East", in *South Asian Archaeology 1987*, Rome, 1990, pp. 493-505.

Delougaz, P., "Architectural reproductions on steatite vases", *Iraq*, 24, 1962, pp. 90-95.

Deppert-Lippitz, B., *Griechischer Goldschmuck*, Mainz, 1985.

Desroches, Ch., K. Michałovski, "Catalogue des objets", in *Fouilles franco-polonaises : Rapports, III, Tell Edfou 1939*, Paris, 1950, pp. 161-327.

Devoto, G., A. Molayem, *Archeogemmologia : Pietre antiche, glittica, magia e litoterapia*, Roma, 1990.

Dihle, A., "Die entdeckungsgeschichtlichen Voraussetzungen des Indienhandels der römischen Kaiserzeit", in *ANRW, II, Principat, 9,2*, Berlin, New York, 1978, pp. 546-580.

Dikshit, M.G., "Notes on some Indian amulets", *Bulletin of Prince of Wales Museum of Western India*, 1951-1952, No. 2 (1953), pp. 86-99.

Dikshit, M.G., "Beads from Ahichchhatrā, U. P.", *Ancient India*, 8, 1952, pp. 33-63.

Dikshit, M.G., "Studies in ancient Indian Glass (I), Glass as mentioned in Kautilya's Arthasastra", *EW*, 1-2, 15, 1964-1965, pp. 62-68.

Dikshit, M.G., "A brief study of the glass industry at Kapadwany", *Museum and Picture Gallery, Baroda*, 20, 1968, pp. 1-9.

Dioscurides : *Pedanii Dioscuridis Anazarbei de materia medica libri quinque*[2], ed. M. Wellmann, Berolini, 1958 ; *Des Pedanos Dioskurides aus Anazarbos Arztneimittellehre in fünf Büchern*, transl. J. Berendes, Stuttgart, 1902 (repr. Schaan, 1983).

*Diverses recherches archéologiques en Afghanistan* : see J. Hackin, J. Carl, J. Meunié, *Diverses recherches* ..., 1959.

*Drevnjaja Baktrija. Materialy Sovetsko-Afganskoj Arxeologičeskoj Èkspedicii* ("Ancient Bactria. Materials of the Soviet-Afghan Expedition"),*Vyp. 2* (vol. 2), ed. I.T. Kruglikova, Moscow, 1979.

During Caspers, E.C.L., "The Indian ivory figurine from Pompei – A reconsideration of its functional use", *South Asian Archaeology* 1979, ed. H. Härtel, Berlin, 1981, pp. 341 sqq.

Durrani, F.A., "Stone vases as evidence of connection between Mesopotamia and the Indus Valley", *Ancient Pakistan*, 1, 1964, pp. 51-96.

Eichholz, D.E., *Pliny, Natural history,* London, Cambridge, 1962.

Erdosy, G., "Early historic cities of Northern India", *South Asia Studies*, 3, 1987, pp. 1-23.

Erdosy, G., "Taxila, Political history and urban structure", in *South Asian Archaeology 1987*, ed. M. Taddei, Rome, 1990, pp. 657-674

Faccenna, D., *Sculptures from the Sacred Area of Butkara I (Swat, W. Pakistan), Catalogue*, by M. Taddei *(IsMEO, Reports and Memoirs, 2)*, Roma, 1962-1964.

Ferguson, J., "China and Rome", in *ANRW, II, Principat, 9,2*, Berlin, New York, 1978, pp. 581-603.

Finot, L., *Les questions de Milinda*, Paris, 1923.

Fischer, K., "Eine Reitergruppe in Vorderansicht aus Swāt nach dem Vorbild von Quadriga-Darstellungen", in *Orientalia Iosephi Tucci Memoriae Dicata*, Roma, 1985, pp. 355-370.

Fischer, K., "How were love scenes on Gandhāran stūpas understood by contemporary worshippers", in *South Asian Archaeology 1983*, Naples, 1985, pp. 629-639.

Fleming, D., "Darius I's foundation charters from Susa and the Eastern Achaemenid Empire", *Afghan studies*, 3-4, 1982, pp. 81-87.

Flinders Petrie, W.M., *Objects of daily use*, London, 1927.

Forbes, R.J., *Studies in ancient technology*, Leiden, 1964-1972 (9 vol.).

Foucher, A., *Art gréco-bouddhique du Gandhâra*, Paris, 1905-1951 (4 vol.).

Foucher, A., "Représentations de Jâtaka dans l'art bouddhique", in *Mémoires concernant l'Asie orientale*, Paris, 1919, III, pp. 1-52

Foucher, A., "Deux Jātaka sur ivoires", in J. Hackin and others, *Nouvelles recherches*, 1954, pp. 83-87.

*Fouilles d'Aï Khanoum I (Campagnes de 1965, 1966, 1967, 1968), Rapport préliminaire*, published under the direction of P. Bernard *(MDAFA, 21)*, Paris, 1973 (2 vol.).

Francfort, H.-P., "Le plan des maisons gréco-bactriennes et le problème des structures de «type megaron» en Asie Centrale et en Iran", *Le Plateau Iranien et l'Asie Centrale des origines à la conquête islamique. Leurs relations à la lumière des documents archéologiques, Paris, 22-24 mars 1976 (Colloques internationaux du C.N.R.S., n° 567)*, Paris, 1977, pp. 267-280.

Francfort, H.-P., *Les palettes du Gandhara (MDAFA, 23)*, Paris, 1979.

Francfort, H.-P., *Fouilles d'Aï Khanoum III, Le sanctuaire du temple à niches indentées, 2. Les trouvailles (MDAFA, 27)*, Paris, 1984.

Francfort, H.-P., *Fouilles de Shortugaï. Recherches sur l'Asie centrale protohistorique (Mémoires de la Mission archéologique française en Asie Centrale, 2)*, Paris, 1989 (2 vol.).

Francfort, H.-P., J.-Cl. Liger, "L'hérôon au caveau de pierre", *BEFEO*, 63, 1976, pp. 25-39.

Francfort, H.-P., M.-H. Pottier, "Sondage préliminaire sur l'établissement protohistorique harappéen et post-harappéen de Shortugaï (Afghanistan du N.-E.)", *Arts Asiatiques*, 34, 1978, pp. 29-79.

Franz, H.G., *Buddhistische Kunst Indiens*, Leipzig, 1965.

Frechkop, S., R. Lavocat, "Sous-ordre des Sélénodontes ou Ruminants", in *Traité de zoologie*, t. 17, fasc. 1, Paris, 1955, pp. 568-693.

Frye, R.N., *The history of ancient Iran*, München, 1984.

Fussman, G., "Chronique des études kouchanes (1978-1987)", *JA*, 275, 1987, pp. 333-400.

Fussman, G., "Le *Périple* et l'histoire politique de l'Inde", *JA*, 279, 1991, pp. 31-38.

Garczynski, P., "Campagne de fouille 1978 à Aï Khanoum (Afghanistan) : IV. Le palais. La cour dorique", *BEFEO*, 68, 1980, pp. 39-43, 86-91, pl. XXXII-XXXIII.

Gardin, J.-Cl., P. Gentelle, "Irrigation et peuplement dans la plaine d'Aï Khanoum de l'époque achéménide à l'époque musulmane", *BEFEO*, 63, 1976, pp. 59-99.

Gasparri, C., "Vasi antichi in pietra dura a Firenze e Roma", *Prospettiva*, 19, 1979, pp. 4-13.

Gentelle, P., *Données paléogéographiques et fondements de l'irrigation (Prospections archéologiques en Bactriane orientale [1974-1978], 1 ; Mémoires de la Mission archéologique française en Asie Centrale, 3)*, Paris, 1989.

Ghailani, L. Al- : see Al-Ghailani, L.

Ghirshman, R., *Bégram, Recherches archéologiques et historiques sur les Kouchans (MDAFA, 12)*, Cairo, 1946.

Ghirshman, R., *Parthes et Sassanides*, Paris, 1962.

Ghirshman, R., "L'art animalier aulique achéménide", *Monuments Piot*, 60, 1976, pp. 1-27.

Ghosh, A., "The pillars of Aśoka, their purpose", *EW*, 17, 1967, pp. 273-275.

Ghosh, A. and others, *Ajantā murals*, New Delhi, 1967.

Ghosh, A. (ed.), *Indian Archaeology* : see *Indian Archaeology ... – A Review.*

Ghosh, A. (ed.), *Jaina art and architecture* : see *Jaina art and architecture.*

Ghosh, R.S.M., "The use of glass in ancient India", *JBORS*, 10, 1924, pp. 194-201.

Ghurye, G.S., *Indian costume (bhāratīya ve.sabhū.sā)*, Bombay, 1951.

Glover, I.C., *Early trade between India and Southeast Asia : A link in the development of a world trading system (The University of Hull, Centre for South-East Asian studies, Occasional papers, 16)*, 1989.

Gobert, I., *La vie publique et privée dans l'Inde ancienne (II^e siècle av. J.-C. - VIII^e siècle environ), 2, Le mobilier*, Paris, 1976.

Gokhale, B.G., "Bharukaccha/Barygaza", in *India and the ancient world*, Leuven, 1987, pp. 67-79.

Gordon, D.H., "Early Indian terracottas", *Journal of the Indian Society of Oriental Art*, 11, 1943, pp. 136-195.

Gorelick, L., A.J. Gwinnett, "Close work without magnifying lenses? A hypothetical explanation for the ability of ancient craftsmen to effect minute detail", *Expedition*, 23-2, 1981, pp. 27-34 ; *idem*, "Discussion of suggestions from readers of Expedition", *Expedition*, 23-4, 1981, pp. 15-16.

*Gorodskaja kul'tura Baktrii-Toxaristana i Sogda, Antičnost', Rannee Srednevekov'e, Materialy Sovetsko-Francuskogo Kollokviuma (Samarkand, 1986)* ("Urban culture of Bactria-Tokharistan and Sogd, Materials of the Soviet-French Colloquium [Samarkand, 1986]"), Tashkent, 1987.

Gouin, Ph., "Les petits objets", in *Fouilles d'Aï Khanoum I*, 1973, pp. 195-201.

Grassé, P.-P. (dir) : see *Traité de zoologie.*

Greifenhagen, A., *Schmuckarbeiten in Edelmetall*, Berlin, 1970-1975 (2 vol.).

Grenet, Fr., "L'onomastique iranienne à Aï Khanoum", *BCH*, 107, 1983, pp. 373-381.

Grenet, Fr., "Mithra au temple principal d'Aï Khanoum ?", in *Histoire et cultes de l'Asie centrale préislamique*, 1991, pp. 147-151.

Groom, N., *Frankincense and myrrh. Study of the Arabian incense trade*, London 1981.

Guillaume, O., *Fouilles d'Aï Khanoum II, Les grands propylées sur la rue principale (MDAFA, 23)*, Paris, 1983.

Guillaume, O., "Contribution à l'étude d'un artisanat bactrien préhellénistique", in *L'Archéologie de la Bactriane ancienne*, 1985, pp. 257-272.

Guillaume, O., A. Rougeulle, *Fouilles d'Aï Khanoum VII. Les petits objets (MDAFA, 31)*, Paris, 1987.

Gupta, P.L., *The Amaravati hoard of silver punch-marked coins*, Hyderabad, 1963.

Gupta, S.P., *The roots of Indian art (A detailed study of the formative period of Indian art and architecture : third and second Centuries B.C. - Mauryan and Late Mauryan)*, Delhi, 1980.

Hackin, J. and others, *Nouvelles recherches archéologiques à Begram (ancienne Kâpicî)(1939-1940) (Rencontre de trois civilisations : Inde - Grèce - Chine) (MDAFA, 11)*, Paris, 1954 (2 vol.).

Hackin, J., "Catalogue descriptif des objets découverts à Begram", in J. Hackin and others, *Nouvelles recherches*, 1954, pp. 157-313

Hackin, J., J. Carl, J. Meunié, *Diverses recherches archéologiques en Afghanistan (1933-1940) (MDAFA, 8)*, Paris, 1959.

Hadot, P., Cl. Rapin, "Les textes littéraires grecs de la trésorerie d'Aï Khanoum", *BCH*, 111, 1987, pp. 225-266.

Härtel, H., "Some results of the excavations at Sonkh. A preliminary report", *German Scholars in India*, New Delhi, 1976, 2, pp. 69-99.

Härtel, H., J. Auboyer, *Indien und Südostasien (Propyläen Kunstgeschichte, 16)*, Berlin, 1971.

Hakemi, A., "Are the models of buildings discovered at Shahdad, models of the temples of the 3rd Millenium B.C. ?", in *South Asian Archaeology 1987*, Rome, 1990, pp. 459-473.

Hallade, M., *Arts de l'Asie ancienne, I, l'Inde (Publications du Musée Guimet, 5)*, Paris, 1954.

Harle, J.C., *The art and architecture of the Indian Sub-Continent*, London, 1986.

Harle, J.C., *Indian art in the Ashmolean Museum*, Oxford, 1987.

Havell, E.B., *The ancient and medieval architecture of India*, London, 1915.

Heinrich, E., *Die Paläste im alten Mesopotamien (Denkmäler antiker Architektur, 15)*, Berlin, 1984.

Hemmy, A.S., "System of weights at Mohenjo-daro", in *Mohenjo-daro*, ed. J.H. Marshall, London, 1931, pp. 589-598.

Higgins, R.A., *Greek and Roman jewellery*, London, 1980.

Hinüber, O. von, "Das Nandyāvarta-Symbol", in *XVIII. Deutscher Orientalistentag (ZDMG*, Suppl. II), ed. W. Voigt, Wiesbaden, 1974, pp. 356-365.

*Histoire et cultes de l'Asie centrale préislamique. Sources écrites et documents archéologiques. Actes du Colloque international du CNRS (Paris, U.N.E.S.C.O., 22-28 novembre 1988)*, Paris, 1991.

Hopkins, E.W., "Notes from India. 1. Bridles in sculpture and painting", *JAOS*, 19/2, 1898, pp. 29-36.

Horne, Ch., "Notes on an ancient Indian vase with an account on engraving thereupon", *JRAS, ns*, 5, 1871, pp. 367-375.

Hornell, J., *The sacred Chank of India : A monograph of the Indian conch (Turbinella pyrum), Madras Fisheries Bureau, Bulletin no. 7*, Madras, 1914.

*Horti Lamiani* : see *Le Tranquille dimore degli dei.*

Huntingford, G.W.B., *The Periplus of the Erythraean Sea, by an unknown author, with some extracts from Agatharkhidēs 'On the Erythraean Sea'*, transl., London, 1980

Huot, J.L., "Le métier de l'orfèvre à Larsa", in *L'archéologie de l'Iraq du début de l'époque néolithique à 333 avant notre ère, Paris 1978*, Paris, 1980, pp. 113-118.

*India and the ancient world : history, trade and culture before A.D. 650, P.H.L. Eggermont jubilee volume*, ed. G. Pollet *(Orientalia Lovaniensia Analecta, 25)*, Leuven, 1987.

*Indian Archaeology 1958-59 – A Review*, ed. by A. Ghosh, New Delhi, 1959. *Indian Archaeology 1961-62 – A Review*, ed. by A. Ghosh, New Delhi, 1964. *Indian Archaeology 1962-63 – A Review*, ed. by A. Ghosh, New Delhi, 1965. *Indian Archaeology 1964-65 – A Review*, ed. by A. Ghosh, New Delhi, 1969.

*Indian archaeology, New perspectives*, ed. R.K. Sharma, Delhi, 1982.

*De l'Indus aux Balkans, Recueil à la mémoire de Jean Deshayes*, Paris, 1985.

Ingholt, H., *Gandhāran art in Pakistan*, New York, 1957.

Irwin , J., "'Asokan' pillars : The mystery of foundation and collapse", in *India and the ancient world*, Leuven, 1987, pp. 87-93.

*Jaina art and architecture*, A. Ghosh, ed., New Delhi, 1974-1975 (3 vol.).

Janaki, V.A., *The commerce of Cambay from the earliest period to the nineteenth century*, Baroda, 1980.

Jarrige, J.-Fr., "A propos d'un foret à tige hélicoïdale en cuivre de Mundigak", in *De l'Indus aux Balkans*, 1985, pp. 281-292.

Jayaswal, P., "Historical data in the Gārgī-Saṃhitā and the Brahmin Empire", *JBORS*, 14, 1928, pp. 397-421 and 15, 1929, pp. 129-135.

Jusupov, X., *Drevnosti Uzboja*, Aškhabad, 1986.

Kaiser, W.B., "Ein Meister der Glyptik aus dem Umkreis Alexanders des Grossen", *JDAI*, 77, 1962, pp. 227-239.

Kala, S.C., *Terracotta figurines from Kauśāmbī*, Allahabad, 1950.

Kālidāsa : *Works of Kālidāsa*, ed., intr. and transl. C.R. Devadhar, vol. I, 1966 (repr. Delhi, 1985). *Oeuvres choisies de Kalidasa*, transl. H. Fauche, Paris, 1865. A. Bergaigne et P. Lehugeur, *Sakuntala, Drame en sept actes mêlé de prose et de vers, [de] Calidasa*, Paris, 1884. Kālidāsa, *Çakuntalā riconosciuta, Dramma in sette atti*, a cura di M. Morani, Milano, 1982.

Kalota, N.S., *India as described by Megasthenes*, Delhi, 1978.

Kauṭilīya : *The Kauṭilīya Arthaśāstra. Part II*, transl. and comm. by R.P. Kangle, Bombay, 1972[2]. *Part III. A study*, Bombay, 1965.

Keller, O., *Die antike Tierwelt*, Leipzig, 1909-1913 (2 vol., repr. Hildesheim, 1980).

Kenoyer, J.M., "The Indus bead industry : contributions to bead technology", *Ornament*, 10-1, 1986, pp. 18-23.

*Koj-krylgan-kala*, see S.P. Tolstov, B.I. Vajnberg, *Koj-Krylgan-kala*.

Koldewey, R., *Die Tempel von Babylon und Borsippa (WVDOG, 15)*, Leipzig, 1911.

Koldewey, R., *Das Wiedererstehende Babylon, die bisherigen Ergebnisse der deutschen Ausgrabungen*[4], Leipzig, 1925 (repr. Zürich, 1981).

Kosambi, D.D., *The culture and civilisation of ancient India in historical outline*, Delhi, Bombay, 1966.

Košelenko, G.A., "Les traditions de la Bactriane ancienne et les étalons culturels du monde hellénistique", in *L'archéologie de la Bactriane ancienne*, 1985, pp. 269-272.

Kurz, O.,"Le rinceau d'acanthe de la plaque d'ivoire n° 329 (fouilles 1937)", in J. Hackin and others, *Nouvelles recherches*, 1954, pp. 55-57.

La Fuÿe, A. de, N.T. Belaiew, "Archéologie, métrologie et numismatique susiennes. Examen des documents pondéraux", in *Mission de Susiane (MMAP, 25)*, Paris, 1934, pp. 134-141.

Lal, B.B., "Examination of some ancient Indian glass specimens", *Ancient India*, 8, 1952, pp. 17-27.

Lal, B.B., "Studies in early and mediaeval Indian ceramics – Some glass and glass-like artefacts from Bellary, Kolhapur, Maski, Nasik and Maheshwar", *Bulletin of the Deccan College Research Institute*, 14, 1953, pp. 48-58.

Lal, B.B., "Examination of rods of glass-like material from Arikamedu", *Ancient India*, 14, 1958, pp. 139-143.

Lal, B.B., "Excavations at Hastināpura and other explorations in the Upper Gangā and Sutlej basins 1950-52", *Ancient India*, 10-11, 1954-1955, pp. 5-151.

Lamotte, E., *Histoire du bouddhisme indien, des origines à l'ère Saka*, Louvain, 1958 (repr. 1967).

La Rocca, E., "Il lusso come espressione di potere", in *Le tranquille dimore degli dei*, 1986, pp. 3-35.

Laufer, B., "Asbestos and Salamander : an essay in Chinese and Hellenistic folk-lore", *T'oung Pao*, 16, 1915, pp. 299-373 ; published also in B. Laufer, *Sino-Tibetan studies*, 1987, t. 1, pp. 219-293.

Laufer, B., *Sino-Tibetan studies : selected papers on the art, folklore, history, linguistics and prehistory of sciences in China and Tibet*, collected by H. Walravens, New Delhi, 1987 (2 vol.).

Law, B.C., "Śakala, an ancient Indian city", *EW*, 19, 1969, pp. 401-409.

Lecuyot, G., "Ajxanum. Žiliščnoe stroitel'stvo" ("Ai Khanum : the habitations"), in *Gorodskaja kul'tura*, 1987, pp. 59-67 (in Russian).

Lecuyot, G., "Résidences hellénistiques en Bactriane, résidences parthes en Iran et en Mésopotamie. Diffusion ou communauté d'origine ?", *Mesopotamian history and environment Series I, Northern Akkad project reports*, 8, 1993, pp. 31-45, pl. 1-2.

Lefebvre des Noëttes, R.-J.-E.-C., *La force motrice animale à travers les âges*, Nancy, 1924.

Lefebvre des Noëttes, R.-J.-E.-C., *L'attelage, le cheval de selle à travers les âges : contribution à l'histoire de l'esclavage*, Paris, 1931 (2 vol.).

Lemlejn, G.G., "Fragmenty kamennyx izdelij iz raskopok v Staroj Nise" ("Fragments of stone objects from the excavations of ancient Nisa") *(TrJuTAKE, 8)*, Aškhabad, 1958, pp. 381-389.

Leriche, P., *Fouilles d'Aï Khanoum V. Les remparts et les monuments associés (MDAFA, 29)*, Paris, 1986.

Le Rider, G., *Suse sous les Séleucides et les Parthes : les trouvailles monétaires et l'histoire de la ville (Mission de Susiane ; MMAI, 38)*, Paris, 1965.

Leroi-Gourhan, A., *Évolution et techniques. L'homme et la matière*[2] *(Sciences d'aujourd'hui)*, Paris, 1971.

Levi, M.A., *I nomadi alla frontiera. I popoli delle steppe e l'antico mondo greco-romano (Centro ricerche e documentazione sull'antichità classica. Monografie, 13)*, Roma, 1989.

Lévi, S., *Le théâtre indien (Bibliothèque de l'École des Hautes Études, IVe Section, fasc. 83)*, Paris, 1890 (2nd reprint 1963).

Lévi, S., "Alexandre et Alexandrie dans les documents indiens", in *Mélanges Maspero, II, Orient grec, romain et byzantin*, Cairo, 1934-1938, pp. 155-164.

Levy, E., "Trésor hellénistique trouvé à Délos", *BCH*, 89, 1965, pp. 503-566.

Lipinsky, A., *Oro, argento, gemme e smalti. Tecnologia delle arti dalle origini alla fine del medioevo 3000 a.C.-1500 d.C.*, Firenze, 1975.

Littauer, M.A., J.H. Crouwel, *Wheeled vehicles and ridden animals in the ancient Near East*, Leiden, Köln, 1979.

Litvinskij, B.A., *Ukrašenija iz Mogil'nikov zapadnoj Fergany* ("The ornaments of the tombs of the Western Ferghana"), Moscow, 1973.

Litvinskij, B.A., A.V. Sedov, *Tepai-Šax : kul'tura i svjazi kušanskoj Baktrii* ("Tepai-Šax. Culture and contacts of Kushan Bactria"), Moscow, 1983.

Litvinskij, B.A., A.V. Sedov, *Kul'ty i ritualy kušanskoj Baktrii. Pogrebal'nyj obrjad* ("Cults and rituals of Kushan Bactria. Funerary customs"), Moscow, 1984.

Loewenthal, A.I., D.B. Harden, "Vasa Murrina", *JRS*, 39, 1949, pp. 31-37.

Loth, A.-M., *La vie publique et privée dans l'Inde ancienne (IIe siècle av. J.-C. - VIIIe siècle environ), 9.1, Les bijoux*, Paris, 1972.

Loth, A.-M., *La vie publique et privée dans l'Inde ancienne (IIe siècle av. J.-C. - VIIIe siècle environ), 7, Les costumes*, Paris, 1979.

Lucas, A., *Ancient Egyptian Materials and Industries*, 4e ed by J.R. Harris, London, 1962 (repr. London, 1989).

Lyonnet, B., "Découvertes de sites de l'âge du bronze dans le Nord-Est de l'Afghanistan : leurs rapports avec la civilisation de l'Indus", *Annali dell'Istituto Universitario Orientale di Napoli*, 37, 1977, pp. 19-35.

Lyonnet, B., "Les nomades et la chute du royaume gréco-bactrien : quelques nouveaux indices en provenance de l'Asie centrale orientale. Vers l'identification des Tokhares – Yueh-Chi ?", in *Histoire et cultes de l'Asie centrale préislamique*, 1991, pp. 153-161.

Lyonnet, B., *Prospection archéologique de la "Bactriane orientale" (Afghanistan du N.E.). Etude de la céramique: typologie, étude comparative et chronologie. Essai sur l'histoire du peuplement depuis le Chalcolithique jusqu'à la conquête arabe (Editions Recherche sur les civilisations)*, Paris, 1995 (forthcoming).

Mackay, E.J.H., "Household objects, tools, and implements", in *Mohenjo-daro*, J. Marshall, ed., London, 1931, pp. 456-480.

Mackay, E.J.H., "Personal ornaments", in *Mohenjo-daro*, J. Marshall, ed., London, 1931, pp. 509-548.

Mackay, E.J.H., "Bead making in ancient Sind", *JAOS*, 57, 1937, pp. 1-15.

*Mahābhārata : Le Mahabharata, poème épique de Krishna-Dwaipayana, plus communément appelé Véda-Vyasa, c'est-à-dire le compilateur et l'ordonnateur des Védas*, by H. Fauche, Paris, 1863-1870 (10 vol.). *The Mahabharata of Krishna-Dwaipayana Vyasa (transl. into English prose from the original Sanskrit xt)*3, by P.C. Roy, New Delhi, 1970-1975 (12 vols). *The Mahābhārata*, transl. and ed. by J.A.B. Van Buitenen, Chicago, London, 1973-1978 (3 vol.). *Storia di Śakuntalā (Śakuntalopākhyāna), Mahābhārata, I, 62-69*, a cura di D. Sagramoso Rossella, Venezia, 1991.

Mankad, D.R., "Yuga Purāṇa : A critically edited text of the Yuga-Purāṇa", *Journal of the Uttarpradesh Historical Society*, 1947, pp. 32-64.

Marshall, J.H., *Excavations at Bhītā (ASIAR 1911-12)*, Calcutta, 1915, pp. 29-94.

Marshall, J.H., "The monuments of ancient India", in *Cambridge history of India*, I, 1922, pp. 555-588.

Marshall, J.H., *Taxila. An illustrated account of archaeological excavations carried out at Taxila under the orders of the Government of India between the years 1913 and 1934*, Cambridge, 1951 (3 vol., repr. Varanasi, 1975).

Marshall, J.H., ed., *Mohenjo-daro* : see *Mohenjo-daro*

Marshall, J.H., A. Foucher, *The monuments of Sāñchī : with the texts of inscriptions edited, translated and annotated by N.G. Majumdar*, Calcutta, London, 1930 (3 vol., repr. Delhi, 1982) (abbrev. : *Sāñchī*).

Martini, M., "Le gemme degli Horti Lamiani", in *Le tranquille dimore degli dei*, 1986, pp. 149-150.

Masson, M.E., G.A. Pugačenkova, *Parfjanskie ritony Nisy (TrJuTAKE, 4)*, Aškhabad, 1959, Moscow, 1956. English translation : *The Parthian Rhytons of Nisa (Monografie di Mesopotamia, 1)*, Florence, 1982.

McCrindle, J.W., *The invasion of India by Alexander the Great : as described by Arrian, Q. Curtius, Diodoros, Plutarch and Justin*2, 1898 (repr. New Delhi, 1983).

*Mélanges Maspero. L'Orient ancien*, Cairo, 1934-1938 (3 vol.).

Menander (*Milinda's questions*) : see *Milindapañha*.

Mendleson, C., "More monkey business", *Anatolian Studies*, 33, 1983, pp. 81-83.

Metzler, D., "Das Pferd auf den Münzen des Labienus – ein Mithras-Symbol?", in *Studien zur Religion und Kultur Kleinasiens*, Leiden, 1978.

Meunié, J., "Qol-i-Nader, une petite fondation bouddhique au Kapiça", in J. Hackin, J. Carl, J. Meunié, *Diverses recherches*, 1959, pp. 115-127.

*Milindapañha* : T.W. Rhys Davids, *The questions of King Milinda (Sacred books of the East, 35, 36)*, Oxford, 1890-1894 (2 vols). L. Finot, *Les questions de Milinda*, Paris, 1923. I.B. Horner, *Milinda's questions (Sacred books of the Buddhists, 33)*, London, 1969 (2 vol.).

Miller, J.I., *The spice trade of the Roman Empire 29 B.C to A.D. 641*, Oxford, 1969.

Milne, J.S., *Surgical instruments in Greek and Roman times*, Oxford 1907 (repr. Chicago, 1976).

Minns, E.H., *Scythians and Greeks*, Cambridge, 1913.

Miroschedji, P. de, "Fouilles du Chantier Ville Royale II à Suse (1975-1977). I. Les niveaux élamites", *Cahiers de la DAFI*, 12, 1981, pp. 9-136.

Miroschedji, P. de, "Vases et objets en stéatite susiens du Musée du Louvre", *Cahiers de la DAFI*, 3, 1973, pp. 9-79.

Mitchiner, M., *The early coinage of Central Asia*, London, 1973.

Mitchiner, M., *Indo-Greek and Indo-Scythian coinage*, London, 1975-1976 (9 vol.). Vol. 1 : *The early Indo-Greeks and their antecedants*, vol. 2 : *The apogee of the Indo-Greeks ; circa 160 to 120 BC.*

Mitra, D., "East India", in *Jaina art and architecture*, t. 1, 1974, pp. 69-84.

Moeller, V., "Das *Nandyāvarta*-Symbol ?", *ZDMG*, 129, 1979, pp. 149-154.

*Mohenjo-daro and the Indus civilization, Being an official account of archaeological excavations at Mohenjo-daro carried out by the Government of India between the years 1922 and 1927*, ed. J.H. Marshall, London, 1931 (3 vol., repr. 1973).

Mooren, L., "The date of *SB* V 8036 and the development of the Ptolemaic maritime trade with India", *Ancient Society*, 3, 1972, pp. 127-133.

Morgan, J. de, "Découverte d'une sépulture achéménide à Suse", in J. de Morgan, G. Jéquier, *MDP, 8*, 1905, pp. 29-58.

Morgan, J. de, G. Jéquier and others, *Recherches archéologiques, Deuxième série (MDP, 7)*, Paris, 1905.

Moynihan, E.B., *Paradise as a garden in Persia and Mughal India*, New York, 1979.

Mukerjee, R., *The flowering of Indian art, The growth and spread of a civilization*, London, 1964.

Mukherjee, B.N., "The problem of attribution of the Reh inscription", *UNESCO, International Association for the Study of the Culture of Central Asia, Information Bulletin*, 11, Moscow, 1988, pp. 43-48.

Mukhopādhyāya, G., *The surgical instruments of the Hindus*, Calcutta, 1913 (repr. 1979).

Murthy, K.K., *The Gandhara sculptures : a cultural survey*, Delhi, 1977.

Murthy, K.K., *Nāgārjunakoṇḍā : a cultural study*, Delhi, 1977.

Murthy, K.K., *Hair styles in ancient Indian art*, Delhi,1981.

Musche, B., *Vorderasiatischer Schmuck zur Zeit der Arsakiden und der Sasaniden (Handbuch der Orientalistik, 7, Kunst und Archäologie. 1 : Der alte Vordere Orient, 2 : Die Denkmäler, B : Vorderasien)*, Leiden, New York, 1988.

Nagaraju, S., *Buddhist architecture of Western India (c.250 B.C.-c.A.D. 300)*, Delhi, 1981.

Nalesini, O., "Bricks and roofs tiles", in G. Verardi and others, *Harigaon Satya Nārāyaṇa*, Rome, 1988, pp. 72-75.

Narain, A.K., *The Indo-Greeks*, Oxford, 1957 (repr. Delhi, 1980).

Narain, A.K., "The earliest Brāhmī inscription outside India", *JAOS*, 106, 1986, pp. 797-801.

Narain, A.K., "Notes on some inscriptions from Ai Khanum (Afghanistan)", *Zeitschrift für Papyrologie und Epigraphik*, 69, 1987, pp. 277-282.

Narain, A.K., "On the foundation and chronology of Ai-Khanum : A Greek-Bactrian city", in *India and the ancient world*, Leuven, 1987, pp. 115-130.

Narain, A.K., "On some Greek inscription from Afghanistan", *Annali dell'Istituto Universitario Orientale di Napoli*, 47, 1987, pp. 269-392.

Narain, A.K., P.K. Agrawala, *Terracotta human figurines (Excavations at Rājghāt [1957-58 ; 1960-65] part IV)*, Varanasi, 1978.

Narain, A.K., P. Singh, *Small finds (Excavations at Rājghāt [1957-58 ; 1960-65] part III)*, Varanasi, 1977.

Naudou, J., "Symbolisme du miroir en Inde", *Arts Asiatiques*, 13, 1966, pp. 59-82.

Nielsen, K., *Incense in ancient Israël*, Leiden, 1986.

Norman, K.R., "Studies in the Minor Rock Edicts of Aśoka", *JRAS*, 1991, pp. 243-253.

Ogden, J., *Jewellery of the ancient world*, London, 1982.

Oliver, A., "Rock crystal vessels in Antiquity", *Muse*, 7, 1973, pp. 29-35.

Orchard, J.J., *Equestrian bridle-harness ornaments (Ivories from Nimrud [1949-1963], fasc. 1, part 2)*, Aberdeen, 1967.

*Orientalia Iosephi Tucci Memoriae Dicata*, Roma, 1985.

Paris, R.-M., *Camille Claudel 1864-1943*, Paris, 1984.

*The Periplus of the Erythraean Sea : travel and trade in the Indian Ocean by a merchant of the first century*, transl. by W.H. Schoff, New York, 1912 ; *The Periplus of the Erythraean Sea, by an unknown author, with some extracts from Agatharkhidēs 'On the Erythraean Sea'*, transl. by G.W.B. Huntingford, London, 1980 ; *The Periplus Maris Erythraei*, ed., trans. and comment. by L. Casson, Princeton, 1989.

Petrie, W.M.F., see Flinders Petrie.

Picard, O., "Sur deux termes des inscriptions de la trésorerie d'Aï Khanoum", in *Hommages à Lucien Lerat*, Paris, 1984, pp. 679-690.

Pidaev, S.R., "Steklo srednevekovogo Termeza" ("Medieval glass ware of Termez"), *ONU*, 1986-7, pp. 53-58.

Piggott, S., "Throne fragments from Pāṭaliputra", *Ancient India*, 4, 1947-48, pp. 101-103.

Pičikjan, I., *Kul'tura Baktrii. Axemenidskij i ellinističeskij periody* ("The culture of Bactria. Achaemenid and Greek periods"), Moscow, 1991.

Pitschikjan, I.R., *Oxos-Shatz und Oxos-Tempel. Achämenidischen Kunst in Mittelasien (Antike in der Moderne)*, Berlin, 1992.

Pliny, *Natural History*, vol. X, *Libri XXXVI-XXXVII (The Loeb Classical Library)*, by D.E. Eichholz, London, Cambridge, 1962.

*Plutarch's Moralia*, transl. of H.N. Fowler (*The Loeb classical library*), Cambridge, London, 1969.

Pollard, J., *Birds in Greek life and myth (Aspects of Greek and Roman life)*, London, 1977.

Popplow, E., *Pferd und Wagen im alten Orient*, Berlin, 1934.

Possehl, G., "Cambay beadmaking : an ancient craft in modern India", *Expedition*, 23-4, 1981, pp. 39-47.

Poster, A.G., *From Indian earth. 4,000 years of terracotta art*, New York, 1986.

Ptolemaeus: see Ronca, I., *Ptolemaios*.

Pugačenkova, G.A., *Xalčajan* ("Khalčajan"), Taškent, 1966.

Pugačenkova, G.A., L.I. Rempel', "O 'zolote bezymjannyx carej' iz Tillja-Tepe (k probleme stilja i svjazej)" ("Regarding the gold of the anonymous kings of Tillja-Tepe, Problems of style and connections"), in *Iz Istorii kul'turnyx svjazej narodov Srednej Azii i Indii*, M.M. Khajrullaev and others, ed., Taškent, 1986, pp. 5-24.

Pugačenkova, G.A. and others, *Dal'verzintepe, Kušanskij gorod na Juge Uzbekistana* ("Dal'verzintepe, Kushana town of Southern Uzbekistan"), Taškent, 1978.

Râmacandra de Râjanallûr, *Çakuntalâ, drame indien, version tamoule d'un texte sanscrit*, translated into French by G. Devèze, Paris, 1888.

Ramin, J., *La technique minière et métallurgique des Anciens (Latomus, 153)*, Bruxelles, 1977.

Rapin, Cl., "Les inscriptions économiques de la trésorerie hellénistique d'Aï Khanoum (Afghanistan)", *BCH*, 107, 1983, pp. 315-372.

Rapin, Cl., "The Greeks in Afghanistan : Ai Khanum", in *Greek colonists and native populations. Proceedings of the First Australian Congress of Classical Archaeology held in honour of A.D. Trendall, Sydney, 9-14 July, 1985*, Canberra, Oxford, 1990, pp. 329-342.

Rapin, Cl., "Ellinističeskaja sokrovišnica Ajxanum" ("The Hellenistic treasury of Ai Khanum"), in *Gorodskaja kul'tura*, 1987, pp. 108-119.

Rapin, Cl., "La trésorerie hellénistique d'Aï Khanoum", *RA* 1987, pp. 41-70.

Rapin, Cl., *Fouilles d'Aï Khanoum VIII, La trésorerie du palais hellénistique d'Aï Khanoum. L'apogée et la chute du royaume grec de Bactriane (MDAFA, 33)*, Paris, 1992.

Rapin, Cl., "Les sanctuaires de l'Asie Centrale à l'époque hellénistique. Etat de la question", *Etudes de Lettres (Université de Lausanne)*, 1992, 4, pp. 101-124.

Raschke, M.G., "New studies in Roman commerce with the East", in *ANRW, II Principat, 9,2*, Berlin, New York, 1978, pp. 604-1361.

Rau, W., *Zur vedischen Altertumskunde (Abhandlungen der geistes- und sozialwissenschaftlichen Klasse, 1983.1)*, Wiesbaden, 1983.

Ray, N., *Maurya and Post-Maurya art : a study in social and formal contrasts*, New Delhi, 1975.

Reinach, Th., *Mithridate Eupator roi de Pont*, Paris, 1890 ; *Mithradates Eupator, König von Pontos*, Leipzig, 1895 ; *Mitridate Eupatore re di Ponto (I cento libri, 10)*, Milano, 1960.

*Records of the Grand Historian of China* : see B. Watson (ed.).

Renou, L. and J. Filliozat, *L'Inde classique, Manuel des études indiennes*, Paris, 1947-1953 (2 vol.).

*La Residenza imperiale degli* horti *Lamiani* : see *Le Tranquille dimore degli dei.*

Reuther, O., "Parthian architecture", in *Survey of Persian art from prehistoric times to the present*, A.U. Pope, ed., I, 1938, pp. 410-444.

Rice, E.E., *The grand procession of Ptolemy Philadelphus*, Oxford, 1983.

Richter, G.M.A., *The furniture of the Greeks, Etruscans and Romans*, London, 1966[2].

Richter, G.M.A., *The engraved gems of the Greeks, Etruscans and Romans*, London, 1968-1971 (2 vol.).

Robert, L., *Noms indigènes dans l'Asie Mineure gréco-romaine (Bibliothèque archéologique et historique de l'Institut français d'archéologie d'Istanbul, 13)*, Paris, 1963.

Robert, L., "Les inscriptions", in *Fouilles d'Aï Khanoum I*, 1973, pp. 208-211 ; *idem*, "Inscriptions grecques nouvelles de la Bactriane", *CRAI* 1968, pp. 416-457.

Robin, Chr., "L'Arabie du Sud et la date du *Périple de la Mer Érythrée* (Nouvelles données)", *JA*, 279, 1991, pp. 1-30.

Rocher, L., *The Purāṇas (A history of Indian literature, 2.3)*, Wiesbaden, 1986.

Ronca, I., *Ptolemaios, Geographie, 6,9-2,1, Ostiran und Zentralasien, Teil I (Reports and Memoirs, 15,1)*, Rom, 1971.

Root, M.C., *The King and kingship in Achaemenid art. Essays on the creation of an iconography of Empire (Acta Iranica, 19)*, Leiden, 1979.

Rosenfield, J.M., *The dynastic arts of the Kushans*, Berkeley, Los Angeles, 1967.

Rostovtzeff, M., *Iranians and Greeks in South Russia*, Oxford, 1922.

Rougé, J., "La navigation en Mer Érythrée dans l'Antiquité", in *L'Arabie et ses mers bordières*, 1988, pp. 59-74.

Rowland, B., "The vine-scroll in Gandhara", *Artibus Asiae*, 19, 1956, pp. 353-361.

Rowland, B., *The art and architecture of India : Buddhist, Hindu, Jain (Pelican history of art)*, London, Baltimore, 1971.

Rtveladze, E.V., "Novye drevnebaktrijskie pamjatniki na Juge Uzbekistana" ("Recent Bactrian ancient monuments in the south of Uzbekistan"), in *Baktrijskie drevnosti*, Leningrad, 1976, pp. 93-103.

Ruben, W., *Kālidāsa. Die Menschliche Bedeutung seiner Werke*, Berlin, 1956.

Ruben, W., *Die Gesellschaftliche Entwicklung im alten Indien, 5, Die Entwicklung der Dichtung im alten Indien (Akademie der Wissenschaften der DDR, Veröffentlichungen des Instituts für Orientforschung, 67)*, Berlin, 1973.

Saldern, A. von, H. Hoffman, P.F. Davidson, *Greek gold : jewellery from the Age of Alexander*, Mayence, 1965.

*Sāñchī* : see J.H. Marshall, A. Foucher, *The Monuments of Sāñchī.*

Sarianidi, V., *Bactrian Gold : from the excavations of the Tillya-tepe necropolis in Northern Afghanistan*, Leningrad, 1985 ; text in French : *L'or de la Bactriane. Fouilles de la nécropole de Tillia-tépé en Afghanistan septentrional*, Léningrad, 1985.

Sarianidi, V., *Die Kunst des alten Afghanistan*, Leipzig, 1986.

Schafer, E.H., "Orpiment and realgar in Chinese technology and tradition", *JAOS*, 75, 1955, pp. 73-89.

Schafer, E.H., *The golden peaches of Samarcand, a study on T'ang exotics*, Berkeley, Los Angeles, London, 1985 (repr. of the ed. of 1963).

Schlumberger, D., "Aï Khanoum, une ville hellénistique en Afghanistan", *CRAI* 1965, pp. 36-46.

Schmidt, E.F., *Persepolis II : Contents of the Treasury and other discoveries (OIP, 59)*, Chicago, 1957.

Schoff, W.H., *Parthian stations of Isidore of Charax*, Philadelphia, 1914 (repr. Chicago, 1976).

Schoff, W.H., *The Periplus of the Erythraean Sea : travel and trade in the Indian Ocean by a merchant of the first century*, transl., New York, 1912.

Sedlar, J.W., *India and the Greek world. A study in the transmission of culture*, Totowa, 1980.

Seligman, C.G., H.C. Beck, "Far Eastern glass : Some Western origins", *The Museum of Far Eastern Antiquities. Stockholm. Bulletin*, 10, 1938, pp. 1-64.

Sharma, G.R., *Reh inscription of Menander and the Indo-Greek invasion of the GanΔgā Valley (Studies in history, culture and archaeology, 1)*, Allahabad, 1980.

Sherkova, T., "The nature of contacts between the Kushan kingdom and the Eastern Mediterranean (on the basis of archaeological evidence from Bactria)", *The International Association for the Study of the Cultures of Central Asia. Information Bulletin, Issue 1*, Moscow, 1982, pp. 47-55.

Singh, S.D., *Ancient warfare with special reference to the Vedic period*, Leyde, 1965.

Sinha, B.C., *Tree worship in ancient India (Worship in India Series, 1)*, New Delhi, 1979.

Sivaramamurti, C., *Amarāvatī sculptures in the Madras Government Museum (Bulletin of the Madras Govt. Museum, N.S., 4)*, 1956.

Sivaramamurti, C., *L'art en Inde*, Paris, 1974.

Sivaramamurti, C., *The art of India*, New York, 1977.

Smith, G.F.H., *Gemstones*, London, 1972.

Smith, V.A., *Asoka, the Buddhist emperor of India*, Oxford, 1910.

Smith, V.A., *A History of fine art in India and Ceylon*, 3rd ed. revised by K. Khandalawala, repr. Bombay, 1969 (first ed. Oxford, 1911).

*South Asian Archaeology 1983, Papers from the Seventh International Conference of the Association of South Asian Archaeology in Western Europe, held in the Musées Royaux d'Art et d'Histoire, Brussels*, J. Schotsmans and M. Taddei, ed., Naples, 1985.

*South Asian Archaeology 1987, Proceedings of the Ninth International Conference of the Association of South Asian Archaeologists in Western Europe, held in the Fondazione Giorgio Cini, Island of San Giorgio Maggiore, Venice*, M. Taddei, ed., Rome, 1990 (2 vols.).

Spagnoli, M.M., "The symbolic meaning of the club in the iconography of Kuṣāṇa kings", *EW*, 17, 1967, pp. 248-267.

Sparreboom, M., *Chariots in the Veda*, thesis, Leiden, 1983.

Spruytte, J., *Études expérimentales sur l'attelage*, Paris, 1977.

Srivastava, A.L., *Nandyāvarta. An auspicious symbol in Indian art*, Allahabad, 1991.

Sse Ma T'sien : see B. Watson, *Records of the Grand Historian of China* and E. Chavannes, *Les Mémoires historiques de Se-Ma Ts'ien.*

Staviskij, B.Ja., *La Bactriane sous les Kushans. Problèmes d'histoire et de culture*, Paris, 1986.

Stern, Ph., "Les ivoires et os découverts à Begram - Leur place dans l'évolution de l'art en Inde", in J. Hackin and others, *Nouvelles recherches*, 1954, pp. 19-54.

Stern, Ph., "Aspects plastiques de l'ancien théâtre indien et peintures murales d'Ajanta (influences réciproques)", in *Les théâtres d'Asie*, Paris, 1961, pp. 49-68.

Stern, Ph., M. Bénisti, *Évolution du style indien d'Amarāvatī*, Paris, 1961.

Strabo, *The geography of Strabo*, transl. by H.L. Jones (*The Loeb classical library*), Cambridge Mass., London, 1917>.

Stronach, D., *Pasargadae : A report of the excavations conducted by the British Institute of Persian Studies from 1961 to 1963*, Oxford, 1978.

Stronge, S., N. Smith, J.C. Harle, *A golden treasury. Jewellery from the Indian Subcontinent (Victoria and Albert Museum, Indian series)*, London, 1988.

Stutley, M., *The illustrated dictionary of Hindu iconography*, London, Boston, 1985.

Stutley, M. and J., *A dictionary of Hinduism : its mythology, folklore and development 1500 B.C.- A.D 1500*, London, 1977.

Taddei, M., "Neue Forschungbelege zur Gandhāra-Ikonographie", *Aus dem Osten des Alexanderreiches*, Köln, 1984, pp. 154-175.

Taddei, M., "Two notes on Gandharan iconography. 1. More on the meditating monkey from Tapa Sardâr", *EW*, 35, 1985, pp. 271-272.

Tarn, W.W., *The Greeks in Bactria and India*$^2$, Cambridge, 1951 (3d ed. Chicago, 1985, with preface and bibliography, by F.L. Holt).

Tartamella, E., *Corallo, storia e arte dal XV al XIX secolo*, Palermo, 1985.

*La Terra tra i due fiumi. Venti anni di archeologia italiana in Medio Oriente. La Mesopotamia dei tesori*, Torino, 1985.

Thapliyal, U.P., *Foreign elements in ancient Indian society 2nd cent. B.-C. to 7th cent. A.D.*, New Delhi, 1979.

*Les théâtres d'Asie*, Study put together by J. Jacquot, Paris, 1961.

Theophrastus, *De lapidibus*, D.E. Eichholz ed., Oxford, 1965.

Thompson, D., *Stucco from Chal Tarkhan-Eshqabad near Rayy*, Warminster, 1976.

Thompson, D'Arcy W., *A glossary of Greek birds*$^2$, Oxford, London, 1936.

Thompson, D.B., "The Tazza Farnese Reconsidered. Das ptolemaische Ägypten", in *Akten des Internationalen Symposions Berlin, 1976*, Berlin, 1976, pp. 113-121.

Thoraval, J., J.-Cl. Liger "Campagne de fouille 1978 à Aï Khanoum (Afghanistan) : V. Le palais : sondages sur la cour sud", *BEFEO*, 18, 1980, pp. 44-45.

Tjuljaev, S.I., *Iskusstvo Indii* ("The art of India"), Moscow, 1988.

Tolstov, S.P., B.I. Vajnberg, *Koj-Krylgan-kala, Pamjatnik kul'tury drevnego Xorezma IV v. do n.è.- IV v. n.è.* ("Koj-Krylgan-kala, Monument of the culture of ancient Chorasmia") *(Trudy Xorezmskoj Arxeologo-Ètnografičeskoj Èkspedicii, 5)*, Moscow, 1967.

Tosi, M., "The Northeastern frontier of the ancient Near East : Marginal notes to V.M. Masson's and V.I. Sarianidi's *Central Asia. Turkmenia before the Achaemenids*, London, 1972", *Mesopotamia*, 8-9, 1973-74, pp. 21-76.

*Traité de zoologie. Anatomie, systématique, biologie*, P.-P. Grassé, ed., t. 17, *Mammifères. Les ordres : anatomie, éthologie, systématique*, Paris, 1955 (2 vol.).

*Le Tranquille dimore degli dei. La residenza imperiale degli* Horti *Lamiani, Roma, maggio-settembre 1986, Campidoglio, Palazzo dei Conservatori*, M. Cima and E. La Rocca, ed., Roma, 1986.

Upadhyaya, B.S., *India in Kālidāsa*, Allahabad, 1947.

Vallat, F., "Deux inscriptions élamites de Darius I$^{er}$ (DSf et DSz)", *Studia Iranica*, 1, 1972, pp. 3-13.

Van Ooteghem, J., *Pompée le Grand bâtisseur d'empire*, Namur, 1954.

Venturo, D., "I vasi murrini. Il contributo delle fonti classiche", *Antiqua*, 11, 1978, pp. 45-48.

Verardi, G. and others, *Harigaon Satya Nārāyaṇa, Kathmandu. A report on the excavations carried out in 1984-1988 (IsMEO. Reports and memoirs, 22)*, Rome, 1988.

Vessberg, O., A. Westholm, *The Swedish Cyprus Expedition, IV, Part 3, The Hellenistic and Roman periods in Cyprus*, Stockholm, 1956.

Veuve, S., *Fouilles d'Aï Khanoum VI. Le Gymnase. Architecture, céramique, sculpture (MDAFA, 30)*, Paris, 1987.

Veuve, S. and others, "Campagne de fouille 1978 à Aï Khanoum (Afghanistan) : VI. Bâtiment public en bordure de la rue principale", *BEFEO*, 68, 1980, pp. 46-50.

Viennot, O., *Le culte de l'arbre dans l'Inde ancienne (Annales du Musée Guimet)*, Paris, 1954.

Vigneron, P., *Le cheval dans l'antiquité gréco-romaine (des guerres médiques aux grandes invasions) (Contribution à l'histoire des techniques, t. 1)*, Nancy, 1968.

*The Vishńu Puráńa, a system of Hindu mythology and tradition*, transl. by H.H. Wilson, London, 1864-1877 (repr. Calcutta, 1972).

Vogel, J.Ph., *La sculpture de Mathurâ (Ars Asiatica, 15)*, Paris, Bruxelles, 1930.

Vogelsang, W., "Early historical Arachosia in South-East Afghanistan. Meeting-place between East and West", *Iranica Antiqua*, 20, 1985, pp. 55-99.

Walker, C.B.F., "Some Mesopotamian inscribed vessels", *Iraq*, 42, 1980, pp. 84-86.

Warmington, E.H., *The commerce between the Roman Empire and India*[2], London, New York, 1974.

Watson, B. (ed.), *Records of the Grand Historian of China, translated from the Shih chi of Ssu-ma chien*, 2, London, 1961.

Wetzel, F., E. Schmidt, A. Mallwitz, *Das Babylon der Spätzeit (WVDOG, 52)*, Berlin, 1957.

Wheeler, R.E.M., "Arikamedhu : An Indo-Roman trading-station on the East Coast of India", *Ancient India*, 2, 1946, pp. 17-124.

Wheeler, R.E.M., "Iran and India in Pre-Islamic times : a lecture", *Ancient India*, 4, 1947-48, pp. 85-101.

Wheeler, M., *Flames over Persepolis*, London, 1968.

White, L., *Technologie médiévale et transformations sociales (Civilisations et sociétés, 13)*, Paris, La Haye, 1969 (English ed., 1965).

Whitehouse, D., "Carnelian in the Persian Gulf", *Antiquity*, 49, 1975, pp. 129-130.

Whitehouse, D., "Excavations at Kandahar, 1974, first interim report", *Afghan Studies*, 1, 1978, pp. 9-39.

Wiesehöfer, J., "Beobachtungen zum Handel des Achämenidenreiches", *Münstersche Beiträge zur antiken Handelsgeschichte*, 1, 1982, pp. 5-15.

Wild, J.P., *Textile manufacture in the Northern Roman provinces*, Cambridge, 1970.

Wilhelm, Fr., H.G. Rawlinson, "India and the modern West", in *A cultural history of India*, Oxford, 1975, pp. 470-486.

Will, Éd., *Histoire politique du monde hellénistique (323-30 av. J.-C.)*[2], Nancy, 1979-1982 (2 vol.).

Wolley, C.L. and others, *Ur excavations, 2, The Royal Cemetery. A report on the Predynastic and Sargonic graves excavated between 1926 and 1931*, New York, 1934.

Woodcock, G., *The Greeks in India*, London, 1966.

Wright, P.W.M., "The bow-drill and the drilling of beads, Kabul, 1981", *Afghan Studies*, 1982, 3-4, pp. 95-101.

Xénophon, *L'art équestre*, Ed. Delebecque, ed., Paris, 1958.

Young, R.S., *The Gordion excavations final reports. I. Three great early tumuli*, Philadelphia, 1981.

Zazoff, P., *Jagddarstellungen auf antiken Gemmen*, Hamburg, Berlin, 1970.

Zazoff, P., *Die antiken Gemmen*, München, 1983.

Zimmer, H., *The art of Indian Asia, its mythology and transformations (Bollingen Series, 39)*, New York, 1968 (2 vol., repr. Princeton, 1983).

# TABLE OF ILLUSTRATIONS

Authors of the plans and designs : G. Lecuyot, J.-Cl. Liger, Cl. Rapin.

## MAPS AND PLANS



## SMALL OBJECTS (DESIGNS)

## PHOTOGRAPHS

I

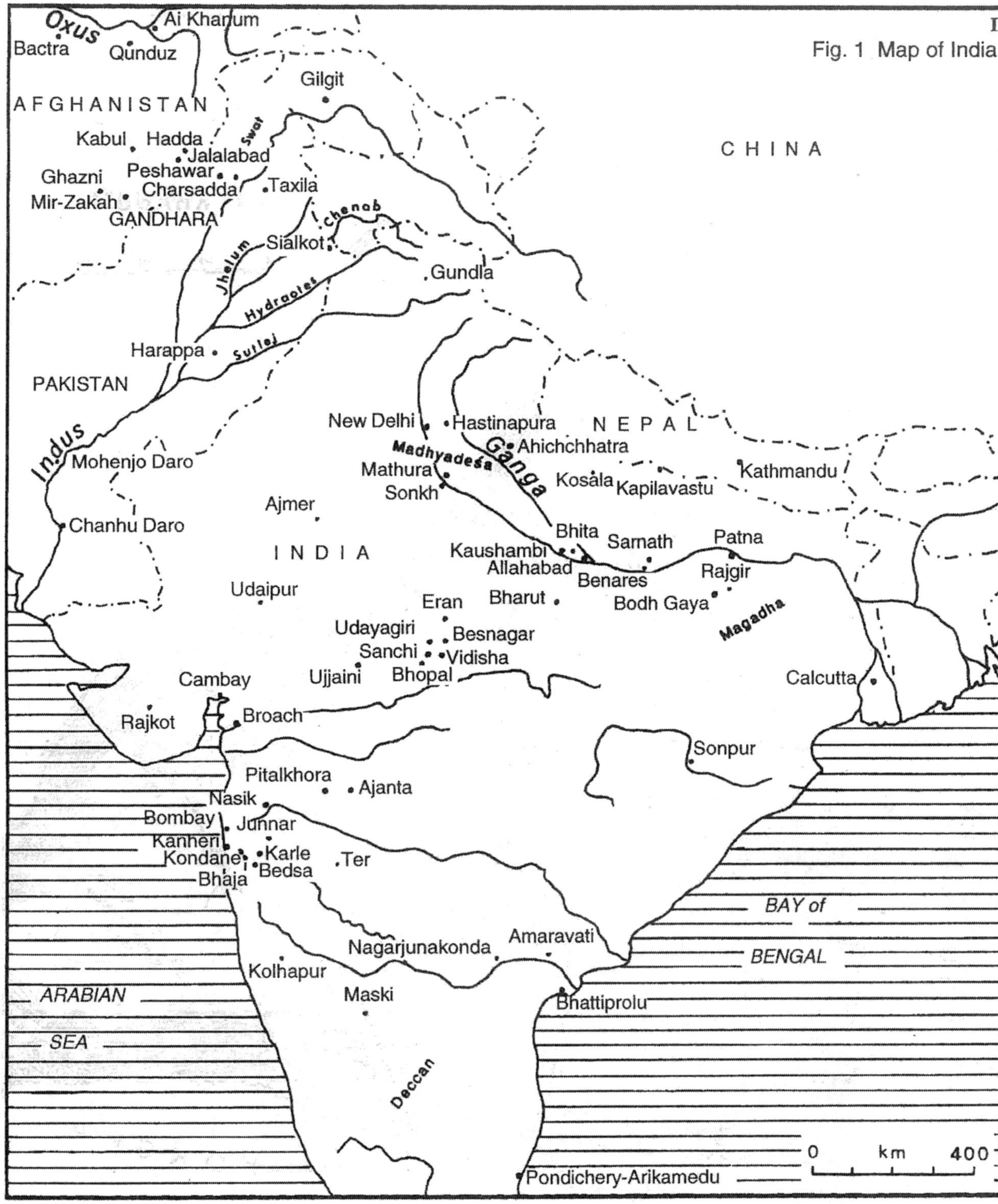


Fig. 1 Map of India

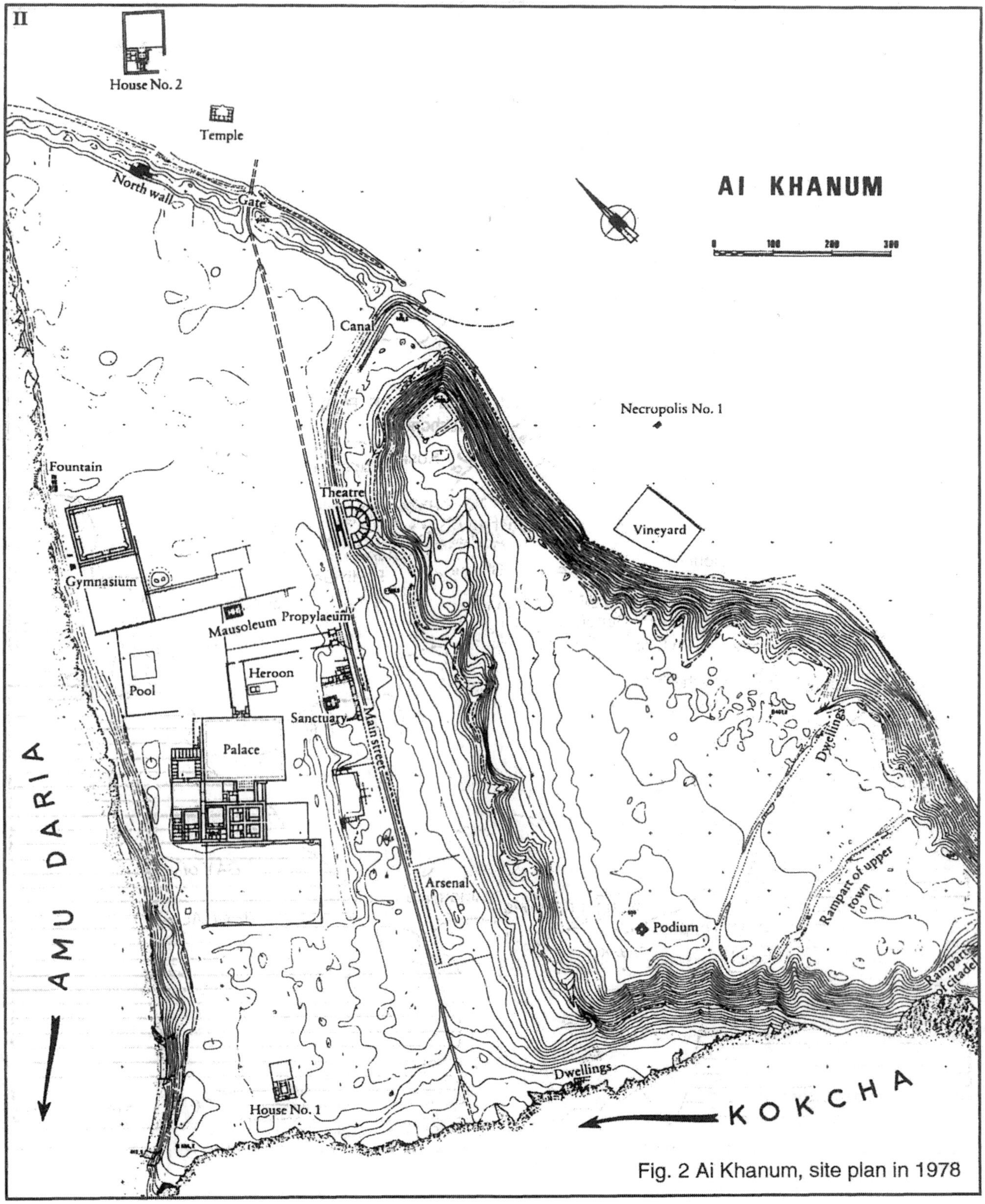


Fig. 2 Ai Khanum, site plan in 1978

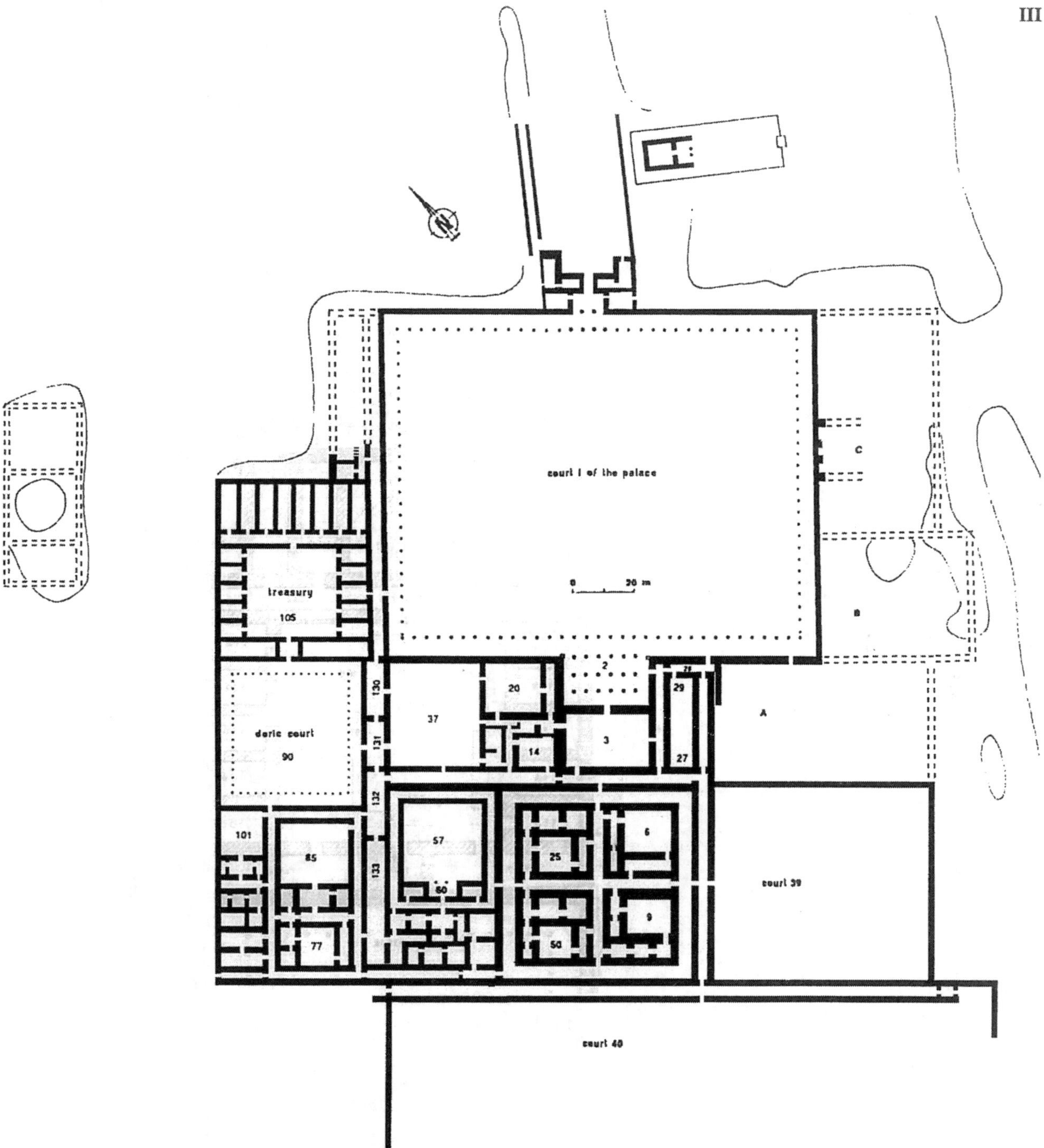


Fig. 3 – Ai Khanum, plan of the palace with dots indicating the supposed location of the buildings

IV

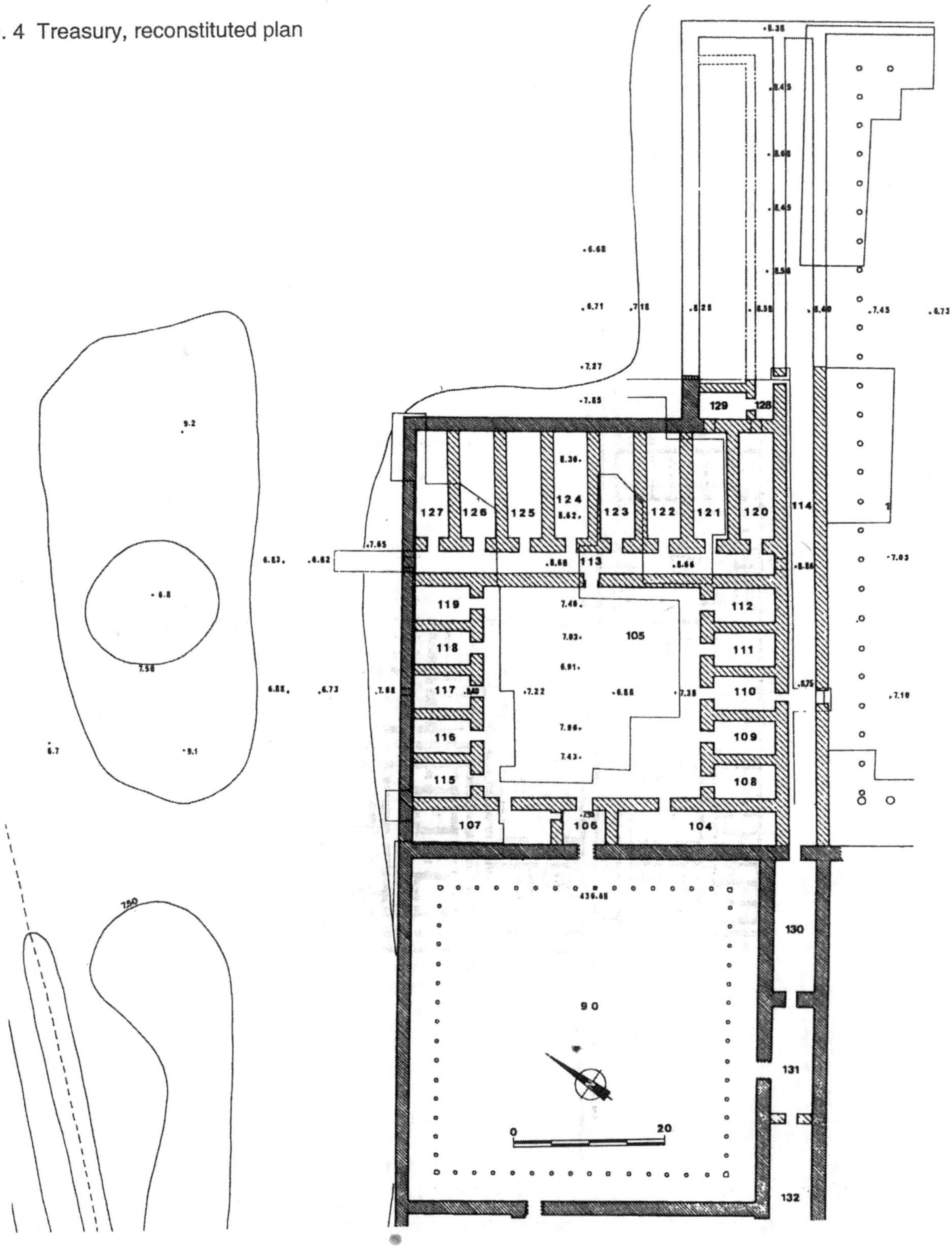


Fig. 4 Treasury, reconstituted plan

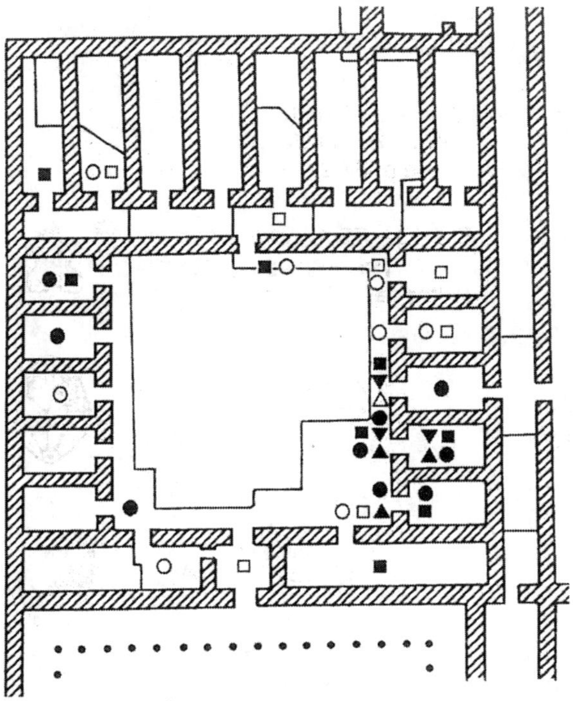

Fig. 5. Map showing the distribution of the finds of the Indian throne in the treasury

(in white: isolated finds. In black: multiple finds)

- ▲ Bronze nails (S3)
- ▼ Schist nails (S14)
- ■ Rock crystal S15
- ● White and banded agate (S17 and S18)

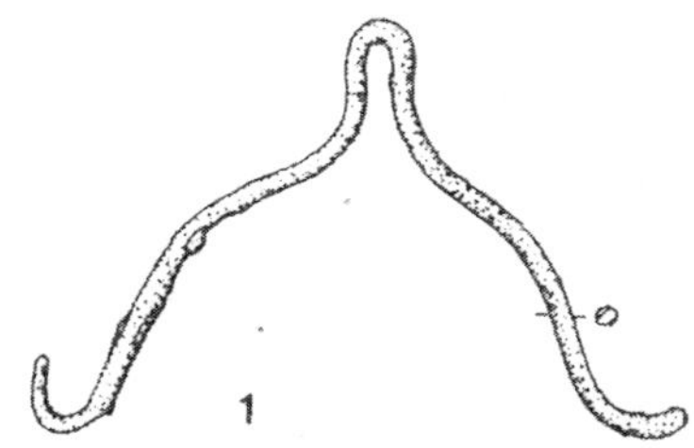


Fig. 6 – D3-1 : handle of ink-pot [1:2] (see p. 17, 123)

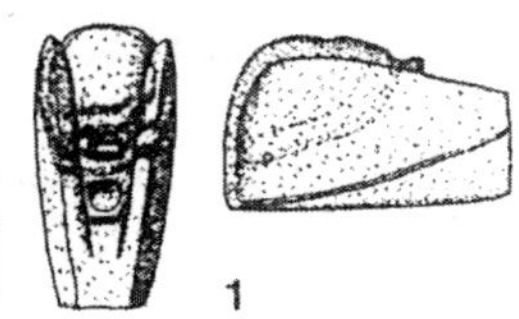


Fig. 7 – E17-1 : pendant - weight in agate [1:2] (see p. 18, 30, 123)

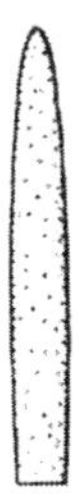

Fig. 8 – I17-1 : polisher in agate [format 1:2] (see p. 38, 123)

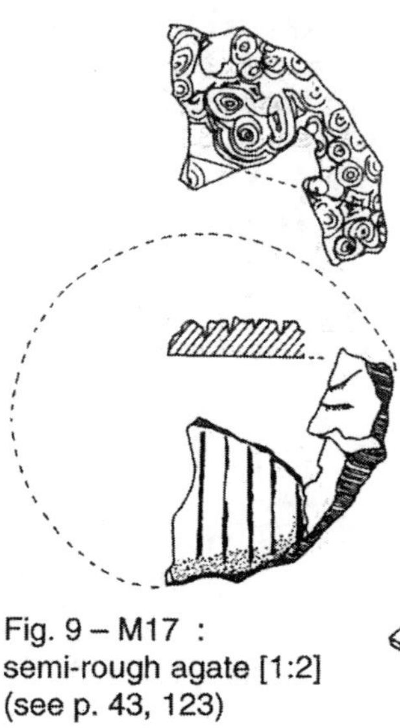

Fig. 9 – M17 : semi-rough agate [1:2] (see p. 43, 123)

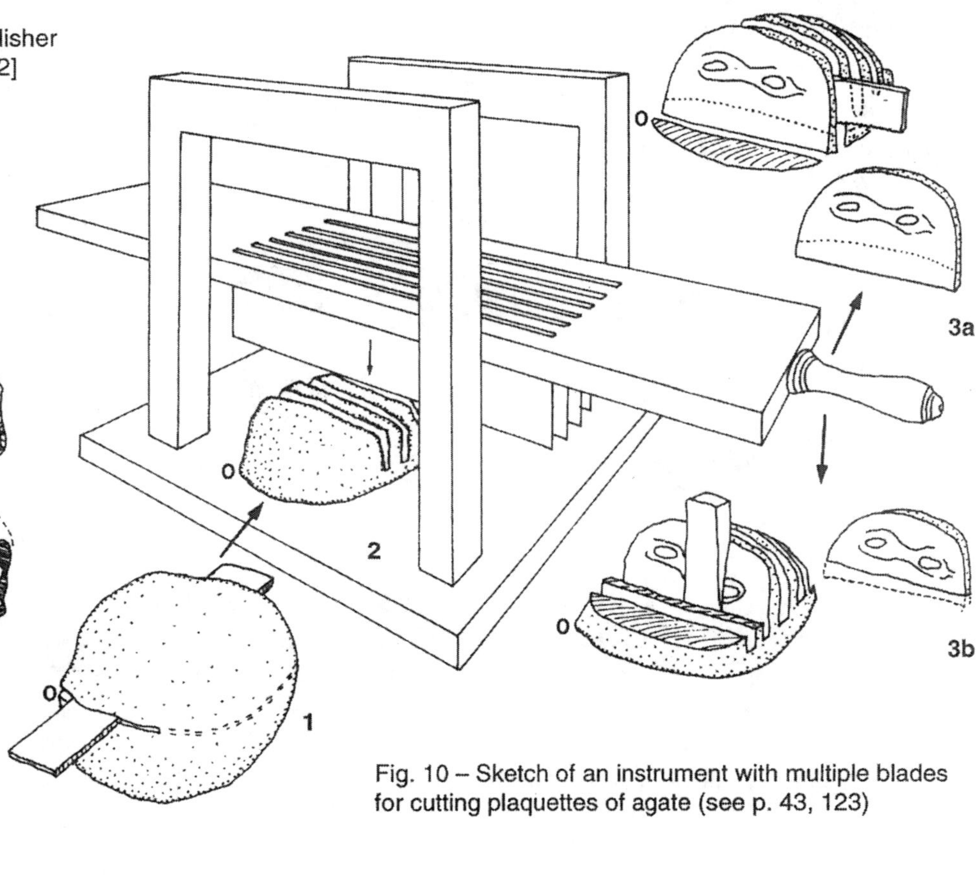


Fig. 10 – Sketch of an instrument with multiple blades for cutting plaquettes of agate (see p. 43, 123)

VI

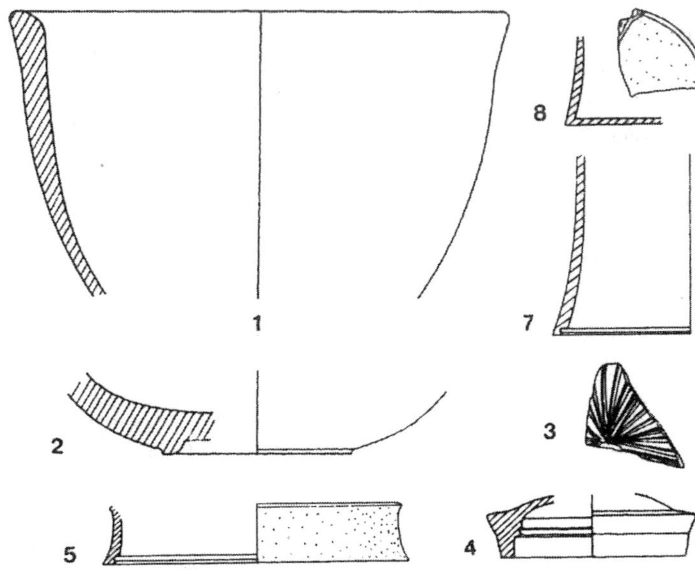

Fig. 11 – N15 : Vessel in rock crystal [1:2] (see pp. 24-26, 124)

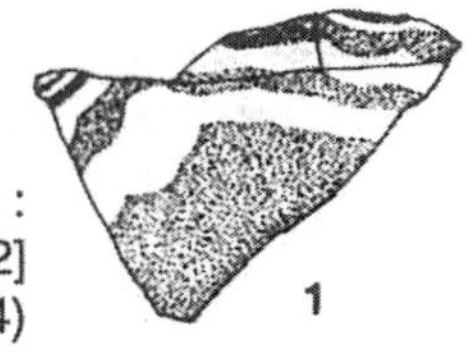

Fig. 12 – N17 : Vessel in agate [1:2] (see p. 24-27, 124)

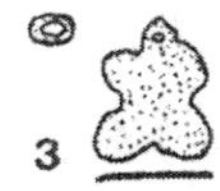

Fig. 13 – O3-1 : anthropomorphic pendant of bronze [format 1:2] (see p. 38, 124)

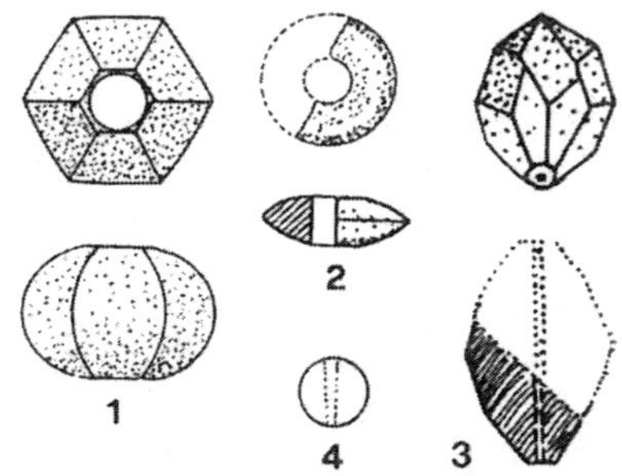

Fig. 14 – O15 : beads in rock crystal [1, 2, 4 : format 1:2; 3 : format 1:1] (see p. 30, 124)

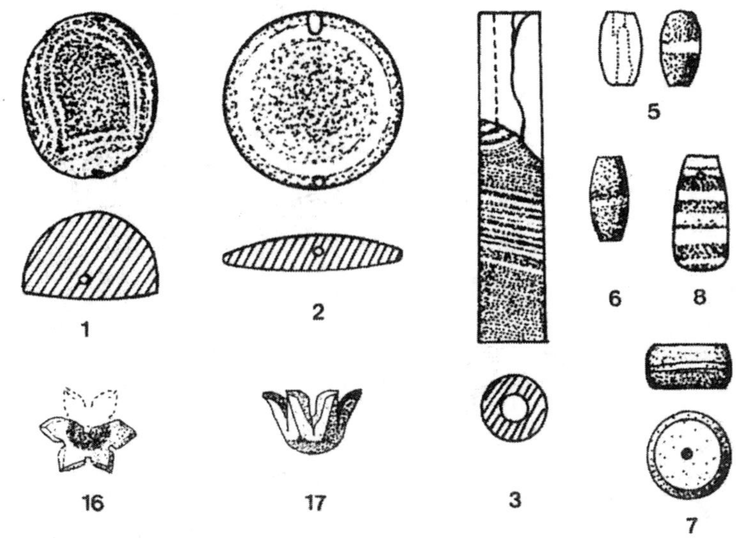

Fig. 15 – O17 : beads in agate [1, 2, 3, 6, 7, 8 : format 1:1 ; 5, 16, 17 : format 2:1] (see pp. 30-31, 38, 124-125)

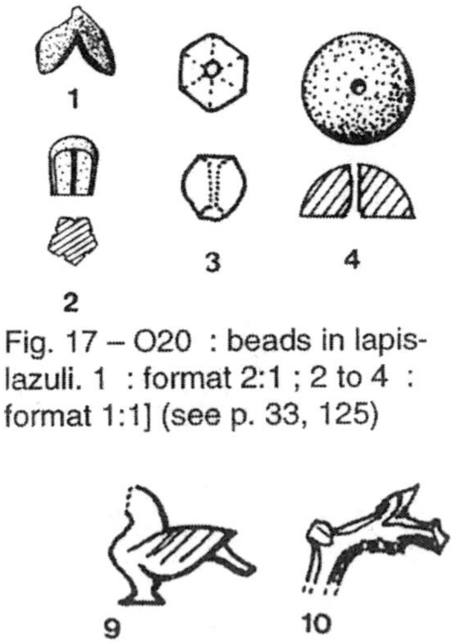

Fig. 17 – O20 : beads in lapis-lazuli. 1 : format 2:1 ; 2 to 4 : format 1:1] (see p. 33, 125)

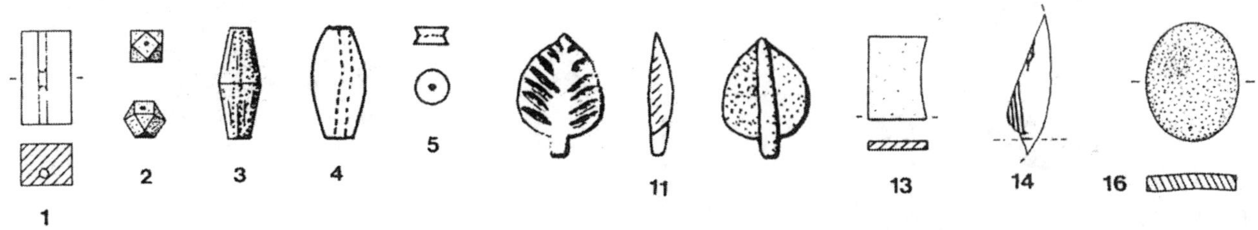

Fig. 16 – O19 : carnelian [1, 2, 3, 5 : format 1:1 ; 9 to 11 : form 2:1 ; 13, 14, 16 : form.1:2] (see pp. 31-32, 35, 125)

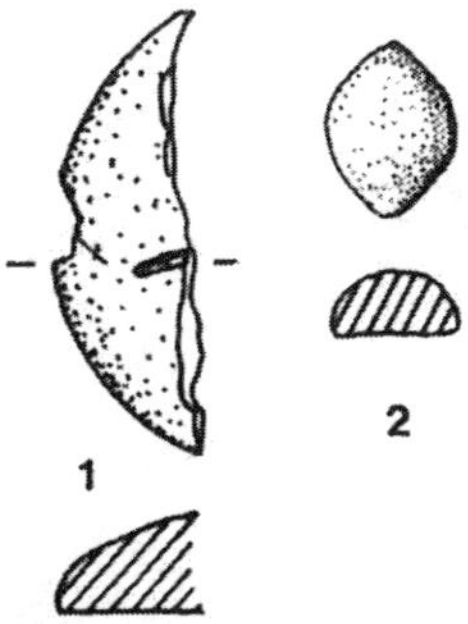


Fig. 18 – O23 : garnet [1:1] (see p. 34, 126)

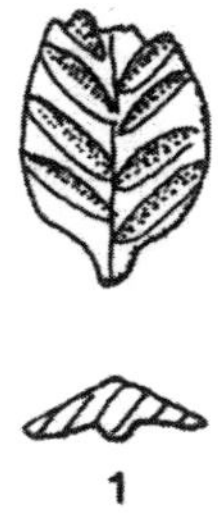


Fig. 19 – O24-1 : blue stone [2:1] (see p. 35, 126)

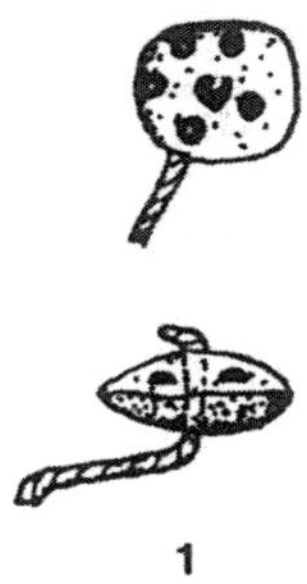


Fig. 20 – O25-1 : peridot [2:1] (see p. 126)

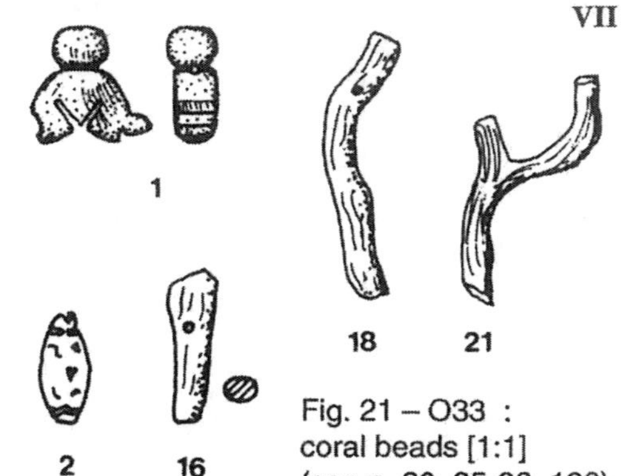


Fig. 21 – O33 : coral beads [1:1] (see p. 20, 35-36, 126)

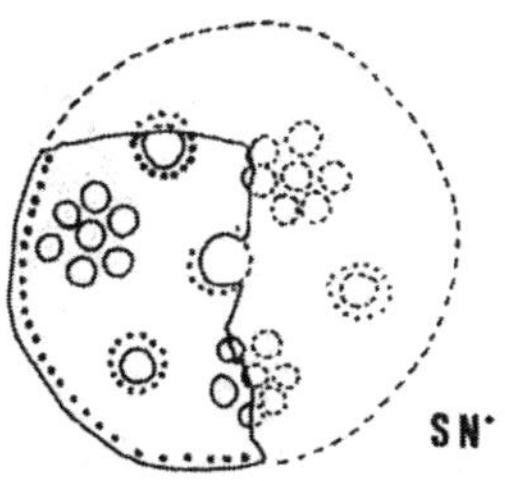


Fig. 22 – O34 : round piece of shell, accidental find [1:2] (see pp. 36-37, 126)

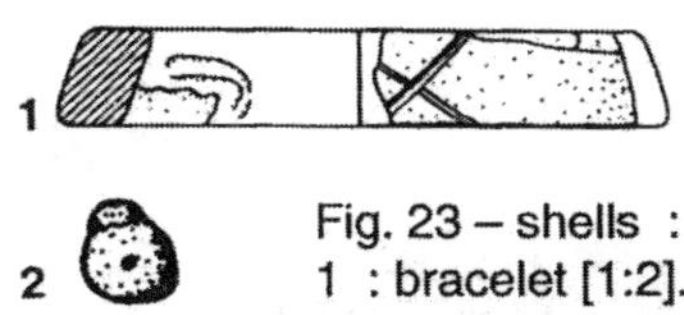


Fig. 23 – shells :
1 : bracelet [1:2].
2 : mother of pearl bead [1:1] (pp. 36-37, 126)

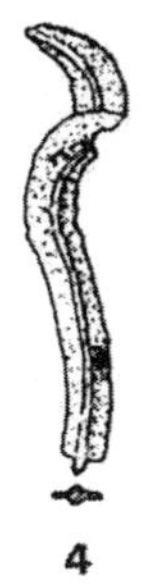


Fig. 24 – Bronze surgical instrument [format 1:2] (see p. 37, 127)

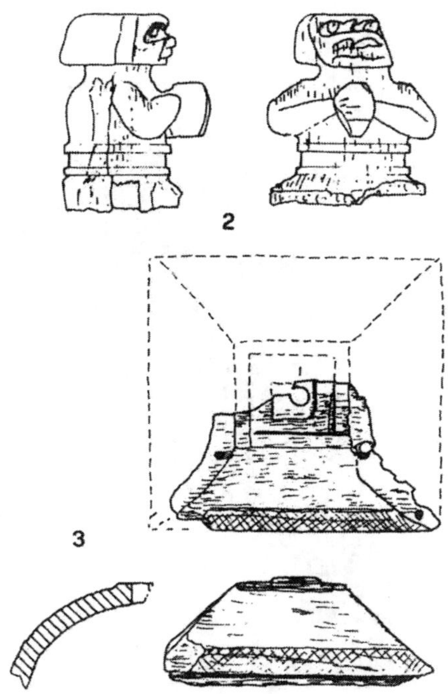


Fig. 25 – R35: Decorative elements in ivory. 2 : monkey ? : [format 1:1].
3 : lid of pyxide [format 1:2] (see p. 38, 127)

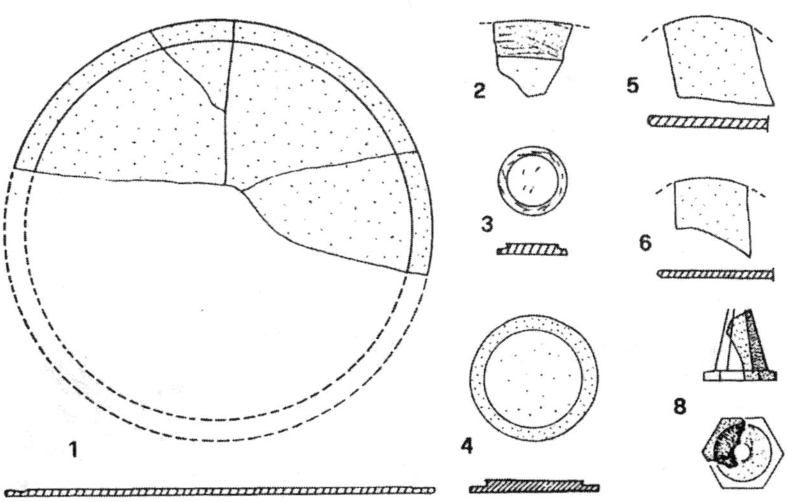


Fig. 27.1 – S15 : Indian throne, elements in rock crystal [1:2] (pp. 41-49)

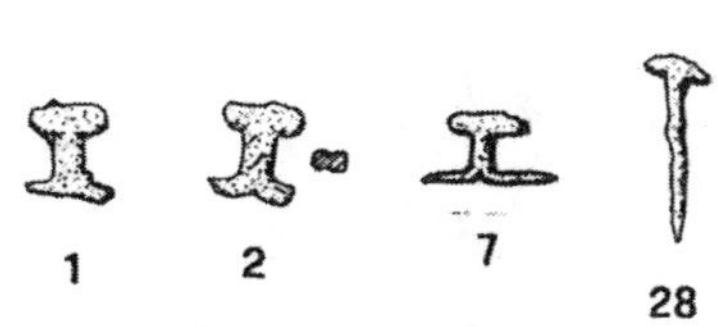


Fig. 26 – S3 : Indian throne, bronze elements for fixing [format 1:2] (see pp. 41-49, 127-131)

VIII

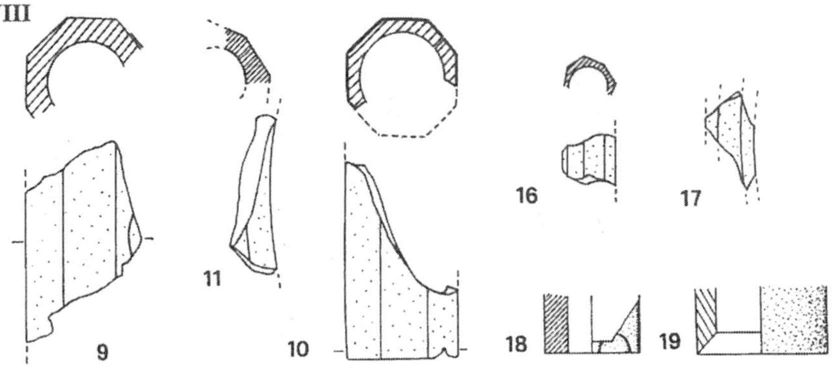


Fig. 27.2 – S15 : Indian throne, elements in rock crystal [format 1:2] (pp. 41-49)

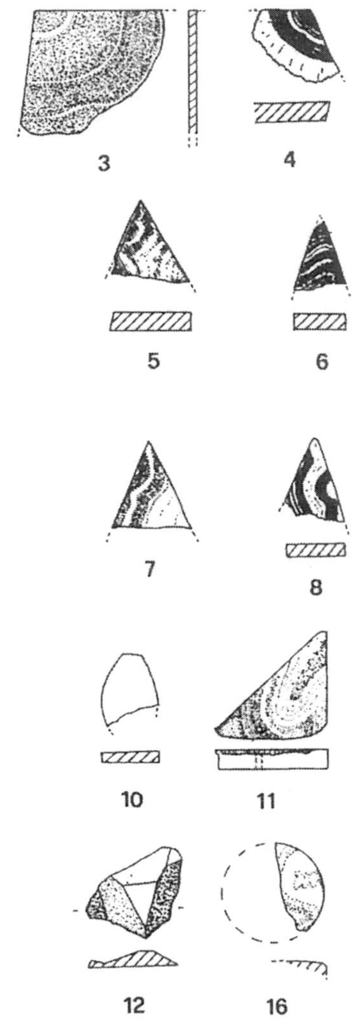


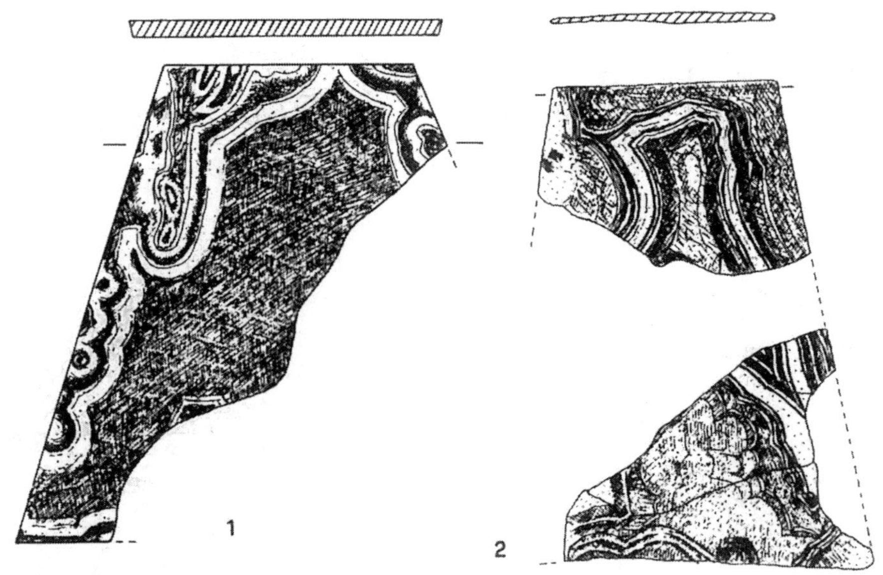


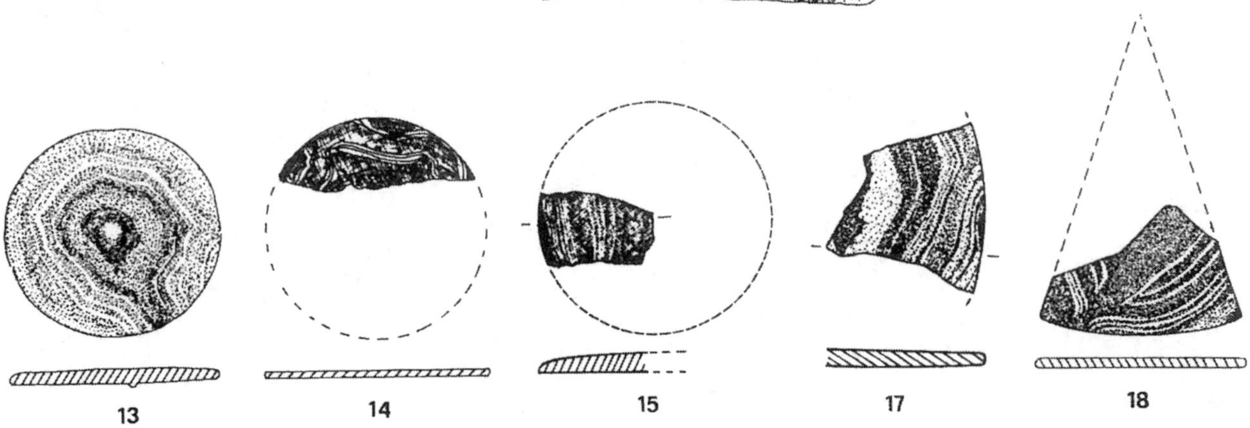


Fig. 28.1 – S17 : Indian throne, elements in banded agate, 1 to 18 [format 1:2] (see pp. 41-49)

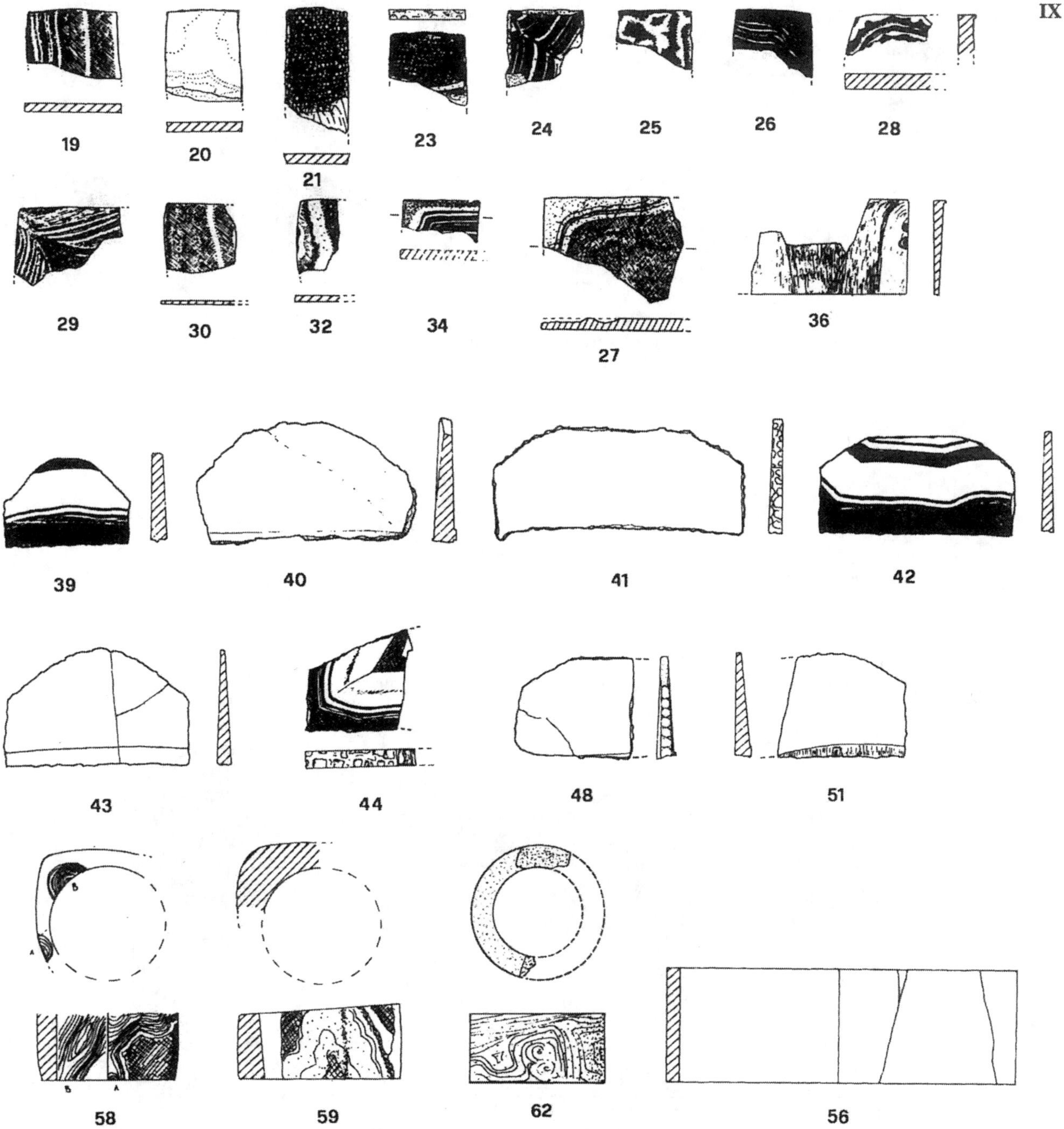


Fig. 28.2 – S17 : Indian throne, elements in banded agate, 19 to 58 [format 1:2] (see pp. 41-49)

X

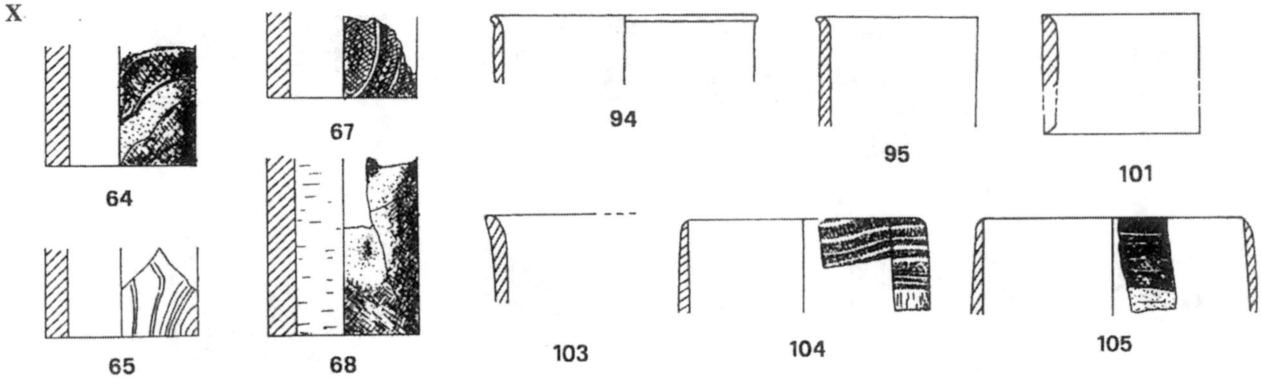


Fig. 28.3 – S17 : Indian throne, tubular elements in banded agate, 64 to 68 ; 94 to 105 : bracelets in agate? [format 1:2] (see pp. 30-31, 130)

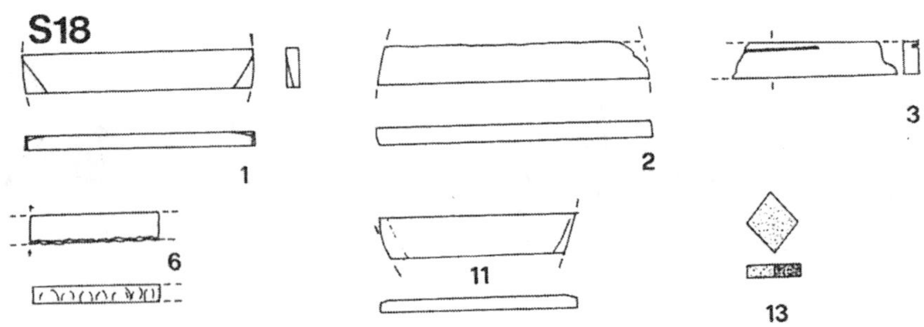


Fig. 29 – S18 : Indian throne, elements in white "porcelain" agate [format 1:2] (see p. 46, 131)

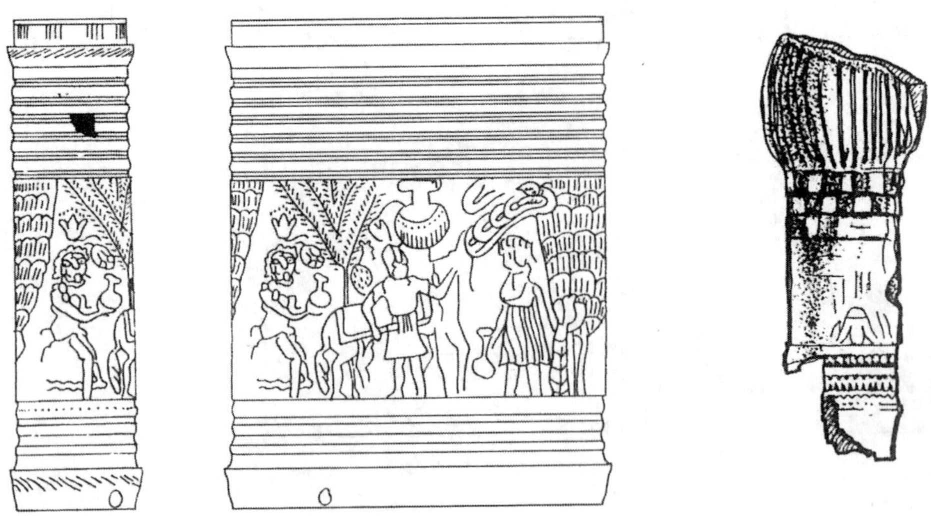

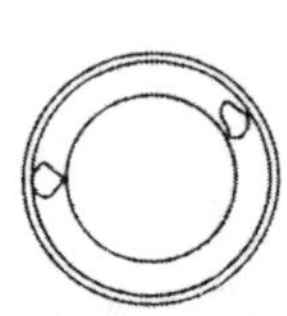

Fig. 29b – Horn cylindre with the representation of an Indian myth, from the Oxus temple at Takht-i Sangin (Tadžikistan) from I.R. Pitschikjan, *Oxos-Schatz und Oxos-Tempel,* Abb. 19 (see p. 50)

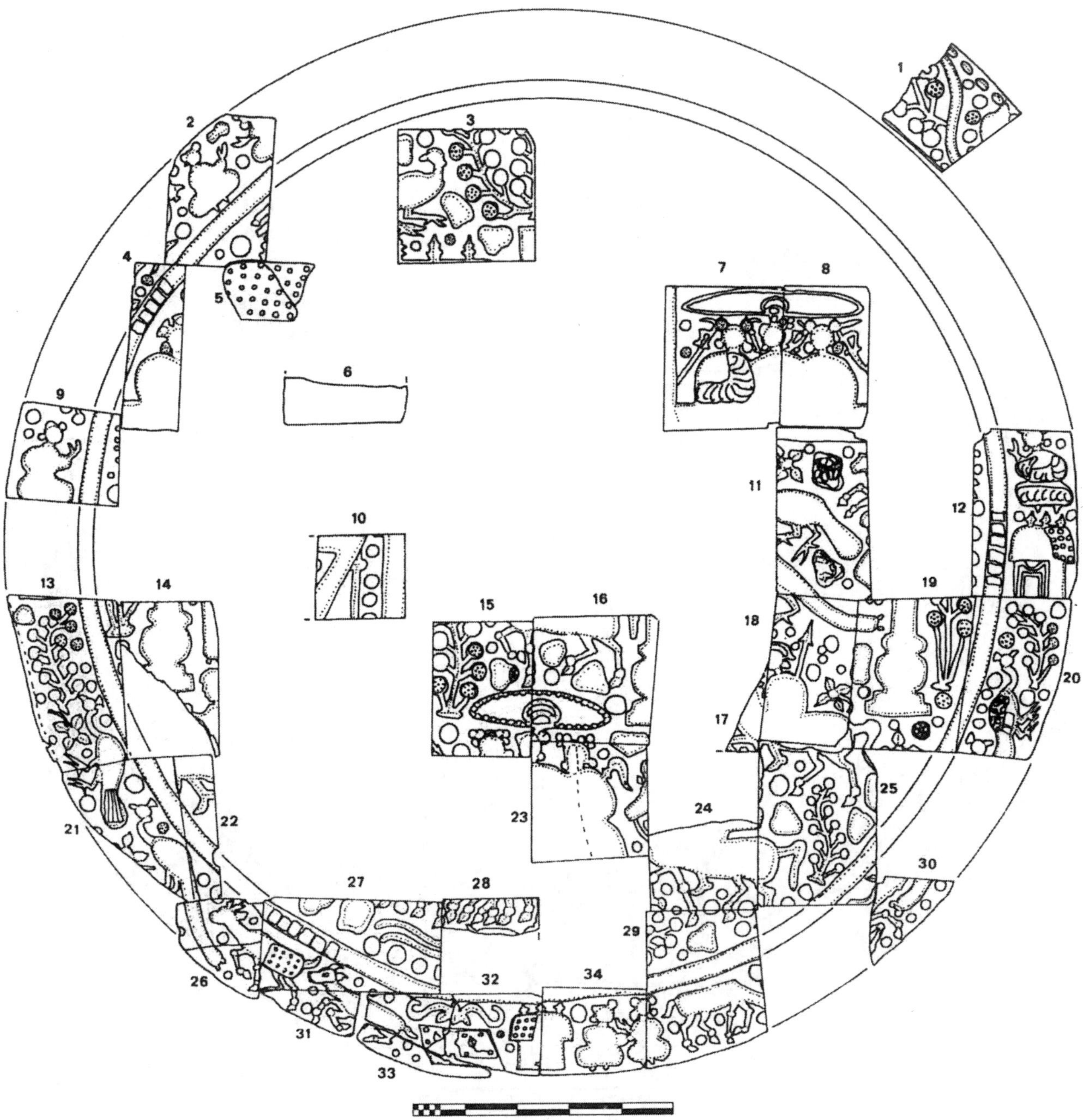


Fig. 30 – Indian plaque (Q) : inventory of the plaquettes
(see pp. 51-102, 132-142)

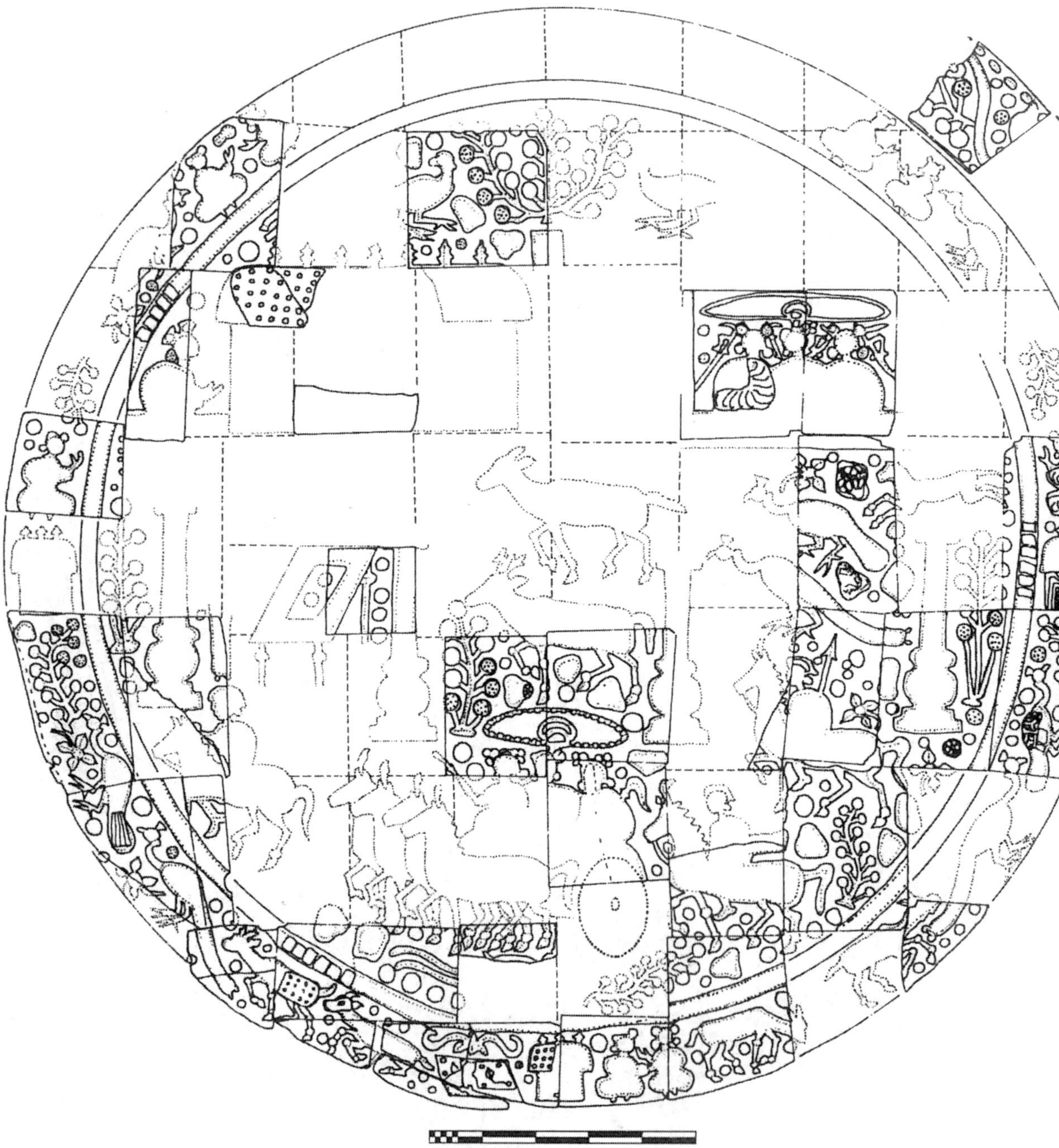

Fig. 31 – Indian plaque (Q) : reconstituted design

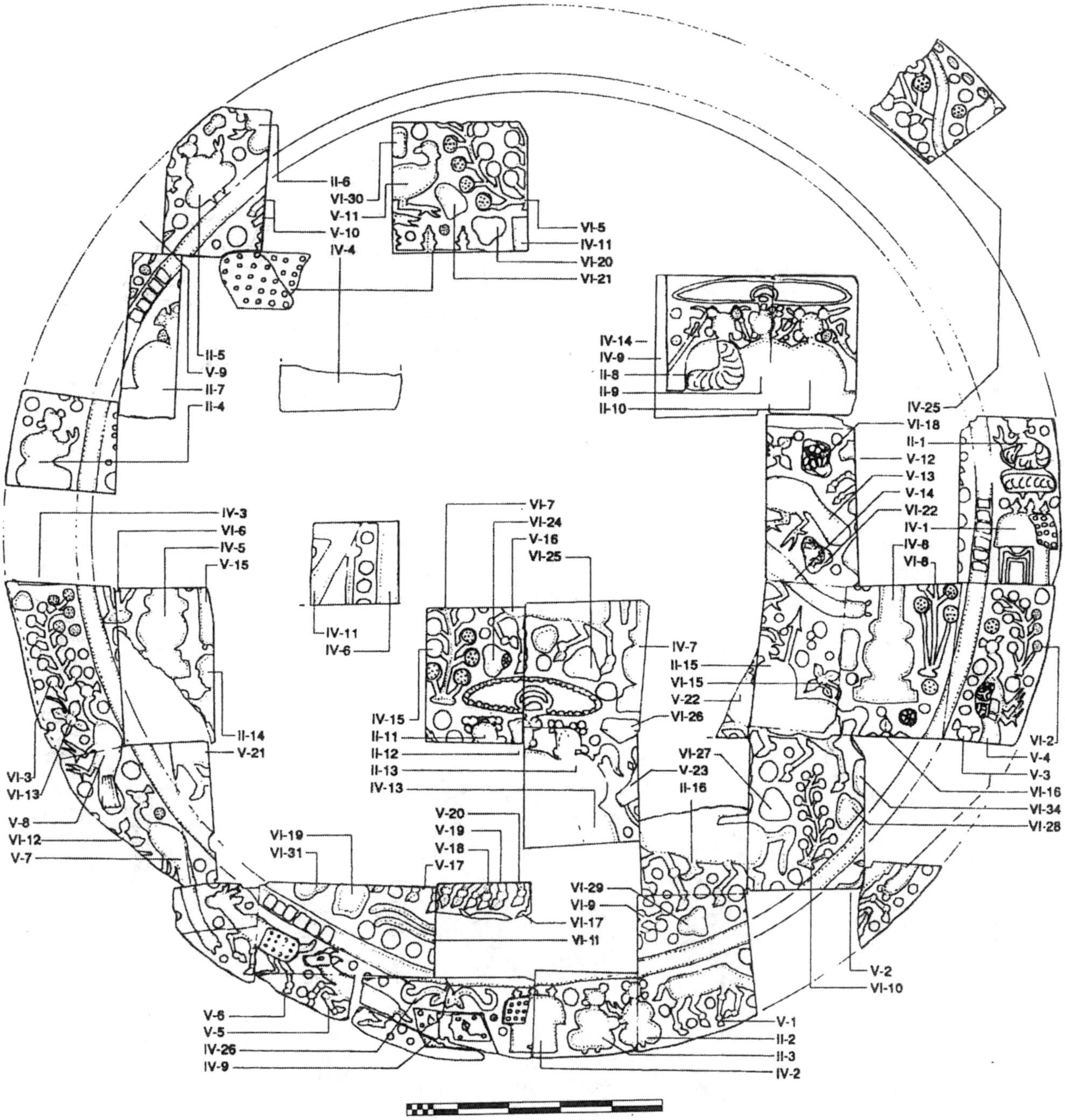


Fig. 32 – Indian plaque (Q) : the motifs
(see pp. 133-138)

XIV Fig. 33 – Indian plaque (Q) : glass inlays [format 2:1]. See pp. 139-142

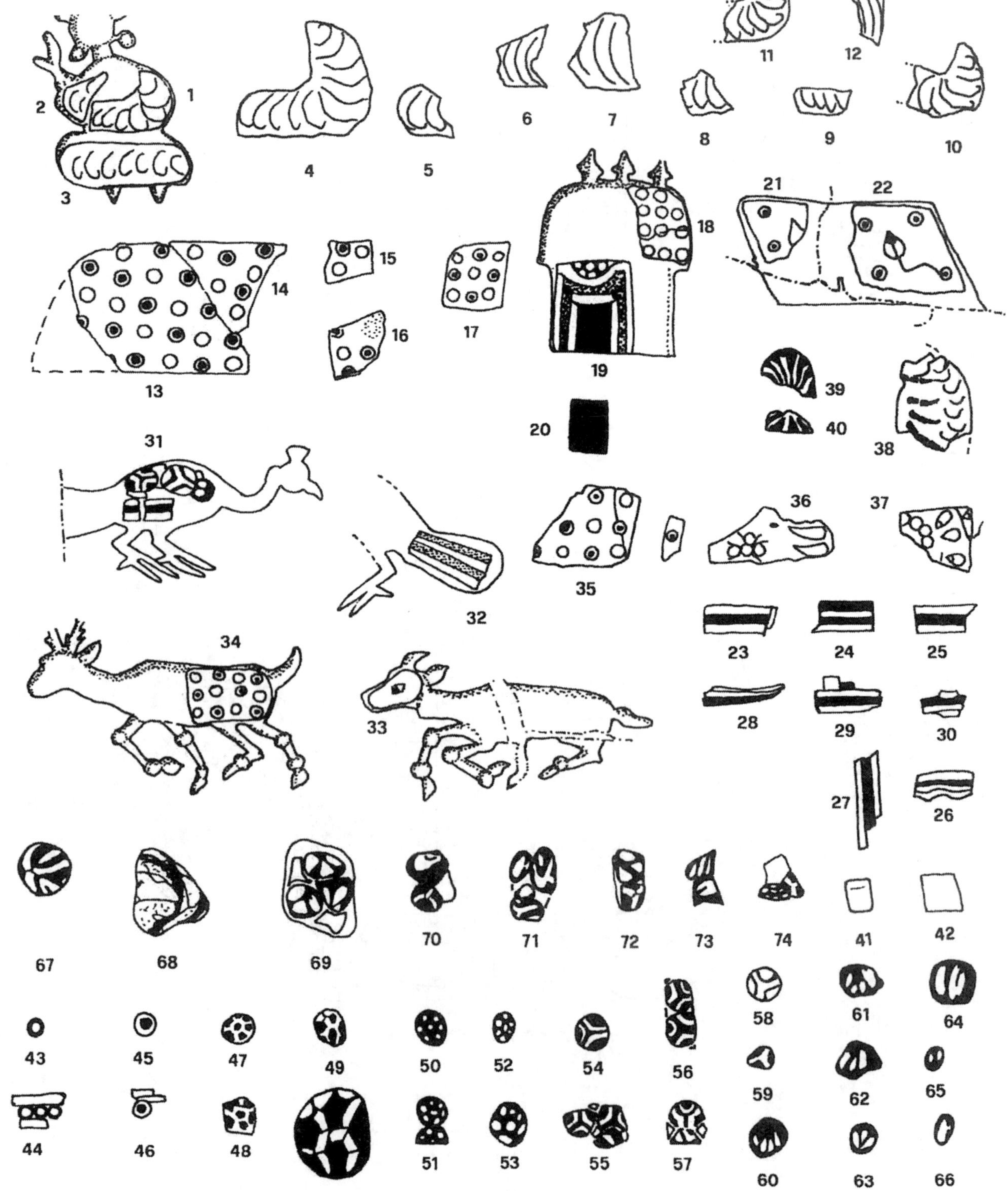

Fig. 34 – Indian plaque (Q) : patterns (see p. 142)

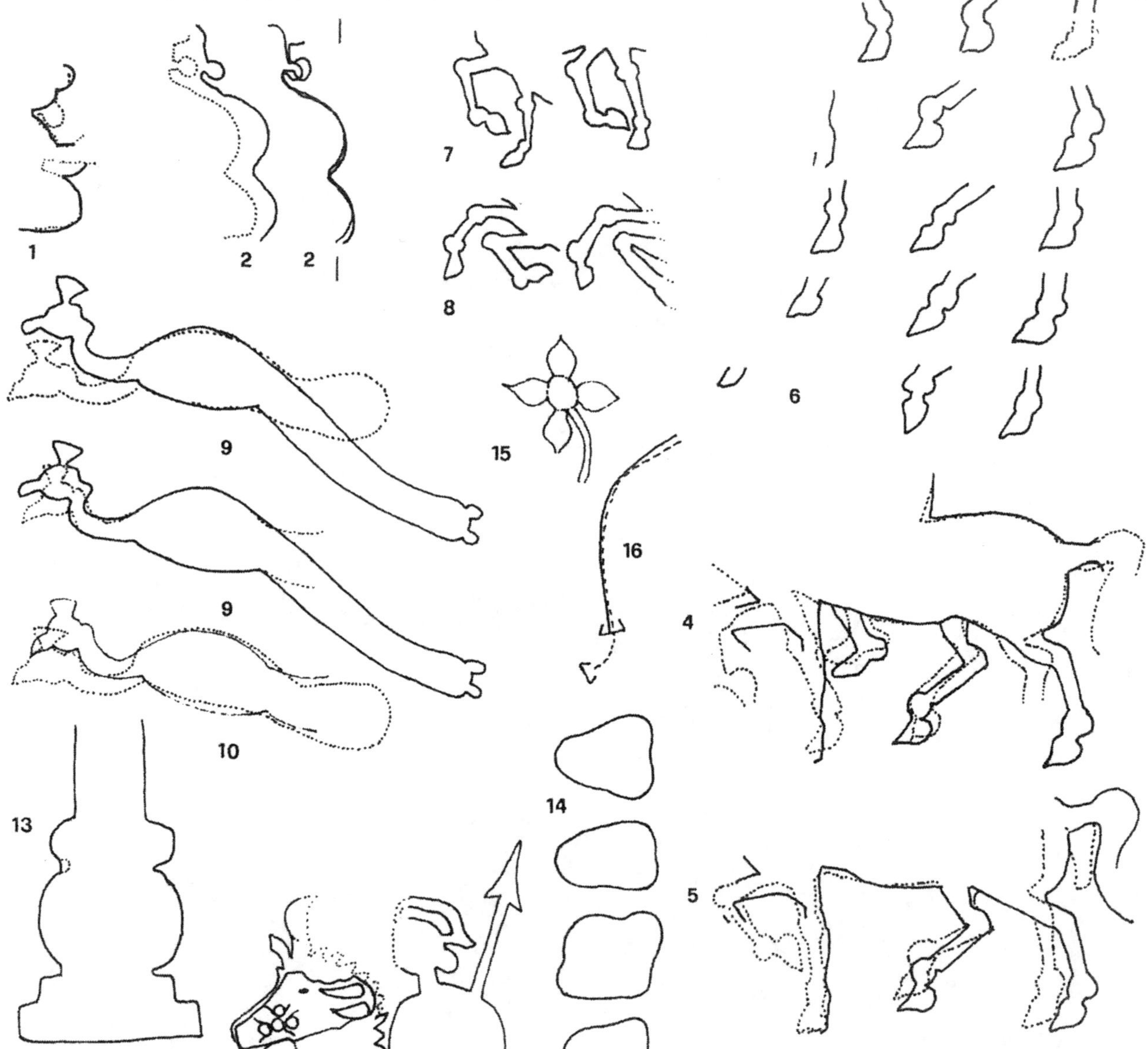


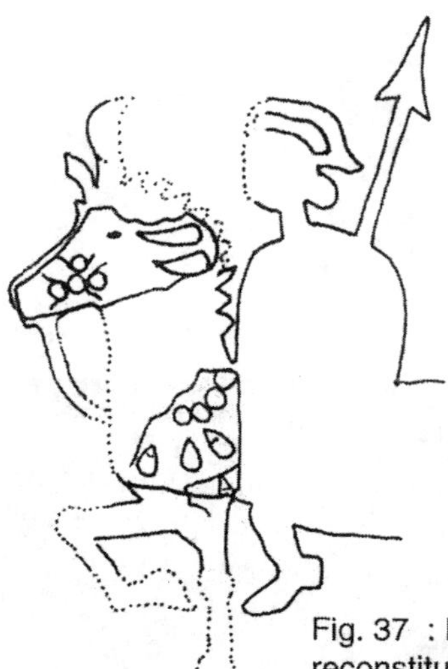

Fig. 37 : hypothetical reconstitution of a cavalier

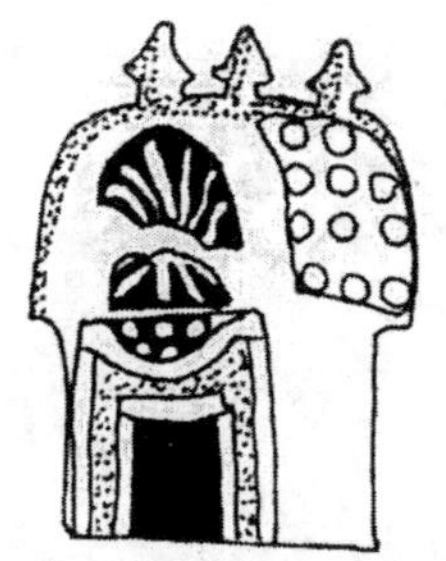

Fig. 35 : hypothetical reconstitution of the building on the right border

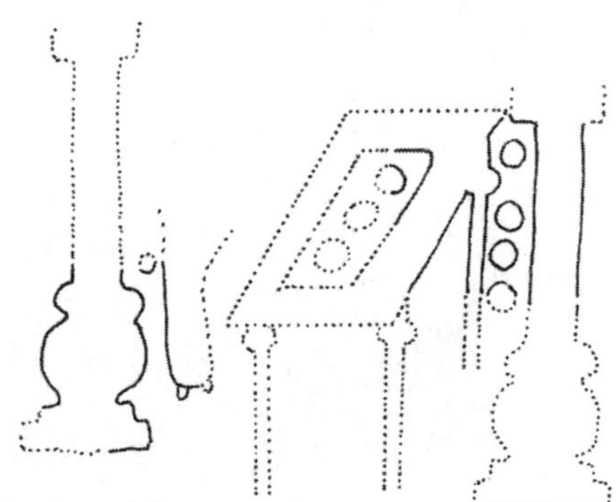

Fig. 36 : hypothetical reconstitution of the central area

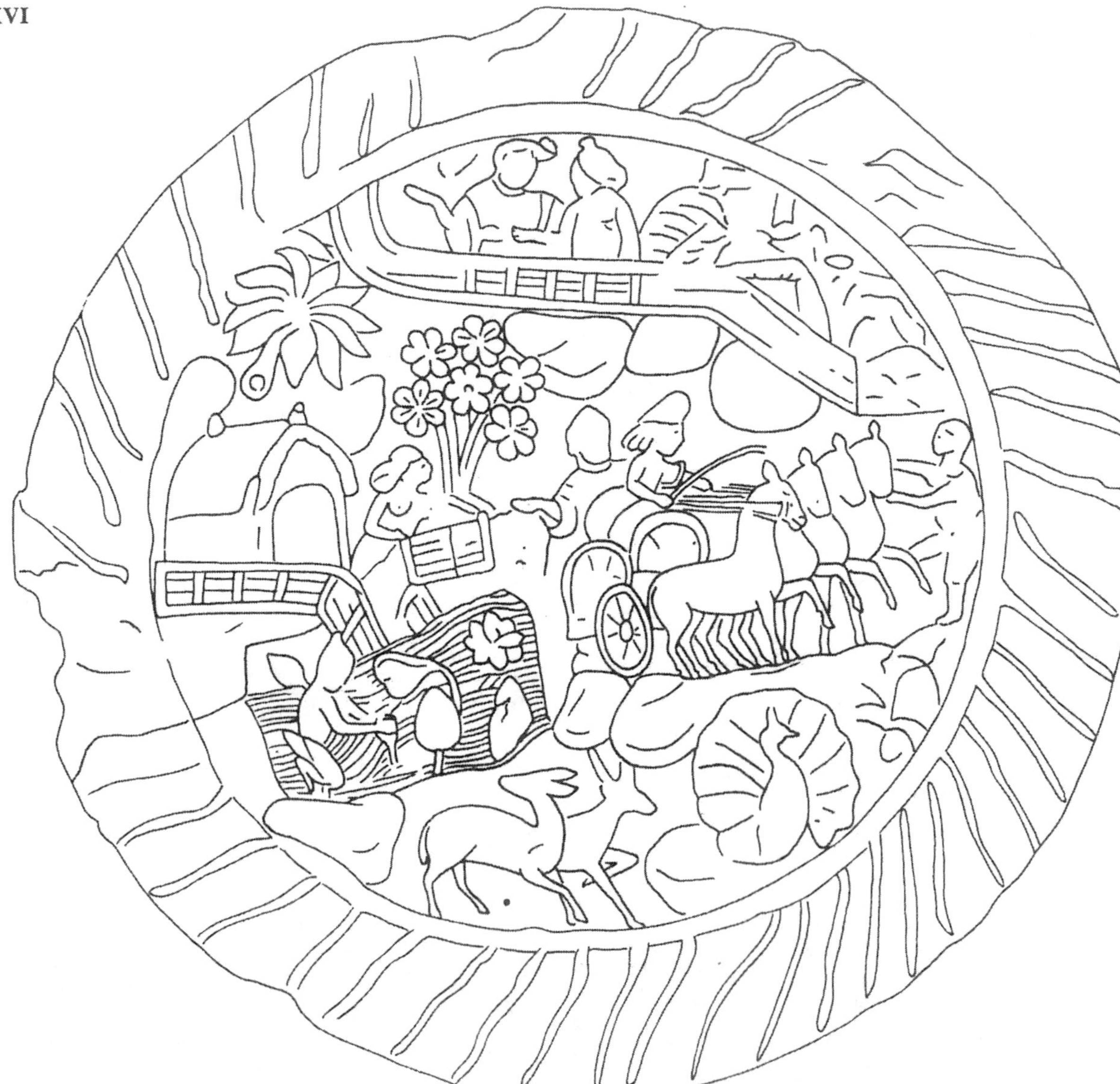

Fig. 38 – Terracotta plaque of Bhita
diam.: 7.5 cm (design of G. Lecuyot based on J.H. Marshall, *ASIAR* 1911-12, pl. XXIV) (see pp. 64-66)

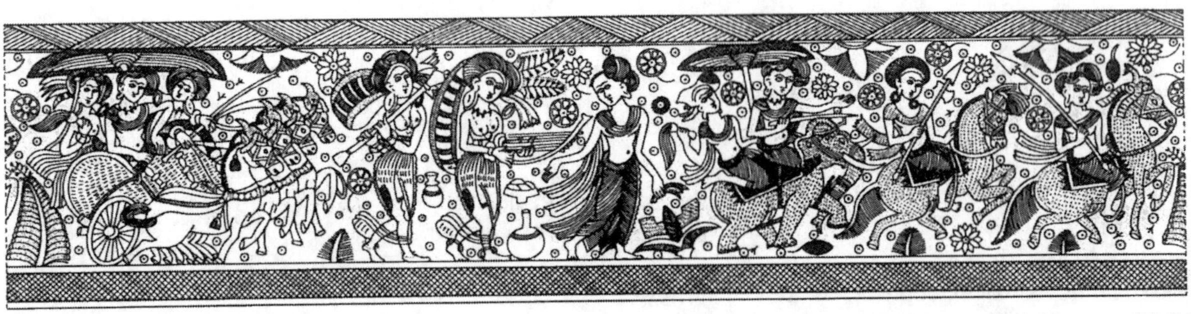

Fig. 39 – Bronze vase from Gundla (design from *The crossroads of Asia*, Cambridge, 1992, p. 164) (see pp. 67-71)

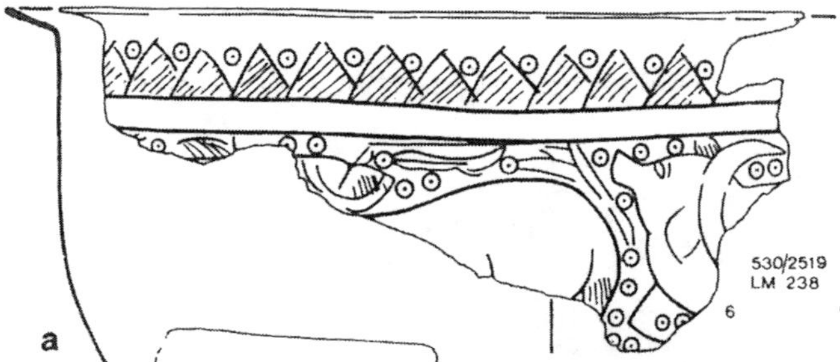


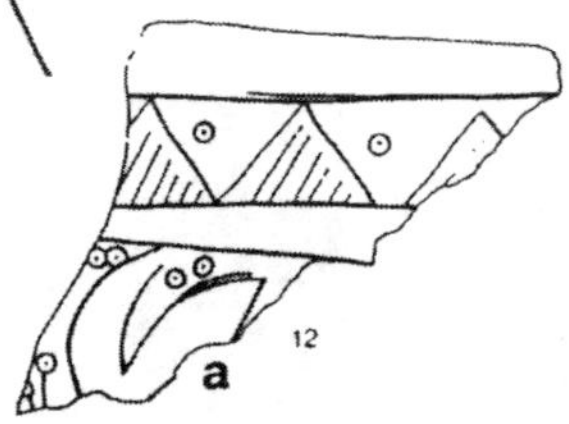

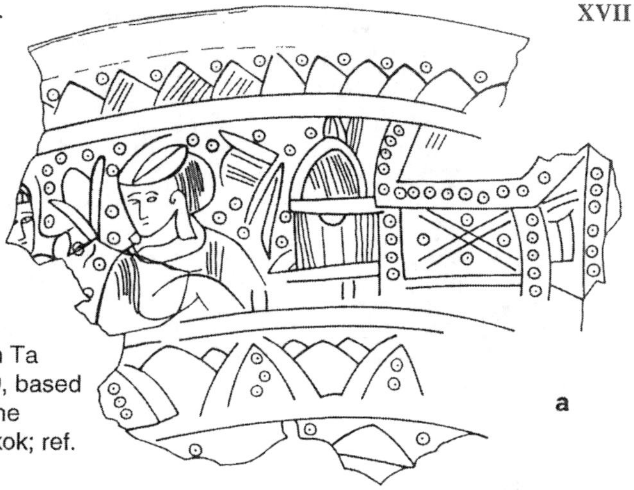

– a (fig. 40 to 42). Ban Don Ta Phet (design made in 1989, based on the object exhibited in the National Museum of Bangkok; ref. 530/2519 LM 238) [1:2]

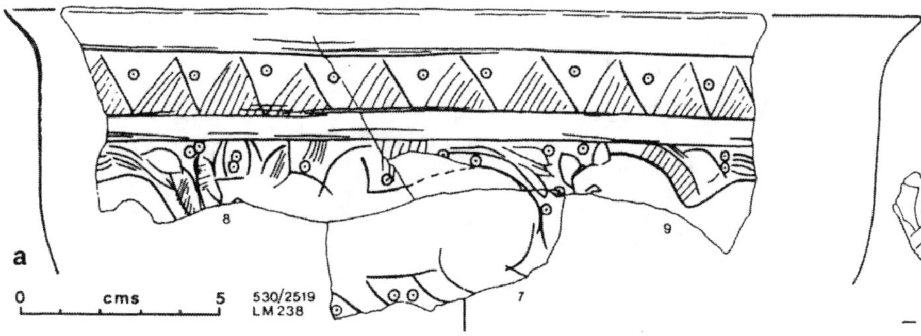


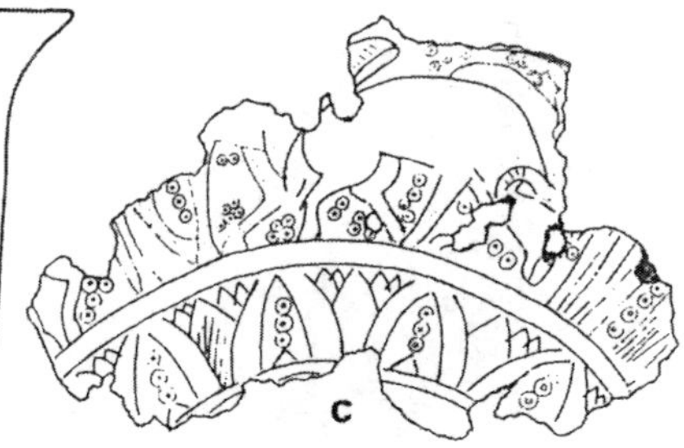

– c. (fig. 44) Khao Jamook, probably fragment of the vase 1 (=b)

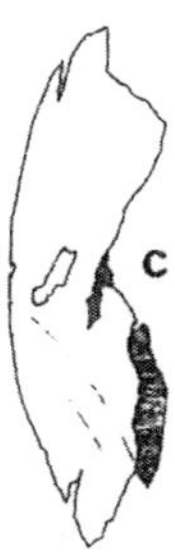

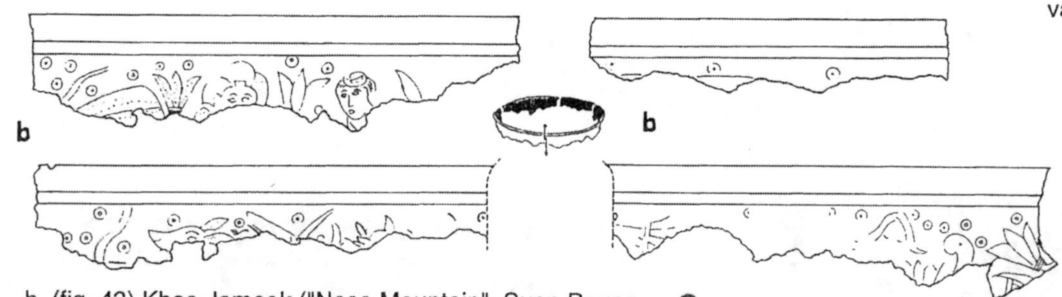

– b. (fig. 43) Khao Jamook ("Nose Mountain", Suen Peung District, Ratchaburi Province), vase 1. Diam.: 14,2 cm [1:4]

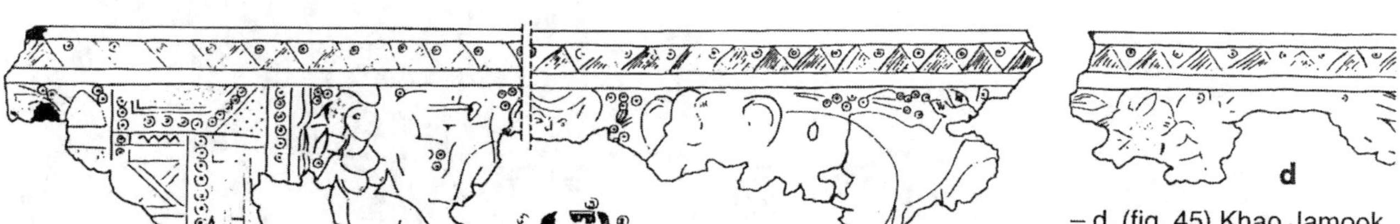

– d. (fig. 45) Khao Jamook, vase 2. Diam.: 11 cm [1:4]

Fig. 40 to 45 – Bronze vases of Thailand (based on I.C. Glover, *Early trade between India and Southeast Asia*, p. 38 and 40 and unpublished designs graciously furnished by the author) (see p. 71)

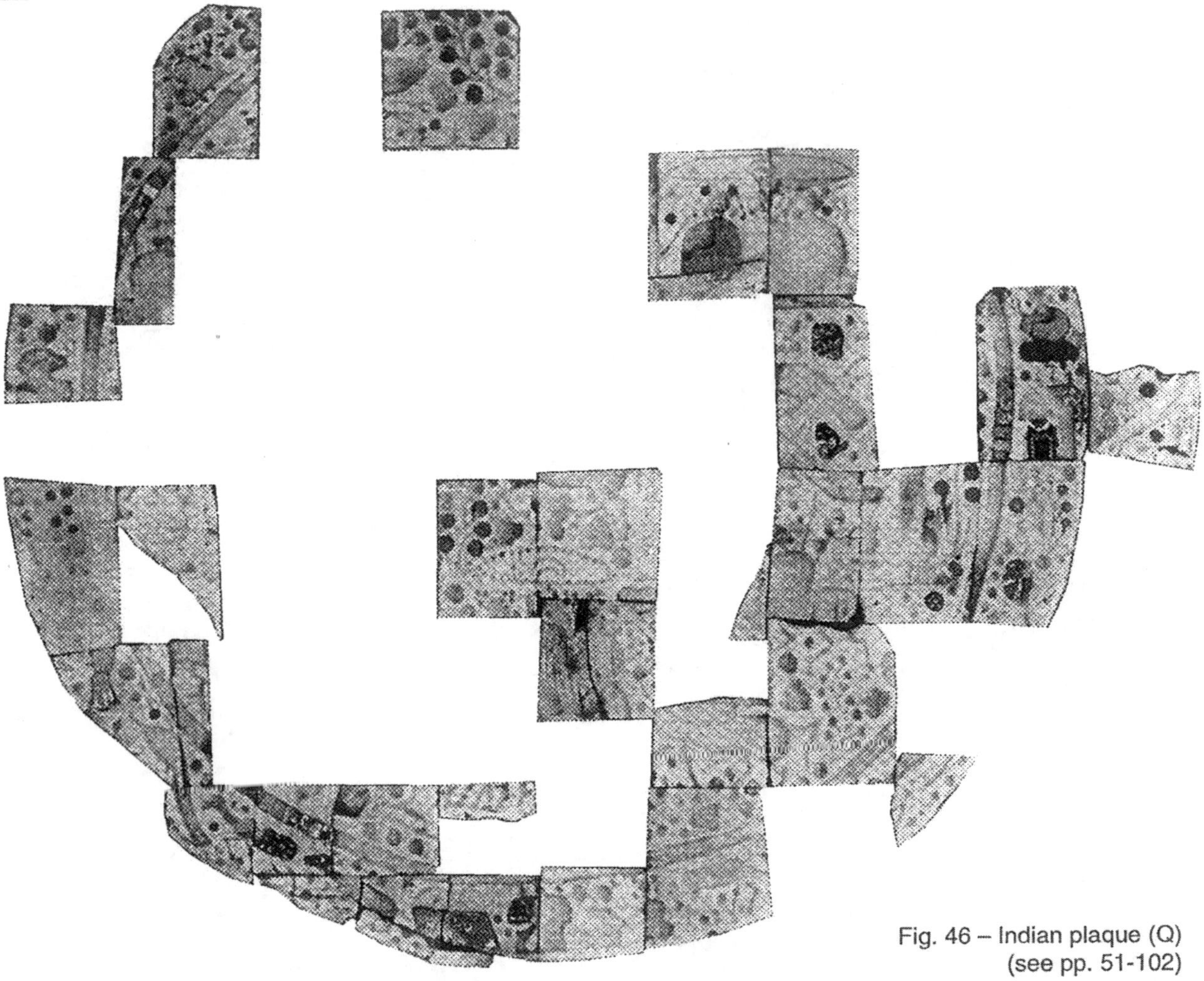

Fig. 46 – Indian plaque (Q)
(see pp. 51-102)

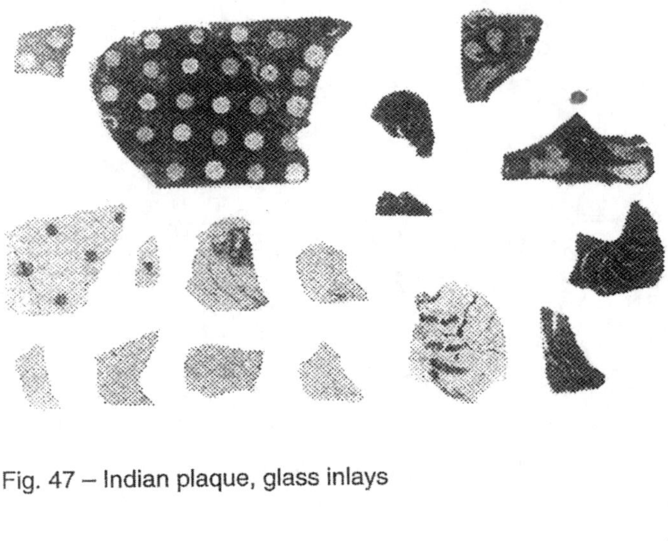

Fig. 47 – Indian plaque, glass inlays

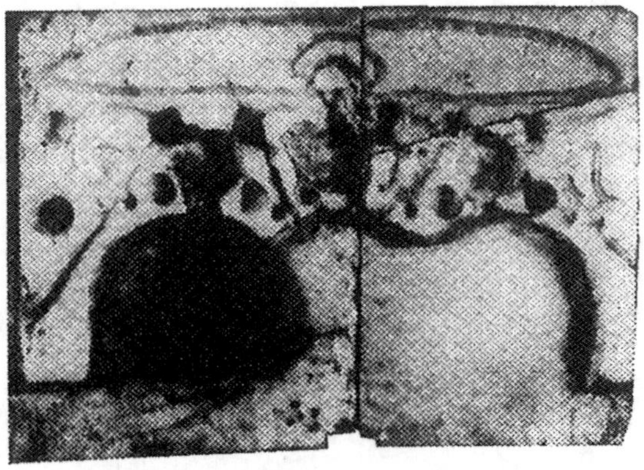

Fig. 48 – Indian plaque, Śakuntalā

Fig. 49-52 – Indian plaque (Q) (see pp. 51-102)



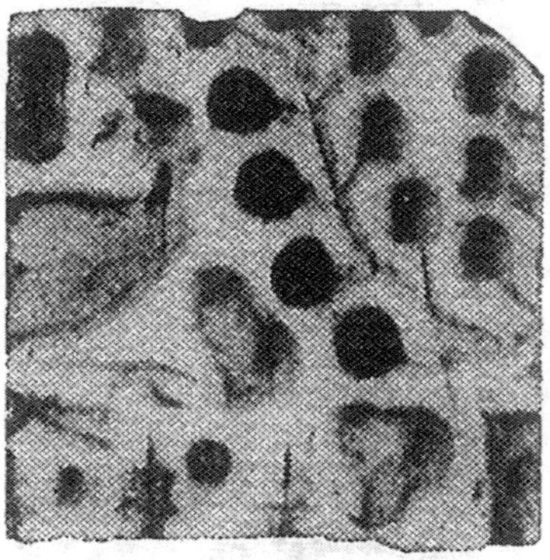

Fig. 49

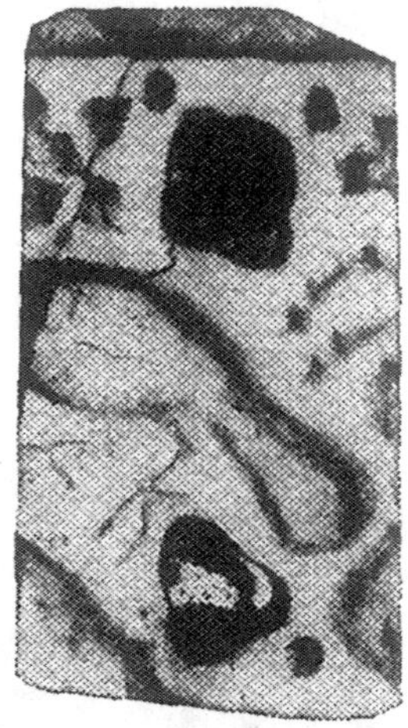

Fig. 50

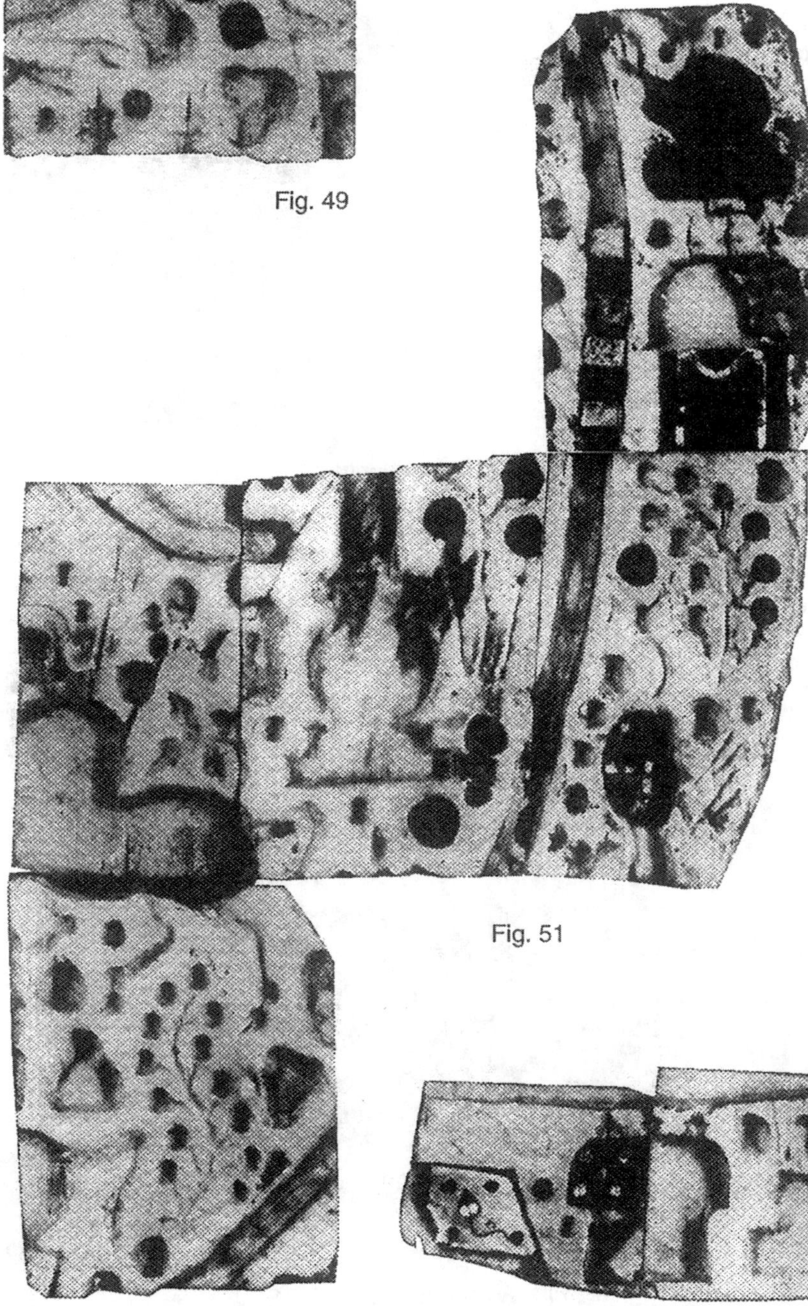

Fig. 51

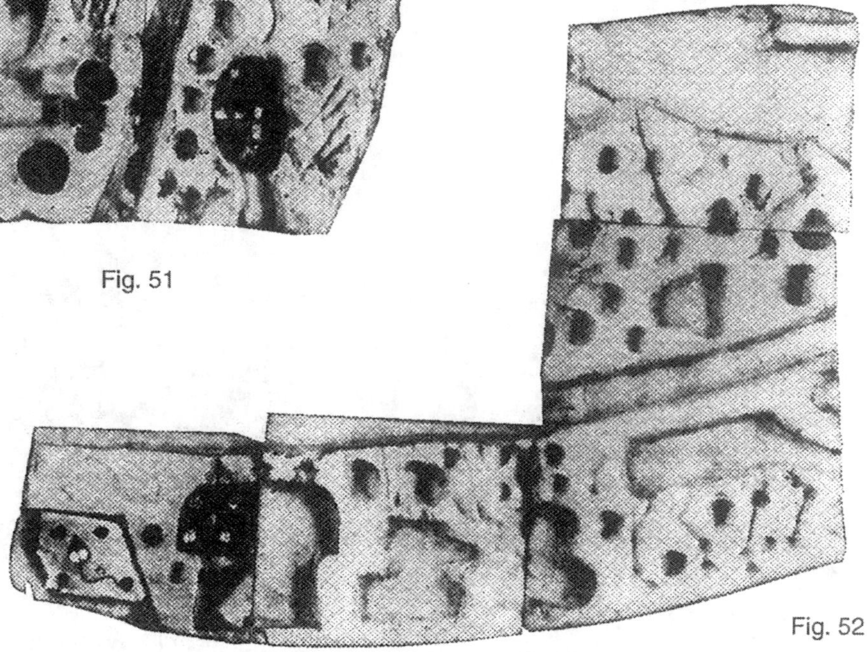

Fig. 52

Fig. 53

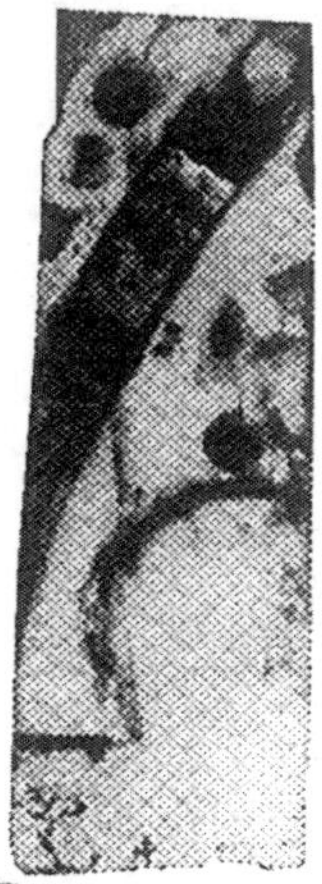

Fig. 54

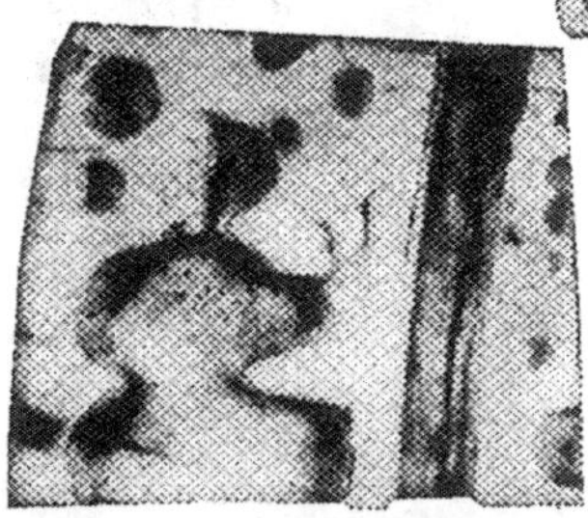

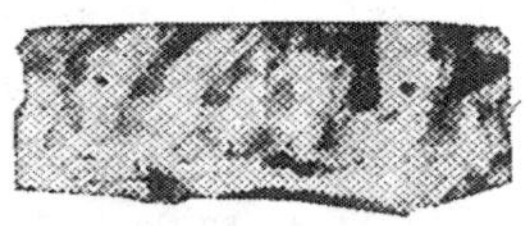

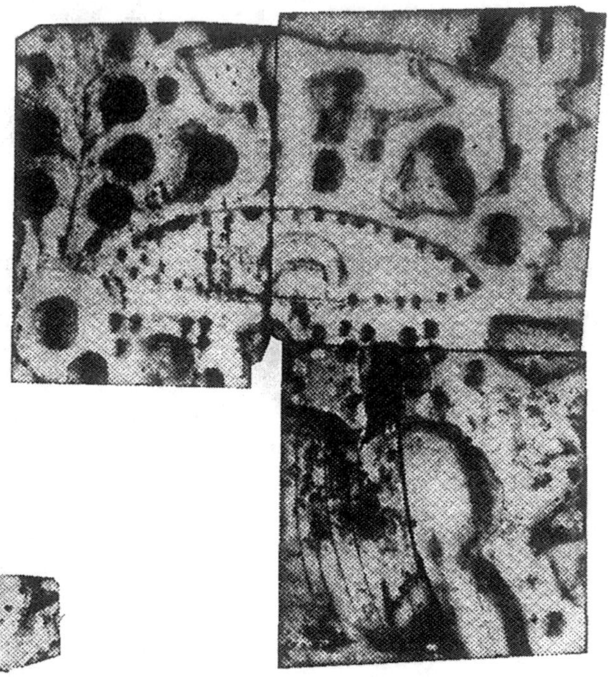

Fig. 55, quadriga

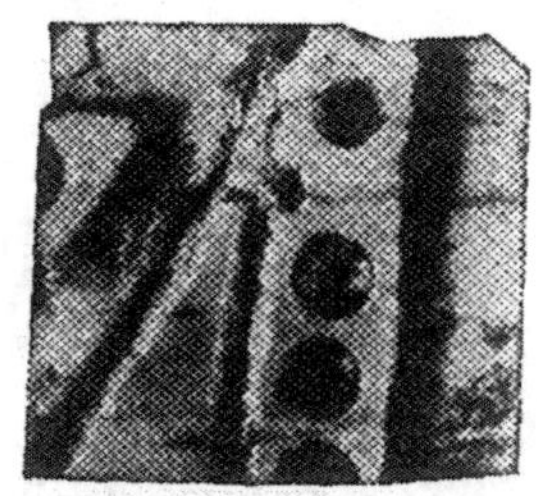

Fig. 57

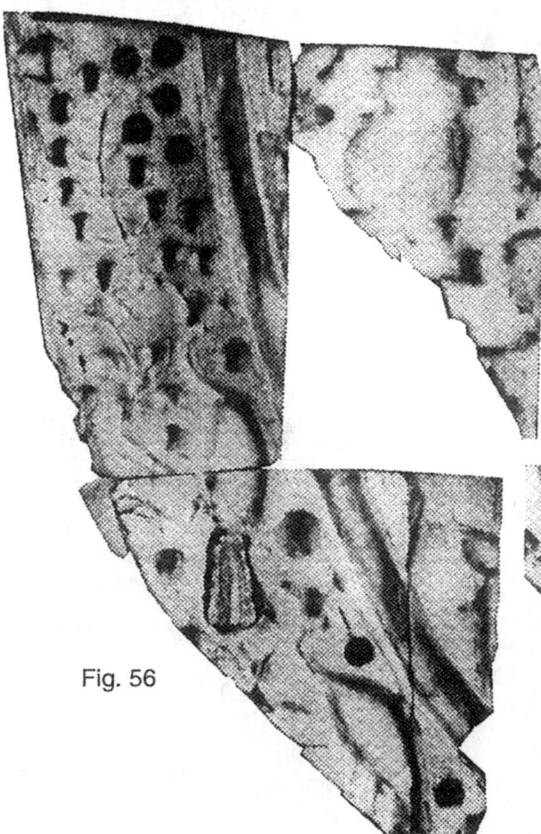

Fig. 56

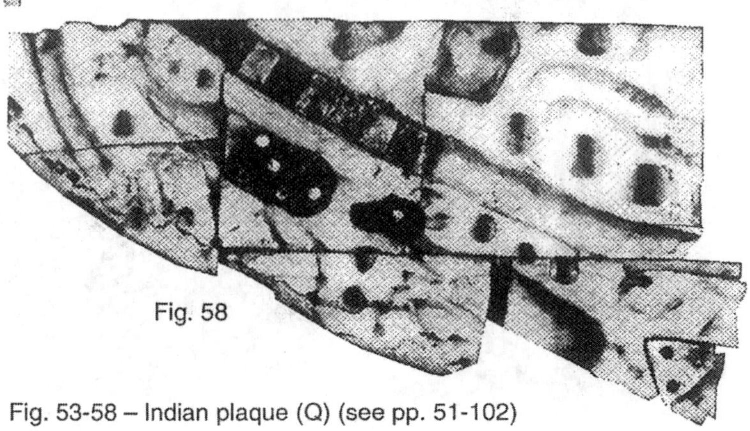

Fig. 58

Fig. 53-58 – Indian plaque (Q) (see pp. 51-102)

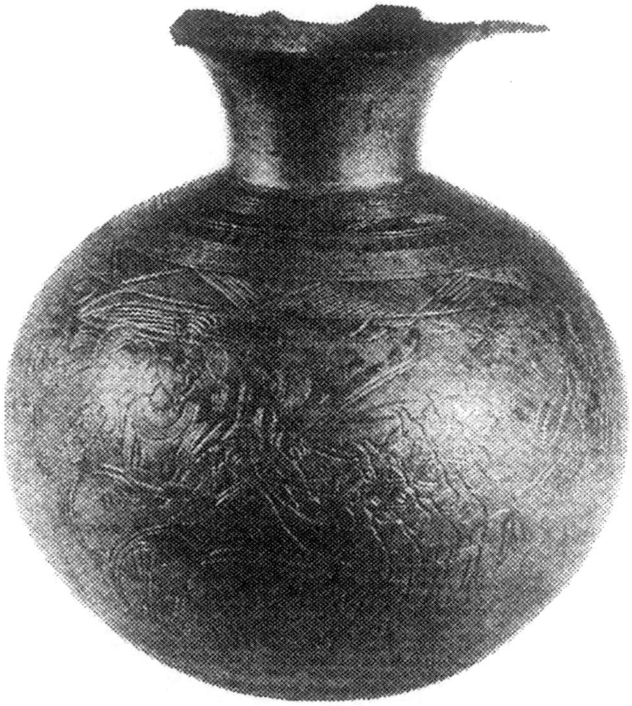

Fig. 59a – Bronze vase from Gundla (photograph, British Museum) (see pp. 67-71)

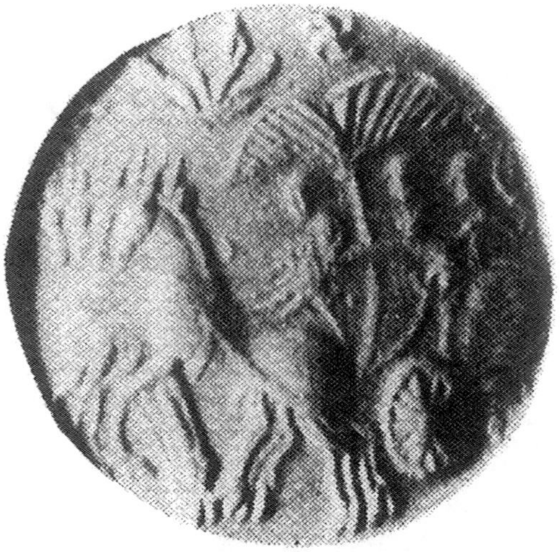

Fig. 60 – Intaglio in bronze from the Houghton Collection (photograph, P. Callieri) (see p. 79)

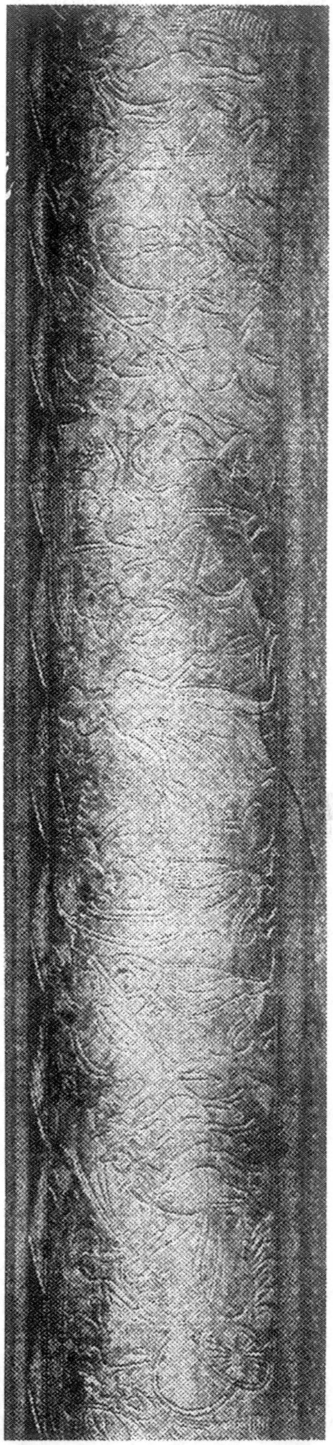

Fig. 59b – Bronze vase from Gundla. Detail of the frieze (photograph, British Museum)